NORMANDY: THE SAILORS' STORY

NORMANDY
THE SAILORS' STORY

A Naval History of D-Day and
the Battle for France

NICK HEWITT

YALE UNIVERSITY PRESS
NEW HAVEN AND LONDON

For information about this and other Yale University Press publications, please contact:
U.S. Office: sales.press@yale.edu   yalebooks.com
Europe Office: sales@yaleup.co.uk   yalebooks.co.uk

Set in Adobe Caslon Pro by IDSUK (DataConnection) Ltd
Printed in Great Britain by TJ Books Limited, Padstow, Cornwall

Library of Congress Control Number: 2023952214

ISBN 978-0-300-25673-4

A catalogue record for this book is available from the British Library.

10 9 8 7 6 5 4 3 2 1

Contents

CONTENTS

Plates

1. Bodies of Canadian soldiers on the beach after Operation Jubilee, 19 August 1942. History and Art Collection / Alamy.
2. Quadrant, the Quebec Conference of 17–24 August 1943. Official US Navy photograph, National Archives, 80-G-178042.
3. Admiral Sir Bertram Ramsay, Naval Commander, Expeditionary Force, with Air Marshal Tedder and Rear-Admiral Vian before the invasion, 1944. RMM 1986/174/10 © National Museum of the Royal Navy.
4. Rear-Admiral Alan Kirk, USN, aboard his flagship USS *Augusta*, 9 June 1944. Associated Press / Alamy.
5. Sailors pose aboard a completed Phoenix caisson in Portsmouth Dockyard, March 1944. Official US Navy photograph, National Archives, 80-G-251981.
6. German soldiers erecting beach obstacles. Bettmann / Getty Images.
7. *LCT-1169* is commissioned, cheered on by the women who built it, 1943. piemags / Alamy.
8. Preparation for the Normandy landings, Slapton Sands, Devon, 1944. Bridgeman Images.
9. USS *LST-289* limps into Dartmouth Harbour, 28 April 1944. Official US Navy photograph, National Archives, 80-G-283502.
10. RM Commandos embark, 1944. RMM 2015/140/541 © National Museum of the Royal Navy.

11. The Allied invasion fleet off the Normandy coast, 6 June 1944. INTERFOTO / Alamy.

12. US troops crouch inside a 'Higgins Boat' LCVP on their way into Omaha Beach, 6 June 1944. US Coast Guard Collection, National Archives, 26-G-2340.

13. HM midget submarine *X-23* comes alongside the Headquarters Ship HMS *Largs*, 6 June 1944. RNSM 2393C © National Museum of the Royal Navy.

14. Infantry with bicycles wade ashore from an LCI during the Normandy landings, 6 June 1944. RMM 1986/174/22 © National Museum of the Royal Navy.

15. Commodore Cyril Douglas-Pennant and Royal Marines. RMM 1986/174/33 © National Museum of the Royal Navy.

16. HMS *Warspite* bombards German batteries around Le Havre, 6 June 1944. piemags / Alamy.

17. US Rhino ferry *RHF-3*, 6 June 1944. US Coast Guard Collection, National Archives, 26-G-2335.

18. 'Jesse James', a US Army DUKW amphibious truck, brings supplies ashore, 11 June 1944. Official US Navy photograph, National Archives, 80-G-252737.

19. Unloading supplies from the US Navy's *LCT-583* at low tide, 15 June 1944. Official US Navy photograph, National Archives, 80-G-253001.

20. Omaha Beach in the immediate aftermath of the invasion. US Coast Guard Collection, National Archives, 26-G-2517.

21. The aftermath of the 'Great Gale' of 19–22 June. Official US Navy photograph, National Archives, 80-G-286431.

22. The minesweeper USS *Tide* sinking off Utah Beach, 7 June 1944. Official US Navy photograph, National Archives, 80-G-651677.

23. A German *Schnellboot* at speed. Popperfoto / Getty Images.

24. Royal Navy Motor Torpedo Boats returning from a dawn patrol off Cherbourg. piemags / Alamy.

25. Men on a US Rhino ferry drop to the deck as a German aircraft passes over, 11 June 1944. Official US Navy photograph. National Archives, 80-G-252834.

Maps, Figures and Tables

Maps

Figures

Table

Glossary and Abbreviations

AA	anti-aircraft
ANCXF	Allied Naval Commander-in-Chief, Expeditionary Force
ASDIC	early name for sonar, supposedly derived from Anti-Submarine Detection Investigation Committee
ATB	Amphibious Training Base (US)
AVRE	Armoured Vehicle Royal Engineers
B-Dienst	*Funkbeobachtungdienst*, German naval wireless intercept service
BDQ	Trawler Registration
Beetle	pontoons used in the Mulberry Harbour to support roadways
BIGOT	security category above Top Secret, supposedly derived from reversing TOGIB (To Gibraltar)
BLO	Bombardment Liaison Officer
blockship	ship deliberately sunk for various purposes
blue on blue	friendly fire
BS	Battleship
BUCO	Build-Up Control Organisation
BYMS	British Yard Mine Sweeper

GLOSSARY AND ABBREVIATIONS

Captain (D)	the senior office of a flotilla of destroyers
casemate	fortified gun emplacement
CB (Seabees)	US Navy Construction Battalions
C-in-C	Commander-in-Chief
COPP	Combined Operations Pilotage Party
COREP	Control Repair Organisation
Corncob	codename for blockship
Corvette	small anti-submarine warship
COSSAC	Chief of Staff, Supreme Allied Commander
COTUG	Tug Control Organisation
CW	Commission Worthy (potential officer, British)
D-Day	used for planning purposes to identify the first day of any military operation before the actual date is known
DD Tank	Duplex Drive amphibious tank
DE	Destroyer Escort (US, known as frigates to the British)
DF	Destroyer Flotilla
DUKW (Duck)	amphibious truck, derived from General Motors' corporate code for 1942 (D); utility/amphibious (U); all-wheel drive (K); and two powered rear axles (W)
E-boat	German *Schnellboot*, roughly equivalent to British motor torpedo boats and US PT Boats. Name derives from Allied short-hand for 'enemy boat'
EG	Escort Group (British)
Enigma	German military cipher machine, also used to describe signals traffic sent using it
ETF	Eastern (British) Task Force
fascine	bundle of wooden rods used to fill in ditches and trenches
FAT	*Flächenabsuchender Torpedo*, German long-range pattern-running torpedoes

GLOSSARY AND ABBREVIATIONS

FDT	Fighter Direction Tender
FFI	Forces françaises de l'intérieur (the French Resistance)
Flag Officer	a naval officer senior enough to fly a command flag, usually a Commodore or an Admiral, depending on their nationality
flail	rotating drum fitted with chains, mounted to the front of a tank or other armoured vehicle to detonate mines
flak	anti-aircraft fire, from the German *Flugabwehrkanone* (anti-aircraft gun)
FOB	Forward Observer Bombardment (British)
FOBAA	Flag Officer British Assault Area
Free French	French military forces who continued to fight on under General Charles de Gaulle after France's surrender in June 1940
FUSA	First United States Army
FUSAG	fictitious First United States Army Group in D-Day deception
Gee/QH	navigation system developed for precision bombing for the RAF
GNAT	German Navy Acoustic Torpedo (British), or *Zaunkönig*
Gooseberry	breakwater formed by sinking blockships
HNorMS	His Norwegian Majesty's Ship
HAIS	oil pipeline system named after the designer (Hartley), the Anglo-Iranian Oil Company (his employer) and Siemens, which manufactured it
HAMEL	oil pipeline system named after its designers, Hammick and Ellis
hard	sloped concrete ramp used to load landing craft
HDML	Harbour Defence Motor Launch
HE	high explosive

GLOSSARY AND ABBREVIATIONS

Headache	German-speaking wireless intercept personnel (British)
H-Hour	used for planning purposes to identify the first hour of any military operation before the actual time and date are known
HQ	headquarters
ITMA	*It's That Man Again*, popular wartime radio show
jg	junior grade (officer, US)
Kite	exceptionally strong, self-righting and self-burying anchors unique to the Mulberry Harbour
Kleinkampfverbände	literally 'small battle units', used to describe a range of small submersibles and boats (see also abbreviation *K-Verbände*)
Kriegsmarine	Nazi Germany's navy
LBE	Landing Barge Electrical
LBK	Landing Barge Kitchen
LBO	Landing Barge Oil
LBV	Landing Barge Vehicle
LBW	Landing Barge Water
LCA(HR)	Landing Craft Assault (Hedgerow), armed with a 24-barrel spigot mortar for destroying minefields and beach defences
LCC	Landing Craft (Control)
LCF	Landing Craft (Flak)
LCG	Landing Craft Gun
LCI	Landing Craft Infantry, sometimes with (S) for small or (L) for large
LCM	Landing Craft Mechanised
LCOCU	Landing Craft Obstacle Clearance Units
LCP	Landing Craft Personnel
LCT	Landing Craft Tank
LCT(A)	Landing Craft Tank (Armoured)
LCT(CB)	Landing Craft Tank (Concrete Buster)
LCT(R)	Landing Craft Tank (Rocket)

LCVP	Landing Craft Vehicle and Personnel
LG	*Lehrgeschwader*, German air force operational training unit
LSI	Landing Ship Infantry
LST	Landing Ship Tank
Luftwaffe	Germany's air force
Marinegruppenkommando West	Naval Group West
Marineküstenbatterie	Naval Coastal Artillery Battery
MGB	Motor Gun Boat (British)
ML	Motor Launch (British)
MMS	Motor Mine Sweeper
monitor	flat-bottomed, shallow-draught warship with heavy guns designed for coastal bombardment
MSF	Minesweeping Flotilla
MT	motor transport
MTB	Motor Torpedo Boat
NCDU	Naval Combat Demolition Units (US)
NCO	non-commissioned officer
Neptune	Operation Neptune, the assault phase of Operation Overlord
NID	Naval Intelligence Department (British)
NOIC	Naval Officer in Charge
NSFCP	Naval Shore Fire Control Parties
OB West	*Oberbefehlshaber West*, the German Army's supreme command in the West
OBE	Order of the British Empire
OKW	*Oberkommando der Wehrmacht*, the Supreme Command of the German Armed Forces
Overlord	Operation Overlord, the Allied liberation of Nazi-occupied Europe
PC	Patrol Craft (US)
Phoenix	concrete caissons used to form the outer breakwater of the Mulberry Harbour.

pillbox	small concrete defensive structure
PLUTO	pipeline under the ocean
POW	prisoner of war
PT Boat	Patrol Torpedo Boat (US)
QH	*see* Gee/QH
R-boat	*Raumboot*, a German motor minesweeper
RCT	Regimental Combat Team (US)
Rhino ferry	simple motorised raft
RNR	Royal Naval Reserve (British), often professional seamen in civilian life
RNVR	Royal Naval Volunteer Reserve (British), often amateur sailors in civilian life
ROC	Royal Observer Corps
SAP	standard armour-piercing, a type of shell
SC	Submarine Chaser (US)
Schnellboot	*see* E-boat
Sfltl	*Schnellbootflottille*, E-boat flotilla
SHAEF	Supreme Headquarters Allied Expeditionary Force
SP gun	self-propelled gun, tracked artillery
StP	*Stützpunkt* (strongpoint)
TBS	talk between ships, secure short-range radio system
TH	Trinity House
TF	Task Force (US)
TIS	Theatre Intelligence Section
TURCO	Turn Round Control Organisation
U-boat	*Unterseeboot*, German submarine
UDT	Underwater Demolition Team (US)
Ultra	Allied intelligence obtained by decrypting Enigma signals (*see* Enigma)
Vichy France	collaborationist regime established after the fall of France in 1940; its capital was the town of Vichy as Paris was occupied by the Germans

Vorpostenboot	literally 'outpost boat', a German naval patrol boat
VPfltl	*Vorpostenflottille*, patrol boat flotilla
Whale roadway	sections used in the Mulberry Harbour
WIR	weekly intelligence report (British)
WN	*Widerstandsnest*, literally 'resistance nest' – a German defensive position
WRNS (Wrens)	Women's Royal Naval Service (British)
WTF	Western (US) Task Force
X-Craft	British miniature submarine
Zfltl	*Zerstörer-Flottille*

Acknowledgements

The contribution made by sailors to victory on D-Day and in the wider Normandy campaign has been a golden thread running through my life ever since my parents took me to the beaches when I was 15 years old, and I first saw the extraordinary, megalith-like remains of the Mulberry Harbour wallowing in the Seine Bay off Arromanches. Neptune/Overlord has informed my career since it began, and over the years I have learned from and been inspired by dozens of veterans and museum peers, academics and writers, broadcasters and enthusiasts. This brief acknowledgement can never be exhaustive, but I am profoundly grateful to them all.

In the summer of 1996, I began working for the Imperial War Museum aboard its historic cruiser HMS *Belfast*. Conversations with the members of the HMS *Belfast* Association were my gateway to the Seine Bay. In November 2010, I moved to Portsmouth, where I was briefly responsible for Portsmouth Naval Base Property Trust's beautifully restored Neptune veteran Motor Gun Boat *MGB-81*, and met Alan Watson and the Medusa Trust, who operate the D-Day navigational leader *HDML-1387*. Later, I was lucky enough to joyride in PNBPT's operational landing craft *F-8*, a later model but functionally identical to those which hit the beaches in 1944.

In 2014, I spent five action-packed days off Normandy interpreting sonar imagery for the Channel 5 documentary *D-Day's Sunken Secrets*. Much to my astonishment, I also found myself making two submersible dives, one accompanied by D-Day COPP veteran Jim Booth, an extraordinary human who had not been in a submarine since June 1944. Visiting the remains of the *Susan B Anthony* with him was a career highlight I doubt will ever be surpassed. In the same year, I joined the National Museum of the Royal Navy, and Director General Professor Dominic Tweddle sent me to Birkenhead to look at a rather rusty funnel protruding from some unappealing water in Birkenhead Docks. This turned into a seven-year labour of love heading up NMRN's project to restore *LCT-7074*, the last surviving Neptune Landing Craft (Tank).

Each of these jobs has been an incredible adventure, opening my eyes to the full panoply of the Seine Bay experience. I will always be profoundly grateful to IWM, PNBPT and NMRN for paying me to play with their incredible toys. I am also very grateful to my present employers, Orkney Islands Council, for patiently indulging my writing even though it has almost nothing to do with my job as Culture Team Manager.

Like any writer I did not 'discover' anything: I was helped to find it by wonderful curators and archivists. The team at the National Archives at Kew were their usual efficient and helpful selves. There has been much high-profile discussion of a diminished service at TNA since the pandemic, but this was absolutely not my experience. IWM's Sound Archive remains an incredible resource, digitised and free to use, as is the rather less-well-known BBC People's War Archive, and I am extremely grateful to both. At the NMRN, I would like to single out my former colleague Heather Johnson for putting key files under my nose. Andrew Whitmarsh, Curator of the D-Day Story in Portsmouth and my former partner on the *LCT-7074* restoration, performed similar magic for his own very rich collections. I am grateful to the editors and publishers of those works from which I have cited extracts, and for the owners of the copyright of the photographs reproduced in the book for permission to publish them.

Throughout this project I have enjoyed access to the unique archive of *The Naval Review*, founded in 1912 as a 'safe space' for naval officers to correspond on professional matters. As a wholly civilian historian, being invited to join has been an extraordinary

ACKNOWLEDGEMENTS

privilege, and in particular I would like to thank Emma Rowlands, the Secretary, for encouraging me.

This book has also been immeasurably enriched by conversations and chance exchanges, often on social media, with an eclectic and inspiring range of folk, far too many to name but every one of whom has added to the sum total of my knowledge or helped me think about things differently. Stephen Fisher and Alan Watson, in particular, have from the outset been beyond generous with their time, knowledge and expertise. Huge thanks to my dear friends Andy and Tamsin Clark for giving me free accomodation and lovely company within easy reach of the National Archives for weekend after weekend, and to Peter and Helen Bristow for their very timely offer of assistance with German translation. Thanks are also due to Andrew Baines, Peter Caddick-Adams, Jane Furlong, Peter Hart, Chris O'Flaherty, Richard Hargreaves, John Rawlinson, Matthew Sheldon, Dominic Tweddle and Jonathan Ware for their support and encouragement along the way.

I am enormously proud to be publishing under the Yale University Press imprint, and I am hugely grateful to Jo Godfrey and her colleagues Lucy Buchan, Chloe Foster, Rachael Lonsdale, Frazer Martin, Meg Pettit and Katie Urquhart for being so supportive and encouraging. Even now when I look at the historians with whom I am sharing a publisher, I feel a slight sense of disbelief. Of them all, the one that leaps out is Professor Andrew Lambert, Laughton Professor of Naval History at King's College London, to whom I will always remain deeply indebted for inspiring me to choose the naval history path at KCL back in 1993. Andrew was one of the anonymous peer reviewers whose constructive feedback helped Yale make their decision, and I am tremendously grateful for his kind words, advice and guidance, along with that of Dr Tim Benbow, also of KCL, who took the time to review the manuscript in the minutest detail, making a number of small but incredibly helpful and pertinent suggestions. Other peer reviewers at proposal and first draft stage remain anonymous, but I am very grateful to them for their feedback.

Importantly, as the saying goes, any errors remain absolutely mine alone.

ACKNOWLEDGEMENTS

Finally, I would like as always to thank my mum Rosalie and my now fully grown 'children' Cerys and Daniel for their continued faith in me, and my extraordinarily patient partner, Hana, who has had my back ever since this journey began back in 2019, with a perhaps overly casual 'I think I'm going to pitch another book!'

Preface

Any success achieved by the British Armies has been made possible
only by the magnificent support given us by the Royal Navy.
Field Marshal Sir Bernard Law Montgomery, May 1945[1]

The naval history of the Normandy campaign cast a spell on me
early in my career, and I have returned to the subject repeatedly
in print, online and on camera. I was once asked which historical event
I would like to have seen and I answered 'D-Day' without hesitation,
although I immediately caveated that D-Day was terrifying, stressful
and dangerous, and I would certainly not wish to have taken part. But
to have witnessed the scale of it would have been extraordinary.

In 2008, while working aboard the Imperial War Museum's
(IWM) historic cruiser HMS *Belfast*, I wrote a short article for *The
Mariner's Mirror*, the journal of the Society for Nautical Research,
about that ship's participation in Operation Neptune, the assault
phase of Operation Overlord, the Allied liberation of Nazi-occupied
Europe.[2] I was convinced there was a bigger story, and I was delighted
when, a few years later, the IWM invited me to write a book on the
same subject, entitled *Firing on Fortress Europe*.[3]

And yet, this still wasn't enough. Every time I approached the
story of the Allied navies in the Seine Bay, it got bigger. *Belfast* was
just one ship, with a very specific role on the Normandy gunline
supporting the army by bombarding shore targets. Thousands of

PREFACE

other sailors made Neptune happen. They crewed landing ships, tiny assault landing craft, and wallowing motorised barges. They spotted for the big guns. They swept mines and protected the flanks of the invasion from attack. They sank blockships under fire and helped to build the famous Mulberry Harbours. Later, they repaired devastated French ports. Ashore, they planned, organised and delivered the entire operation from draughty offices and underground bunkers, everywhere from Orkney to Falmouth.

And yet the more I read, the more I realised that these sailors were largely absent from the literature, particularly from more recent publications, even though Neptune/Overlord is widely recognised as the greatest, most complex amphibious operation in history, and amphibious operations depend on ships and sailors. At most, readers will find one or two, usually operating landing craft, and usually on 6 June 1944. Sailors appear as passive facilitators, an adjunct to the troops, whose only role was to ferry them to the beaches. There are more books about paratroopers than there are about sailors, and this book is an attempt to redress that balance.

This is not another book about D-Day, another book about Operation Neptune or indeed about Operation Overlord. (Sometimes this narrative will refer to these two intimately linked operations as Neptune/Overlord.) Neptune began at 2330 on 25 May, when the signal went out for sealed orders to be opened; half an hour later the military holding camps on the south coast were sealed. It ended, according to the British Naval Staff History, on 3 July, when the last of the senior officers who had led the assault were withdrawn and new headquarters were established ashore:

> The withdrawal of all these officers and the transfer of the two naval commands to the shore marked the stabilisation of the naval position in the assault area ... this was the official end of Operation 'Neptune'.[4]

The demanding work of the Allied navies to protect, support and sustain the invading army did not end with what was a fairly perfunctory change in command structure. Sailors continued to live, work, fight and die in the Seine Bay for weeks after Neptune ended, and indeed continued to risk their lives in European waters until Overlord ended with the final unconditional surrender of Nazi Germany on 7 May 1945, effective from 8 May in the West and 9 May in the Soviet Union.

This book presents the work of the Allied navies as a forgotten naval battle, which I have called the Battle of the Seine Bay, although geographically it spread well outside that congested and vulnerable body of water.[5] It began sometime after August 1943, when the Allied political and military leadership, acting on the advice of their planners, finally decided that the invasion would take place on the Normandy coast. When it ended is equally debatable, but I have chosen 12 September 1944, when the German naval base at Le Havre fell, and the Seine Bay became largely secure, although the ongoing work of the Allied navies continued up the Channel coasts of France, Belgium and the Netherlands, at Walcheren and in the Scheldt and even on the Rhine, and huge quantities of supplies continued to flow across the beaches well into the autumn.

To an extent, much of what the Royal Navy did during the Second World War could be argued to have been enabling work for Neptune, notably the series of amphibious operations in the Mediterranean and the long struggle to secure the sea lanes across the Atlantic, without which D-Day would have been impossible. These events have been well related by others, and it was important to avoid the temptation to 'mission creep' into a general naval history of the Second World War in the west.[6] Similarly, the strategic decision-making process which led to an invasion in Normandy in 1944 has been effectively covered by other writers, so I have confined myself to the briefest contextual summary of the key events of 1939–44.[7]

All ranks are given as in 1944, and I have not footnoted final ranks attained. To assist with narrative flow, honorifics, titles and decorations have generally been omitted, unless relevant to establish character or experience. Similarly, I have generally left out the complicated nuances of the Royal Navy's arcane caste system for commissioned ranks, as I do not believe it is hugely important to know whether someone was Temporary, Acting or Temporary/

PREFACE

Acting in their role. I have similarly often omitted their status as regular (RN, USN) or reservist (RNR, RNVR, USNR); the distinctions had blurred significantly by 1944, and the vast majority of those who fought in the Seine Bay were 'hostilities-only' personnel of one form or another.

German and other European ranks are given in the relevant language, as British equivalents are not always entirely accurate. Ships are introduced for the first time with their national prefix (HMS, USS) and afterwards the name only is given. Metric equivalents are provided for measurements except in direct quotation. Naval formations are usually abbreviated after first introduction, so the British 1st Minesweeping Flotilla abbreviates to 1st MSF, and the German *1.Schnellbootflottille* abbreviates to *1.Sfltl.* Where possible, all times are taken from contemporary sources and the twenty-four-hour clock is used throughout, so 0900, 2300, etc.

At least 200,000 Allied sailors took part in Neptune, and countless more fought the wider Battle of the Seine Bay. They secured the invasion area, successfully landed a huge army along 50 miles of heavily defended coastline, and then protected, sustained and supported it for months. Sailors in the Seine Bay were not taxi drivers. They were active combatants, maintaining a ceaseless watch by day and by night, turning the Seine Bay into the greatest defended encampment in history. Victory in the Second World War depended on them.

This is their story.

Prologue: Death in the Seine Bay
0502, 6 June 1944

I have to report that H.Nor.M.S 'SVENNER' was sunk at 0530 on the 6th June by enemy action.

Kapteinløytnant Tor Holthe, Royal Norwegian Navy[1]

On the night of 5/6 June 1944, Korvettenkapitän Heinrich Hoffmann, commanding the German *5. Torpedobootsflottille* at the occupied French port of Le Havre astride the estuary of the River Seine, was in his cabin aboard his flagship, the torpedo boat *T-28*, preparing for a routine minelaying operation in the Channel. Shortly after midnight, one of Hoffmann's signallers knocked and stepped inside to hand him an important signal, a warning order alerting him to the presence of enemy units steaming south towards the Baie de la Seine, or Seine Bay, the huge inlet of the English Channel which stretched nearly 100 kilometres along the coast of Normandy from Le Havre in the east to the tip of the Cotentin Peninsula at Cap Barfleur in the west. The 34-year-old miner's son from Marburg called his commanding officers aboard for a quick conference, then sent them back to their ships to prepare them for sea.

At 0330, Hoffmann's three serviceable ships, the big fleet torpedo boats *T-28*, *Jaguar* and *Möwe* – equivalent in size and capability to Royal Navy destroyers – slipped out of Le Havre, accompanied by six armed trawlers from *15. Vorpostenflottille* (Patrol Boat Flotilla). As he ploughed steadily south, Hoffmann heard above the sounds of the sea and the steady beat of *T-28*'s engines a constant drone from multiple aircraft engines overhead.[2] At 0502, as dawn started to break, he saw that the horizon ahead was hazy, despite the general absence of cloud. Rightly concluding that this was an artificial smokescreen he pushed his tiny force into the gloom to try to establish what was going on. Emerging at the other side nine minutes later, Hoffmann was shocked to discover a huge force of Allied warships spread out across the Seine Bay, including six battleships or heavy cruisers and between fifteen and twenty destroyers, all heading south; 'curiously', he later noted in the Flotilla War Diary, 'the flotilla was yet to be fired upon'.[3] Feeling as if he was 'sitting in a row boat', Hoffmann ordered his ships to full speed ahead, hoisting his red attack flag. Shortly afterwards, he sent the prearranged signal 'Toni Dora Sechs' (TD6), and each ship launched torpedoes: six from *T-28*, and five each from the other two ships.[4]

The British quickly got over their surprise. The battleship HMS *Warspite* reported engaging 'twelve enemy destroyers' with its main armament at 0604 – proving just how difficult it was to identify small fast-moving targets in poor visibility – and huge waterspouts began to erupt around the heavily outgunned Germans, who fired back with little effect.[5] Shortly afterwards, a huge explosion rocked the trawler *V-1545*, which began to sink by the stern. As its sister ship *V-1511* stopped to pick up survivors, Hoffmann took his torpedo boats in again to draw the British fire, then wisely concluded he had probably done all he could.[6] Zigzagging frantically, the German ships vanished back inside the smokescreen and by 0645 they were tied up alongside in Le Havre. Remarkably, Hoffmann's torpedo boats had just two men lightly wounded, although the number killed, seriously wounded and missing aboard the flimsy *Vorpostenboote* was much higher.[7]

The attack caused some frantic manoeuvring among the bombarding warships. The headquarters ship HMS *Largs* was forced to lurch hard astern and to port, horrified sailors watching a torpedo pass just a few metres in front of the bow.[8] More 'tinfish' narrowly missed the old battleship HMS *Ramillies*, her survival being attributed by one veteran to the fact that the commanding officer, Captain

Gervase Middleton, was wearing a traditional Maori *piu piu* (flax kilt) which had been presented to the ship for luck earlier in the war![9] Middleton himself acknowledged his good fortune, but also his alert lookouts whose report 'saved me'. Middleton continued:

> I was just going to turn the ship back broadside on to the destroyers to engage them, but hearing this I kept her as she was and then watched as no less than five torpedoes went by parallel to me, three to port and two starboard within fifty yards. If I had been across their line several must have hit me … we were all lucky except a small ship beyond me, who stopped one of those that missed me.[10]

That 'small ship' was the Norwegian-manned destroyer HNorMS *Svenner*. There was little the commanding officer, 30-year-old Kapteinløytnant Tor Holthe, could do, as his ship was stationary and he was waiting for minesweepers to clear the way to his bombarding position. Holthe never even saw his assailants. 'Shortly after 0530 a torpedo track was discovered on port beam coming from approximately South East', he wrote in a brief report two days later. 'Full ahead and hard a port were ordered but before the ship had started moving the torpedo struck about midships between the boiler rooms.'

As his stricken ship heeled over to starboard, Holthe, who had first seen action in 1940 when the Germans invaded his country, reluctantly gave the order to abandon ship and his men leapt overboard. At 0540, realising there was no hope of saving his command, he joined his men in the water; shortly afterwards the destroyer broke in two and sank, the bow and stern resting on the seabed and pointing forlornly skywards in a giant V.[11] Many of the survivors were picked up by *Svenner*'s sister ship, HMS *Swift* – Lieutenant-Commander John Gower defying orders and taking his destroyer in close to pick up soaked, shocked men from the water. 'We rescued about eighty', he remembered, 'which made a tremendous handful of extra bodies to look after, some being wounded.'[12] Thirty-two Norwegians and one British sailor died.

Seaman Gunner Edward Wightman watched *Svenner*'s end from his action station aboard *Ramillies*. The destroyer's fate was a grim illustration that the Seine Bay was going to be a dangerous place for sailors. 'Bodies and wreckage, rafts, timber etc floated past', he recorded in his diary. 'Poor chaps – leaves a nasty taste in the mouth.'[13]

Hoffmann's attack on *Svenner* is often the only naval action to appear in accounts of D-Day and the Battle of Normandy. Sometimes, the destroyer's loss is even used as shorthand to imply a lack of action, an absence of genuine 'peril', for ships and sailors involved in Operation Neptune: 'the sole serious attempt by the Kriegsmarine to interfere with the landings'.[14]

Nothing could be further from the truth. *Svenner's* destruction was just one shot in a very long campaign.

✳ 1 ✳
The Long Road Back:
Returning to Europe
May 1940–August 1943

The great design for the return of Allied Forces to the Continent
of EUROPE had its beginnings at Dunkirk . . .

History of COSSAC, May 1944[1]

To an extent, the Royal Navy embarked upon the Second World
War assuming it would replicate the First.

Of course, technology had changed. Aircraft had become more
capable since the Armistice of 11 November 1918. Most nations
possessed some sort of independent or semi-independent air force,
and many had enthusiastically embraced a philosophy – arguably a
cult – that strategic bombing against the enemy's military-industrial
complex could win wars, advocated by air power theorists and melo-
dramatically propagated by popular novelists like H.G. Wells.[2] At
sea, even the most dedicated devotee of big-gun battleships could see
that new technology such as submarines and aircraft carriers would
play a significant role in any future conflict and on land the tank
would be a key component of any modern army.

However, the underlying strategic assumptions about the new war
were largely similar to 1914. A small but scalable British Expeditionary
Force would join a larger French Army to defend the French frontier.
At sea, the Royal Navy's Home Fleet would relocate to its old 1914–18
base, Scapa Flow in Orkney, and keep Nazi Germany's smaller
Kriegsmarine bottled up in the North Sea, while the Strait of Dover

was closed to German warships and submarines by an impenetrable barrier of mines, light forces and aircraft. The German submarines (*Unterseebooten*, or 'U-boats'), which had nearly brought Britain to its knees in 1917, would be defeated by the new wonder weapon ASDIC (today's sonar), which used sound waves to echo-locate submerged submarines. Globally, Allied warships would swiftly hunt down and destroy enemy commerce raiding surface ships, just as they had in 1914–15.[3] The destruction of the German 'pocket battleship' *Admiral Graf Spee* in the South Atlantic on 13 December 1939 seemed to provide an early indicator that it would be business as usual for the Royal Navy and its allies.

The fall of first Norway and then, catastrophically, the Netherlands, Belgium and France to German attack in the spring and early summer of 1940, and Fascist Italy's entry into the war on the Axis side, changed everything. More than eighty years on, knowing that the war was ultimately won by the Allies, it is hard to convey the scale of this catastrophe. Britain was never 'alone', of course: the Empire could still call upon vast resources and reserves of manpower from Canada, Australia, much of Africa and the entire Indian sub-continent to support its war effort, and the United States government, although neutral, was sympathetic. But that support lay thousands of miles away, and had to be brought to Britain by sea, simply to ensure its survival. To actually win the war, a British army would have to return to the continent, this time without the support of a powerful continental ally. Although this was recognised by many planners and decision makers from the outset, it cannot be emphasised enough just how utterly inconceivable it seemed in that bleak summer of 1940.

Returning would require an assault landing of an army by the navy on a hostile shore, an amphibious operation of unprecedented scale and complexity, and such operations were and remain arguably the most challenging and risky of military undertakings. Amphibious operations had been rare and often shambolic in 1914–18, perhaps the most famous example being the Allied landings at Gallipoli in April 1915, when assaulting troops climbed over the bulwarks of open rowing boats or staggered down ramps from the converted collier *River Clyde*, suffering appalling losses. Gallipoli and the carnage which often characterised frontal assaults during the First World War haunted many British decision makers, notably Winston Churchill, who admitted after the war that 'the fearful price we had to pay in human life and blood for the great offensives of the First World War was graven in my mind. Memories of the Somme and Passchendaele ... were not to be blotted out by time and reflection.'[4] This perhaps explains why amphibious tactics and technology were largely neglected during the interwar period, but the catastrophe of 1940 meant that for the British and later the Western Allies, this new war in Europe would have to be an amphibious one. At its peak, Germany eventually controlled an unbroken line of coast stretching from the Spanish frontier to Arctic Norway, and along the Mediterranean from the French Riviera to the Dardanelles. Aggressive, confident use of amphibious warfare could convert this into a vulnerability. Ultimately, only sea power would permit a re-entry into the continent.

There was a mountain to climb. To take just one example, the first tank landing craft, the TLC Mark 1, did not appear until November 1940; eventually around 800 of what became known as Landing Craft Tanks, or LCTs, would be needed to deliver Operation Neptune, alongside thousands of other specialised amphibious ships and craft.[5] Given that so much hinged on the availability of these vessels, they feature heavily in the succeeding chapters. The terms 'landing craft' and 'assault shipping' will henceforth often be used interchangeably and generically to refer to the great variety of shipping used to put an army ashore on a defended coast.

In order to land an army, sailors not only had to learn how to put soldiers ashore safely under fire, but also how to keep them supplied with ammunition, provisions, fuel and weaponry, how to provide them with heavy gunfire support, how to treat and evacuate their casualties and myriad other vital tasks. In an amphibious landing, the entire base infrastructure for the invading army either had to remain on the 'near shore' from whence the invasion came, or it had to remain afloat. Either way it would fall to sailors to provide it and protect it. Although valuable work had been carried out before the war by the Inter-Service Training and Development Centre, established at Fort Cumberland near Portsmouth in May 1938, and by the

Royal Marines' Mobile Naval Base Defence Organisation, this was largely focused on small-scale raiding, not major amphibious landings. In 1940, very few people could even have conceived the scale of the effort which would be required four years later.

One of them was Churchill, despite his inner fears. Even in 1940, with the Empire on the defensive and defeat a possibility, the thrusting, aggressive, newly installed Prime Minister was turning his mind to the offensive. On 7 July 1940, he sent a memo to Herbert Morrison, the Labour politician who had become Minister of Supply in the new wartime coalition, demanding progress on 'designing and planning vessels to transport tanks across the sea for a British attack on enemy countries'.[6] Later in the month he established a new tri-service organisation, Combined Operations Command, with a specific remit to develop amphibious warfare. Its first Chief was the 68-year-old Gallipoli veteran, Admiral of the Fleet Sir Roger Keyes, and at first the focus was on small-scale raids against the enemy-occupied European coast, drawing on plans sketched out by a staff officer, Colonel Dudley Clarke. Clarke was in turn inspired by the actions of the Boer 'Commandos' which had harassed Imperial forces during the First Boer War in South Africa (1899–1902), and this was ultimately what the new raiding forces were titled. Lieutenant-General Sir Alan Bourne, Adjutant-General of the Royal Marines, was tasked with recruiting volunteers from the Army to carry out the raids and finding the necessary naval personnel and ships to deliver them to the far shore and recover them afterwards.[7]

Commandos instilled a confident, offensive spirit at a time when the British Army could do little but remain on the defensive in the main theatre of war. They gave British soldiers and sailors battle experience, and an opportunity to both learn the amphibious techniques which would be so vital when the time finally came to return to the continent, and damage enemy morale by showing that they could strike anywhere and at any time. Men and equipment were in short supply, so the early raids were small in scale, but over time they expanded into fairly major operations.

On 27 October 1941, Churchill selected Captain Lord Louis Mountbatten, a dashing 41-year-old naval officer and member of the

British royal family who had distinguished himself at sea on a number of occasions since the war began, to replace Keyes as Director of Combined Operations. The Mountbatten era coincided with some dramatic changes in Britain's fortunes. Since 22 June 1941 the country had again been fighting with a powerful if erratic continental ally, the Soviet Union, and the opposing German Army had become correspondingly more stretched. The threat of a German invasion was much diminished. Aid from the United States had grown exponentially since the famous Lend-Lease Act of March 1941, and US entry into the war seemed a possibility. With a return to the continent more likely, the time was right for a more professional, strategic Combined Operations. Mountbatten was promoted, first to Commodore and then to Acting Vice-Admiral. Despite his youth and relatively junior rank, he was brought onto the Chiefs of Staff Committee, the collective professional heads of the armed forces, at the same time being granted the honorary ranks of Lieutenant-General in the Army and Air Marshal in the Royal Air Force, a move which did not meet with universal approval. Although he liked and respected Mountbatten, General Sir Alan Brooke, Chief of the Imperial General Staff from December 1941, noted acerbically that 'Mountbatten's inclusion in the COS was a snag ... he frequently wasted both his time and ours ... at times he was apt to concern himself with matters outside his sphere.'[8]

Nevertheless, Mountbatten's enhanced influence was a strong statement about the future importance of Combined Operations, and some of the Commando raids which followed were much larger, more complex experiments in tri-service collaboration – a number of them, and the larger assault landings which followed, are shown on Map 1. Nearly 600 commandos took part in an attack on Vågsøy on 27 December 1941 (Operation Archery), fighting a pitched battle against German mountain troops in the streets of the small Norwegian town. On 27–28 February 1942, paratroops made a daring raid on Bruneval, north of Le Havre on the Normandy coast, capturing German radar equipment and technical personnel before withdrawing by sea (Operation Biting). Finally, in Operation Chariot on 28 March 1942, the so-called Greatest Raid of All, hundreds of

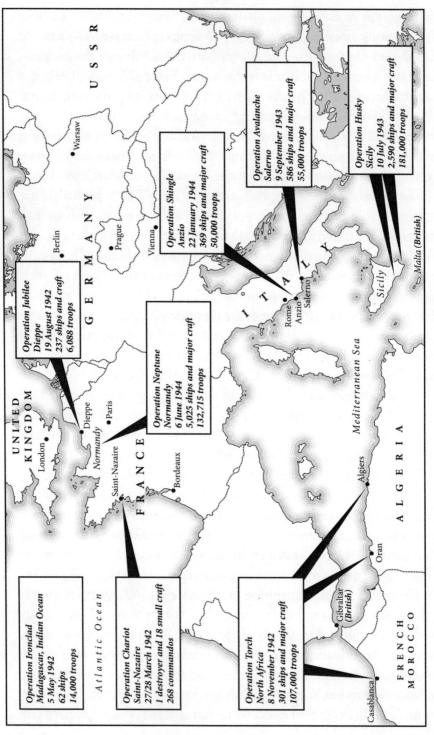

Operation Ironclad
Madagascar, Indian Ocean
5 May 1942
62 ships
14,000 troops

Operation Chariot
Saint-Nazaire
27/28 March 1942
1 destroyer and 18 small craft
268 commandos

Operation Torch
North Africa
8 November 1942
301 ships and major craft
107,000 troops

Operation Jubilee
Dieppe
19 August 1942
237 ships and craft
6,088 troops

Operation Neptune
Normandy
6 June 1944
5,025 ships and major craft
132,715 troops

Operation Shingle
Anzio
22 January 1944
369 ships and major craft
50,000 troops

Operation Avalanche
Salerno
9 September 1943
586 ships and major craft
55,000 troops

Operation Husky
Sicily
10 July 1943
2,550 ships and major craft
181,000 troops

Map 1. Assault landings, 1942–5.

commandos smashed facilities in the French port of Saint-Nazaire and the Royal Navy slammed the obsolete, explosive-filled destroyer HMS *Campbeltown* into the gates of the huge Normandie Dock, the only dock on the west coast of France capable of receiving the German battleship *Tirpitz*. Although the cost was high, the operation was successful, as *Campbeltown* exploded shortly afterwards, putting the dock out of commission for years. Further afield, in May 1942 the British staged a successful amphibious landing against the Indian Ocean island of Madagascar, which was defended by French troops from the pro-Axis Vichy regime established after the 1940 surrender. Codenamed Ironclad, this often-overlooked operation represented a quantum leap in amphibious capability. Assault transports and troopships landed a force of three entire brigades, reinforced by tanks and Commandos, and supported by nearly fifty warships and nine squadrons of carrier-borne aircraft; this was the first time the Royal Navy's Fleet Air Arm had supported an amphibious operation. Ironclad also saw the first use of an improvised Landing Ship Tank (LST), a type which would prove essential in the more ambitious operations which would follow.[9]

Filled with confidence, Combined Operations turned its collective mind to an operation of still greater scale. With the US in the war since the Japanese attack on Pearl Harbor on 7 December 1941, an invasion of occupied Europe was inevitable, and the Americans were in a hurry. Although they had agreed with the British that Germany constituted the more serious threat and as a consequence had committed themselves to a policy of 'Germany First' at the First Washington Conference (22 December 1941–14 January 1942), popular opinion in the US demanded retaliation against the Japanese. The result was years of wrangling, with the Americans impatient to invade and bring the European war to an end, and the British more cautious.

This so-called Second Front Debate has been much misrepresented. Most informed Americans understood perfectly well that it would take months, if not years, to prepare an invasion of occupied Europe, which could only take place when sufficient US troops and military equipment had crossed the Atlantic. Moving this vast force across the English Channel in turn required the construction of huge numbers of transport and assault ships. The Allies had to learn how to conduct large-scale amphibious operations, and the US Army desperately needed combat experience. Germany's military-industrial complex had to be degraded as much as possible, through aerial bombing and through a grinding war of attrition against the Soviet Army on the Eastern Front. Finally, to ensure that this vulnerable armada could make the crossing as safely as possible, control of the sea and the skies above it had to be guaranteed.

1 July 1943 was estimated to be the earliest possible date for a re-entry to the continent. On 27 March 1942, US Army planners presented an outline invasion plan – optimistically entitled Operation Roundup – to President Franklin D. Roosevelt, requiring forty-eight Allied divisions and around a million troops. The build-up of forces in the UK, code-named Bolero, was to begin immediately, along with a sustained aerial bombing campaign. Dubbed the Marshall Memorandum, after General George C. Marshall, the US Army's Chief of Staff, it was approved by Roosevelt on 1 April 1942. The location of the proposed invasion was yet to be determined, but it was likely to take place somewhere between Boulogne and Le Havre.[10] The only circumstances in which an earlier landing might take place were if Soviet resistance disintegrated or, conversely, the Red Army delivered such an overwhelming blow in the east that Germany was on the verge of collapse, in which case a hastily improvised operation, Sledgehammer, would take place near Cherbourg. The British, although dubious about the United States' ability to deliver the resources required in little over a year, formally accepted the Marshall Memorandum on 14 April 1942. Given that at this time the Allies were being thrown back on all fronts by overwhelming Japanese, German and Italian forces, this was an extraordinarily confident decision.

Some significant figures, notably Churchill, still preferred a more peripheral strategy, usually in the Mediterranean. 'You must remember', one Churchill confidante apparently told Marshall, 'you are fighting our losses on the Somme.'[11] But most British decision makers recognised that victory would only come with the return of Allied boots to northern European soil. The mature debate was not about 'if' but about 'when and where'. While the bulk of the military and naval forces were British, the British got the final say, and preferred to defer the landings until Germany was weaker and the Allies stronger. As more US troops arrived and the Americans grew in confidence and political shrewdness, eventually the British were relegated to the role of junior partner and the decision was taken out of their hands.

At first, planners believed that without the successful capture of an operational port through which supplies and reinforcements could flow to the battle front, no amphibious landing could succeed. In early 1942, Mountbatten and the Combined Operations planning team prepared an ambitious raid on the French coast involving regular infantry and armoured formations, delivered by Royal Navy landing craft with strong naval and air support. The objective was to seize and hold the port of Dieppe for a limited period of time. Dubbed Operation Jubilee, it took place on 19 August 1942, and it was a disaster. Of more than 6,000 mostly Canadian troops who landed, 980 were killed, 635 were wounded but brought home and 2,010 were taken prisoner.[12] The RAF lost over 100 aircraft with 102 men killed wounded and taken prisoner, while the Royal Navy lost 33 landing craft and a destroyer, with 523 sailors killed, wounded or captured. However, valuable lessons were learned about the importance of beach reconnaissance, air superiority and effective, overwhelming naval gunfire support, including the provision of cheap, expendable inshore fire control craft (see Chapter 4). Significantly, another lesson was the need to form permanent, coherent naval assault forces, ensuring efficient co-ordination of forces while afloat and immediately after landing. Above all, Jubilee confirmed the need for an alternative to capturing a heavily defended port.[13] All of this helped ensure Neptune's success nearly two years later. Whether these important lessons were worth the very high cost paid is a debate to be considered elsewhere. Certainly, the Canadian Official Historian argued that they were 'the price paid for the knowledge that enabled the great operation of 1944 to be carried out'.[14]

What was abundantly clear was that the Allies were not ready to invade and the Germans were still too strong, particularly in the air. While the build-up of sea, land and air forces continued, along with efforts to degrade German strength at sea, in the air and (in Russia) on land, the Americans reluctantly conceded at the hastily convened Second Washington Conference (19–25 June 1942) that landings in northern France in 1942 were impossible and even 1943 was probably unlikely. While planning continued, at British insistence the Allies committed to a sequence of operations in the Mediterranean, with the eventual aim of opening up vital sea lanes and driving Italy out of the war. Here, further experience could be gained and US troops be committed into action in Europe without the huge risks inherent in a cross-Channel operation.

The first was an amphibious landing on the coast of Vichy French-occupied North Africa, Operation Torch. Combined with an offensive by General Bernard Montgomery's 8th Army, presently dug in and facing General Erwin Rommel's Deutsches Afrikakorps to the west of Alexandria, at the other end of the North African littoral, the ambition was to annihilate all German–Italian forces in North Africa and lay the groundwork for further operations in southern Europe, as well as open up the Mediterranean to Allied shipping. The more myopically land-focused critics of the Mediterranean strategy often overlook the very real benefits of this last point. With the Mediterranean a dangerous, contested space, most vulnerable Allied merchant shipping was forced to take the longer route around the Cape of Good Hope before transiting either the Red Sea, to supply Montgomery, or the Indian Ocean to supply forces in the Far East. Every ship using this route was tied up for months. Safe access to the Mediterranean meant shorter journeys and faster turnaround times, which by extension created more shipping capacity – an essential prerequisite for any invasion of northern France.

For largely political reasons Torch was constructed as an almost entirely US-led operation. This gave US commanders vital combat experience, notably the Commander-in-Chief, Lieutenant-General Dwight D. Eisenhower, an experienced staff officer who had been largely responsible for shaping the US Army's 'Germany First' strategy before the war began. Torch helped Eisenhower develop the wholly integrated Allied command structure, which would serve him well in Italy, and then in Normandy. Bringing US troops into action against Germans and Italians would also motivate US popular opinion in favour of 'Germany First'. Finally, the Vichy French in North Africa had no reason to love the British after the Royal Navy's destruction of their fleet at Mers-el-Kébir on 3 July 1940, which had cost the lives of 1,297 French sailors, so it was expedient to badge as many participants as possible as American in the hope of bringing about an early capitulation.

Launched on 8 November 1942 and coinciding with Montgomery's dramatic victory over Rommel at El-Alamein (23 October– 4 November) thousands of kilometres to the east, Torch took the Vichy French – and the Germans – entirely by surprise, thanks to excellent intelligence and operational security. Three assault forces landed at Casablanca, Oran and Algiers. The first two were entirely American; Algiers was a British sector but again, the first waves of assault troops were American. At sea, as during Neptune, it was a very different story. The Western Naval Task Force at Casablanca, which sailed directly from the United States, was entirely American, totalling 91 warships and 31 transports, all under the overall command of Rear-Admiral Henry Kent Hewitt, USN, but most of the ships which made up the Eastern and Central Task Forces were British, and the entire operation afloat was under the command of Admiral Sir Andrew Cunningham, RN, as Naval Commander Expeditionary Force.

Torch was not without its learning points. The expectation had been that the Vichy French would rapidly change sides and join General Charles de Gaulle's Free French, but this assumption showed a lamentable failure to understand the intricacies of French politics, and resistance was fierce in places, notably Casablanca. At Oran, an attempted *coup de main* to seize the harbour was bloodily repulsed with the loss of the two small warships carrying the assault force, reinforcing the key lesson from Dieppe, that taking a defended port from the sea was almost impossible. Elsewhere, heavy surf proved to be a significant obstacle. In some places the mountainous waves reached nearly 5m in height, swamping landing craft and causing further chaos when subsequent forces arrived to find the beaches cluttered with wrecks. 'Conditions on the beaches ... presented a scene of the greatest confusion', ran one official account; 'lorries, jeeps, light tanks and stores were piling up so fast that they could only be kept above the high water mark with the greatest difficulty ... crews of stranded landing craft were wandering round aimlessly or tinkering ineffectively with their craft.'[15] It is worth emphasising just how disastrous this situation would have been on the French coast, with more motivated and resolute German opposition waiting to take advantage. It provides another excellent illustration of just how much the Allies had to learn before they could return to the continent. However, Torch was still a success. Three days later, Admiral François Darlan ordered a general ceasefire, bringing the fighting to an end in Algeria and Morocco. Unfortunately, before the Allies could exploit their success, the Germans moved into neighbouring Tunisia at the invitation of the Vichy government, beginning a long, grim slog of a campaign through the winter which did not end until May. Torch also led to a German occupation of the whole of mainland France – much of the south had been under Vichy administration – and Corsica.

In January 1943, with the campaign in North Africa still raging, Churchill, Roosevelt and their military commanders, the Combined Chiefs of Staff, held a conference in newly liberated Casablanca, codenamed Symbol. Stalin was invited to attend but declined as the Battle of Stalingrad had reached a critical stage. Key decisions included the policy of accepting nothing less than an unconditional German surrender, and the commitment to a combined strategic bombing campaign from the UK against Germany. The Americans lobbied hard for an invasion of north-west Europe in 1943, and the British pushed back equally hard, arguing instead for a continued Mediterranean strategy to draw down more German forces from France and continue their attrition on the Eastern Front, maintain momentum and make best use of the huge Allied armies now in theatre. Reluctantly, the Americans agreed. The invasion of France was deferred, although the build-up of forces continued, and planning began for an invasion of Sicily in the spring.

However, crucially, the Americans were able to push through the creation of an Anglo-American planning staff for the invasion of France, led by the British Lieutenant-General Frederick Morgan. Its title, COSSAC, was an acronym derived from his title: Chief of

Staff to the Supreme Allied Commander, although no Supreme Commander had been appointed yet, making the task extremely challenging. Sir Alan Brooke apparently appointed Morgan with the 'pithy' words 'Well there it is, it won't work but you must bloody well make it!'[16] COSSAC's first task was to determine the precise location for the invasion. The availability of suitable beaches and the limited range of air cover during the assault meant there were only two viable options: the shortest but most obvious crossing from Dover to the Pas-de-Calais, which also offered the most direct route into Germany, or Normandy's Seine Bay.[17]

At Casablanca it was also decided that the Allied bombing offensive by the US 8th Air Force and the RAF's Bomber Command should now prioritise destroying German airpower, to ensure total control of the air prior to an invasion. This would be achieved by destroying German aircraft factories on the ground and German fighters in the air, in turn forcing yet more fighters to be withdrawn from the west to defend the Reich. This was confirmed in a directive issued by the Combined Chiefs of Staff on 10 June 1943, which gave this huge operation the codename Pointblank, its primary task 'the destruction of the German fighter force and the industries which supplied it'.[18] The Allied planners also acknowledged that an essential prerequisite for the invasion was providing sufficient resources, at sea and in the air, to defeat Germany's U-boats in the North Atlantic. Without a decisive victory in the Atlantic, the safe and timely arrival of the vast forces required to undertake an invasion of France could not be guaranteed. The Battle of the Seine Bay would have been infinitely costlier had it been subject to interference by an undefeated Luftwaffe and U-bootwaffe.

These decisions were reiterated at the Third Washington Conference (Trident, 11–25 May 1943), when the Americans reluctantly conceded that no invasion of France could take place before May 1944, but it was clear that the Americans were now imposing their will more effectively: although the Mediterranean offensive would continue from Sicily on to the Italian mainland, a firm target date of 1 May 1944 was set for the invasion of France, now codenamed Overlord, and the British accepted that troops and ships would have to be withdrawn from the Mediterranean to support it. Even Churchill, after speaking eloquently and at length about every possible Mediterranean or Balkan diversion, made it clear that 'His Majesty's Government earnestly desired to undertake a full scale invasion of the Continent from the United Kingdom as soon as a plan offering reasonable prospects of success could be made.'[19] British opposition to Overlord has been overstated at times. Even Brooke, no cheerleader for US strategy or, indeed, US strategists, and deeply pessimistic about the prospects for any cross-Channel operation, nevertheless recorded in his diary while attending Trident that the ultimate goal of any peripheral approach was to 'force a dispersal of German forces, help Russia, and thus eventually produce a situation where cross-Channel operations are possible'.[20]

Operation Husky, the invasion of Sicily, took place on 10 July 1943. Husky was the second largest amphibious operation of the war after Overlord, involving more than 2,500 ships and 180,000 troops landing along nearly 100 miles of coast. The opposition was also the fiercest to date. At Licata, US landing craft were heavily engaged by shore batteries, and the minesweeper USS *Sentinel* was sunk after repeated attacks by German dive bombers, with the loss of ten lives.[21] Air attack was a constant threat, by day and by night. Off Gela, the destroyer USS *Maddox* was also bombed and sunk, with even heavier loss of life: 211 officers and men. In the same sector, the US Navy provided an object lesson on the value of naval gunfire by targeting and driving off a counter-attack by Italian light tanks.

More lessons were learned in the Sicily landings. The Anglo-American senior command structure failed to work properly, with inter-Allied and inter-service relationships almost dysfunctional at times. Beach organisation, although an improvement on Torch, remained poor. The accompanying airborne landing was a disaster, with US paratroops being very badly scattered and more than 200 soldiers drowning when British gliders landed in the sea. The subsequent land campaign took longer than expected and ended with the remarkable German evacuation of its largely intact army across the Strait of Messina to the Italian mainland on the night of 11/12 August.

Sicily was followed by landings on mainland Italy, at Salerno in Operation Avalanche (9 September) and across the Strait of Messina in Operation Baytown a few days later. Avalanche was a close-run affair, saved once again to a significant extent by effective naval gunfire support. When the Italian front stagnated, one final major landing, Operation Shingle, was undertaken at Anzio, south of Naples, on 22 January 1944. An effort to outflank the defending Germans, the landings at Anzio instead also became bogged down for months.

In the meantime, between 28 June and 2 July 1943, with less than a year to go, Mountbatten chaired a conference, codenamed Rattle, at HMS *Warren*, formerly the Hollywood Hotel in the Scottish town of Largs, which was coincidentally the name of one of the headquarters ships which would take part in Neptune. Twenty generals, eleven air marshals and air commodores and eight admirals, including five Canadians and fifteen Americans, thrashed out the relative merits of Normandy and the Pas-de-Calais, and concluded that the German defences in the Pas-de-Calais were too formidable, the beaches too narrow and road exits too congested to make a landing viable. The advantages of a short sea crossing were also illusory, as the invasion forces would still have to come from ports all around the southern English coast. It would have to be Normandy.[22]

This 'COSSAC Plan' was taken to a further inter-Allied conference, Quadrant, held in Quebec between 17 and 24 August, where it was endorsed by Churchill, Roosevelt and the Combined Chiefs. They also endorsed the construction of artificial ports, codenamed Mulberry, to offset the requirement to land near a heavily defended port, and thus mitigate against another Dieppe scenario.[23] Quadrant also committed the Allies to a simultaneous landing in the south of France, codenamed Anvil, which was to become a source of considerable Anglo-American friction. In theory it was intended as a diversion to tie down German forces in the south of France, and a means of opening up the port of Marseille, but it would also draw resources away from the Mediterranean campaign, resented by some Americans as an irrelevant British-inspired sideshow motivated by imperial concerns.

From a naval perspective, this point of view is arguably simplistic and unjust. For the Allied navies, the Mediterranean was a vast classroom, in which a string of progressively more challenging amphibious operations taught vital skills to sailors of all ranks. Neptune's future Naval Commander-in-Chief, the formidable Admiral Sir Bertram Ramsay, RN, and his two principal subordinates, Rear-Admiral Alan Kirk, USN (Commander Western Naval Task Force) and Rear-Admiral Sir Philip Vian, RN (Commander Eastern Naval Task Force) all gained vital experience in the Mediterranean, as did many of their senior officers and thousands of their sailors. The Mediterranean provided a hard core of experienced personnel, in some cases forming entire ship's companies of everything from landing craft to battleships. However, the Battle of the Seine Bay would require thousands more ships and sailors – more than twice as many as Husky.

It is time, therefore, to return to the United Kingdom, to examine the extraordinary efforts being made to prepare for the Normandy operation: building ships, recruiting and training sailors, planning history's most complex amphibious landing and, firstly, doing every-thing possible to ensure that the Allied navies dominated the Seine Bay, the English Channel, and the wider maritime battlefield which surrounded them.

✳ 2 ✳
Owning the Channel: Operations in Home Waters
January 1943–June 1944

You went to sea looking for trouble – that was the idea!
Able Seaman Bernard Howe, MTB-739[1]

By June 1944 the Royal Navy and its allies had established a qual-
itative, quantitative and psychological dominance over the
enemy which was arguably the most essential ingredient for victory
in the Seine Bay, but it could never be taken for granted. It had to be
earned.

The Royal Navy greatly outnumbered Germany's Kriegsmarine,
but numerical superiority was not enough. The British were grossly
overextended: as well as home waters, the fleet had to provide forces
for the Mediterranean, the Indian Ocean and the Arctic, as well as
countless smaller deployments. The United States Navy did almost
all the heavy lifting in the Pacific and the Royal Canadian Navy
(RCN), which expanded from a tiny coast defence force to become
the world's third largest navy by 1945, gradually took over much of
the responsibility for the Battle of the Atlantic, but this meant neither
service had much to spare for the waters around the United Kingdom.[2]
If the Kriegsmarine combined local superiority with good planning
and a little luck, it could achieve success against the odds, as it did
during the famous 'Channel Dash' in February 1942, when the
battlecruisers *Scharnhorst* and *Gneisenau* and the heavy cruiser *Prinz
Eugen* passed through the Strait of Dover on their way back to

21

Germany. A similar triumph during Neptune/Overlord could be disastrous.

Not every operation in home waters was directly conceived as an enabling action for Neptune/Overlord but indirectly, almost everything helped. Prior to January 1943, much of the Royal Navy's time was spent in defensive work: minesweeping, escorting coastal convoys and trying to intercept German light naval forces raiding from occupied Europe.[3] But from the start of 1943, as the Official Historian writes, 'our various forces were now far more active in the enemy's coastal waters than his were in our own. And, as harbingers of an even more important swing of the pendulum, Combined Operations bases and training establishments were now springing up all around our coasts.'[4]

Much of this offensive action was carried out by the small warships of the Royal Navy's Coastal Forces, working alongside aircraft from the Fleet Air Arm and the Royal Air Force's Coastal Command to strike German naval and merchant shipping from the Norwegian fjords to the Bay of Biscay. Among the most important targets were Germany's *Schnellbooten*, fast, well-armed motor torpedo boats known as 'E-boats' to the Allies, which could inflict damage out of all proportion to their size if well-handled.[5] Even a small number of E-boats could wreak havoc among vulnerable invasion traffic. They had been virtually invulnerable in the first years of the war: too heavily armed to be threatened by any of the flimsy British craft which could match their speed, and too fast to be caught by anything bigger. It was a full year before the Royal Navy managed to sink one. But by 1943, the balance was shifting thanks to a combination of new, more powerful, Allied aircraft and fast attack craft available in much larger numbers; well-trained, experienced crews; and innovative tactics, notably the use of radar and wireless interception which took advantage of the incessant chatter which was the E-boats' Achilles heel.

Anthony Rushworth-Lund was a Fleet Air Arm pilot with years of combat experience in the Mediterranean. In April 1943 he joined 841 Squadron, flying anti-E-boat patrols in converted Albacore torpedo bombers out of RAF Manston. The Albacores were vectored on to their targets from a control room in Dover or using their own primitive radar equipment, but the last stages of interception always relied on the old-fashioned 'Mk 1 Eyeball'. 'This was all at night, absolute non-moon stuff', Rushworth-Lund recalled, 'so you had to be able to see these things. Obviously if they were moving, they left a nice wake in the water and you'd pick that up.'[6]

The slow biplanes made ideal, stable platforms for rocket attacks on enemy shipping. 'If you got rockets into a boat it almost certainly would sink', Rushworth-Lund recalled, 'we looked all around and couldn't see any sign of it at all after that so we'd always assume it was sunk.'[7] The Albacores were seen as such effective anti-shipping platforms that when the Fleet Air Arm squadrons were withdrawn on 1 June 1943 to meet a pressing need for trained air crews to serve aboard aircraft carriers, the RAF requested a small number of the naval biplanes for continued service in coastal waters. RAF aircraft made 572 attacks between January and May 1943, sinking twenty-two ships. Offensive minelaying was another key tool. During the same period, the RAF laid 6,559 mines in the Channel and the North Sea, sinking another seventy-four ships and damaging ten.[8]

The fast attack craft of the Royal Navy's Coastal Forces were just as effective. Coastal Forces had begun the war as a small group of largely experimental craft, manned primarily by young reservists with courage and enthusiasm but limited training and expertise. By September 1943 it had grown exponentially in numbers, experience and capability, with the key Royal Navy commands at Portsmouth, Plymouth, Dover and the Nore boasting nearly 350 Motor Torpedo Boats (MTBs, the principal platform for attacking enemy shipping), Motor Gun Boats (MGBs) and Motor Launches (MLs). Many crews operated highly capable British Power Boat Mark V MGBs and later Fairmile D MTBs, nicknamed 'Dog Boats': powerful, formidably armed craft which finally gave Coastal Forces the ability to take on and defeat E-boats. Albert Morrow, from Vancouver, commanded *MTB-726* in the all-Canadian 65th MTB Flotilla:

These were Dog Boats . . . We were fitted with four supercharged Packard engines, 1500 horsepower apiece and four propellers so

we sounded like a bomber taking off and we had a top speed of
... 40 knots, but when we got all our armament on and that kind
of thing it was about 38 knots. We were pretty hard hitting! We
had a semi-automatic anti-tank gun up forward with a 36-inch
recoil. We had a rocket firing machine beside that, then on either
side of the bridge going aft we had two turrets of twin 0.5s. Up on
the bridge we had two banks of .303 Vickers anti-personnel and
then after the bridge itself was a turret of Oerlikon twin 20mms,
and then aft of that again on the stern was the 'Chicago Piano',
the 40mm.[9]

According to Able Seaman Bernard Howe of *MTB-739* 'you went
to sea looking for trouble – that was the idea', sometimes night
after night if the weather conditions permitted.[10] The same three
boats of the 14th MTB Flotilla, for example, fought actions against
German convoys off Saint-Valery-en-Caux on the nights of 8/9 and
10/11 September 1943, sustaining damage on both occasions and
claiming an enemy craft sunk on the first night.[11] Morrow vividly
described the breathless nature of these actions, fought at high speeds
in the dark:

> We had to make sure we had [a] 90-degree angle on the bow
> because that would present a broader target to us ... to get into
> the best range was 800 yards but meanwhile if we were discov-
> ered, we were being fired on. If anybody tells you they've never
> been afraid ... he's either a liar or dead drunk! ... You're really
> scared, and as soon as you fire your torpedoes, then you usually
> can turn on a parallel course, Order 1 we called it ... and open fire
> with everything we had. Well, then your fear, your nervousness,
> goes then because you're hitting back.[12]

The sheer number of operations precludes describing every action,
but the events which follow give some flavour of the intensity during
this crucial period, as the Royal Navy stamped its authority on these
vital waters. The Battle of the Seine Bay can perhaps be said to have
begun in October 1943, when it instituted a series of offensive sweeps

close to the occupied French coast, codenamed Tunnel, which were intended to wear down the Kriegsmarine, disrupt German shipping and gain control of the Channel. These sweeps were directed by Ultra intelligence, obtained by codebreakers at Bletchley Park by deciphering German Enigma signals. The second Tunnel took place on the night of 22/23 October, and it was a disaster. Six destroyers set off with the cruiser HMS *Charybdis* on a still, squally night, expecting to intercept the German blockade runner *Münsterland*. At 0135, the cruiser detected what turned out to be five German fleet torpedo boats of *4. Torpedobootsflotilla*. Shockingly quickly, the destroyer *Talybont*'s German-speaking 'Headache' (wireless intercept) operator heard the enemy force shake out into line ahead, and then fire torpedoes. *Charybdis* was hit twice, at 0145 and 0150, the second exploding in the engine room and bringing the cruiser to a stop. The destroyer HMS *Limbourne* immediately fired illuminating flares, possibly a poor decision as a minute later, a torpedo hit her too, detonating the forward magazine and blowing off the bow.[13] The unseen German torpedo boats left and the remaining destroyers were left to pick up the pieces. *Charybdis* sank within half an hour. *Limbourne* stayed afloat but despite repeated efforts, could only steam in circles. Towing the destroyer also proved impossible, 'owing to a very large portion of the ship's side projecting at right angles to the ship rendering her unmanageable', according to Lieutenant Edward Baines, CO (Commanding Officer) of *Talybont*.[14] *Limbourne*'s CO and First Lieutenant being 'concussed and incoherent', the decision to abandon was taken by a 'a conference of available officers', after which the ship was torpedoed by *Talybont* and later by HMS *Rocket*. The rest of the force lingered until 0600 picking up survivors, before heading home under a protective umbrella of RAF fighters.

The defeat was attributed mainly to the fact that the ships had never worked together. 'In peace time it was agreed a night encounter was the most difficult battle of all', commented the highly experienced Roger Hill, commanding the destroyer HMS *Grenville*, who led the battered force home, 'flotillas were trained night after night ... yet here we were in wartime taking a hotchpotch of destroyers without any practice or training and going over to the enemy coast to look for a flotilla of Elbing Class destroyers who all went the same speed and were . . . accustomed to working together'.[15] *Charybdis* was also an inappropriate ship for the job, and was new to the Channel. Tragically the cruiser's captain, George Voelcker, had confessed to Hill good humouredly that he was 'more experienced as an anti-aircraft cruiser' just before the force sailed, when the latter had tried to have the operation postponed allowing time for more training.[16] 462 men died in *Charybdis*, and another 39 in *Limbourne*. It was an inauspicious start which made it clear the Royal Navy still had a great deal of work to do before the Channel could truly be considered a safe operating environment for the invasion.

That work continued the night after the Tunnel disaster, when Coastal Forces craft and Royal Navy destroyers fought one of the biggest E-boat battles of the war. Twenty-eight raiders came out to attack two convoys passing each other off the Norfolk coast near Cromer. Like most such actions, it was chaos: a frenzy of small craft operating at incredibly high speeds, weaving in and out of plodding rows of merchant ships, and fought mostly in the dark except for the occasional starshell which illuminated the mayhem in its brief glare. In all six MGBs and two MLs took part, divided into pairs which operated independently as Units Y, R, V and S. Destroyers from the convoy escorts provided heavier firepower.

Unit Y, MGBs *603* and *607*, had perhaps the most dramatic success of the night. Arriving on the scene at 0103, the two boats sat quietly, following events using hydrophones and tracking enemy movements by watching for gunfire and listening to radio traffic. At 0153, the MGB crews leaped into action, increasing speed and turning on their radar, when they detected contacts less than 2,000 metres away. Starshell revealed two E-boats, one on fire. 26-year-old Lieutenant Mike Marshall, an Oxford rugby blue from north Yorkshire and senior officer in *607*, ordered full speed and both MGBs turned towards the enemy, pouring fire into the stricken E-boat. At this point his equally determined opponent, Korvettenkapitän Werner Lützow in the undamaged *S-88*, the commander of *4. Schnellbootflottille*, altered course to starboard, steering straight for him. Marshall, apparently no more willing to back down from a challenge at sea than he was on the rugby field, ordered his helm to port and turned *607* to ram, taking heavy fire as he did so. '*MGB 607* struck the enemy amidships at practically full speed at 0214', he wrote in his report; 'own boat was thrown clear by speed of enemy and engines were then stopped as considerable damage to bow was suspected.'[17]

As Marshall watched from his wallowing, badly damaged boat, *S-88* slipped beneath the waves. Shortly afterwards, the second E-boat, Leutnant zur See Dietrich Howaldt's *S-63*, which had been on fire throughout the action, 'blew up with a colossal explosion throwing debris some 200 feet into the air', just as *603* closed to investigate. Forty survivors were recovered, although Lützow was not among them; he was last seen lying in the debris of *S-88*'s bridge with a catastrophic head injury.[18]

Somehow Marshall nursed his mangled command home at a stately 3 knots. The action cost the lives of five of his crew, but thanks to his efforts and those of the other crews, almost the entire German E-boat force in the West failed to sink a single merchant ship. The only British loss was the escort trawler *William Stephen*, which was caught alone after straggling astern of the convoy.

A few weeks later, the Royal Navy scored another startling success, this time in the Bay of Biscay. Allied Ultra intelligence derived from German signals sent using the Enigma cipher machine and deciphered by the now-famous codebreakers at 'Station X', the Government Code and Cypher School at Bletchley Park, indicated that seven blockade-running merchant ships were preparing to leave various French ports and five loaded ships were returning with cargoes of vital raw materials from Japan. Although these materials were important, the quantities carried in a single ship were small, and intercepting blockade runners had as much to do with establishing dominance at sea as it did with destroying cargoes. Operation Stonewall was established as a standing cruiser patrol operating out of Plymouth and Horta in the Portuguese Azores, supported by strong air patrols. The notionally neutral Horta was a strange place to be: Commander Felix Lloyd-Davies, Executive Officer of HMS *Glasgow*, recalled how 'there was no black out . . . the ship had to put her deck lights and things on for the first time in the war.

We were there for Christmas in 1943 and we were going to give a big children's party!'[19]

That party never took place. At 1911 on 23 December, *Glasgow* was ordered to sea after a patrolling US aircraft sighted an inbound merchant ship. HMS *Enterprise* and the New Zealand-manned cruiser HMNZS *Gambia* also joined the patrol line. The first blockade runner slipped through the net but by this point multiple aircraft had reported more enemy ships at sea; by 1100 on Christmas Eve, Admiral Sir Ralph Leatham, the Commander-in-Chief at Plymouth, had concluded that 'it had become quite obvious that blockade running was in full swing'.[20] The aircraft had also sighted enemy destroyers, which the Kriegsmarine had ordered to sea in a standing operation to escort incoming blockade runners. On the 27th, the searches bore fruit when a Czech-crewed B.24 Liberator of 311 Squadron attacked the blockade-runner *Alsterufer*, which was set on fire and later abandoned. However, it was the last phase of this confused and protracted battle which brought real benefits in the Seine Bay six months later. *Glasgow* and *Enterprise* were ordered to combine and search for the German destroyer force. The two cruisers rendezvoused at about 0300, in pitch dark and heavy seas, and then spent a frustrating day responding to confused and inconsistent air reports before, at 1335 on the 28th, *Glasgow* obtained a radar contact, then spotted masts and signalled 'Enemy in sight'.[21]

The contact turned out to be eleven enemy destroyers, but the British cruisers had placed themselves between the Germans and their base, and the senior officer, Captain Charles Clarke of *Glasgow*, did not hesitate to engage. 'The Chief Yeoman on the Bridge was the first person to sight them', Felix Lloyd-Davies recalled, 'and when he said the enemy is in three columns consisting of eleven ships it rather took the smile off our faces, as it meant there were about double the number we expected!'[22] Not everyone was so nonchalant. Ordnance Artificer Albert Pitman of *Glasgow* remembered the cruiser's Gunnery Officer exclaiming over the Tannoy 'Enemy in sight . . . my Christ it's eleven German destroyers! We're for it!'[23]

Clarke intended to make the most of his opportunity. 'My intention was to engage any destroyer which looked like closing to her effective range', he wrote in his report. 'I would "stand my ground" until more than one attained this range, when I would turn away to reduce the closing rate.'[24] Albert Pitman remembered this process being rather more dramatic: 'Nobby Clarke took the *Glasgow* in', he recalled. 'He was an ex-destroyer skipper. Bows on to the first Narvik [class destroyer], gave her the forward turrets, [then] slewed round and gave her the after turrets and ran out again.'[25]

Glasgow altered course and opened fire at 1346. The older *Enterprise* conformed to *Glasgow*'s movements, her Canadian skipper, Captain Harold Grant, breaking out his battle ensigns and opening up with his own guns two minutes later. The German force consisted of five large Narvik Class destroyers and six Elbing Class fleet torpedo boats divided into two flotillas, with the senior officer being Kapitän zur See Hans Erdmenger of *8.Zerstörer-Flottille*. They fought bravely but were poorly co-ordinated and the weather conditions did not favour them. 'We'd . . . forced them to fight the action in a rather heavy sea which helped us because of course being destroyers their foremost guns are more difficult to work than ours', Lloyd-Davies recalled:

> At one point they formed a semi-circle and they all fired their torpedoes . . . we then turned at high speed and steamed out and the nearest torpedo only came within about two hundred yards of us. After that we went back into action again and the Germans now appeared to be demoralised and started trying to make off in small numbers. Our gunnery was extremely efficient and we were putting every German ship out of the line after about four or five salvoes.[26]

For the first forty-five minutes the Germans fought together, joined at 1400 by a lone Focke-Wulf Condor patrol aircraft, which launched an ineffective glider bomb attack before being driven off. Five minutes later *Glasgow* was hit just below the bridge, wrecking the light anti-aircraft guns and killing two sailors.[27] The torpedo attack was much more effective than Lloyd-Davies's casual reflections imply: according to the official report it was delivered with 'considerable accuracy' and *Glasgow* had to make an emergency turn.[28] But the British fire was heavy and accurate, and at 1428 the German force split, the main body retiring to the south under cover of a smokescreen while Erdmenger took *Z-27* and the fleet torpedo boats *T-22*, *T-25* and *T-26* to the north, with *Enterprise* and *Glasgow* in hot pursuit. This diminished German force was now catastrophically outgunned, and all four ships were damaged; the end was not long in coming. By 1515, *Z-27* was stopped and on fire after a shell hit from *Enterprise* wrecked the boiler room, *T-22* was retiring at speed under a smokescreen, and *Glasgow* and *Enterprise* were engaging *T-25* and *T-26*, both of which were battered into submission and then sunk with torpedoes by *Enterprise*. *Glasgow* finished off the wrecked *Z-27*, closing to under 2,000 metres while firing continuously and then torpedoing it; *Z-27*'s magazine blew up at 1637 and the destroyer sank in four minutes. 532 German sailors were killed, including Erdmenger.

At this point Clarke broke off the action. Both ships were almost out of ammunition and developing faults from a long period of high-speed manoeuvring. Albert Pitman was in *Glasgow*'s B Turret, where 'the seals on the recoil cylinders blew and there was recoil fluid everywhere', and the gun crew were apparently resorting to firing harmless practice shells.[29] The elderly *Enterprise*, launched in 1919, was in even worse shape: Captain Wood reported a long list of defects, including the failure of radar, rangefinders and compasses, and one gun was jammed in a permanently elevated position.[30] The two cruisers were ineffectively harassed by German Heinkel 177 bombers for forty-five minutes as they made for home, but the most dangerous moment came at 1933, when a lone aircraft dropped a stick of bombs just off *Glasgow*'s port bow. The raider turned out to be American, Clarke noting wryly that 'it appears this was a friendly gesture'.[31]

The battle was a resounding success, perhaps overlooked because it came two days after the destruction of the German battlecruiser *Scharnhorst* in the Barents Sea. Even a victory could be hard on both ships and men though: when *Glasgow* returned to Plymouth after burying the two fatalities, the ship's damage was so severe that it was unable to return to sea, which meant a welcome week's leave for the ship's company.

At the end of 1943, Dover Command initiated a series of complex standing operations codenamed Operation Dandy and Operation Dusty, co-ordinating large numbers of Coastal Forces boats with shore battery fire and air support to attack targets passing through the Channel. Seven such operations were carried out in January and February 1944. On the night of 29/30 January, for example, when intelligence reported that a German *Sperrbrecher* (a large, heavily armed auxiliary minesweeper) was due to pass west with a strong escort, eleven boats supported by three Albacores were deployed to intercept. They failed to stop the *Sperrbrecher*, although a German minesweeper was stopped and set on fire.[32] Five of the same boats and two fresh craft went out again the following night, although on this occasion the attack was abandoned.

High-speed actions in the dark were stressful and exhausting, even if nothing happened. At times, they must have been terrifying. Leading Telegraphist Leslie Sprigg joined the Lowestoft-based *MTB-695* at the end of 1943. On the night of 6/7 March 1944 he took part in an attack on the heavily defended harbour at Ijmuiden in the Netherlands, an E-boat base. Lieutenant-Commander Donald 'Richie' McCowen, a 38-year-old New Zealander and the flotilla commander, took six boats into the harbour entrance just as a German convoy was forming up, and in a wild, chaotic action sank or damaged several enemy ships. Most of McCowen's boats escaped undamaged, but *695* did not. 'I had heard the sound of shells hitting us', Sprigg recalled, 'when suddenly there was a terrible scream from just above me. I ran up the few steps to the chart room and John Morrish fell back on to me. A shell had pierced the splinter mat and hit him. He died almost at once.'[33] Sub-Lieutenant John Morrish, from Farnborough, was just 20 years old. He was *695*'s navigating officer. Killed with him was 27-year-old David Wickham, who had just been appointed to a staff job and was travelling as a passenger to gain experience. Sprigg made his way up to the bridge when there was a sudden crash and a horrific lurch: out of control, *695* had run into the boat ahead. He found chaos. The Commanding Officer, Lieutenant

Douglas MacFarlane, was badly wounded and instructed Sprigg to take the wheel, although he did not actually leave the bridge. MacFarlane refused medical attention for the five hours it took 695 to limp back to Lowestoft, and promptly collapsed from loss of blood soon after his battered boat had tied up alongside.[34]

The exhausting pace of operations accelerated during the spring of 1944, with much activity directed at the crucial Seine Bay. Although the location of Neptune was still a tightly kept secret, more perceptive sailors might have looked at discarded track charts and made a reasonably accurate guess. The other giveaway was the huge amount of defensive minelaying around the future assault area. Minelayers and Coastal Forces craft alone laid 2,867 mines during this period, with thousands more being dropped by the Royal Air Force.[35]

A pair of actions fought over three nights by British and Canadian warships against the German *Torpedobootsflottille*, victors of the Tunnel battle in October 1943, vividly illustrate the intense fighting to secure the Seine Bay and its immediate hinterland. On the evening of 25 April, the cruiser HMS *Black Prince* sortied from Plymouth with the Royal Canadian Navy destroyers *Athabaskan*, *Haida* and *Huron* and the RN destroyer *Ashanti*, all powerful fleet destroyers of the Tribal Class. Together they formed Force 26, under the command of Captain Dennis Lees in *Black Prince*, and this was another Tunnel operation to harass enemy shipping along the Brittany coast. This time a Coastal Forces unit had been allocated to 'lurk' outside the French port and a radar-equipped RAF Halifax bomber was going to sweep the coast to look for targets.[36] These carefully placed assets found nothing at all, and it was mostly luck which brought Force 26 into action with the German torpedo boats *T-27*, *T-24* and *T-29*, under the command of Korvettenkapitän Franz Kohlauf, who had led the operation in which *Charybdis* and *Limbourne* had been sunk.[37]

Kohlauf was guided by radar ashore and tried to avoid the Anglo-Canadian force, but the Allied warships had their own radar and after a twenty-minute pursuit *Black Prince* opened fire at 0220, initially with starshell. The conditions were not ideal: it was profoundly dark and Kohlauf's force were making smoke, meaning the torpedo boats were 'practically invisible', but in addition this was not, perhaps, the Royal Navy's most efficient action. Twice the destroyers fouled *Black Prince*'s line of fire, and both guns in the cruiser's B Turret went out of action.[38] At 0252 alert lookouts spotted a torpedo on *Black Prince*'s starboard side, the cruiser altered course violently to comb the tracks and it ran perilously close alongside.

By this point the outgunned Germans were in a bad way. *T-27* had been hit four times and Kohlauf had ordered it into the nearby port of Morlaix, although the torpedo boat fired all six torpedoes at *Black Prince* before leaving.[39] The cruiser's 'Headache' operator fortunately picked up a signal and Lees altered course again to evade. *Black Prince* never rejoined the action, but the destroyers continued the pursuit.

At 0325, Commander Harry DeWolf's HMCS *Haida* sighted Kohlauf's flagship *T-29*, damaged and out of control after repeated hits. *Haida* and *Athabaskan* pounded the torpedo boat at close range after both ships missed with torpedoes. 'In spite of being stopped and on fire', Lees wrote later, 'the enemy fought with great gallantry and returned fire with close range weapons until about 0340', when *T-29* was 'literally a blazing wreck'. At this point *Ashanti* and *Huron* took over: 'each hit increased the fires which now burned with an intense white heat accompanied by frequent explosions'. The remarkably resilient *T-29* did not finally sink until 0420, taking Kohlauf and 137 of his crew with her.[40] *Ashanti* and *Huron* managed to collide while forming up to head home, bringing a clumsily fought and incomplete victory to an end. Overall, the action was not well received, Captain Antony de Salis, the Royal Navy's Director of Torpedoes and Mining, commenting acerbically that 'torpedo fire is scarcely mentioned by the Senior Officer of the Force and the congratulatory paragraphs appear to indicate his satisfaction with the torpedo performance of his force, which D.T.M does not share'.[41] The destroyers had fired eighteen torpedoes, mostly against a stationary target, but managed no confirmed hits. Lees also came in for criticism for disengaging *Black Prince*.

A few nights later, *Haida* and *Athabaskan* took on *Torpedobootsflottille* again when they were patrolling mid-Channel in a belated effort to protect the invasion exercise in Lyme Bay, code-named Tiger, which had been attacked by German E-boats with horrendous loss of life (see Chapter 5). Acting on Ultra intelligence and guided by excellent radar tracking, the two destroyers intercepted their old adversaries, *T-24* and *T-27*, which were making for Brest to repair battle damage. The result was 'an unsatisfactory action in which, quite unnecessarily, we swapped a "Tribal" for an "Elbing"'.[42] The Canadians made contact at 0402 and opened fire ten minutes later. The two German ships turned away, made smoke and returned fire, at the same time launching all their torpedoes, one of which hit *Athabaskan* aft and stopped her. Minutes later *Haida* hit *T-27*, setting it on fire, holing it below the waterline and wrecking the steering. Kapitänleutnant Werner Gotzmann, desperate to save his ship, apparently ran *T-27* aground near Vierge, where the torpedo boat continued to burn and was subsequently abandoned.

A few minutes earlier *Athabaskan* had been rocked by a huge secondary explosion, followed by a vast, swollen mushroom of smoke, when burning fuel reached the magazine: the destroyer sank just after 0430. *Haida* rescued forty-two survivors, many badly burned, before DeWolf dropped his boats and made for home, wary of being caught so close to the French coast when dawn broke. For the same reason, support by two British destroyers and a pair of MTBs was cancelled. Eighty-five men were rescued by the Germans, but remarkably six more and three from *Haida* returned to Plymouth in *Haida*'s cutter, inspirationally commanded by Leading Seaman William Maclure of *Haida*, who described his actions matter-of-factly to the subsequent Board of Enquiry. 'At 540 we got the motor started and I was picking up men, looking especially for those who were wounded', he recalled. 'At ten to seven we saw three German minesweepers headed for the survivors. We got the engine started and went as fast as we could go. The sweeper chased us for half an hour and came up within half a mile of us.'[43]

Maclure's harrowing voyage took another fourteen hours. The tiny craft was repeatedly buzzed by aircraft from both sides, and the cutter's unreliable engine broke down again for what must have seemed an eternity but was in fact around two hours. The survivors were finally picked up by an RAF rescue launch at 2145. When asked whether he ever considered making for the French coast and the relative safety of a prisoner-of-war camp, Maclure laconically replied 'no sir, I wanted to keep as far away from it as possible'.[44] He was Mentioned in Despatches for his actions.

128 men died, including *Athabaskan*'s celebrated commanding officer, Lieutenant-Commander John Stubbs, DSC, DSO.[45] Once again, the Canadians were criticised for their poor torpedo use, Rear-Admiral Wilfred R. Patterson, Assistant Chief of the Naval Staff (Weapons), writing that 'it is apparent that we forgot all about torpedoes'.[46]

The following night, illustrating how important it was to neutralise every German naval asset which might influence operations in the Seine Bay in June, three Swordfish torpedo bombers from 838 Naval Air Squadron were sent to finish off the beached *T-27*. The raid was a disaster, with all three aircraft being shot down and all nine aircrew killed. According to one account, the orders had been sent to 838 by mistake, and the mission was intended to be allocated to the RAF's formidable rocket-equipped Typhoon fighter-bombers rather than the elderly Swordfish.[47] *MTB-673* finally finished off *T-27* on 4 May, leaving the torpedo boat capsized and sinking.

Although the lion's share of responsibility for securing the Seine Bay in the final weeks before Neptune fell to the British and the Canadians, other Allied naval forces played their parts. One of the most aggressive players was Capitaine de Corvette André Patou's Free French destroyer *La Combattante*, formerly the Royal Navy's HMS *Haldon*. On the night of 25/26 April, *La Combattante* and HMS *Rowley* intercepted a large force of E-boats from two combined flotillas, Kapitänleutnant Berndt Klug's *5.Schnellbootflottille* and Korvettenkapitän Gotz von Mirbach's *9.Schnellbootflottille*. In what Patou described as 'a rather confused melee', *La Combattante* put three 4-inch shells into Leutnant zur See Bernhard Teenhausen's *S-147*, setting the E-boat on fire. 'By 0404', wrote Patou, '[S.147] was completely stopped, a blazing wreck, from which came the sounds of exploding ammunition.' Patou circled *La Combattante* around the fatally wounded E-boat, pouring in fire until the crew abandoned it. The French destroyer picked up eleven survivors; *S-147* blew up and sank at about 0440.[48]

La Combattante returned to the fray on 13 May, engaging E-boats in company with *MTB-680* and *MTB-608*. Patou handled his ship well again, prompting Admiral Sir Charles Little, Commander-in-Chief at Portsmouth, to praise *La Combattante*'s excellent efficiency, especially in gunnery, and the Commanding Officer's 'keen tactical sense'. This time, the French destroyer first damaged an E-boat and then went on to sink Oberleutnant zur See Sobottka's *S-141*. Among the twenty killed in this boat was Oberleutnant zur See Klaus Dönitz, eldest son of the Kriegsmarine's Commander-in-Chief, Grand Admiral Karl Dönitz, who was aboard as an observer. It had been his twenty-fourth birthday.[49]

It took patience as well as courage to secure the Seine Bay area. Operation Maple was a huge undertaking to build an impenetrable mine barrier around the bay, to protect the invasion fleet from E-boats sortieing from Le Havre and Cherbourg. As well as the purpose-built minelayers HMS *Apollo* and HMS *Plover*, this involved four flotillas of motor launches and five MTB flotillas, a total of fifty-eight Coastal Forces craft, supported by RAF heavy bombers.[50] In total, 4,000 air-laid and 3,000 surface-laid mines were in place before the invasion, all of them, remarkably, fitted with 'sterilisation clocks' to render them harmless when the invasion armada passed overhead.[51] Operation KN6, carried out on the night of 22 May, provides a fairly typical illustration of the very painstaking nature of this work. Four MTBs under the command of 25-year-old Lieutenant David Shaw, Senior Officer of the 14th Flotilla, sortied from Gosport to lay just eight mines, naval mines being bulky and MTBs having limited carrying capacity.[52]

May saw the effort to smash the Kriegsmarine in and around the Seine Bay build up to a crescendo, as the invasion approached. The Fleet Air Arm sent two squadrons back to the Channel, including 854 Squadron, flying highly capable US-built Grumman TBM Avenger aircraft out of RAF Hawkinge in Kent. 22-year-old Sub-Lieutenant Eric 'Ricky' Rickman joined the squadron during this period. Like the Coastal Forces crews, Rickman and his fellow aviators spent much of their time looking for trouble on what were known as 'Rover Patrols', when up to six radar-equipped Avengers would take off at regular intervals and search the enemy-held coast from the Hook of Holland down to Le Havre and Dieppe. If the observer got a radar contact, Rickman would set a course to intercept, looking for the tell-tale phosphorescent wake which indicated a ship under way. Rickman recalled:

> What you then do, is ... overfly the ship and go half a mile past it, drop a parachute flare ... [a] brilliant white light. You then turn immediately and do a semi-circle round ... and you can see this black shape of the ship in the flare path in the water ... open bomb doors, forty-five degrees, press the button and the best of luck. Except that in my case it was the worst of luck ... I did eight attempts and they were all near misses ... it's like playing darts.[53]

Rickman's luck eventually changed when he dropped two bombs straight down the centreline of his target ship, feeling the blast from the subsequent explosions pushing the underside of his aircraft. Naval warfare is sometimes mischaracterised as somehow cleaner than war on land, but this was rarely the case, and certainly not for Rickman, who had experienced the Blitz as a teenage bicycle messenger in Raynes Park, south-west London. This was an opportunity to hit back after years of frustration:

> I went down to fifty feet and circled round about a hundred yards around this burning ship and I could see characters running down the escape ladders [and] companion ways into the sea ... these were the first Germans I'd ever seen, the Germans who'd made my mother sob when the bomb dropped a few yards from our house ... I said [to the gunner] Vic turn your turret round and have a go at these buggers.[54]

On a subsequent Rover patrol Rickman and his crew bumped into a heavily armed flak ship. 'All hell broke loose, cannon fire, yellow-red-orange, three streaks of cannon shells were going up in front of me

... we were surrounded by about eight guns all firing up at us ... I figured they were forty feet between them only, I've got a fifty-four foot wing span.' Turning his aircraft on its side and dropping to fifty feet above sea level, Rickman got away as quickly as he could. 'It was', he recalled, 'like being a drunken parrot in an incandescent cage.'[55]

With so many exhausted young men fighting confused, fast-paced battles in the dark, accidents were inevitable. On 28 May, just days before Neptune, the relentless Patou in *La Combattante* identified two small fast-moving targets and opened fire, undoubtedly confident that his ship would be chalking up another 'kill'. Unfortunately, his targets on this occasion were a pair of Dog Boats, *MTB-732* and *MTB-739*. The *739*'s Australian CO, Sub-Lieutenant William Fesq, frantically fired recognition flares, but *La Combattante*'s efficient gunners battered *732* with 4-inch shells: within minutes the MTB caught fire, blew up and sank, with the loss of 25-year-old Lieutenant Albert Randell and sixteen of his crew. The condition of the fourteen survivors from this strategically inconsequential 'blue on blue' skirmish when they were eventually admitted to the Royal Naval Hospital at Haslar, in Gosport, is an object lesson on the brutal reality of naval warfare: lacerations, fractures, gunshot and puncture wounds and burns.[56] According to one participant, Seaman Gunner Bernard Howe of *739*, the consequences could have been far worse, as Fesq was on the point of torpedoing *La Combattante* when he spotted the French destroyer's own recognition signal and held his fire.[57]

Further afield, the Home Fleet and the Royal Air Force kept a watchful eye on the Kriegsmarine's fast-diminishing pool of heavy ships, lurking in Norwegian and Baltic bases, interspersed with sudden, violent efforts to neutralise them. The Royal Navy's determination to keep a strong force in northern waters, while at the same time asking for increased US support for Neptune, was incomprehensible and irritating to many Americans, notably the US Navy's irascible Chief of Naval Operations, Admiral Ernest J. King, but the threat seemed real enough, and the British were still scarred by the huge efforts required to deal with these highly capable marauders earlier in the war. The principal threat was a German sortie against the precious Atlantic convoy lanes, but the stakes had perhaps never been higher than they were in June 1944, with the forthcoming Normandy campaign dependent on the troops and men crossing the Atlantic. In the modern language of 'risk assessment', the likelihood of a German battle group making a sortie southwards to interfere with the invasion was undoubtedly low, but the consequences of one successfully doing so were potentially disastrous and so, in addition, the watch on the north could arguably also be considered the Seine Bay's northern flank. By June 1944, the threat had significantly diminished. *Scharnhorst* had been sunk. The battleship *Tirpitz* had been badly damaged by X-Craft miniature submarines in September 1943, and then battered again from the air by Fleet Air Arm carrier aircraft in April 1944 just before returning to service, keeping it out of the fight until the end of June. However, the pocket battleships *Lützow* and *Admiral Scheer* and the heavy cruisers *Prinz Eugen* and *Admiral Hipper* were still afloat in the Baltic, alongside three light cruisers and a sprinkling of smaller units. It is really only hindsight which confirms that most of these ships were very poorly manned and maintained by this stage of the war.

It should be reiterated that as far as the participants were concerned, this activity was not always explicitly linked to Neptune/ Overlord. These operations, and many more besides, often had their own specific objectives. But whether it was the Home Fleet's patient vigil at Scapa Flow, or the innumerable actions fought by small craft and aircraft in the Channel and the North Sea, this hard work whittled down the Kriegsmarine's limited number of warships and eroded the confidence and will to fight of its sailors and officers, making the Seine Bay a safer operating environment for the vast armada which was about to enter it.

Safety could never be entirely guaranteed, however, and many of the ships and crews on which success depended were new and untested. To provide further insurance against failure, extraordinary attention was paid to planning, intelligence and deception, and once again, sailors were at the heart of it.

3
Backroom Boys and Girls: Planning, Intelligence and Deception
October 1943–June 1944

There was no such thing as a typical day.

'Ginger' Thomas, Women's Royal Naval Service[1]

While thousands of sailors risked their lives afloat, others were at the heart of the intricate planning work and intelligence gathering that preceded the landings.

Planning

Neptune's architect was the remarkable Admiral Sir Bertram Ramsay. Consigned to the retired list just before the war, he was recalled to service in August 1939 as Flag Officer, Dover, where he remained for two years, overseeing Operation Dynamo, the evacuation from Dunkirk between 26 May and 3 June 1940, and, rather more embarrassingly, the February 1942 'Channel Dash'. Ramsay was appointed to command the naval force for the wildly optimistic Sledgehammer and Roundup proposals in 1942, but when these were abandoned he went to the Mediterranean as Cunningham's deputy for Torch and then as commander of the Eastern Task Force for Husky, where he persuaded Cunningham and Montgomery to change their 'operationally unacceptable' plan to land British and US forces at opposite ends of the island, more than 150 miles apart.[2]

Ramsay thus returned to England in July with expertise in Combined Operations and the confidence to speak 'truth to power'. He was appointed Allied Naval Commander Expeditionary Force (ANCXF) on 25 October 1943, initially working within Morgan's COSSAC organisation, then establishing his own headquarters, supported by his able Chief-of-Staff, Rear-Admiral George Creasy, described by one contemporary as 'the last man to get flustered or to neglect even the smallest and unimportant facets of a problem'.[3] In December 1943, Eisenhower was appointed Supreme Commander, with Montgomery as Commander of 21st Army Group and overall ground forces commander for the invasion, and Air Chief Marshal Sir Trafford Leigh-Mallory as overall air commander.

When Ramsay began work in January 1944, he was faced with an immediate crisis: Eisenhower and Montgomery believed strongly that the COSSAC plan which had been endorsed at the August 1943 Quadrant Conference in Quebec was flawed. In fairness Morgan was perfectly aware of the limitations of his plan, but he was relatively junior, and had limited authority to push back against restrictions imposed on him, in particular the limited availability of shipping and the requirement to deliver Anvil, writing after the war that 'almost all of us knew . . . that the most critical of all the critical items . . . of supply of war materials was landing craft and shipping'.[4] He also lacked the formidable knowledge of the challenges and pitfalls inherent in amphibious operations, built up by those who had spent three years delivering landings in the Mediterranean, although COSSAC observers had been present at Husky.[5] Morgan had to work with what he had: 'The assault . . . was to be launched with a short air bombardment of the beach defences, after which three assault divisions would be landed on the Caen beaches, followed by the equivalent of two tank brigades and a regimental combat team.'[6] Two divisions were to be preloaded in landing craft for the follow-up waves, so in total enough assault shipping was required for five divisions. The operation also involved a small airborne landing to capture the key town of Caen and commando operations on the peripheries.

'[Eisenhower] had then told me he had only a sketchy idea of the plan and that it did not look too good', Montgomery recalled; 'he directed me to act as his representative in London until he himself could get there'. By 1 January, while still in the Mediterranean, Montgomery had reviewed the COSSAC plan in detail and spelled out his impressions in writing to Churchill: the plan, he wrote, 'is on too narrow a front and is confined to too small an area' and as a consequence was 'impracticable'.[7] Eisenhower and Montgomery's concerns were largely informed by new intelligence indicating significant strengthening of the German defences in France, derived from aerial photo-reconnaissance, the French Resistance, documents captured in Italy, stolen plans of the Atlantic Wall, and intercepted signals sent by the Japanese Military Attaché in Berlin after he toured the defences in November 1943. Among the challenges identified were increased numbers of combat divisions, new beach obstacles, additional coastal gun batteries and preparations for the demolition of ports.[8]

The revised plan was a huge expansion, adding an additional two assault divisions preloaded in landing craft to the original three, and a landing by three airborne divisions. It extended the invasion beaches to the east as far as Ouistreham on the estuary of the River Orne and to the west up the side of the Cotentin Peninsula, a total increase of the assault area from 20 miles to 50. Three assault areas became five, famously codenamed (from west to east) Utah, Omaha, Gold, Juno and Sword, with Gold and Utah being the new additions. The soldiers understood perfectly well that providing shipping for this expansion would present a formidable challenge to their naval colleagues. Ramsay took it on the chin, recording in his diary following a 5 January meeting with Montgomery and Leigh-Mallory, Commander of the Allied Expeditionary Air Force, that 'I pointed out the costs of what this implied and that the bill must be met by Admiralty for increased force.'[9]

The 'bill' was paid initially by deferring the proposed date for Neptune by a month from 1 May to 1 June 1944, to allow for another month's construction of the precious assault craft. This was moved again to a final window of 5, 6 or 7 June, which offered the best compromise between a low tide to allow assaulting troops to see, avoid and neutralise German beach obstacles, and sufficient light to allow effective bombardment from air and sea. This was also subject to the vagaries of the weather, as relatively calm seas were essential for the seaborne landing and fog would probably rule out the airborne drops. Additional assets were derived from the Americans reluctantly agreeing to defer Anvil to August, and King belatedly supplying additional warships for gunfire support.

The expanded Neptune was planned down to the minutest detail incredibly quickly. Montgomery, Ramsay and Leigh-Mallory issued the Initial Joint Plan on 1 February 1944. Ramsay's Naval Outline Plan followed on 28 February. The British landings alone involved eleven flag officers and seventy-two captains, according to a Seniority List drawn up on 15 May 1944.[10] Inevitably, an inter-Allied command team of such strong personalities was not without friction. Ramsay was a hard task master, and struggled with both Sir Philip Vian, who he referred to privately as both 'a little helpless' and 'a queer creature', and Rear-Admiral Alan Kirk – 'not a big enough man to hold the position he does'.[11] To further complicate matters, Ramsay had to work alongside the C-in-Cs of the various naval Home Commands, some of whom were senior to him, and the Americans still reported to their own C-in-C, Naval Forces Europe, Admiral Harold 'Betty' Stark, a former Chief of Naval Operations, for administrative purposes. Without exception, senior officers accepted the authority of their theoretical juniors with no complaint. It is, perhaps, hard to comprehend in today's meritocratic and largely deference-free society what a significant gesture this was in 1944. Given these complexities and the extraordinary pressures under which these men were operating, an element of tension at all levels of command was perhaps hardly surprising, but the underlying point is that the team succeeded despite it.

There were two principal challenges, the first being 'the breaking of the strong initial crust of the coastal defences by assault together with the landing of the fighting army formations'.[12] The British assault formations would be landed by the Eastern Naval Task Force, under Vian, with Royal Navy subordinates Rear-Admiral Arthur Talbot (Force S, Sword Area), Commodore Cyril Douglas-Pennant (Force G), Commodore Geoffrey Oliver (Force J) and Rear-Admiral

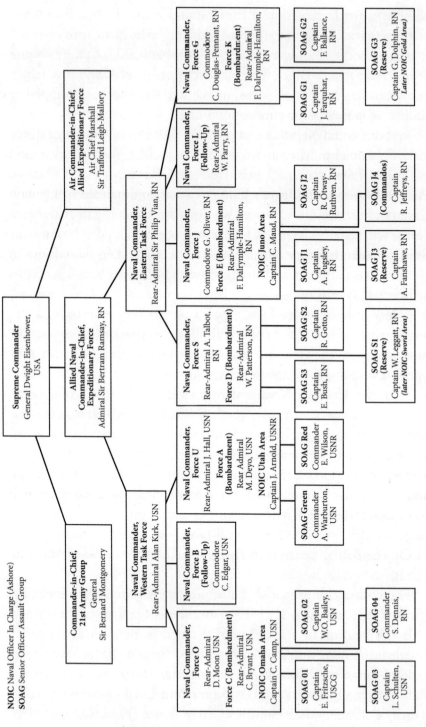

NOIC Naval Officer In Charge (Ashore)
SOAG Senior Officer Assault Group

Figure 1. Naval command structure: Operation Neptune.

Supreme Commander
General Dwight Eisenhower, USA

Air Commander-in-Chief, Allied Expeditionary Force
Air Chief Marshall Sir Trafford Leigh-Mallory

Allied Naval Commander-in-Chief, Expeditionary Force
Admiral Sir Bertram Ramsay, RN

Commander-in-Chief, 21st Army Group
General Sir Bernard Montgomery

Naval Commander, Eastern Task Force
Rear-Admiral Sir Philip Vian, RN

Naval Commander, Western Task Force
Rear-Admiral Alan Kirk, USN

Naval Commander, Force G
Commodore C. Douglas-Pennant, RN
Force K (Bombardment)
Rear-Admiral F. Dalrymple-Hamilton, RN

Naval Commander, Force L (Follow-Up)
Rear-Admiral W. Parry, RN

Naval Commander, Force J
Commodore G. Oliver, RN
Force E (Bombardment)
Rear-Admiral F. Dalrymple-Hamilton, RN
NOIC Juno Area
Captain C. Maud, RN

Naval Commander, Force S
Rear-Admiral A. Talbot, RN
Force D (Bombardment)
Rear-Admiral W. Patterson, RN

Naval Commander, Force U
Rear-Admiral J. Hall, USN
Force A (Bombardment)
Rear Admiral M. Deyo, USN
NOIC Utah Area
Captain J. Arnold, USNR

Naval Commander, Force B (Follow-Up)
Commodore C. Edgar, USN

Naval Commander, Force O
Rear-Admiral D. Moon USN
Force C (Bombardment)
Rear-Admiral C. Bryant, USN
NOIC Omaha Area
Captain C. Camp, USN

SOAG G1
Captain J. Farquhar, RN

SOAG G2
Captain F. Ballance, RN

SOAG G3 (Reserve)
Captain G. Dolphin, RN
Later NOIC Gold Area)

SOAG J1
Captain A. Pugsley, RN

SOAG J2
Captain R. Otway-Ruthven, RN

SOAG J3 (Reserve)
Captain A. Fanshawe, RN

SOAG J4 (Commandos)
Captain R. Jeffreys, RN

SOAG S2
Captain R. Gotto, RN

SOAG S3
Captain E. Bush, RN

SOAG S1 (Reserve)
Captain W. Leggatt, RN
(later NOIC Sword Area)

SOAG Green
Commander A. Warburton, USN

SOAG Red
Commander E. Wilson, USNR

SOAG 02
Captain W.O. Bailey, USN

SOAG 04
Commander S. Dennis, RN

SOAG 01
Captain E. Fritzsche, USCG

SOAG 03
Captain L. Schulten, USN

William Parry (Force L, the British initial follow-up). The Americans were led by Kirk as Commander Western Naval Task Force, with US Navy subordinates Rear-Admiral Don Moon (Force U), Rear-Admiral John Hall (Force O), and Commodore Campbell Edgar (Force B, the US initial follow-up). Each assault force consisted of assault shipping, supported by allocated units for minesweeping, shore bombardment and escort. The assault forces were subdivided into smaller groups, each assigned a particular sector, and within each sector were a number of colour-coded beaches. So, for example Assault Group J2 in Oliver's Juno Area was commanded by Captain Robert Otway-Ruthven in the headquarters ship HMS *Waveney*, a converted frigate. Otway-Ruthven was responsible for landing the 8th Canadian Infantry Brigade in Nan Sector, facing the villages of Bernières-sur-Mer and Saint-Aubin, which incorporated Nan White and Nan Red beaches.[13]

There were of course some differences between the assault areas, but in general terms the plans were broadly similar (see Figure 2). Screened by the bombardment, the assault craft started their journey to the beaches at 'lowering positions' 7–8 miles offshore, or 'transport areas' in the US sectors, which were 10–11 miles out, a precaution against German coastal defence guns which had unfortunate consequences. The moment of landing, known as H-Hour, varied according to the tide and the natural and artificial obstructions in any given sector; ultimately there were several H-Hours, spread over one hour and twenty-five minutes, with the Americans landing earlier, which Ramsay worried might cause confusion and compromise the element of surprise.[14]

On the British beaches the assault infantry were accompanied by specialised armour, the Armoured Vehicles Royal Engineers or AVREs: tanks equipped with flails to beat paths through minefields; fascines or small assault bridges to cross ditches and craters; and monstrous petard mortars which fired an 18kg explosive charge for destroying bunkers. In theory, the first to land were the swimming Duplex Drive or DD tanks, so called because of their twin propulsion systems of conventional tracks for land and propellers for water, which were deployed from LCTs offshore and swam in. The

Americans declined the use of almost all of these so-called 'Funnies', in part because most were based on British Churchill tank hulls and logistically it was complex to add an entirely different tank to their order of battle, with all the resultant challenges around spares and maintenance. The only exceptions were the DD tanks, which were based on the US M4 Sherman hull.

Landing alongside the assault troops and the specialised armour were the sailors and combat engineers of the British Landing Craft Obstacle Clearance Units (LCOCU) and the US Naval Combat Demolition Units (NCDU), deployed to clear as many beach obstacles as they could in the very short window available before the rising tide covered them again. More sailors arrived to help bring order to the chaos of the assault areas, including the US Navy's Beach Battalions, and as part of the tri-service Beach Groups in the British sector, the RN Beachmasters with their Beach Commandos and Beach Signal Sections (the roles of all these highly trained specialists will be explained in Chapter 5). If all went well, by the evening the follow-up forces would arrive, followed the next morning by the first build-up convoys and convoys delivering components for the Mulberry Harbours.

At every level, the naval officers were in command at sea, as noted in the Naval Staff History: 'Until the army was firmly established ashore the command of each Naval Task and Assault Force *and of the military forces embarked* was exercised by their respective naval commanders.'[15] Whether it was naval captains and army brigadiers surveying events from headquarters ships or very junior and very young officers lurching ashore in assault landing craft, strong relationships were built and decisions were often mutually agreed, but in the event of a disagreement, it was the sailors who made the final call while the force was afloat. Otway-Ruthven's final Operational Order, issued on 26 May, makes this crystal clear: at no point in the document is there any reference to direction being provided by Army officers while afloat. COs are warned to watch for instruction from Otway-Ruthven, his deputy (Commander Robert 'Red' Ryder, a veteran of Saint-Nazaire and Dieppe who had been awarded the Victoria Cross for his actions during the former operation), or the Principal

Beachmaster, all naval officers. The Army were simply 'the load'. 'GET YOUR LOAD TO THE FAR SHORE. REMEMBER OUR OBJECT!' Otway-Ruthven exhorted in capitals.[16]

To make all this possible, further plans were developed to cover the loading, assembly and passage to Normandy of the army, drawing on a military document called the 'Q Appreciation', which outlined the full requirements of the army 'in men, vehicles, equipment, ammunition and everything else that the fighting soldier would need'. In essence, the Army outlined its requirements in the Q Appreciation, and the naval planners then worked out how to embark it all and ship it across to the right place.[17] There was also a Minesweeping Plan, and a Naval Bombardment Plan, which organised the movements of four strong Bombarding Forces, A and C in Kirk's Western Task Force and D and E in Vian's Eastern Task Force.

The significant step change in the effectiveness of naval shore bombardment during the Second World War, built up in earlier amphibious operations and reaching a peak of efficiency during Neptune, is rarely given the recognition it deserves. Shore bombardment was not a natural activity for sailors: it was a difficult skill which had to be learned. Less than thirty years earlier, shore bombardment had proven largely useless against Ottoman defences at Gallipoli. How was it, then, that by 1944 a fleet could be sent into hostile waters to engage fixed defences which were 'the most formidable ever tackled hitherto in a seaborne assault'?[18] The fundamental nature of naval gunnery had not changed. Rather, there had been a quantum shift in the quality of rangefinding equipment, spotting, intelligence, training and inter-service co-operation, which meant identifying and hitting targets ashore without harming friendly troops had become almost second nature.

The Neptune bombardment plan divided German defences into four broad categories, with heavy coastal defence batteries (120mm–155mm guns) in reinforced concrete emplacements the top priority, as they had the ability to threaten the fleet at sea, followed by smaller batteries in concrete emplacements, batteries sited in the open and the beach defences which immediately threatened the assaulting troops: pillboxes, gun shelters, mortar pits and trenches.[19] These

As employed in Operation Neptune
Approximate situation at H–20 minutes
(frontage ships and craft not to scale)

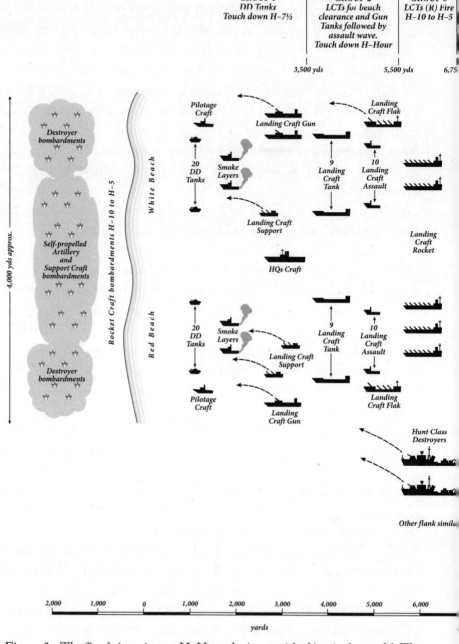

Figure 2. The final situation at H–Hour during an ideal 'typical assault'. The
reality on most beaches would turn out to be very different, thanks to what the
nineteenth-century strategist Carl von Clausewitz famously called 'friction':
intervention by the enemy, the weather and other unpredictable factors.

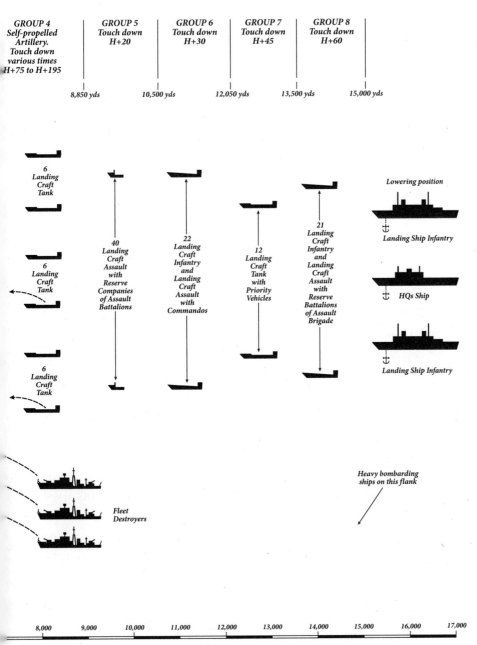

GROUP 4
Self-propelled
Artillery.
Touch down
various times
H+75 to H+195

GROUP 5
Touch down
H+20

GROUP 6
Touch down
H+30

GROUP 7
Touch down
H+45

GROUP 8
Touch down
H+60

8,850 yds   10,500 yds   12,050 yds   13,500 yds   15,000 yds

6
Landing
Craft
Tank

6
Landing
Craft
Tank

6
Landing
Craft
Tank

40
Landing
Craft
Assault
with
Reserve
Companies
of Assault
Battalions

22
Landing
Craft
Infantry
and
Landing
Craft
Assault
with
Commandos

12
Landing
Craft
Tank
with
Priority
Vehicles

21
Landing
Craft
Infantry
and
Landing
Craft
Assault
with
Reserve
Battalions
of Assault
Brigade

Lowering position

Landing Ship Infantry

HQs Ship

Landing Ship Infantry

Fleet
Destroyers

Heavy bombarding
ships on this flank

8,000   9,000   10,000   11,000   12,000   13,000   14,000   15,000   16,000   17,000

yards

defences would be dealt with by a combination of air and sea bombardment. Strategic bombing began well in advance of D-Day, although to protect the location of the invasion German defences all around the occupied European coast were hit. Air attacks on Normandy reached a crescendo on the night of 5/6 June when heavy bombers dropped a hundred tons of bombs on each of ten coastal batteries, medium bombers pounded six more early on D-Day, and more bombers returned to assist in 'drenching' the beach defences prior to the assault.[20]

Each assault area had an allocated bombardment force. Force A, allocated to Utah Area and commanded by Rear-Admiral Morton Deyo, consisted of one battleship (the veteran USS *Nevada*), the Royal Navy big-gun bombardment monitor *Erebus*, five cruisers, a Dutch gunboat and eight US Navy destroyers. Rear-Admiral Carleton Bryant's Force C at Omaha boasted the other two US Navy battleships (*Texas* and *Arkansas*), the British cruiser *Glasgow*, the Free French cruisers *Georges Leygues* and *Montcalm*, nine US and three British destroyers. Supporting Force S was Bombardment Force D, commanded by Rear-Admiral Wilfred Patterson in the cruiser HMS *Mauritius*, with the RN battleships *Warspite* and *Ramillies*, the monitor *Roberts*, four more cruisers, including the elderly Polish-manned *Dragon*, and fifteen British destroyers. Rear-Admiral Frederick Dalrymple-Hamilton commanded both Force E at Juno and Force K at Gold from HMS *Belfast*, with the cruiser *Diadem* and eleven destroyers in the former and four cruisers, the Dutch gunboat *Flores* and thirteen destroyers in the latter. Finally, in reserve and able to be deployed anywhere as needed were Vian's flagship HMS *Scylla*, Kirk's flagship USS *Augusta*, seventeen US destroyers, two British cruisers and the powerful Royal Navy battleships *Rodney* and *Nelson*, although the latter was held back at Milford Haven.[21] Once in theatre, the Flag Officers commanding the bombarding ships would be under the command of the Assault Force commanders, regardless of seniority. Each heavy ship was allocated a bombardment berth and given a bearing and distance to steam from a light buoy laid by the minesweepers.[22]

Each bombarding force could draw on eight squadrons of Spitfire and Seafire spotting aircraft and teams of Forward Observers (FOBs) ashore: in the British sectors there were eleven FOB parties in Force G, ten in Force J and eight in Force S, plus an additional six parties with the 6th Airborne Division, seven supporting various Commandos and one liaising with the Americans at Omaha. Seventy-eight Bombardment Liaison Officers worked aboard the supporting ships.[23] The Americans deployed three Naval Shore Fire Control Parties (NSFCPs) with each assault infantry regiment of the 1st Infantry Division (Omaha) and 4th Infantry Division (Utah), seven NSFCPs with the 29th Infantry Division (Omaha), an NSFCP with each of the 2nd and 5th Ranger Battalions and the 101st Airborne Division, plus Naval Gunfire Liaison Officers attached to the Army's artillery, and specially trained army spotters with the 82nd Airborne Division, which dropped further inland.[24]

Main and subsidiary targets for the initial bombardment were allocated well in advance, in the British areas by Vian and in the US sectors by the individual assault force commanders, reflecting the US Navy's doctrine emphasising delegation and decentralised command.[25] Ships were to open fire 'either when the assaulting convoys came within range of them, or when it became light enough for the enemy to spot the fall of his shot ... whichever was later'.[26] It is this instruction which has given rise to apparently endless arguments about 'which ship fired' first – with each assault force landing at different times there was NO general 'open fire' order across the entire invasion area, and consequently no way to verify for sure precisely who let fly the first shell, but it would certainly have been in the Western (US) area.

Big ships were allocated coastal batteries. Some smaller warships were also assigned targets, but most commanding officers 'were given discretion, giving priority to (a) guns firing on our own forces (b) pill-boxes (c) suspected machine-gun posts and (d) possible observation posts'.[27] Shortly before the assault, smaller warships and fire support landing craft would close in and carry out 'drenching fire' on the beach, with the intention of suppressing the defenders during the vital last moments as the landing craft closed and their vulnerable passengers tried to get ashore.

Gaining a full understanding of enemy defences in the tightly controlled coastal zone was challenging, and there were errors, not so much regarding the location of defences but about what they were equipped with. Famously, for example, when United States Rangers stormed the heavy 155mm coastal battery at Pointe du Hoc, overlooking both Omaha and Utah Areas, they found the guns had been removed, and when British paratroops captured Merville Battery, which threatened Sword, the guns were smaller than expected. Nevertheless, thanks to the efforts of reconnaissance pilots and the talented (and often overlooked) analysts who painstakingly interpreted their photographs, along with the French Resistance, agents, codebreakers and countless others, the information provided to the bombarding warships was impressively comprehensive.

A surviving draft fire support plan for Gold Area shows the level of detail provided, and the complete integration of the air and naval bombardment packages. Nine priorities for air bombardment were identified, including heavy coastal batteries at Longues-sur-Mer, Arromanches and Mont Fleury, and beach defences in the towns of Arromanches, La Rivière and Le Hamel.[28] Each was allocated either one or two 'boxes' of strategic bombers, a combat box being a US 8th Air Force tactical formation, normally consisting in 1944 of thirty-six B-17 Flying Fortresses. The plan records the precise bomb loads the aircraft would carry and when they would be over the target area, offers supporting notes, and then goes on to provide the same level of detail for the naval bombardment which would follow.[29]

So, for example, one of the highest priority targets was the *Marineküstenbatterie* (Naval Coastal Battery) at Longues-Sur-Mer, *Widerstandsnest* ('resistance nest') *48* in German defence parlance.[30] *WN48* lay between Gold and Omaha and was equipped with four modern 150mm naval guns (albeit manned by soldiers in June 1944) fully enclosed in concrete casemates set back from the shore. Fire was controlled from an observation post on the cliff edge, connected to the gun positions by underground armoured cables, and the whole site was surrounded by minefields, barbed wire and machine gun positions.

The Support Plan allocated two boxes of bombers to *WN48*, whose objective was to 'destroy or so neutralise guns that they cannot bring fire to bear on shipping on US or XXX Corps front', XXX

Corps being the principal headquarters for the invading British and Canadian troops on D-Day. The plan goes on to point out that 'the bty [battery] is well to flank and may be bombed at any period with any type of bomb without affecting beaches or exits'.[31] This type of target was identified as a Category A target, 'on which the most effective, destructive type of attack should be applied – without restriction!' The loads were thus to be 100% heavy 'cratering' bombs, to be delivered over a half-hour period from H-Hour minus twenty minutes to H-Hour plus ten minutes.[32] For air attacks before D-Day, Longues was a Priority Two target, the highest priority being the partly completed 122mm battery at Mont Fleury, which was immediately behind Gold Area, but Longues moved up to Priority One for fighter bomber attack on D-Day itself.[33] Between H minus 40 and H plus 320, *WN48* would also be bombarded by the cruiser HMS *Ajax*. For the first three hours *Ajax* would have to share a spotter aircraft with her sister ship *Argonaut*, which was targeting *WN50*, a 105mm battery at Vaux-sur-Aure.[34]

For the subsequent drenching fire, the plan allocated warships, support landing craft and military artillery firing from landing craft during the approach to a series of coded locations, and details very specifically their fire plan. So, for example, between H minus sixty and H minus ten, two destroyers were to carry out Serial Fourteen, a fire mission against a target improbably codenamed Sofa (Sofa was actually *WN36*, a 50mm anti-tank gun emplacement on the beach at Asnelles-sur-Mer). This would involve one round of standard armour-piercing (SAP) ammunition per gun, per minute, for the first twenty minutes, half a round of SAP per gun, per minute, for the next twenty minutes (that is, one round every other minute), and then finally rising to a crescendo of three rounds per gun, per minute, until fire lifted ten minutes before the troops hit the beach.[35] This extraordinary level of precision and detail was repeated right across the assault area.

For individual ships, this was drilled down to a concise set of orders. So, the battleship HMS *Warspite*'s main target was *WNTrou017*, a 150mm battery in the grounds of the chocolate box Manoir du Grand Bec at Villerville, opposite Le Havre on the northern side of the Seine Estuary. *Warspite*'s secondary target was a partially completed 380mm *Marineküstenbatterie* at Le Grand Clos, north of Le Havre.[36] If these targets had already been destroyed by air attack, *Warspite's* instructions were to 'search for targets of opportunity' until observers called for fire from ashore. The ship had a dedicated spotting aircraft, callsign 'Airedale', available from forty minutes before sunrise for twelve hours, and the same aircraft would then be 'on call' to provide further support if needed for another three hours.[37] Ranging fire should be a single round of high-explosive shell, but 'fire for effect' should be a full salvo of 15-inch (380mm): in *Warspite's* case this meant six guns, as one of her twin turrets had been wrecked by a German *Fritz X* glider bomb off Salerno.

Once these meticulously planned fire missions had been completed, ships could be expected to be given further targets of opportunity by their spotting teams ashore or in the air, and to be reallocated to different sectors as needed. The Bombardment Plan also included an invaluable system for ammunition resupply at depots back in the UK, whereby lighters were kept afloat and loaded with the precise outfit of ammunition required for specific ships, so that they could turn around and return to the gunline as quickly as possible.[38]

The second challenge for the fleet came immediately after the assault formations were established: 'to commence and continue without pause . . . their reinforcement at as high a rate as possible'.[39] Supplying and supporting the army meant filling the Seine Bay with depot and repair ships, survey ships, buoy layers, telephone cable ships, salvage vessels, stores ships, tugs, colliers, oilers and tankers, as well as the huge forces required to support the construction of the Mulberry Harbours.

Until Cherbourg was liberated and operational, the hopes of the logisticians rested on one fantastical proposition: that in the absence of a port, one could be taken across the channel. The reasoning behind it was simple – the need for a large deep water port was as obvious to the Germans as it was to the Allies, and the former had clustered their strongest defences around their ports. This had already provoked debate around artificial harbours, initiated by, among others, Churchill, who challenged Mountbatten in May 1942 to develop piers for use on beaches; 'don't argue the matter', he wrote acidly, 'the difficulties will argue for themselves'.[40] The Dieppe Raid in August 1942 had been in part a final test to see whether the German defences could be overcome. They could not. As one 1947 War Office report, co-authored by Rear-Admiral Harold Hickling, a New Zealander who ran Mulberry B at Arromanches, and his military opposite number, Brigadier Ian Mackillop, a senior quartermaster from 21st Army Group, made clear, Dieppe 'gave us a practical and costly lesson . . . a frontal attack on any suitable major port would prove a very bloody, and maybe lengthy, operation'.[41]

Rear-Admiral John Hughes-Hallett, naval commander at Dieppe, supposedly commented afterwards that if a port could not be captured it would be necessary to take one across.[42] A long period of experimentation with three different designs followed, one involving adjustable 'Spud' pier heads and a flexible steel roadway, one, the Hughes Pier, consisting of steel bridges mounted on concrete caissons which could be towed over and sunk, and a third, the improbably named 'Swiss Roll', which was a floating mat made of timber and canvas. At Quadrant, the Combined Chiefs approved a proposal for two artificial harbours, and Mulberry was born. The Hughes Pier was discarded in autumn 1943 and the Swiss Roll, belatedly, a few months later, leaving the Spud system as the final design.[43]

Each Mulberry would consist of a series of piers formed of mile-long sections of roadway known as Whales, running across pontoons called Beetles, connected to the Spud pier heads which could be jacked up and down, allowing the roadway to be used whatever the state of the tide. Exceptionally strong, self-righting and self-burying anchors known as Kites, unique to the Mulberry Harbours, held the Beetles in place. Different versions of the pier head were built to discharge LSTs and conventional freighters, and the roads were rated to carry different types of vehicles, a heavy one for tanks and a lighter one for lorries. The piers and the adjacent beaches were protected by three lines of defence from the elements: a harbour wall made from huge prefabricated concrete caissons (Phoenix), an outer breakwater formed from floating 2,000-ton steel structures called Bombardons, and an inner line of old freighters and warships (Corncobs) scuttled to form a barrier codenamed 'Gooseberry'. Each of the five assault areas would have a Gooseberry, with complete Mulberry Harbours at Saint-Laurent in Omaha Area (Mulberry A) and Arromanches in Gold (Mulberry B).

Mulberry required huge amounts of raw material, including vast quantities of steel which to this day some argue would have been better used to construct more landing craft. The Phoenix caissons alone required a million tons of concrete, 70,000 tons of steel reinforcing and 1.5 million square yards of shuttering.[44] Some were constructed on the Thames, in huge improvised docks excavated from the foreshore and kept dry using pumps, until their earth 'gate' was demolished and the finished caisson floated free.[45] Mulberry also occupied 23,000 people working for twenty-five construction companies across forty-five to fifty sites.[46] Incredibly, both huge facilities had to be designed and built in just seven months. The components were constructed in conditions of great secrecy but the structures were not easy to hide, especially from the air. The challenge was to conceal their purpose: the vast Phoenix caissons, for example, were at various times fitted with railway tracks and dummy gun batteries or festooned with elaborate aerials, rumours were encouraged that they were floating forts, troop transports or petrol tankers, and some components were berthed to the east of the embarkation ports, indicating that they were connected to a landing around Calais.[47]

The Phoenix caissons were sunk in secluded locations until required, which was fine in theory but something of a nightmare in practice, as they proved exceptionally difficult to recover; 'far and away the biggest salvage job of the war', according to US Navy Captain Edward Ellsberg, who refloated Phoenix units at Selsey Bill.[48] These elaborate efforts were not in vain: although there is evidence that the occasional Luftwaffe reconnaissance aircraft overflew Mulberry components, General Günther Blumentritt, von Rundstedt's Chief of Staff at OB West, said after the war that 'we had no idea, not any report, that [the Allies] were developing artificial harbours'.[49]

More ships and sailors had to be allocated to the laying of another innovation, the 'pipe line under the ocean' (PLUTO), intended to secure the invading army's vital fuel supplies.[50] This had been proposed to Mountbatten by Commander Thomas Hussey, but experts from the oil industry had been tasked with working out the detail. Two options had been considered: the HAIS system, based on a submarine telegraph cable and named after the designer (Hartley), the Anglo-Iranian Oil Company (his employer) and Siemens, which manufactured it; and the HAMEL system, a welded pipe which could be wound on to a rotating drum, designed by a pair of engineers named Hammick and Ellis. Both versions were used in the final PLUTO project, which also required a network of pipes across the UK, and pumping stations on the Isle of Wight and at Dungeness. Two simpler systems, Tombola and Amethea, were also developed to connect storage tanks in the assault area to tankers offshore. Pluto was a naval responsibility and required over a thousand officers and men, mostly drawn from cable-laying specialists in the Merchant Navy.[51]

Co-ordination of this effort, the 'Build Up', involved hundreds of thousands of men and women, overseeing the safe and timely delivery of as many as eight convoys and up to twelve landing craft groups a day, and the Build Up Plan was a correspondingly huge piece of work, with sections dealing with a range of impenetrable acronyms: BUCO (Build-Up Control Organisation), TURCO (Turn Round Control) and COREP (Combined Operations Repair Organisation), which will be explained in Chapter 11.

Every formation of ships, and every individual craft within it, no matter how small and apparently insignificant, had its own clearly assigned role, and every single commanding officer, even those in comparatively minor war vessels like landing craft, received his own voluminous set of Neptune orders, which in theory could not be shared with anyone else until shortly before the invasion. In the case of landing craft, these orders would tell them precisely where they would anchor or berth prior to the operation, who they were going to pick up, where they would collect them and where they would deliver them. Each set of orders contained Ramsay's own ANCXF Orders – around 1,000 pages of typescript, broken down into sections which detailed each phase of the operation in chronological order, beginning with preliminary minelaying by the Royal Navy and RAF (ON2) and ending with

ON21 (Pluto) and ON22, a doubtless gratefully received glossary.[52] These were accompanied by corresponding sets of orders from Task Force and lower commanders.[53] Otway-Ruthven's J2 Operation Order, for example, was another thirty-one pages.[54] Ramsay's orders were first issued to a small group of senior commanders on 24 April 1944. Two days later he relocated his headquarters to Southwick House, outside Portsmouth, from where he would direct the invasion, and where further planning continued. The final plan was 'frozen', with no further amendments permitted, at 0900 on 12 May.[55]

The incredibly detailed final plan irritated some Americans who had been taught at the US Naval War College to issue broad general instructions to subordinates and then leave them to work out the detail. Kirk was particularly critical. 'The landing became, in the eyes of the British, what they called a "set piece"', he said in a 1962 inter-view, 'in other words, no initiative was possible ... this was to be a somewhat formalised affair.'[56] However, initiative was not helpful in a complicated operating environment like the Seine Bay. As the historian and Ramsay biographer Andrew Gordon has written, manoeuvring nearly 7,000 vessels, from tiny assault landing craft to 30,000-ton battleships, in the confined waters of the Seine Bay 'could quickly have become a shambles had they been "playing jazz" rather than following an orchestrated script'.[57]

Much of the detailed planning was carried out at Norfolk House in London, which was the home of the Supreme Headquarters Allied Expeditionary Force (SHAEF) until Eisenhower relocated to a bigger site in Bushy Park, to the south-west of London, in April. By 1944, Britain had 'combed out' almost its last reserves of men from all but the most essential war work to join the fighting services, and much essential support for the planning teams came from women, many of them 'Wrens' from the Women's Royal Naval Service (WRNS). Ginger Thomas was a 22-year-old Wren from Swansea who joined COSSAC in 1943, working directly for Morgan, who stayed on as Eisenhower's Deputy Chief of Staff for Intelligence and Operations. Thomas remembered Morgan as energetic and hard-working, in fact a 'workaholic'. 'It was', she recalled, 'a privilege to work for such a wonderful man. I was very proud to have that job.'

In fact, so good was her relationship with the man who always called her 'Sailor' that they remained friends until the day he died.[58]

Thomas was accommodated in a nurses' hostel between Chalk Farm and Belsize Park, and travelled to Norfolk House every day on the Underground, remaining there all day and sometimes into the small hours of the next morning, with no home leave for a year. At the weekends she went to stay with a cousin in Shaftesbury and slept solidly for two days, before returning to do it all over again. She accompanied Morgan everywhere, taking dictation, minuting meetings and typing up his correspondence. 'We all realised that it was very hush hush, and very important . . . it was also a little bit frightening, because I never thought I would be involved in anything so important. Whether the invasion plans would be successful was a big worry in my little mind.' The headquarters was buzzing with activity and there was, she remembered, 'no such thing as a typical day'.[59] Thomas paints a vivid picture of the atmosphere at SHAEF as the clock ran down to the invasion; everyone focused on their individual responsibilities, quietly confident, but acutely aware of their responsibility for the lives of thousands of soldiers, sailors and airmen.

Lieutenant-Commander (E) R.P. Cowey was part of a small team of naval engineers working at Norfolk House under Engineer Rear-Admiral Geoffrey Morgan (no relation to the general). Their very specific function was to 'assess and arrange emergency repair services, stores and fuel on the beaches and in liberated ports for craft taking part in the landing'.[60] All these functions were to be delivered by a shore-based Mobile Land Repair Unit on the beach near Courseulles for patching up broken landing craft, and later by a fully equipped Depot Repair Ship.

Cowey arrived in October 1943 and was given the original COSSAC Outline Plan to study. This meant he would have been privy to the most sensitive information of all: where the landings were to take place and, later on, when. This meant Cowey and the other engineers were subject to the highest level of security possible for Overlord, a level above Top Secret. This was known as BIGOT and personnel who were cleared to that level were said to be BIGOTed.[61] Certainly security at Norfolk House was incredibly tight. Only one door was used and after passing inside, personnel had their passes scrutinised and could be searched. Norfolk House passes gave the holder access to the Admiralty, the War Office, Combined Operations Headquarters, and Montgomery's 21st Army Group Headquarters at St Paul's School, Hammersmith (Montgomery's old school), but this arrangement was not reciprocal. Offices were searched at night to ensure no papers were left out.

Kathleen Cartwright was a teleprinter operator at Norfolk House, part of Naval Party 1745, which consisted of some 100 Wrens who reported directly to Ramsay and worked around the clock, following the naval watch system. When important messages came through, they were sealed, stamped by the Duty Officer and then delivered to the Admiralty by whichever Wren received it, whatever time it arrived. Never having been out late at night in her home town of Dewsbury, Cartwright's greatest fear was a message arriving in the middle of the night. 'Sure enough, on one occasion it did, at 3 a.m.', she remembered. 'It was totally black outside and I ran all the way to Admiralty House at the top of the Mall and back again.'[62]

Not every Wren was as well informed as Cartwright and Thomas. Paulina Nichol was a Wren working in 'a strange secret hideout in the cellars of the old Berkeley Hotel'. Nichol was a trained meteorologist, but this did not help her work out what on earth she might be doing to contribute to the invasion:

> We were sat down in front of sheets of huge sheets of statistics with columns and columns of figures and all we had to do was add the figures up. This was part of a plan to discover . . . how best to choose the day for the invasion. This was to do with phases of the moon. It was some slightly crackpot theory that a chap had who'd written in to the Air Ministry . . . this being before the days of calculators, they used us as calculators. We never really saw the end product of this curious experiment.[63]

Intelligence

Nichol may not have been wholly clear about the importance of her role, but obtaining and evaluating information about the weather formed a vital element of the vast, sweeping range of operations to gather, assess and disseminate intelligence prior to Neptune. Ordinary Seaman Harold Checketts, a 24-year-old from Worcestershire, had retrained as a meteorologist after surviving the destruction of HMS *Prince of Wales* in December 1941. After an idyllic year in the Maldives, he was recalled to the less exotic surroundings of Lee-on-Solent 'to be inducted in the English weather' by a young Wren meteorologist named Jean, his future wife. From there he went to a site near Beer in Dorset 'to watch the waves coming up and down poles, hundreds of them . . . fitted into the sea, to see how swell hits the shore and what it does as it comes in . . . does it go higher, does it go quicker?'[64]

The weather could not be controlled or managed, and the only thing worse than having to cancel the landings because of bad weather would have been a failure of forecasting leading to the invasion armada being broken up en route, as the resultant loss of life and shipping would probably have ruled out another attempt for years. The role of the forecasters in the final days and hours before D-Day, and in particular that of Eisenhower's chief meteorologist, RAF Group Captain James Stagg, has been well documented, but the painstaking work of gathering and interpreting weather data for months before-hand is perhaps less widely understood.[65] After three weeks in Dorset, Checketts was reunited with his wife-to-be and another Wren, Pam Pinks. They were rushed by lorry to join Stagg's team at Southwick House, reporting to Stagg's RN subordinate, Instructor-Commander John Fleming. Checketts' job was to plot onto charts a relentless flow of weather information coming in by teleprinter – 'that sort of horrible machine behind the door':

> This little, tiny place on the map would hold an enormous amount of information for someone who could decode the plotting you'd done. The wind direction was on there, the temperature was on there, the humidity was on there, the barometric pressure was on there. We knew what was going on, of course, you couldn't help it, but we didn't interpret. We didn't draw any lines, we didn't draw any fronts, we didn't draw any isobars . . . that was done by the

two Lieutenants . . . as quickly as they could get hold of the charts. They more or less snatched them from us sometimes to get at it because they'd got to present it to Commander Fleming.[66]

Distinguishing purely 'naval' elements from the wholly integrated Allied intelligence operation is not easy. A tri-service Anglo-American Theatre Intelligence Section (TIS) was incorporated into SHAEF, but this included a specifically naval section of officers and Wrens reporting to Ramsay. Their responsibilities including a continuous watch over German naval movements, prisoner-of-war interrogations, photographic interpretation and psychological propaganda. Intelligence relevant to the invasion was also obtained through the wider work of the Naval Intelligence Department (NID), and through Ultra. Ramsay's intelligence team also directed the euphemistically named 30 Assault Unit, a joint Royal Navy and Royal Marines commando unit headed initially by James Bond author Ian Fleming (no relation to the meteorologist), which would gather enemy documents and equipment and send it back for analysis after the invasion.

NID distributed a weekly intelligence report (WIR) around the fleet, summarising recent events at sea worldwide. WIR213, issued on 17 April 1944, profiled German perspectives of the forthcoming invasion, obtained from a neutral source with wide-ranging contacts among the German 'aristocracy and higher bureaucracy'.[67] It concluded that although most Germans had lost almost all faith in final victory, particularly in the East, many felt that their fate was irrevocably bound up with that of the Nazi Party. The coming invasion was no secret, but the thoughts of those Germans who inadvertently contributed to the intelligence profile reveal a serious underestimation of Allied determination to defeat them. Knowledge of this underestimation was arguably one of the greatest weapons with which the invading Allies were provided. The unidentified author wrote:

Though the Germans do not know much of what is happening outside their own country, they do know by bitter experience their own internal hardships; and of these they believe that the British know little, and the Americans nothing whatsoever. Through their immense loss in action of both life and material they have been made conscious of the full depth of human suffering. Therefore, they argue 'as we should never have allowed our leaders to get us into this mess, had we only known how dreadful it would be, it now seems probable that the leaders of the western democracies would never be permitted by their people . . . to bring upon them the same hardships and casualties purely to inflict upon us the full measure of defeat'.[68]

According to this snapshot of German public opinion, 'the Germans now wait anxiously, nay even hope, for the great invasion', believing they could smash it with heavy loss of life, prompting the Western Allies to agree to a compromise peace, which would in turn allow Germany to transfer all its forces to the east and hold off the Russians.[69]

Painstaking analysis of the weather and enemy intentions illustrates the desk-based element of intelligence gathering. Other work was more hazardous. One of the most significant risks associated with Neptune was a lack of precise information about the beaches, including the gradients and the materials they were formed from – this had caused significant issues at Dieppe and during Torch. Later on, following a huge increase to the numbers and variety of beach obstacles initiated following the appointment of Generalfeldmarschall Erwin Rommel as General Inspector of Western Defences in November 1943, additional intelligence about the types of defences the assault troops might encounter became an urgent requirement. Beach gradients could be calculated using aerial photography, specifically six carefully spaced lines of images, taken during the first two or last two hours of daylight, and on a day when wind speed did not exceed 20 knots.[70] 140 Squadron RAF took the photos, and the Royal Engineers analysed them and calculated the gradients. Further information came from a national appeal for souvenir postcards showing European beaches, which Wren Ginger Thomas recalled being 'stuck on the wall' in various Norfolk House offices.[71] The American 10th Photo Reconnaissance Group began a detailed survey of Rommel's new obstacles in early May 1944, using an extreme low-level flying technique known as 'dicing'.[72]

However, geological samples could only be obtained by putting ashore small covert survey parties, known as Combined Operations Pilotage Parties or COPPs, from Coastal Forces craft or miniature submarines. Because of the overwhelming requirement to protect the location of the invasion, COPP parties were landed all around the coast of occupied Europe. Only one group was caught, on the night of 17/18 May, and fortunately they were operating in the Pas-de-Calais, precisely where the Allies wanted the Germans to think the invasion would take place. The survey parties themselves tended to be navigation specialists, but their work was directed by a Commander from the Royal Navy's Hydrographic Department and Surveying Service on Ramsay's planning staff.[73]

The COPP surveys were codenamed Postage Able. The first took place on New Year's Eve 1943, when two Royal Engineers, Major Logan Scott-Bowden and Sergeant Bruce Ogden-Smith, swam ashore from a modified Landing Craft Personnel (LCP) near Luc-sur-Mer. The second was more complicated, and longer. Scott-Bowden and Ogden-Smith went across in the miniature submarine *X-20*, commanded by Lieutenant Ken Hudspeth, a 25-year-old Australian from Echuca, Victoria, who had already been awarded the Distinguished Service Cross for his part in the attack on *Tirpitz* in September 1943. With them was Lieutenant-Commander Nigel Clogstoun-Willmott, a Royal Navy Navigator and the progenitor of the COPP programme.

X-20 remained in the Seine Bay for four days, surveying the beaches at Vierville-sur-Mer, Moulins, Saint-Laurent and Colleville-sur-Mer which would eventually become Omaha Area. Methodically, the divers swam ashore by night collecting beach samples in condoms, then recording echo-soundings and carrying out periscope surveys of the beaches by day. It was exhausting, perilous work, broken up by unpleasantly close encounters with the enemy, who could be clearly seen improving the defences as the COPP team watched. Although the team were supposed to move on to Sword Area, by the end of their work at Omaha they were exhausted, the weather was worsening and conditions in the boat were becoming very uncomfortable, so the mission was cut short and the submarine returned safely to Portsmouth.[74]

Survey teams also landed covertly to survey the proposed sites for the Mulberry Harbours, using LCPs fitted with special compasses and a naval variant of the RAF Gee Navigation system known as QH, as well as underwater exhausts and a blackout canopy for covert operations. These surveys were run by a pair of Hydrographers, Lieutenant F.M. Berncastle and Lieutenant N.C. Glen, working out of a block of flats in West Cowes on the Isle of Wight.[75]

Berncastle and Glen set off on their first survey run to the site of the British Mulberry B near Arromanches on the night of 23 October 1943, taking in three LCPs which were towed halfway over by MGBs. 'At about sunset we cast off the tow and went south under our own power, arriving off the French coast around midnight.' Anchoring one LCP as a marker, the two officers used the remaining boats to run lines of soundings inshore 'in the form of a star', going as close inshore as possible and fixing their positions using the silhouettes of houses, which could then be plotted against RAF reconnaissance photographs back in the UK. At 0400, the three boats left the Seine Bay and returned to England. They returned on five more occasions, surveying the American Mulberry site, and some of the beaches.[76]

The work was undoubtedly hard and stressful. On one occasion the team were almost illuminated by German flares, the echo sounders were unreliable and 'it was not unusual to solve the problem by hitting the amplifier with one's fist'. It was cold and uncomfortable, and hot food was impossible to supply until the surveying parties were issued with cans of self-heating soup, reserved for the assault troops but apparently made available on Vian's express orders.[77] Twice bad weather prevented the MGBs from coming out to meet them and the tiny LCP had to return to Newhaven under its own power.

It should be emphasised that for all its extraordinary resources and reach, Allied intelligence was not flawless. At one point Naval Intelligence vanished down a curious rabbit hole leading to a mysterious German asset called the 'W-boat'. In March 1944 an entire panel was established under the chairmanship of the Admiralty's Director of Anti-Submarine Warfare, Captain Clarence Howard-Johnston, to consider countermeasures against this apparently serious threat.[78] W-boats were believed to be very small submersible or semi-submersible E-boats, with an extraordinarily high speed of 40 knots (74km/h) on the surface or 30 knots submerged, twin torpedo tubes and a range of 600 miles on the surface, and were considered to be 'about four times as dangerous as a normal E-boat'.[79] Instructions were issued for some MTBs to have their torpedo tubes removed and replaced by large numbers of small depth charges. Directed by ASDIC-equipped MLs or frigates, the MTBs were supposed to move in a line and saturate the enemy approach path with depth charges, at best an imprecise method of attack. Other proposed countermeasures included smoke, illuminants and pyrotechnic sonobuoys.[80] Unfortunately, the predatory W-boats never existed. They appear to have been a peculiar amalgam of intelligence concerning three German weapons systems: the Type XVII U-boats, full-size submarines with an experimental hydrogen peroxide propulsion system designed by Hellmuth Walter which did indeed provide a very high submerged speed, but these were slow on the surface and never entered frontline service; high-speed explosive motor boats known as *Linsen*, which did not carry torpedoes; and a variety of miniature submersibles, which were torpedo-carrying vessels but painfully slow. Intelligence gathering was an art not a science, and intelligence reports were painstakingly constructed using information often obtained in tantalisingly small quantities from a range of often unreliable sources.

Deception

Before leaving the work of the 'backroom boys and girls' it is important to briefly touch on the work of those involved in the byzantine efforts to convince the Germans that the invasion would take place at a different date and time, or in a different location, or would even involve different and often entirely fictional soldiers, sailors and airmen. These were the people who the historian Thaddeus Holt has dubbed 'The Deceivers'.[81] Although thousands of sailors contributed to these deception operations, most had no idea that they were doing so. Few sailors were active contributors and the reality was that the most effective elements were not inflatable tanks and landing craft, but a carefully cultivated network of double agents, feeding bogus information back to their German handlers. The stories of these remarkable individuals, foremost among whom was Juan Pujol García, better known as Garbo, fall well outside this narrative.[82]

Deception began long before D-Day. In 1943, the Allies staged a series of operations designed to convince the German that an invasion was coming that year: Tindall, a wholly fictitious threat to Norway; Starkey, a landing in the Pas-de-Calais; and Wadham, an American-run threat to invade Brittany a few weeks after the fictitious Starkey. Starkey was interesting in the context of the Battle of the Seine Bay as its secondary objective was to draw the Luftwaffe into a battle of annihilation over the Channel as part of the Pointblank directive, and as such it involved a staged amphibious landing on 9 September 1943.[83] Preceded by heavy bombing raids, over 300 ships set off for France from the Solent and Dungeness, coming within 10 miles of the enemy-held coast near Boulogne. Unfortunately, Starkey failed in its primary objective as most of the German armed forces with the exception of (according to Morgan) a solitary junior officer in the coast artillery ignored it altogether, and the hoped-for air battle never took place.[84]

The more extensive and significant D-Day deception plan, Fortitude, took place in 1944. Fortitude South relied on fictitious agent reports and vast quantities of false wireless traffic to convince the Germans that Neptune was a diversion and the real invasion would be carried out in the Pas-de-Calais, by the wholly fictitious First United States Army Group, or 'FUSAG'. A parallel operation, Fortitude North, maintained the illusory threat to Norway, playing to one of Hitler's greatest obsessions. The architect of Fortitude, Colonel David Strangeways, had a naval opposite number, Lieutenant-Commander Alec Finter, who had run naval deception operations in the Mediterranean, and the Admiralty contributed three Mobile Deception Units, codenamed CLH. These were transmitters in vans, manned by telegraphists who had been specially trained to simulate the wireless traffic of an assault force.[85] As the invasion approached, work also began to identify the locations and frequencies of German radar installations, so that they could either be bombed, jammed or deceived as the operation was underway. The operation, codenamed Knitting, was carried out by a converted Coastal Forces boat, *MTB-255*, and the results informed Operations Taxable and Glimmer, which took place on D-Day (see Chapter 6).[86]

The hard work of the deceivers, the planners and the intelligence gatherers were at least as important as the stoicism and courage of those who served afloat in ensuring victory in the Seine Bay. None of their efforts, however, would matter if sufficient ships could not be built, borrowed or transferred in time for the invasion.

* 4 *
Build, Borrow and Beg:
Assembling the Armada
June 1943–June 1944

From the naval point of view there are serious objections, such as increased naval requirements that we alone cannot meet . . .
Admiral Sir Bertram Ramsay, 20 January 1944[1]

The fleet required for the Seine Bay was already colossal, even before Neptune expanded to five assault areas. Morgan described his initial allocation as a 'pitifully small' lift, but the Admiralty's initial response to Ramsay's outline of his far greater requirement was simply to ask him to reduce it by 40 per cent. 'This', a contemporary wrote mildly, 'Admiral Ramsay felt himself unable to do', and after some significant negotiations the Admiralty accepted his argument. The great push to secure ships began.[2]

The need for landing craft alone was enormous. As well as the five assault divisions, thousands of supporting troops had to be landed, from engineers and specialised armoured vehicles to Commandos, Rangers and naval Beach Parties. They would travel in vessels ranging from tiny assault landing craft capable of carrying a platoon of infantry soldiers, through medium-sized Landing Craft Mechanised (LCMs) and Landing Craft Vehicle and Personnel (LCVPs) which could lift one tank, and larger LCTs like *LCT-7074*, to oceangoing Landing Ships and troopships. Other specialised craft provided additional firepower and logistical support.

More warships would be assembled for the Bombardment Forces, the largest force of minesweepers ever assembled would bring them safely to the assault areas, and yet more ships would provide convoy escort and anti-submarine screening and carry out countless other tasks. The British Naval Staff History lists 7,016 ships and vessels taking part in Neptune from battleships (7) and cruisers (23), through minesweepers (287) and Coastal Forces craft (495), to the ubiquitous 'major landing craft' (1,211). Around a seventh of the fleet comprised merchant ships, including coasters, tankers and stores ships.[3] In Portsmouth Command alone, the requirements for landing craft berths expanded from 1,200 for the proposed Sledgehammer in April 1942 to 2,500 for Roundup in July 1942, and finally a staggering 3,000 for Overlord.[4]

Even the vast resources of the United States were stretched to the limit to provide these ships, given the competing demands of a global maritime war. To give just one example, producing assault shipping was pointless if there were insufficient merchant ship hulls to send troops and equipment across the Atlantic, so landing craft had to be traded off against Liberty ships. Then again, mercantile hulls were pointless if they were going to be sunk by U-boats, so anti-submarine escorts were also essential. But, to turn the wheel full circle, there was no point in transporting all those troops, tanks and guns across to the UK if there were insufficient landing craft to take them on to France.[5] Other shipbuilding resources were diverted to the Mulberry Harbours and PLUTO. The insidious influence of inter-Allied politics played its part: when the British vetoed Sledgehammer in 1942, the Americans diverted nearly all of their June 1942 landing craft production to the Pacific.[6]

Some ships were newly built for Neptune, and others were converted, including Landing Ships Infantry (LCI) and headquarters ships adapted from ocean liners or warships, and landing craft fitted out for inshore bombardment work. Some hulls were transferred from other theatres, notably the Mediterranean, and arrived at the last possible moment. Even then the fleet was only barely large enough. Additional 'lift' was improvised, assault craft were loaded to their maximum capacity and the military had to make some tough compromises: each assault division, for example, was restricted to 2,500 vehicles instead of the 3,200 which were originally intended.[7]

Some ships were barely seaworthy. When Lieutenant-Commander Alan Villiers, naval reservist and later celebrated writer and adventurer, brought back two flotillas of Landing Craft Infantry (Large) (LCI(L)) from Malta at the end of 1943, he described them as 'old and much used'. 'The nineteen LCI(L)', he went on, 'were the oldest British LCI(L) in existence and most of them had nearly 3,000 engine hours to their credit, without proper refit.' All had taken part in multiple assault landings in the Mediterranean.[8]

Bill Perks was a seaman aboard the destroyer HMS *Walker*, which had been launched in 1917, and had years of gruelling service in the North Atlantic behind her. *Walker* was battered by an Arctic gale shortly before D-Day, and huge waves had cracked the stanchions in the mess deck which held the structure together. In different circumstances *Walker* would have gone into drydock or given her age simply been scrapped, but *Walker* had a job to do, escorting Convoy E2B2Z to Omaha Area. 'We thought "well we'll go back home"', Perks recalled, but instead 'We went into Iceland where they . . . got some big, thick planks of wood and shored it all up . . . we were still shored up with temporary repairs when we went to D-Day.'[9]

Perhaps the most iconic assault ship of the Second World War was the Landing Ship Tank, or LST. LSTs were the largest ships capable of discharging their loads directly on to an open beach, and there were never enough of them, prompting Churchill to rage to Marshall that 'history would always wonder how the fate of two great empires was tied up in some goddamned things called LSTs!'[10]

The first three LSTs were improvised by the British from unusually shallow-draught oil tankers and trialled at Madagascar, after which a purpose-built design was approved, but it was American ingenuity which simplified the concept for mass production, and it was American manufacturers which rolled them out by the hundreds. John C. Niedermair was a designer in the Bureau of Ships in Washington when the British requirement arrived in November 1941. 'I got busy and made a few sketches', he recalled. 'The craft had to meet two conditions. One, it had to be able to cross the ocean and have enough draft to get there. Then when it got to the landing area the crew needed to pump the ballast tanks dry and go on to the beach.'[11]

By October 1942 a prototype had been completed by the Dravo Corporation of Pittsburgh, Pennsylvania. Over that winter, Niedermair put the ship through a series of trials at Norfolk Navy Yard, Virginia. Then came the crucial beaching trial, at Quonset, Rhode Island. 'They hit the beach at about ten knots', Niedermair recalled. 'That's pretty high for a landing craft and most captains don't like to hit the beach like that ... as we were approaching the beach that speed of ten knots seemed to get faster and faster. I began to look around to see what I would hang on to! Well, we hit the beach and ... it wasn't any problem.'[12]

By the end of the war, 1,573 LSTs had been built in the USA alone, many by inland companies with no previous shipbuilding experience. Once they had been built, they were collected by hastily assembled crews. Christopher Clitherow arrived in Philadelphia as part of the ship's company of HMS *Royal Sovereign*, which was in for a very long refit. Two-thirds of the crew were dispersed to other duties, and Clitherow was appointed to take charge of an LST. 'The idea, both of the ships and their function, was entirely new', he remembered, 'we started with completely unbiased minds and no previous records. We had to find out their habits and capabilities, and a fascinating game it proved.' His new command, *LST-415*, was very different to a battleship. 'Right in the bottom', he recalled, 'were fuel and water tanks; some empty, sealed compartments to give buoyancy; the engine and generator rooms; and a large number of ballast tanks, which could be flooded or emptied at will, to tip the bow or stern, or to list the ship sideways. All these extended upwards to just above the waterline.'[13] Above all this was the most important part of the ship. *LST-415* was a big steel shoe box with one job, carrying as much military hardware as possible to 'the far shore' and putting it on the beach:

The tank deck ... extended from the bows to about a hundred feet from the stern and occupied two deck levels. At the fore end of the tank deck was the ramp, a huge square vertical door, hinged at the bottom, which, when hoisted, made a water-tight joint, and when lowered became a platform over which vehicles from the tank deck could drive out. Outside the ramp were two doors opening sideways; these, when closed, formed a ship's bow instead of a square front and also protected the ramp from damage.[14]

There were many differences to get used to in American-built ships: bunks instead of hammocks, no scuttles or portholes in the accommodation spaces, and innumerable gadgets. The catering facilities were apparently 'magnificent'. Downsides included unreliable steering gear, a gyro compass which was 'somewhat frivolous', and diesel engines designed for railway engines.[15] Dennis Watkins commissioned the frigate HMS *Retalick* in Boston after months at sea in the old cruiser *London*. 'I was very pleased indeed', he recalled, 'it was like a little palace to me. Beautifully clean, all electric galley, bunks to sleep in. It was a clean and comfortable ship.'[16] Sometimes, if there was time, these Stateside 'luxuries' were removed by the determinedly austere Royal Navy; Midshipman Ernest Noble remembered the bunks being stripped out of his US-built minesweeper HMS *Gazelle*.[17]

US-built ships also tended to be welded rather than riveted, so they could be built quickly by inexperienced men and women. This also meant that once in service, repairs and alterations could be carried out in hours rather than days, but the new process was not to everyone's taste. When Stan Parker joined the minesweeper *Pylades* in Savannah, Georgia, the welded seams filled him with horror. 'When I saw it, I thought "oh blimey that's not going to be good, all welded" ... in my mind I thought if we get any problems ... the welding would split ... when I first saw it, I thought "I don't like that".'[18]

Christopher Clitherow commissioned *415* into the Royal Navy on 19 January 1943. During a short work-up in Chesapeake Bay, the new ship's company learned to beach and then haul themselves off using a stern anchor and a huge winch, a fundamentally unnatural activity for most sailors. 'Having been paid for many years to keep ships off the beach', he recalled, 'we commenced very slowly!' A few days later they were ordered to New York with five other new LSTs to load up with military equipment and head for the UK. The first voyage in open water in a 300ft-long welded ship was 'terrifying':

> She reacts to a bump like a diving board off which one has just jumped. Unfortunately, one has only jumped in the air and come down again, and now one goes on bouncing, while every conceivable piece of the ship rattles as if its teeth were about to fall out. There is a limit to what you can take of this, apart from the fact that the main breakers of the generators are liable to jump off, plunging the ship in darkness, and putting the steering engine out of action.[19]

In New York, they took on board 400 tons of boxed provisions, 50 crated lorries, 296 jeeps and a US Navy Landing Craft (Tank) Mk V, which was welded onto the upper deck, the American crew joining the LST for the passage across the Atlantic. This was Bolero, the years-long build-up of US troops and equipment in Britain, in action.

Thousands of sailors were sent out from the UK to collect their new ships, crossing the Atlantic in empty troopships returning, then passing through HMS *Asbury*, the Royal Navy's Barracks and Accounting Base in Asbury Park, New Jersey. When Henry Bell brought back his LST, he was one of only three experienced sailors among the ship's company. Bell had already survived the accidental sinking of the cruiser *Curacoa* by the liner *Queen Mary* in October 1942 and was not troubled by an Atlantic gale. 'We came back to New York and loaded up with lorries and aircraft landing mats and all sorts of goods, and also we had a small landing craft on our deck which was crewed by Americans', he recalled. 'We left New York . . . and we hit a gale and the landing mats went over the side and the elevator fell through and the steering fell down . . . I did forty-eight hours on the wheel because the rest of them were being sick.'[20]

29-year-old Royal Navy Lieutenant Colin Madden was second-in-command of a 'flight' of twenty-two flimsy LCI(L)s, responsible for navigating them across the Atlantic from Norfolk, Virginia:

The flight ... was LCI(L) Flight Number 8 ... to do the ocean passage we had about twenty sailors altogether and three officers, and I was one of the ocean captains of one of them ... These ships were built in a matter of weeks, even less. They had as propulsion cight lorry engines in two banks of four. Absolutely basic ... it was quite a long way to go from Norfolk, Virginia, to Gibraltar!

It is only hindsight that provides perspective on the threat from German U-boats and surface raiders at this stage of the war. The horrors of the 'Wolf Packs' were only a few months before, and nobody knew for sure what the Kriegsmarine was capable of. LCI(L)s were slow, unarmoured and almost defenceless targets. 'We were always a little bit frightened', Madden recalled; 'it was pretty easy for one submarine to surface near us and to pick us off one by one.'[21]

Although much of the mass-produced armada came from the United States, Britain's outdated, overstretched shipbuilding industry made a significant contribution. Shipyard workers were the unsung heroes of the Battle of the Seine Bay, and as with the planners, many were women, introduced to the industry on significantly lower rates of pay following a national agreement between the government, shipbuilders and trade unions in July 1941 permitting 'dilution' of the usually skilled (and unionised) workforce, workmen who tradition-ally served long apprenticeships before finally qualifying.[22] Alice Hall worked at R. & W. Hawthorn, Leslie and Company on Tyneside and her story is fairly typical. With no family, she was instructed to leave her job in a string factory and 'go in munitions, go in the forces or go in the shipyard. Well, I'd enough of factories', she recalled, adding in a statement illustrative of the times, 'and Ted [her husband] said I hadn't to go in the forces, so I said I'll go to the shipyard.' Hall was a 'dilutee' and trainee electrician. After six weeks' training, she found herself installing the main telephone exchange deep inside the cruiser HMS *Diadem*, which was completed in early 1944 and would form part of the bombardment forces off Juno Assault Area. The work was hard but fulfilling, Hall remembered: 'we worked long hours and everybody was happy ... I was definitely helping the war effort, and I wasn't when I was making balls of string!'[23]

Most workers were not building anything as dignified as a cruiser. 5,000 small wooden landing craft were constructed in the UK by boatbuilding companies, many on the River Hamble in Hampshire. Bill Miles was coxswain of a Landing Craft Assault (LCA), perhaps the most basic warship in the Seine Bay:

> She was a strong wooden craft with armoured side panels and armoured doors which protected the thirty-five men she carried ... Forward of these doors was the heavy iron bow ramp which was lowered and raised by hand. There were two armoured cockpits port and starboard, one was for the coxswain or helmsman with the steering controls, voice pipe and telegraphs, with which to pass his orders to the stoker in the small engine room at the stern where he sat between two Ford V8 engines which supplied the power to drive the boat through its twin screws at a speed of ten knots. The port side cockpit mounted a Lewis machine gun which was to protect the craft against enemy air attack and to give support fire to the disembarking troops. There were signalling flags and a hand operated bilge pump and a kedge anchor. For hoisting and lowering the craft from the ship's davits was a very strong steel eye fore and aft. She lay low in the water and ... it needed skilful handling to keep her from swamping in rough weather.[24]

Thousands more wooden landing craft rolled out of US boatyards, including the famous 'Higgins Boat' LCVP, which could land a platoon. Its designer, the New Orleans boatbuilder Andrew Higgins, had originally conceived it for the swamps and bayous of Louisiana, believing he would find a ready market among hunters, fishermen and, according to legend at least, 'rum runners' smuggling illegal alcohol to the United States during the Prohibition era. Well over 23,000 LCVPs were produced during the Second World War.

1,200 of the far larger, seagoing LCTs were built in the UK for service in the Seine Bay.[25] British-built landing craft were nowhere near as comfortable as the American LSTs. George Humphries was a 20-year-old telegraphist who was posted to a British-built Landing Craft Tank Mk III, according to him 'the worst craft you can ever go on in the Navy'. 235 Mk III LCTs were completed. They were nearly 60 metres long and displaced 350 tons unloaded. They had a crew of two junior officers and ten seamen, who lived in a tiny mess deck at the aft end of the ship, behind the engines and below the equally small galley, officers' wardroom and bridge. It was impossible to stand upright in much of the unheated mess deck, which was foul with condensation when occupied, and there was insufficient room for all the crew to sling their hammocks; Humphries ended up suspended 4 metres in the air above the open tank deck, with only canvas between his body and the weather. 'The living conditions were abominable', he concluded; 'you couldn't . . . do washing, so you just stunk. Awful . . . Mk IIIs were disgusting.'[26]

At least Humphries served in a purpose-built assault craft, even if the conditions were basic. A lot of capacity had to be improvised, and one simple expedient involved modifying unpowered Thames 'dumb barges', which were really no different to the much-derided Rhine barges with which the Kriegsmarine had intended to invade England back in 1940. The key difference, of course, was that in 1944 the Allies could rely on almost complete control of the air and sea, which made the risks inherent in using such fundamentally unsuitable craft more acceptable. Albert Rogers was a seaman aboard one. 'We had two Chrysler Marine 8-cylinders put on either side port and starboard', he remembered; 'they cut the stern off the back of it and put a ramp to go out into the water and one inboard to go into the hull. In between the two ramps was a big steel bulkhead that had to be lifted up and clamped down with four handles to either side.' The wheelhouse on the deck was 'a glorified overgrown box' with 'four-inch armour plating round about four feet high. They put a steering wheel in it [and] a bell pull for port and starboard [engines].'[27]

By such expedients was a Thames barge turned into the majestic-sounding Landing Barge Vehicle, LBV-121. The stern ramp meant that LBVs had to be beached backwards which, improbably, meant turning these underpowered and ungainly craft bows-on to the weather moments before landing, dropping a kedge anchor and then

going stern first through the pounding surf, an extraordinary challenge to the seamanship of their often young and inexperienced
crews – Rogers was a 20-year-old Londoner with no previous
seagoing experience beyond some elementary rowing and ropework
as a teenager in the Hampstead Naval Brigade (akin to the Sea
Scouts). Stern beaching also tended to wreck the vulnerable rudders
so, incredibly, *LBV-121* carried a pair of huge oars, which on one
occasion the coxswain and leading seaman had to actually use to
steer their ersatz man o'war from Southampton to the Isle of Wight.
The accommodation comprised five bunks and a coal-burning stove
jammed into a tiny locker in the bows.[28] Other adapted barges were
used as floating kitchens for the thousands of sailors afloat for days
in craft too small to have a galley; the first such Landing Barge
Kitchen was improvised during training exercises at the end of
1943.[29] Other barges became small tankers carrying petrol, diesel or
water, and floating workshops known as Landing Barges Emergency
Repair, which were, according to one report, not a success as they
could not be kept dry, had very limited facilities and tended to be
swamped in bad weather.[30] Some, known as Landing Barges Flak,
even carried a pair of Bofors anti-aircraft guns with Royal Artillery
crews.[31]

LBV-121 was one of 159 barges sent to Southampton after May
1942 for conversion by local engineering firms in a process dubbed
Operation Consular. The subsequent installation of engines after
January 1943 was codenamed Haulabout. Once converted, they were
moored on the Rivers Beaulieu and Itchen.

Refit and maintenance work on Neptune-specific ships and
craft at Southampton rose from 70 vessels of all types in January
1943 to a peak of 170 in February 1944.[32] Vice-Admiral Sir Marshal
Clarke, the long-serving Admiral Superintendent at Portsmouth,
produced a lengthy report detailing his establishment's contribution
to assembling the Seine Bay fleet from 1 October 1942. It provides
an extraordinary case study of the accelerating pace of preparations
as D-Day drew closer. 'At the beginning of this period', Clarke
begins, 'preparation for OVERLORD was a comparatively minor
commitment of the Dockyard. For example, in October 1942 the

weekly return of Ships Under Repair showed only four major landing craft in hand.'[33]

Clarke's responsibilities stretched far outside of Hampshire, encompassing satellite shore establishments from Cumbria to Newhaven in East Sussex. Some 15,000 personnel, including 1,200 women, were employed in the principal construction departments, of which between 50 and 60 per cent were working on 'repairs, refits and new construction'. Among the unique projects were the conversion of LCTs into armoured LCT(A) variants, the adaption of eighteen LCTs into LCT(R) rocket landing craft for close-range 'drenching' fire support and the retrofitting of ramp extensions to LCTs to enable them to launch DD amphibious tanks.[34] From April 1944, an extraordinary 406 warships of all shapes and sizes passed through Clarke's hands for refits, including 186 landing craft. In addition, Portsmouth found the capacity to convert three old warships into blockships which would be scuttled as part of the 'Gooseberry' breakwaters. The CO of one, the old battleship HMS *Centurion* (launched in 1911), brought his ship into Portsmouth on 13 May, reporting proudly that his aged and expendable command had reached 17½ knots (a creditable 32km/h) in the final stage of the long journey back from Alexandria, and his ship's company had 'worked well and cheerfully despite discomforts and delays'.[35]

Clarke's command also fitted out the headquarters ships *Largs*, *Hilary* and *Bulolo*, former passenger liners used to direct operations across an entire assault area.[36] HMS *Hilary* returned from the Mediterranean after years of hard service and desperately needed that refit, according to 20-year-old Londoner Frank Luff, a communications rating who had served in the ship since June 1943. The HQ ship was armed with depth charges which were unusable as *Hilary* was too slow to get out of the way of the resulting explosion, a pair of old guns which Luff said wrecked the ship when they were test-fired, and improvised armour around the wheelhouse, bridge and upper decks. As a consequence, *Hilary* was terribly top heavy, so, bizarrely, the ship had 50 tons of beetroot in the keel as ballast to compensate. Two of the ship's upper decks were jammed full of empty oil drums as additional buoyancy aids.[37]

Hilary came back via Gibraltar in December 1943, a journey Luff described as 'one of the most frightening experiences I had in the war'. The convoy was pursued by a U-boat pack, and then slammed by a three-day Atlantic gale:

> We carried six Landing Craft (Personnel) on our sides. We lost all six of these ... they got dragged off the side of the davits. We got our funnel bent. One of the landing craft when it got ripped off ... knocked a hole in the side. To make matters worse ... the buffeting of the ship got so bad that our water tank was split and got contaminated with salt water. We then got informed that fresh water was no longer available for drinking, not until we arrived at port, and the journey instead of taking us three days took us ten days.[38]

Luff and his shipmates were forced to drink evaporated milk and even the stale beetroot juice carried in the hold as ballast. By the time they reached Milford Haven *Hilary* was a wreck, and as the ship entered the Solent salt water in the boilers slowed her down so much she could make no headway against the tide. When the tide turned and *Hilary* finally came in, onlookers cheered because they thought the battered ship had been in action, but just a few months later the liner joined the invasion fleet as headquarters ship for Force J. Phenomenal efforts like this enabled Ramsay and Eisenhower to celebrate the fact that, on the eve of the invasion, 99.3 per cent of all US and 97.3 per cent of all British assault vessels on hand for the invasion were serviceable.[39]

Because of the emphasis on D-Day itself in much of the literature, and the military-centric nature of many narratives, which represent naval forces as merely the delivery system for the Army, assault craft are often the focus for much of the debate around shipping, but the bombardment forces were equally important and in just as short supply. The key difference was that battleships and cruisers could not just be produced at short notice, and also had to carry out other important tasks right up to the eve of the invasion, including providing a covering role against any attempt to intervene by the Kriegsmarine.

This is why, although hundreds of miles away, the Home Fleet's battleships and aircraft carriers should be seen as fully part of the operations in the Seine Bay. In fact, although the Home Fleet watched the north, Ramsay even devised a contingency plan, Operation Hermetic, which involved Vian rushing into the North Sea with his elderly battleships to meet the Germans if they came south: 'it would be a glorious thing', he recorded in his diary on 14 May, 'to wipe out the German Fleet with my Amphibious Operational Warships'.[40]

Glorious fleet actions aside, the main role for battleships and cruisers in the Seine Bay was bombardment. On D-Day itself and in the days which followed, the fleet and the Allied air forces would provide the main source of artillery support for the Army and would be key in trying to suppress the German Atlantic wall defenders during those key moments when the vulnerable invading troops rushed ashore. Afterwards, properly controlled naval firepower would still provide an overwhelming advantage on the battlefield with which military artillery simply could not compare. The heaviest artillery deployed by the Army in Normandy were 7.2-inch (182mm) howitzers by the British and the famous 6.1-inch (155mm) 'Long Tom' field guns by the Americans. British battleships, by contrast, might be armed with 15-inch (380mm) guns. Cruisers could deploy smaller guns in huge numbers: a typical German coastal battery might field four 155mm guns, whereas a light cruiser like HMS *Belfast* could deploy twelve weapons of similar calibre, and a further twelve 4-inch (101mm) guns roughly equivalent to military field artillery.[41] Finding enough battleships and cruisers for the Seine Bay was vital, a lesson which had been driven home at Dieppe.

The British had committed to providing all the gunfire support for Neptune as originally conceived and allocated four battleships and twenty cruisers to the operation, as well as two big gun monitors, shallow-draught vessels designed for shore bombardment. However, the expansion to five assault areas meant asking the Americans for help. Alan Kirk outlined his needs for the US Western Task Force before Christmas. 'I wrote to Dickie Edwards, who was on Admiral King's staff, and I told him ... if they didn't want to have the thing look rather dubious, they'd better assemble the ships.'[42] King prevaricated but eventually agreed to assist. Rear-Admiral Carleton F. Bryant commanded the US Navy's Battleship Division Five, flying his flag in the veteran USS *Texas*, with the even older USS *Arkansas* (commissioned in 1912) under command. Bryant arrived off Northern Ireland in the spring of 1944, and *Texas* and *Arkansas* went through a crash course in naval bombardment, the sailors intently studying carefully disguised scale topographical models of the enemy-occupied coastline. 'They had all the contours. They also had every tree, every fence, every house, every ditch and every dike on them.'[43]

Rear-Admiral Morton L. Deyo brought more welcome US support across on 18 April 1944, in the form of the heavy cruiser *Tuscaloosa* and the battleship *Nevada*, along with the nine destroyers of Destroyer Division (DESRON) 18. William Kirkland was a junior officer in USS *Doyle*. 'None of the officers or men, save perhaps the Commodore, had any idea what they were to do that summer ... by twos and fours the ships sortied daily for drills and high-speed manoeuvring off the coast in the area of Eddystone Light', working alongside their British counterparts and getting to know them socially: 'so passed some pleasant days of Anglo-American camaraderie'.[44] In the end, the US Navy provided three battleships, two cruisers and twenty-two destroyers for the bombardment forces. Among the last arrivals from across the pond were three squadrons of the US Navy's Patrol Torpedo (PT) Boats, equivalent to British MTBs, two of which only arrived in June. They were grouped under the command of the US Navy's swashbuckling PT hero Lieutenant-Commander Robert Bulkeley, who had distinguished himself in the Pacific before moving across to the UK.[45]

Battleships and cruisers could not be risked close inshore where they were vulnerable to mines: their role was to lay off at a distance and carry out precision bombardments of German coastal defence batteries. The close-range 'drenching fire' was supposed to be provided by destroyers, of which there were never enough, so additional gunfire support came from Landing Craft Gun (LCG) and Landing Craft Flak (LCF), LCTs which had been decked over and usually armed with either a pair of old naval guns or 20mm Oerlikon anti-aircraft guns, manned by Royal Marines. If all else failed, the support landing craft were intended to be beached to become stable, static gun platforms, essentially a coastal gun battery in reverse.

The need for cheap, expendable inshore fire control craft had been first identified at Gallipoli in 1915, summarised in the 1919 Mitchell Report of lessons learned, and then investigated in a desultory manner during the interwar years. The first LCF saw service at Dieppe, when their light guns, although effective against low flying aircraft as intended, had 'little effect on the strong and well entrenched German defences'.[46] They were accompanied by smaller Landing Craft Support improvised from the little LCAs and armed with machine guns and smoke mortars, which proved useful but again these were rather lightly armed. Dieppe incentivised the development of more potent 'craft equivalent to a monitor type', bringing about the Landing Craft (Gun) and larger Landing Craft Support, converted from LCIs.[47] These latter were fitted with military anti-tank weapons in small turrets, which were described by one contemporary writer as 'miniature destroyers or waterborne tanks ... equipped to go in advance of the flotilla and break down ... light enemy resistance'.[48] The larger types debuted in Husky, the Sicily landings, which in turn exposed further shortcomings, notably concerning their fire support equipment.

These improvisations were often carried out hurriedly, often by 'structural engineers employing prefabrication methods' rather than proper shipyards. One Admiralty letter admitted that 'all types of landing craft have been built very rapidly and to the minimum standard required'.[49] In the case of the early LCGs this led to a disastrous decision to save time and money by only decking over half of the open tank deck for the gun mounts and leaving the forepart open behind the welded-up ramp. This created a perfect water tank, and *LCG-15* and *LCG-16* were swamped on the night of 25/26 April 1943 on a routine passage from Belfast to Holyhead, with the loss of seventy-three men, along with a further six from the sloop HMS *Rosemary*, which tried to assist. There were only three survivors, one of whom described the fatally open foredeck as looking like a swimming pool, and the pumps failing as flotsam came in with the water and blocked the outlets. After this the remaining LCGs were decked over.[50]

Other precious LCT hulls were converted into the famous LCT(R), vividly recalled by almost every Normandy veteran as formidable weapons systems. In reality they were crude improvisations, converted by welding up the bow doors and plating over the open tank deck, on which were set 1,064 rocket launchers in fixed racks which were loaded by hand, and fired by aiming the entire ship and closing a series of a simple electrical circuits. 'The system . . . was so antiquated it was unbelievable', recalled Eric Lines, a Wireman in *LCT(R)-447*; 'there was this electric board for firing . . . with about 20 or 30 tumbler switches on it . . . the skipper used to say . . . he wanted such-and-such a rack activated. You used to knock all these switches down, and then he would fire whatever he wanted to fire.'[51] Small batches of 64 rockets could be fired for range finding, and the remainder were 'fired for effect' in bigger salvoes.

Everything was in short supply, even the small craft required for communications and other general duties. On 10 January 1944, an urgent meeting was convened at the Admiralty to review the 'urgent operational requirements of small craft which are outstanding'. Eighty-eight Motor Fishing Vessels, fifty-eight Fast Motor Boats and a staggering 256 Harbour Launches had to be found before 31 March. The shortfall was to be met by cutting supplies to the Eastern Fleet, combing out all the principal UK bases, notably Scapa Flow which was to surrender 20 per cent of its harbour craft, and requesting transfers from the Royal Air Force, the Army, warships at sea, and the United States. Converting obsolete MTBs was considered, and thought was even given to a bizarre Dunkirk in reverse by 'using laid-up private motor boats of between 20 and 30 feet', crewed in some cases by the same weekend yachtsmen who had assisted in 1940. Three days later a committee was established to screen all Neptune demands, ensuring that small boats were being allocated efficiently. It was chaired by Admiral Sir Lionel Preston, who had served as Director of the Admiralty's Small Vessel Pool since the Dunkirk evacuation. Flag Officers of harbours, ports and training bases reported their holdings through January. The Flag Officer in Charge at Glasgow noted on 21 January that he could offer up eighteen small craft from the Clyde River Patrol, but that these were 'somewhat fragile' and as they were manned by civilians 'there are no crews available for transfer with craft'. More boats were found in reserve, and detailed estimates were prepared of how many small craft under repair would be ready by 31 March.[52]

So desperate was the need that at one point a press appeal was issued for civilian volunteer crews. 'In connection with the forth-coming operations for the liberation of the occupied countries of Europe', it read, 'there may be an opportunity for yachtsmen and others with motor boat or steam boat experience, to place their serv-ices at the disposal of the Admiralty.' The estimated need was for 1,000 men, but the appeal generated more than 4,000 applications in six weeks and the process was closed on 20 May. Early in the process consideration was even given to 'crews composed entirely of women', although this was vigorously crossed out.[53]

Eventually, through compromise, creativity and sheer hard work, Preston was able to note on 9 May 1944 that 'it was now apparent that the bare requirements of small craft would be satisfactorily met'.[54] In part this was thanks to Admiral King in the US, who had sixty of the US Coast Guard's versatile 83ft cutters sent over for use as rescue boats.[55]

At the very last minute, the final pieces of the puzzle were slotted into place, when even the vital convoy routes were emptied of precious anti-submarine escort and support groups to screen the Seine Bay. Arctic Convoys were suspended from early April 1944 until after the invasion had been successfully delivered, and Western Approaches Command, the key command for the North Atlantic, gave up an extraordinary sixteen escort destroyers, fourteen sloops, twenty-five frigates and sixty-three corvettes.[56]

It was not, of course, just about the ships, although construction of the vast infrastructure required to sustain the fleet falls largely outside the scope of this narrative.[57] By June 1944, Portsmouth Command alone had twenty landing craft bases accommodating 29,000 officers and men of the British Forces S, G and J, all under Rear-Admiral Frederick Buckley as Commodore, Landing Craft Bases. Base infrastructure included dozens of the ubiquitous concrete embarkation hards where troops could board landing craft straight over their ramps, as well as thirteen Landing Craft Repair Bases, accommodation including eight tented camps and 172,000 square feet of storage space.[58]

For the US Western Task Force, Rear-Admiral John Wilkes, USN, was Commander Landing Craft and Bases, Eleventh Amphibious Force, improbably abbreviated in the US style to COMLANCRABELEVENTHPHIB. Wilkes was responsible for 'the readiness and training of all beaching and landing craft'. With his headquarters in Devonport, his empire included ten Amphibious Training Centres, four Advanced Amphibious Training Sub-Bases, and five Supply Depots and Repair Bases, including a vast centre constructed on Exeter Golf Club. The latter accommodated nearly 3,000 officers and men by June 1944, had its own railway spur, and occupied around 300 buildings spread across 95 acres, along with another 75 acres of open storage.[59] Wilkes, described in the US Official History as 'a bundle of nervous energy', was an exceptional officer, whose 'splendid efforts' were singled out by Ramsay in his official Despatch.[60]

The ships and infrastructure were ready. But while construction proceeded at breakneck speed, the crews had to be recruited, trained and prepared for them.

* 5 *
Finding Sailors: Recruitment and Training
June 1943–June 1944

Training was concentrated and carried out at high pressure . . .
Report of Proceedings, Naval Commander Force G[1]

Finding sailors was arguably harder than building ships, particularly for the British, who by this late stage of the war were facing what the Official Historian has called 'an acute shortage of manpower'.[2] For the Army, this eventually led to the breakup of entire infantry divisions to provide replacements as casualties in Europe started to mount.[3]

In August 1943, the Admiralty disbanded the Royal Marines Division and two redundant formations known as Marine Naval Base Defence Organisations, releasing thousands of men to retrain as Commandos or landing craft crews. Royal Marines manned the armament on LCGs and LCFs and provided crews for two-thirds of the LCAs. Including the five battalion-sized Commandos, more than 20,000 took part in Neptune: it was the single biggest deployment in the Corps' history.[4]

In 1944, the Admiralty found more sailors by 'laying up', or taking out of service, four older battleships, five cruisers and forty obsolete destroyers, as well as an entire minelaying flotilla. Personnel were transferred from the Army and the Royal Air Force and most of the latest intake of 18-year-old recruits went into Combined Operations. Every possible sailor was 'combed out' from duties ashore, their duties backfilled by women, thousands of whom joined up in 1943–4, inspired by the words of a recruiting poster exhorting them to 'Join the Wrens – and free a Man for the Fleet!' Similar efforts were underway on the other side of the Atlantic.

Every sailor (or Royal Marine, or US Coastguardsman) went through generic basic training. At this point, both raw recruits and transferred personnel would progress to role-specific training in (for example) landing craft, then formation-level training, before finally becoming small cogs in the huge tri-service exercises which preceded Neptune. This chapter will concentrate mainly on the Combined Operations personnel who were being specifically trained for service in the Seine Bay but, as the invasion drew near, sailors serving in more 'conventional' warships were also brought in. Combined Operations crews had just one role, and a lengthy period to prepare for it, but this was not the case for those who manned the Home Fleet's battleships and destroyers and the Escort and Support Groups, or those who were transferred late in the day from other theatres. Their roles in the Seine Bay were not wildly different to their 'day jobs', but they had to carry on doing those day jobs until the very last moment.

Combined Operations Training Centres were established to meet the enormous requirement for landing craft crews, boat officers and naval beach commandos. In just a few gruelling weeks, young sailors were turned into amphibious warfare specialists. The need for junior officers was particularly acute. In the Royal Navy, many came through a fast-track process known as the 'Y Scheme'. 'You don't want to be just one of the crowd', exhorted a wartime pamphlet; 'when the time comes, you'd like to . . . captain your own small vessel . . . the Navy has a scheme which is designed to help people like you.'[5]

Potential officers could volunteer for the Y Scheme in advance of their call-up, sometimes as young as 16½ years old. While waiting for their call-up they carried out pre-entry training and then, if they passed a selection board, they were observed closely during basic training. If they displayed 'signs of intelligence, resourcefulness, and leadership' they went to their first ships as 'CW' ('Commission Worthy') candidates and spent a minimum of two months at sea as ratings, again under close observation.[6] If they continued to display leadership qualities, they were plucked out and sent to HMS *King Alfred*, a sprawling shore base occupying a former school and leisure centre near Hove, and Lancing College, all in East Sussex. Here they underwent twelve weeks training and emerged as Temporary Acting Probationary Sub-Lieutenants, probably the most insubstantial title the hierarchy-conscious Royal Navy could bestow. At this point, ludicrously, the Service sent them to the Royal Naval College at Greenwich for a short course on Wardroom etiquette, known disparagingly as the 'knife and fork' course. The 20-year-old Brian Haskell-Thomas attended in 1943. 'We were ushered into a room and a Commander came in and said "you have become officers. We are now going to teach you how to be gentlemen"', he recalled. 'One chap stood up and said, "I was a gentleman before I considered joining this organisation!" He was sent outside to put his head under a cold tap. Silly thing to say really.'[7]

Having learned how to eat dinner properly, many new officers found themselves bound for Combined Operations. For many this meant HMS *Lochailort*, the Combined Operations School for junior 'boat officers', at Inverailort Castle near Fort William in Scotland. The course was a gruelling six-week-long resilience test, which some found harder than their subsequent service in the Seine Bay. 'You go through the most rigorous physical examinations and tests . . . you're stretched to your limits all the time,' remembered Bertie Male, a tough former Petty Officer who had been recommended for a commission after being Mentioned in Despatches when his ship was sunk in the Mediterranean.[8]

Every week the young candidates were given tests, and if they failed they were returned to sea, to complete their naval service on the lower deck. The pressure was intense. 'We waded ice-cold streams. We climbed mountains in PT kit in snow and ice. We marched and we did rifle drill. We did assault courses, on and on and on, day after day,' remembered Male. 'Physically you're exhausted and all the time you have to keep up to date with your weekly examinations and your academic studies.'[9] Male passed and was posted to LCTs. Half of his intake failed and were unceremoniously sent back to sea.

The 19-year-old Londoner William Jarman, another Y Scheme entrant who went through *Lochailort* in the bitter winter of 1942/3, remembered some candidates using a discrete code to indicate to their instructors that they had had enough. 'When you lined up for divisions in the morning, the chap who said he wanted to say goodbye normally went straight up to the Commanding Officer and saluted him. Instead of the usual way of saluting with a rifle, [which] is to move your arm across the butt of the rifle ... he'd raise his hand to the cap badge. It was a recognised way of saying "I've had enough, I want you to know this and you can send me home."'[10]

By the end of 1943, potential Combined Operations officers were not even going through *King Alfred*. Instead, they went straight from the lower deck to *Lochailort* and, if they passed a truncated course on landing craft operations, were immediately granted commissions. The urgent requirement to learn how to fold your napkin at Greenwich had also apparently been discarded. Peter Bird, from Cheshire, knew he was being considered for a commission and had already trained on landing craft when he received a peremptory order to go to Inverary. There, a board of senior officers grilled him about his father's occupation, his schooling, his performance at sports and why he wanted to be an officer. Despite replying bluntly that he didn't want to be an officer at all, Ordinary Seaman Bird – the son of a Cheshire sawmill manager – apparently displayed the right qualities because the following day he was on his way to *Lochailort*, where lessons on signals, seamanship and naval history were combined with boxing, assault courses, cross-country runs and brutal swims across the River Ailort in the depths of winter. One particularly sadistic physical training instructor had previously been employed at the 'glasshouse', the Naval Detention Quarters in Preston, and made the trainees climb a rope and cross a roof girder nearly 4 metres above the ground in a Nissen Hut:

> He used to shout the naval order 'still' ... then everybody must absolutely freeze, nobody must move until that's been corrected. So, when we got on this girder, a whole class of us, about a dozen of us, he used to shout 'Still!' and wait there till the first man dropped off and then we were allowed to proceed.[11]

Despite all this Bird passed. Proudly, he went to the castle to 'take tea with the officers' before being given a first class travel warrant for his journey home: 'the first thing I did … was order a huge breakfast, Scottish porridge and bacon and eggs, I thought I was in heaven really … once you qualified then you got the perks'.[12]

All around the country, from Inverary to Hayling Island, young men were rushed through Combined Operations training. Junior ranks had rather less choice in the matter. Dennis Small was a Royal Marine who was redeployed in the huge 1943 restructuring and found himself in a grim hutted camp on the moors in Devon: the washrooms had no roof or hot water, and camp standing orders apparently specified that trainees would run at all times, everywhere they went. Periodically they ran to the nearby town of Budleigh Salterton and back, an experience which ended with a painful bare-foot sprint along a pebble beach to 'harden our feet'.[13] In between there were relentless daily kit inspections. A few times a week they ran to the firing range for some rather more lethal training, running across a gateway before a machine-gunner could react and fire at them. After two months of this, the intake went to South Wales for what would today be called 'adventure training', after which they were sent to join landing craft at one of dozens of Combined Operations training centres scattered around the coast. Number One Combined Training Centre at Inverary, established in July 1941 overlooking Loch Fyne in the west of Scotland, was the largest. The naval element of this tri-service establishment, known as HMS *Quebec*, turned the tough young men who emerged from places like *Lochailort* into landing craft crews. Bill Miles went there to join an LCA Flotilla, recalling that 'men were drowned, injured and killed … which was a high price to pay for a trained assault force'.[14]

Royal Marine Bob Phippen learned basic seamanship driving LCAs on the River Dart under the watchful gaze of their instructors, often First World War veterans. As an NCO, Phippen was made a coxswain, and once he had learned how to operate his tiny, flat-bottomed, blunt-bowed craft, he started to take it out of the shel-tered waters of the Dart into open water, a very different experience during which 'for the first couple of trips … we were all quite seasick'.

Beach landings took place at Slapton Sands, a few miles from Dartmouth, where the entire population had been evacuated to create a vast military training area.[15] Like all landing craft, the challenge was to get the bow onto the beach so that the embarked soldiers could cross the ramp to the beach 'without getting their feet wet'. To assist with this, landing craft deployed a kedge anchor from the stern as they went into the beach, which helped them maintain position, and could then be used to haul them off the beach stern-first. Larger landing craft carried out this process mechanically using a capstan and the ship's engines, but on the little LCAs the crew had to just haul in the anchor cable by hand as quickly as possible to avoid the thick rope fouling the propellers.[16]

Signals training was basic semaphore, hand signalling with flags, as most landing craft were not equipped with radios. Royal Marines 2nd Lieutenant Tony Lowndes did his outside a hotel in Southsea: 'You learn to start with the basics of A–B–C–D–E–F–G with one flag and then the two flags together and all the rest of it', he recalled, 'through the whole alphabet. And we would stand about fifty yards apart and send messages to each other doing these signals.' This was followed by similar exercises at night using signal lamps.[17]

In September 1943, Lowndes moved to HMS *Northney*, the Combined Operations landing craft base, training centre and holding camp which occupied most of Hayling Island. The trainees were accommodated in a former holiday camp where 'the food was absolutely appalling! Breakfast for instance was porridge with a mixed assortment of bugs and sort of things floating around it.' Here, the officer trainees received a crash course in seamanship and basic coastal navigation, all that was required in landing craft as 'you were never ... out of sight of land'. After this they moved down the road to *Northney III* where they were taught the different handling characteristics of the various types of 'minor landing craft', using a battered training flotilla of LCAs, LCMs and LCVPs:

> We used to do just landing: putting the ramp down, pulling it up and then getting off, learning at what stage to chuck the kedge anchor out. Because Hayling Island always is a bit exposed you

get all sorts of winds and changes of tides. The tide goes in and out very quickly in the creeks, so you needed a lot of expertise and a lot of practice . . . you watch your wake and if the wake starts to overtake you, you know you're just about to go aground.[18]

Running aground meant twelve hours marooned on the mud flats in a tiny unheated landing craft. There were worse hazards though: in a later training camp, HMS *Sea Serpent* at Burnham-on-Crouch, Lowndes and his crew of trainee officers fell behind during a navigation exercise and found themselves far out in the North Sea in the dark. Weary and frightened they finally struggled home at 0300, to be greeted by 'a right bollocking from the commanding officer who . . . thought that we'd deliberately gone off on our own and decided to abandon the exercise'.[19]

The next step was to learn to operate as a full flotilla, a coherent unit of landing craft, capable of manoeuvring in formation. Lowndes joined the 802nd LCVP Flotilla as Divisional Officer and second-in-command in Brighton in March 1944. It consisted of twelve LCVPs and a hundred or so junior officers and Marines, led by Lowndes and his CO, with a small team of Royal Navy engineers under a sub-lieutenant to maintain the craft.

Across the Atlantic, thousands of young Americans were learning the same techniques. Many passed through the US Navy's vast Amphibious Training Base, or ATB, at Solomons Island, Maryland. Established in 1942 to train crews for Torch, the accelerating demand for landing craft crews meant that by 1944, Solomons Island was processing a staggering 10,000 sailors at any one time. Situated at the end of a peninsula with almost no room to expand, the ATB was grossly overcrowded and short on supplies, decent accommodation and fresh water. It was also almost impossible to get off the peninsula, so leave – 'liberty' in US Navy parlance – was infrequent. 'The men found themselves in the classic navy hell', wrote the son of one US Navy landing craft veteran, 'no liberty, nowhere to go if they got it, and nothing to do once they got there.'[20]

At Solomons Island, raw recruits fresh from basic training went through a three-week classroom course in basic seamanship. They were then grouped into training crews, given an LCT Mk V from the training flotilla and, like their Royal Navy counterparts, learned how to put them on a beach and get them safely off again. Most of the training LCTs were hopelessly worn out from years of being abused by trainees. Officers were not allocated to crews at this point. Instead, they formed their own crews and trained as a group, then they were matched up with their crew and landing craft once they 'graduated'.[21]

Walter Trombold was the Executive Officer of *LST-55* and met his fellow officers at Solomons Island. Just like their British allies, US landing craft crews were mostly reservists from an eclectic range of backgrounds; the Battle of the Seine Bay was largely fought by 'hostilities only' men. The CO, Lieutenant Alfred Mills, had been a bank executive in New York City. Joel Ferris, the Engineering Officer, had been a farmer in Oklahoma – almost as far from the sea as it is possible to get in the continental USA – and the Communications Officer, John Zimmer, was a former musician. Harry Wright was a college graduate, born and raised in Mexico. The enlisted men were a typical mix, too – a few experienced sailors, notably the senior rates and the engineers, and a much larger group of men 'who had never graduated from eighth grade ... totally unskilled youngsters who just hadn't had a chance to apply themselves in school or anywhere else'.[22] Wartime training could be a life-changing experience for young men like this, who learned skills which opened up opportunities when they returned to civilian life.

The Royal Canadian Navy operated a number of landing craft flotillas, trained by the Royal Navy and operating under RN command. Much to their disgust, Canadians in Combined Operations received British rations rather than the somewhat better RCN fare. 'Although they may consider the food only fair', wrote one British staff officer unsympathetically, doubtless after receiving a litany of complaints from Canadian sailors, 'they can only grin and bear it. No extra concessions are made to Canadians in this respect whatsoever.'[23]

Some sailors, out of boredom or a sense of adventure, volunteered for an anonymous formation named 'Party Funshore', according to rumour an ironic abbreviation for 'Foreign and Unknown Shores'.

Norman Wright was part of a Beach Signals Section, ultimately destined for Sword Area:

> One vehicle contained a large transmitter, the second a large receiver and the third was a workshop ... the Navy's sense of humour in christening us 'Party Funshore' was now becoming apparent. We were dressed in Army Khaki (so as not to stand out from the troops going ashore) ... the whole unit was in charge of a Fleet Air Arm Pilot Sub-Lieutenant, apparently they had a surplus of these ... the second in charge was a Chief Petty Officer who had been at the Battle of Jutland and ... the rear was brought up by yours truly, a humble Petty Officer Radio Mechanic, aged twenty.[24]

Signing up for Funshore might also lead to service with the Royal Navy Beach Commandos, or the Landing Craft Obstacle Clearance Units (LCOCUs). The job of the Beach Commandos was to bring order out of chaos, as part of a much larger tri-service organisation known as a Beach Group. RN Commandos evolved from earlier units known as 'Beach Parties', which had first been trialled in Madagascar. Led by officers known as Beachmasters, their job was to mark out the beaches and control movements, ensuring as far as possible that all assault shipping landed in the right place, at the right time and that the embarked troops got off the beach as quickly and efficiently as possible. They went through a unique training programme at HMS *Armadillo*, a training establishment on Loch Long in Scotland. Combined Operations Headquarters defined a Beach Commando in December 1942 as 'sufficient officers and men to handle the craft required to land a brigade, their attached troops, vehicles and stores'.[25] This consisted of one Principal Beachmaster, three Beachmasters, all of them officers, supported by three Petty Officers, six Leading Seamen, eighteen Able Seamen and thirty-nine Ordinary Seamen. The RN Commandos were lettered, to distinguish them from the numbered Army and Royal Marines Commandos: F, J, L, P, Q, R, S and the mostly Canadian W Commando took part in Neptune.

Able Seaman Albert Cattell trained with G Commando, and recalled months spent roaming the Highlands, landing with the Army:

> The Beachmaster ... stopped in the middle of the beach. You fanned out, you checked the beach for mines and any obstructions in the water. If there was enemy fire we were taught, 'down door and away you go' to secure the perimeter of the beach against the enemy ... then you come back and put these road signs up to guide the craft in.[26]

Sometimes the Commandos had to carry out a grim drill known as a 'deep water reconnaissance', forming a line at right angles to the sea with the tallest man on the seaward side and the shortest on the beach, and then wading along checking for obstructions. 'Without doubt this was one of the most unpopular tasks', recalled Sub-Lieutenant Joe Bramble, Assistant Beachmaster with M Commando, 'especially in the cold waters of a Scottish loch in mid-winter'.[27]

The role of the LCOCUs and their US equivalent, the Navy Combat Demolition Units (NCDUs), has been much misunderstood and distorted by myth and legend, although it was unquestionably hazardous. Although some were trained divers, their role was to go in alongside – not before – the initial assault waves, and work as fast as possible to defuse mines and destroy as many beach obstacles as possible before they were covered by the incoming tide. René Le Roy was half-French and boiling with rage about the fate of his homeland when he joined the Royal Navy at just seventeen in 1942. 'I was a very bitter young man', he recalled, 'I had a hatred of Germans, not Nazis, just Germans ... these ... buggers, who would start another war, creating havoc, destroying homes again, refugees.' Simply being a sailor was not enough, and even the rigours of the Combined Operations officers' training course at Lochailort failed to satisfy him: as a freshly minted midshipman, he went to Appledore in Devon to train for the LCOCUs. At Appledore Le Roy went through an intensive course in underwater swimming, after which he collected a group of twenty-six 'recruits' enthusiastically provided by the Naval Base Commander at Portsmouth from his defaulters – men under punishment – and they all went to nearby Fort Cumberland to learn about explosives. After two weeks the group had progressed to blowing up everything from trees to safes, prompting one comedian to comment that 'this is like a bloody refresher course, I've been inside [prison] once for this!'[28]

On the other side of the Atlantic, Orval Wakefield was 'ready for a change' after weeks sawing timber with the US Navy's famous Construction Battalions, or 'Seabees', so he volunteered for the NCDUs. Of forty potential recruits who turned up for an introductory lecture, only Wakefield and one other stayed beyond the recruiter's grim warning that 'the duty would be extremely hazardous and that those who volunteered would be considered expendable'. Intensive explosives training was provided by civilian explosives experts from the mining and quarrying industries, following which the new recruits joined NCDU 132 at Fort Pierce, Florida: an officer, a Chief Petty Officer and four Petty Officers. By April 1944, they were on their way to the United Kingdom. Although the NCDUs proudly called themselves 'frogmen', as they spent much of their time in water, like the LCOCUs their dangerous and unpleasant work did not involve diving. Most of the time it did not even involve swimming but wading. 'The popular notion of frogmen is of rubber wet suits', recalled Wakefield, 'but we weren't so glamorous. We were outfitted with marine-green coveralls, boots, helmets and the type of sacks that newspaper boys wear . . . full of plastic explosives wrapped in good old navy socks.'[29]

As some sailors served ashore, not all those who would serve afloat in the Seine Bay were even sailors. One group of soldiers deserving an honourable mention were the DUKW drivers. DUKWs were amphibious trucks designed by General Motors in the United States, the initials being GM code for 1942 (D); utility/amphibious (U); All-Wheel Drive (K); and two powered rear axles (W). Inevitably they were nicknamed 'Ducks' and they were an absolutely vital tool for the build-up of supplies and reinforcements once the assault landings had successfully taken place (see Chapter 11). Their drivers were soldiers, who had had a short course in seamanship to drive their vehicles in water. Robert Lunn of the Royal Army Service Corps was posted to Towyn in North Wales for a 'Duck Course', joking that 'we're going to become farmers and look after Ducks'. Driving on land was easy enough but driving afloat was a different matter, and basic seamanship was bewildering: semaphore and Morse Code ('a waste of time because we never used it'), tides, wind, use of the compass and rope work, including splicing rope fenders, and most confusing of all, knots: 'the bowline knot was the knot that you used to tie up alongside a ship ... I couldn't get it. I used to stay up at night!'[30] The DUKWs would be invaluable in the Seine Bay.

Dick Berryman was another soldier who had to learn how to work with the sea services. A 26-year-old from Topsham in Devon, he had joined the Territorial Army before the war, serving in the Royal Artillery. 'There was a call for volunteers', he remembered, 'and the Sergeant-Major said, "your name's going forward, Berryman!"' Doubtless wondering what he had done wrong he found himself, like Lewis Goodwin, at HMS *Dundonald*, doing 'wet landings' and learning how to be a Naval Gunfire Observer, before being permanently assigned to the Combined Operations Bombardment Units.[31] Each Bombardment Unit consisted of a Forward Observer Bombardment, usually a Royal Artillery captain, supported by an Observation Post Assistant, or 'OP Ack', like Berryman, and three naval telegraphists to signal back to the bombarding ships. Other Royal Artillery officers served as Bombardment Liaison Officers aboard warships.[32] Each team operated with a specific ship, allowing the warships to perform the role of artillery. For the soldiers, it meant learning a very different way of doing things:

> There was no question of line and angle of sight and things like that, because your guns were floating about a mile out to sea ... You spotted by the clockwork method. You imagine the target was at the centre of the clock and when you saw the shot fall, then you recorded the shot. You decided from that position that it would either have to go to the east, in which case you'd say '3 o'clock so many hundred'. Or north, you'd say '12 o'clock so many hundred'.[33]

Berryman went to Scapa Flow, where warships honed their bombardment skills by relentlessly shelling the northern tip of the beautiful little island of Papa Westray. Chief Engine Room Artificer Ron Jesse, on board the cruiser HMS *Belfast*, remembered the ship's gunners practising 'like crazy' during this period at Scapa, not just bombardment with the big guns but rehearsing procedures for other threats they might face in the Seine Bay – not that they had any idea of their ultimate destination. 'We expected to be attacked by submarines and ... light craft like torpedo boats', he recalled, 'and so our light guns, our 4-inch guns were given exhaustive practice in shooting at moving targets.'[34]

Other observers were airborne. Former policeman and naval reservist Mike Crosley was a veteran Fleet Air Arm pilot, a Lieutenant-Commander (albeit 'Temporary Acting') who had already spent several years flying Sea Hurricanes in the Mediterranean, narrowly escaping drowning when the aircraft carrier HMS *Eagle* was torpedoed and sunk in August 1942. Crosley attended a bombardment spotting course in Ayrshire in May 1944, now flying Seafires, the Royal Navy's version of the famous Spitfire. Circling overhead, they provided corrections to warships anchored in the Clyde as they methodically pounded the unfortunate isle of Arran. In between, a group of Army officers known as 'C-Balls', an informal acronym for Carrier Borne Air Liaison Section, used models to teach the pilots about the mysteries of land fighting:

> They used hessian, canvas and models of farms, transport, cows, German soldiers, etc, camouflaged as we might expect them to appear from the air ... We sat around the target ... staring down at it as if from our aircraft in real life. Soldiers somewhere underneath then blew puffs of smoke through eye droppers through the hessian to simulate shell bursts. We then had to make corrections to the fall of shot to bring them onto the target.[35]

Like the shore-based Bombardment Units, Crosley and the air spotters generally used the clock code system of correcting fire. Air spotters trained to fly in pairs, with one pilot concentrating on observation while another, known as the 'weaver', flew 2,000ft above and watched for enemy aircraft. Once trained, Crosley and the other pilots went south to await the invasion. They joined 3 Naval Air Fighter Wing: four air observation squadrons totalling forty-eight Seafire LIII aircraft flying out of HMS *Daedalus*, the Fleet Air Arm Base at Lee-on-Solent and commanded by Commander Nigel 'Buster' Hallett. Working alongside them as part of a combined Air Spotting Pool were three RAF squadrons and the only US Navy pilots ever to fly Spitfires. Lieutenant Robert Calland's Cruiser Scouting Squadron 7, or VCS-7, was formed from the embarked aviators in the Western Naval Task Force's battleships and cruisers, whose Curtiss Seagull and Vought Kingfisher floatplanes were too vulnerable to risk running into German high-performance land-based fighters. The US Navy pilots were all experienced bombardment spotters but converting from the biplane Seagulls to the advanced Spitfire Vs must have been a steep learning curve indeed.

With role-specific and formation training complete, the new naval units were allocated to larger formations, and finally to the huge Assault Forces. Exercises and rehearsals grew in scale and complexity, from Assault Force exercises to brigade-level practice landings with the military formations they would deliver to Normandy, and finally to huge comprehensive invasion rehearsals. Some of the assault forces had worked together for a long time, like Force J, which would land the Canadian 3rd Division in Juno Area. Force J evolved from the naval forces which had gone to Dieppe in 1942, and the J designation may well have dated back to this earlier operation, which was code-named Jubilee; certainly, it predated the codename Juno. Force J had also taken part in Husky.

Colin Madden joined this veteran formation in 1943, arriving at HMS *Mastodon* on the Beaulieu River, better known as Exbury House, prewar home of Lionel de Rothschild, on 16 August. Madden was to be Navigating Officer and Staff Officer (Operations) to the Commanding Officer of what would become Assault Group J1, led by Captain Tony Pugsley, a decorated veteran who had commanded destroyers since 1939. Two days later they moved to Lepe House – 'there was no light, there was no hot water, there was no staff, there was nothing' – and two days after that they were deep into their first exercise. 'The jobs we had to do were legion', Madden recalled:

> We had to work during this period at training, at teaching, exercising, planning, having meetings, visiting, lecturing, explaining, writing orders ... we had to get to know the Commanding Officers, the Squadron Officers and as many of the ship's companies of these craft as we possibly could. We had to check the Hards where the craft had to go to load up, which craft should go where and ... what the gradients were ... all over the Solent and Spithead ... Not only did we have to see to the approaches from the sea but we had to also make certain that ... they were also easy to get at from the shore.

With no prior experience, Madden was sent to measure the beach gradient at Bracklesham Beach near Chichester, to assess its suitability for training; 'I did this not particularly well ... all I remember about it was I got extremely wet!'[36]

The pace was relentless. Within a few days of arriving, Madden took part in Exercise Starkey, when Force J's big Landing Ships Infantry (LSIs) joined the feint towards the Pas-de-Calais which was both training exercise and deception operation. Starkey was followed by the improbably named Baby Porpoise, a landing on the beach at Bracklesham which Madden had attempted to survey, in vile conditions which drowned out 5 per cent of the LCTs taking part. Two weeks later Madden personally led a thirty-six-hour-long navigation exercise, steaming LCTs in line, learning how to follow the craft ahead without using lights, and occasionally making simple formation changes. Even steaming in line was a challenge for these underpowered, clumsy craft, particularly when the tide was running and each craft had to steam on an identical 'line of bearing', pointing their bows into the tide at exactly the same angle to offset its effects and keep on the course they intended to follow.[37]

Ludicrously named exercise followed ludicrously named exercise in unremitting succession. After Baby Porpoise came Pirate, exercising with the unpredictable and lethal LCT(R), and Sunbeam, which focused on the complexities of bringing 2,000 troops aboard the LSIs, taking them to sea, transferring them into the tiny assault craft which swung from their davits and then putting them ashore. At the end of 1943, Force J worked with their follow-up forces to practise putting ashore the entire division, an exercise codenamed Push, during which Madden nearly sank aboard an armed (and thus unstable) Landing Craft Support. January 1944 saw a navigation exercise with the support landing craft, the LCGs and LCFs, and Exercise Crab, which provided experience of boarding troops on to the bigger LCTs and LSTs over the concrete embarkation hards.

Force J staged their final solo training exercise, codenamed Sealegs, on 6 February 1944, after which they moved on to much larger, multi-force invasion rehearsals.[38] Soon afterwards, Madden was introduced to HMS *Lawford*, the converted frigate which would be J1's head-quarters ship. 'This is the time when we realised that other things were going on apart from our own little group of J1', he remembered. 'J2 were doing the same as we were, and fitting into our exercises and indeed doing some of the exercises with us. To the east of us Force Sword was forming and to the west of us Force Gold, and they were becoming what was to be known as the Eastern Task Force.'[39]

March saw a full-on assault training exercise, Prank, which timed each stage of the invasion down to the last minute. It was, of course, much easier to stay impeccably on time when the enemy was not interfering, so planners tried to introduce what the strategist Clausewitz called 'friction' whenever they could. In Gold Braid on 27 March, the J1 command team were thrown a curve ball during what should have been a routine exercise focussed on the build-up of reserves after the initial assault, when *Lawford* was ordered back to harbour after six hours and Pugsley was instructed to take on the key role of Captain (Patrols), directing the defensive line of coastal forces craft and armed landing craft which would be thrown around the invasion area to protect the vulnerable transports (see Chapter 12).[40]

Each force went through roughly the same programme of exercises, with some variations depending on when they were formed. Force S had less time to prepare than Force J. Its story, according to a comprehensive report written after Neptune, began in October

1943 'when Force S headquarters was set up at Cameron Barracks, Inverness. Slowly the Force was built up in the Moray Firth area, but it was an uphill struggle from the start, bases, accommodation, repair facilities, water transport and general amenities being totally inadequate.' In November 1943, 3rd (British) Infantry Division moved in nearby and 'for the next four months we shared with our opposite numbers of the 3rd Division the trials and tribulations consequent on trying to make bricks without straw'.[41]

In April, Force Headquarters moved to Portsmouth for final preparations, and took part in a huge exercise focussed on the movement of the all-important build-up forces after the initial assault. It was codenamed Cropper VII and it ran between 22 and 27 April.[42] Peter Bird, who took part as a staff officer with a Landing Barge flotilla, described how, lacking radio, the crews of the improvised barges carried out simple manoeuvres at sea like the men of Nelson's navy a hundred years before, putting up different coloured 'burgees' (swallow-tailed flags) to indicate different formations.[43]

Force G, landing the 50th (Northumberland) Division, had the least time of all the Anglo-Canadian forces to prepare, as like Force U it only came into existence after Eisenhower and Montgomery expanded the landings. Its commander, Commodore Cyril Douglas-Pennant, was appointed on 21 February 1944, and the Force itself came into being in the Portland–Poole area on 1 March, with Douglas-Pennant hoisting his broad pendant ashore in HMS *Purbeck*, formerly the Royal Hotel in Weymouth, Dorset. Force G's learning curve was a steep one: 'training was concentrated and carried out at high pressure as it was realised there was a lot to be achieved in a short time'. Four brigade-size exercises, Smash 1–4, were delivered in swift succession before the Force relocated to Southampton on 26 April to make way for the Americans and progress to the larger invasion rehearsals. Even this very limited training programme meant that Douglas-Pennant's staff could not begin thinking about the invasion itself until May.[44]

The US Forces O and, later, U were based in south-west England and carried out their training on the Devon and Dorset coast, much of it in Lyme Bay at the Amphibious Training Centre at Slapton Sands. The US training programme was originally developed and run by Rear-Admiral John Hall, until Hall moved to command Force O, and was delivered by the staff of 11th Amphibious Force, the umbrella organisation for all US amphibious forces in Europe. Basic training was all carried out in the USA, so US training focused entirely on invasion rehearsals, meshing US and British amphibious techniques to create a unified but not wholly satisfactory combined doctrine.[45] The first series for Force O, codenamed Duck 1–3, ran between January and March 1944. In Fox, the last big exercise Force O carried out in isolation, nearly a hundred major assault craft put ashore elements of two Regimental Combat Teams, equivalent to British brigade groups, on Slapton Sands; it was observed by Ramsay, who pronounced himself 'much impressed'.[46]

The final full-scale invasion rehearsal for Forces S, G, J and O was Fabius, a huge combination of six entirely separate exercises which stretched from Weymouth to Littlehampton. It began on 3 May, delayed slightly by weather, and ran until the following day. Ramsay pronounced himself 'favourably impressed', but the exercise was not without incident. The destroyer HMS *Offa* was shot up by a German aircraft with the loss of three killed and four wounded, and shortly afterwards British Beaufighter fighter-bombers attacked a pair of MTBs, sinking *MTB-708* and wounding eleven officers and men.[47] Veteran Combined Operations officer Jimmy Green commanded some of the British-manned LCAs which would carry US troops into Omaha area on 6 June, and stormed Slapton Sands during Fabius; disconcertingly, his tiny craft were straddled by 14-inch (355mm) shells from the battleship *Texas*, which doubtless added to the realism, as well as giving rise to rumours that Green's entire flotilla had been sunk.[48] Tony Lowndes and his Royal Marine LCVP crews joined Fabius at Hayling Island, and were less than impressed, remembering that 'we were getting in each other's way . . . and there was no proper control of the movement going in and out'.[49] 'A bit chaotic', was Lowndes' verdict, but in the end it didn't matter. There was simply no more time to practice. Although a few small exercises ran well into May, there would be no more big rehearsals. From now until 6 June, the priority would be repairing the hundreds of craft which had been battered into unserviceability during training.

The steepest learning curve fell to the late addition, Force U. Between February and March 1944, Force U and the US Army's 4th Infantry Division went through a crash course of assault landing exercises named after wildlife: Teal, Mallard, Otter 1 and 2, Mink 1 and 2, and Gull, followed by a series of Muskrats and Beaver. Finally, because Utah Area was located on the eastern side of the Cotentin Peninsula, geographically separate from the rest of the assault areas, Force U was given its own separate final invasion rehearsal.[50] Continuing the animal theme, the planners christened it Tiger.

Tiger took place between 26 and 28 April 1944, and was the most significant setback of the training cycle. It began well enough. The US assault troops boarded their transports and went out into Lyme Bay on the night of 26/27 April, behind minesweepers from the 14th and 16th Flotillas. Gradually, they turned back, replicating their journey across the Channel, until they arrived at Slapton Sands, which had a shingle beach and a shallow lagoon behind, just like Utah (see Map 2). The assault wave landed on the morning of

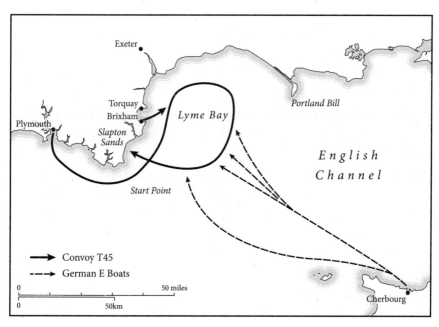

Map 2. Exercise Tiger, 22–30 April 1944.

27 April, following a bombardment by destroyers and cruisers. The next night, a follow-up wave of eight US LSTs left Brixham and Plymouth to form Convoy T4 and make the same journey with the objective of arriving on the morning of D+1. T4 was escorted by the Royal Navy corvette HMS *Azalea*. A second escort, the elderly destroyer HMS *Scimitar*, had been holed in a collision and returned to harbour; crucially, *Scimitar*'s replacement, the equally venerable HMS *Saladin*, never caught up with the convoy.[51]

Command and control were complicated. The convoy and escort were under the overall control of Rear-Admiral Don Moon as Commander, Force U, and under the direct command of Commander Bernard Skahill, USN, as senior officer in *LST-515*, as directed by the standing Plymouth Command War Orders: 'The control of the task force and close escort will be carried out by the senior officer present whether British or American.'[52] Out to sea, four British destroyers and five MTBs divided into four forces formed what turned out to be a rather flimsy screen across the mouth of Lyme Bay, to prevent any incursion by German E-boats. The screen was under the command of Admiral Sir Ralph Leatham, the Royal Navy's Commander-in-Chief at Plymouth. In addition, three MGBs had been deployed as an additional patrol line. Bewilderingly, these were sent out on an instruction from the C-in-C, Portsmouth, but were under the immediate command of the Flag Officer in Charge at Portland, from where they sailed.[53]

18-year-old Londoner John Capon was serving aboard one of the screening destroyers, HMS *Obedient*. Coming on watch just after midnight he saw 'two orange balls of flame':

> I said to Wiggy Bennett 'here Wig, some poor bastard's copped it over there' and then all of a sudden it came back, you know sound takes a bit to travel, it came back 'boom boom' . . . then we saw tracer. We thought it was an exercise.[54]

Unfortunately, it was not part of the exercise. Nine E-boats from Korvettenkapitän Bernd Klug's *5.Schnellbootflottille* and Korvettenkapitän Gotz Freiherr von Mirbach's *9.Schnellbootflottille*, with both senior officers embarked, had swept across from Cherbourg on a routine patrol. The weather was fine, the sea was calm and the visibility was good, but despite this the Germans penetrated the flimsy screen, which they did not even notice, 'with comparative ease'.[55] Communications problems and the thin escort meant that by 0030 they were operating with impunity around the vulnerable convoy, one E-boat commander reporting 'a rather long line [of targets]'.[56]

The British picked up high-speed radar contacts and one destroyer, HMS *Onslow*, briefly sighted an E-boat, only to lose it minutes later. Convoy T4 was ordered to close the shore, standing instructions in the event of an attack, but it was too late: soon afterwards, the chaos of a night action began, with random flares popping up all over Lyme Bay.[57] At 0130, gunfire erupted around the convoy as the German skippers manoeuvred into firing positions and was followed around half an hour later by a succession of torpedo explosions.

LST-507 was hit at 0215 and sank in flames, as the unfortunate corvette *Azalea* started to zig-zag around the now-scattering convoy, seeking but failing to find the enemy.[58] Sergeant Stanley Stout of the 1st Engineer Special Brigade was asleep in a DUKW in the LST's vehicle deck when the torpedo hit. As he ran up the ladder to the deck 'all hell broke loose ... those out in the open were in total panic and many were falling to the deck hit by what seemed to be incoming fire. Just as I went on deck a tremendous explosion shook the ship. It felt like an earthquake', he recalled later, 'with the deck literally jumping up and down.' As Stout watched in horror, stored petrol and ammunition exploded, the embarked vehicles blew up like bombs as their petrol tanks 'cooked off' in the heat, and the ship burst into flames. With many officers dead, there was nobody to organise life-boat drill and the equipment was in any case badly damaged, but Stout eventually got away in a badly overloaded boat, after grabbing a seriously burned comrade's rifle and shooting through the cables.[59] *LST-531* and *LST-289* were torpedoed almost simultaneously about six minutes later: *289*'s stern was blown off but the ship somehow stayed afloat and was escorted into Dartmouth by *Azalea*.

The remaining LST skippers tried to extricate their slow, vulnerable commands. Lieutenant (jg) Stanley Koch, commanding *LST-496*, 'made a ninety degree turn to port, went ahead flank [US Navy jargon for full speed], and gave the order to open fire with aft battery on radar target ... commenced zigzagging endeavouring to present our stern to radar target'.[60] At 0230 Koch steamed for Portland, straining his engines so hard the airline parted on his port motor. They dropped anchor at 0415, three other LSTs following a few minutes later. The E-boats left the scene at 0330 and returned home unscathed.

In the meantime, hundreds of soldiers and sailors were adrift in the bitterly cold waters of Lyme Bay. Arthur Victor was a hospital apprentice on *507* who ended up in a group of seventy-five shocked and traumatised survivors clinging to the side of a raft. One by one 'those without life preservers just let go, struggled a bit, then disappeared', he remembered; 'they died and drifted away, or died and went under, or just died where they were. The man holding on to me from behind died in his Mae West [lifejacket]. I had to stare into the lifeless eyes of someone so close yet unknown to me.'[61] By dawn there were only twenty men left of Victor's group.

Lieutenant-Commander Philip King, CO of *Saladin*, noted grimly in his subsequent report that many soldiers had their lifejackets incorrectly fastened around their waists instead of under their armpits, so when they jumped into the water their heavy packs turned them upside down and they immediately drowned.[62] Rescue did not come until the following day. When the Royal Navy motor launch *ML-303* was ordered to sea, the lower deck rumour was of an attack by the infamous (and fictitious) 'W-boats'. The scene which greeted them was horrific. 'On arrival we found hundreds of dead US soldiers floating and bobbing around', Signalman William Smith vividly described years later:

Their body movements were being accentuated by a heavy swell. They were fully clad with steel helmets firmly fastened. A large proportion had badly burned faces and hands and from a distance we initially mistook them for coloured [*sic*] troops. Having passed through burning oil-covered sea it would seem a fair number had suffocated, and in their death throes had drawn their legs up to their Mae West life jackets, causing them to hunch up with rigor mortis. We pulled them in with boat hooks and set them on the boat sides, along the rails, with their faces facing outboard; we loaded about fifty or so per boat and returned to Portland. The action of placing the bodies facing outwards was to avoid the crew having to look at the damaged and grotesque faces.[63]

As far as possible, everybody had to be accounted for, as any suggestion that the Germans might have recovered prisoners would have been disastrous for security. There was particular concern about a number of BIGOTed officers from the 1st Engineer Special Brigade, although all were eventually found.

Back in Portland, the dead GIs were loaded into ambulances and taken away, many of whom were eventually buried in the military cemetery at Brookwood, Surrey. *ML-303* did two trips out into Lyme Bay; at the end of a long and exhausting day the crew were warned not to speak or write about what they had seen. Aboard HMS *Onslow*, Telegraphist Derek Wellman had been in his tiny Wireless Office, vaguely aware of some low-speed manoeuvring and odd bumping noises along the ship's side but very little else. At 0400 he came off watch and headed to the washroom. Surprised and irritated to find the door tied shut, he pulled the offending rope free and flung open the door to find 'maybe thirty American soldiers. A good many of them had been suffocated with oil ...', Wellman grimly remembered; 'one or two were kind of thrashing about like recently caught whiting, so it was a fairly horrific sight to see. I quickly closed the door and tried to forget what I'd seen.'[64]

Later, Captain James McCoy, *Onslow*'s CO and Captain (D) of the 17th Flotilla, 'cleared lower deck' and addressed everyone who wasn't actually on watch, warning the sailors never to speak of what they had seen. McCoy admitted in a subsequent report that his destroyers' performance had not been good enough, highlighting in particular their poor gunnery, which he attributed to 'no action of any kind since December 1942 and insufficient practise in E-boat warfare while with the Home Fleet in northern waters, with all too little time between operations for practices'.[65] The destroyers did not enjoy the luxury of the months of operation-specific training enjoyed by the assault forces: they were simply too busy. E-boats were not a threat in the Arctic or the North Atlantic.

There is no evidence to support decades of rumours that US servicemen were buried in anonymous mass graves in the Devon countryside, or that there was any kind of 'cover-up', although the news was certainly kept quiet until after D-Day, and the casualties were simply listed among the far longer lists which appeared after the invasion; official histories reference the event, but do not go into excessive detail.[66] A total of 749 US servicemen died and a further 200 were injured, far more than ultimately died on any of the Utah Area beaches on 6 June.

Questions were asked, inevitably, but not for long: the invasion was just weeks away, and everyone was busy. Appallingly, much of the official blame apparently fell on Skahill.[67] The reality was that the Allied navies were desperately overworked and overstretched; mistakes were inevitable but, more importantly, there were always going to be occasions when the enemy simply did their job better. Leatham concluded a long explanatory note to Kirk, copied to Ramsay, by offering his 'profound regret', but went on to offer the following in mitigation:

> Concurrently with the execution of Exercise TIGER, many urgent movements, planning and preparations were in progress for Exercise FABIUS following closely on its heels. A night action with enemy destroyers was fought on 25/26 [see Chapter 2] and plans were being made for another offensive operation on 28th April, thus ... the capacity of the staff was severely stretched.[68]

In addition, Leatham mentioned the high volume of signals traffic caused by both these issues which led to delays in signals being passed on, and the fact that the exercise orders were incomplete and distributed late. In the end, everyone was just far too busy, and far too tired.[69] Afterwards, efforts were made to improve communications between British and US naval vessels and the handling of convoys and escorts, soldiers received better training in the use of their life-jackets and additional small craft were allocated to rescue duties. It was largely the Tiger disaster which prompted the Americans to release additional Coast Guard cutters. Ultimately, the Admiralty concluded that there was no merit in censuring any officer, as appropriate steps had been taken to improve performance.[70]

Kirk was apoplectic, demanding stridently in a BIGOT-protected signal on 4 May that the E-boat base in Cherbourg be bombarded 'by the heaviest naval guns and by the heaviest aerial bombs' to neutralise the threat before the invasion, clearly a nonsensical suggestion when so much effort was being spent trying to conceal the location. Ramsay sent a diplomatic response on the 13th telling Kirk that his proposals had been 'carefully considered' but going on to outline over two carefully constructed pages all the reasons why such a bombardment was not appropriate.[71] Privately, Ramsay dismissed the call as 'hysterical' and was absolutely furious when Kirk went behind his back to raise the issue with Eisenhower, prompting one of the biggest fall-outs the two officers had. In the event, no bombardment took place.[72]

Ultimately the key lesson from Tiger was that it showed just how overstretched Allied naval forces were in early 1944, and what a potent threat the Kriegsmarine remained despite its diminished strength. Tiger grimly demonstrated that no plan, in the words of the old military adage, ever survives contact with the enemy, and that German air and sea forces, however diminished, were still a 'clear and present danger' in the Seine Bay.

6
Final Days: The Dangers of the Sea and the Violence of the Enemy
24 May–6 June 1944

OK. We'll go.

General Dwight D. Eisenhower

'Preserve us from the dangers of the sea, and from the violence of the enemy', run the words of the Naval Prayer, and both would concern Ramsay as the clock ticked down to the assault. Tiger had provided a graphic illustration of the still-potent German threat at sea. Technically, Ramsay's opposite number was 51-year-old Admiral Theodor Krancke, Commander-in-Chief of the Kriegsmarine's Paris-based *Marinegruppenkommando West*, who had reported directly to Großadmiral Karl Dönitz, C-in-C of the Kriegsmarine, since January 1943. In reality, the German command situation was considerably less coherent. Krancke did not enjoy Ramsay's ability to draw on whatever naval assets he needed and, just as significantly, he had no powerful 'Supreme Commander' figure to report to, no Eisenhower.

Instead, there were three senior soldiers, each with different responsibilities: Rommel, as Inspector-General of the invasion defences and Commander of *Heeresgruppe B* (Army Group), Generalfeldmarschall Gerd von Rundstedt, as *Oberbefehlshaber West* (Commander-in-Chief, West), and General Leo Geyr von Schweppenburg, who had control of most of the armoured divisions as commander of *Panzergruppe West*. These three officers fundamentally disagreed with each other on a number of key points falling outside the scope of this narrative, most notably where to deploy the all-important armoured divisions to best prevent a successful landing. In the event, all three reported to Hitler, through *Oberkommando der Wehrmacht* (OKW), the Supreme Command of the German Armed Forces, and it would be the Führer who had the final say. As a final complication, what remained of the Luftwaffe in the West had its own command structure, and ultimately only its Commander-in-Chief, the eccentric and by 1944 thoroughly inept Reichsmarschall Hermann Göring, would determine how it was used. These complexities trickled down to the operational level and conspired to make Krancke's job extremely challenging.

Krancke was profiled for the benefit of Royal Navy officers in WIR 216.[1] A former CO of the pocket battleship *Admiral Scheer*, he was appointed in April 1943. His resources were extremely limited and his plan in the event of invasion was correspondingly simple: on receiving the code word '*Grosslandung*' (large landing), all available surface ships and U-boats were to make for the threatened area at high speed, with all units to be in theatre within the first few hours of the invasion. 'Allied superiority would be terrific and ... German naval participation would be a fight to the end, in other words, self-sacrifice.' Beyond this, Krancke's only other option was to try to increase defensive mining out at sea, which he did as much as he could.[2]

Krancke's anti-invasion plan was tested over a series of exercises, all of which were detected and meticulously analysed in Britain by the Naval Intelligence Department's Operational Intelligence Centre. The findings were then distributed in a series of Most Secret reports for Allied naval officers. Krancke's plan was tested for real during an invasion scare on 29 January 1944, when an aircraft reported a formation of 200–300 landing craft at sea 120 miles south-west of the Biscay port of Lorient. The 'landing craft' were actually fishing boats, but the German response provided an Allied intelligence bonanza:

The enemy reaction was vigorous and prompt and characteristic of a pre-determined plan. The priority of the operation was plainly absolute, and the concentration on the single object complete. The emphasis on disregard of danger from aircraft and mines establishes the acceptance of the view that U-boats are expendable.[3]

E-boats and U-boats were probably the most significant threat facing the Seine Bay armada. On the eve of the invasion there were five E-boat flotillas in the west: Klug's *5.SFltl* and von Mirbach's *9.SFltl* at Cherbourg were the closest threat, but given the speed and range of these craft, *4.SFltl* (Boulogne), *2.SFltl* (Ostend) and *8.SFltl* (IJmuiden) could be in the Seine Bay rapidly if required. In theory each flotilla contained twelve boats, but in practice by 1944 supply problems, action losses and breakdowns meant they were rarely able to deploy so many.[4] Dönitz wrote after the war that there were thirty boats in theatre.[5]

As far as U-boats were concerned, by June 1944 the standard Atlantic submarine, the Type VIIc, had become hopelessly outclassed by Allied anti-submarine forces. The North Atlantic had become a graveyard for U-boats, following the key decision made at Casablanca in January 1943 to provide the modern warships and long-range aircraft required to win the Battle of the Atlantic. Dönitz had withdrawn his submarines in August 1943 after staggering losses – 109 U-boats were lost in all waters between April and July 1943.[6] They were, however, regrouping and German scientists and engineers were frantically trying to provide the older boats with the kind of technology they desperately needed to give them back their edge, while new, more capable submarines came into service. Among other innovations, including extra anti-aircraft guns, homing torpedoes, sonar decoys and radar detection devices, many had by June 1944 been fitted with a device known as a *schnorkel*, an exhaust system which allowed the submarines to use their diesel engines while submerged. This freed them from the requirement to surface to recharge their electric motors, although it was crudely built and the crews loathed it; one U-boat commander described the consequences when the air intake was obstructed, causing a vacuum in the boat: 'the men gasped for air, their eyes bulging ... breathing became ever more difficult; suffocation seemed imminent', he wrote, and the moment when the blockage was cleared provided no relief, 'air was sucked into the boat with a long sigh. The sudden change in pressure burst many an ear drum. Some of the men covered their faces in pain and sagged to the deck plates.'[7]

In the event of an invasion, U-boat crews would be expected to sacrifice themselves on a scale exceeding their near-suicidal efforts in the North Atlantic. The Kriegsmarine has sometimes naively been described as somehow sitting apart from Nazi excesses during the Second World War, but this was demonstrably not the case: there was a reason why Hitler made Dönitz his successor in May 1945. In a special order issued on 27 March 1944, he exhorted that, in the event of an invasion, 'I demand of every commander that he has only one objective in his heart and before his eyes, irrespective of precautions which would normally apply: Attack! At them! Sink them!' In a subsequent order issued on 10 April to all Kriegsmarine units, he chillingly threatened to 'destroy the soldier who does not fight to the very end, and who does not fulfil his duty to the last, with insults and disgrace'.[8] In the months preceding Neptune, a 'rapid response' U-boat force codenamed *Gruppe Landwirt* ('farmer') was gradually assembled in various French bases, its development watched closely by the Allies thanks to Ultra intelligence. On the eve of the invasion, there were fifty-three Type VIIc boats in *Landwirt*, twenty-five equipped with schnorkels. Most were based in the ports scattered along the shore of the Bay of Biscay, notably Brest. More submarines were based in Norway but perfectly capable of reaching the Seine Bay, albeit after a longer and more hazardous passage. Fixing these boats in place was a key objective of the Fortitude North deception.[9]

As far as the surface fleet was concerned, the Kriegsmarine had always operated at a huge disadvantage compared to the Western Allies. On the outbreak of war in 1939, its dismayed Commander-in-Chief, Admiral Erich Raeder, had noted privately that 'our surface fleet was so inferior in strength and numbers . . . that it could do little more than show that it knew how to die valiantly'.[10] In June 1944 there were just fifteen major surface units in the west: eight destroyers and fleet torpedo boats, and five smaller torpedo boats, roughly equivalent to the US-built destroyer escorts. The largest and most capable destroyers were based at Brest, with six torpedo boats in Hoffmann's *Torpedobootsflottille* at Le Havre.

In addition, there were numerous flotillas of minesweepers and patrol boats scattered around the coast, grouped into three *Sicherungsdivisionen* (Security Divisions) under the command of the *Befelshaber der Sicherung West* (Commander-in-Chief, Security, West), Konteradmiral Erich-Alfred Bruenning.[11] Often dismissed out of hand, even by German commentators, as 'of little fighting value', some of these ships were fairly effective.[12] German fleet minesweepers in particular were large, capable warships used for a wide range of tasks; the British nicknamed them 'Channel Destroyers', and they represented a significant threat, although they were only armed with guns, not torpedoes. As well as the minesweepers, there were a variety of armed landing craft (*Artillerieträger* and *Artilleriefährprahme*), *Raumbooten* (R-boats), which were motor minesweepers roughly equivalent to the British MLs, and a range of converted trawlers and other small craft. Helmut Lucke served as a signaller in a typical inshore patrol boat; these were grouped into *Hafenschutzflottillen* (Harbour Defence Flotillas):

> It wasn't the big trawlers that we were on, it was the little wooden ones ... they had a machine gun or two, 2cm and maybe 1.5cm, that's all, they were only very small ... There might have been four or five of us on there including the Captain ... well, 'Captain', he was only like a *Bootsman*, same as a Corporal ... quite a few of them, it was their own boats. They were fishermen in Germany and they [were] called [up] including with their boat.[13]

As well as conventional warships, the Kriegsmarine also planned to deploy an eccentric assortment of miniature submarines, explosive motor boats and human torpedoes, collectively described as *Kleinkampfverbände* (*K-Verbände*), or 'small battle units'. Only one stage removed from suicide weapons thanks to their hasty design and testing, poor quality construction, and the lack of training of their mostly teenaged crews, *K-verbände* had already been used in the Mediterranean, but did not become operational in the Seine Bay until after the invasion. Dönitz placed a great deal of faith in them, and there was a concerted effort to build up stocks in France in early 1944: at Hitler's regular naval conference on 18 January 1944, for example, the Führer approved the construction of fifty midget submarines and an unspecified number of one man torpedoes 'as a defence weapon in case of enemy landings'.[14]

Allied estimates of the threats were reasonably accurate, although the numbers were overestimated. One US briefing paper prepared in April 1944 warned of five destroyers, up to eleven torpedo boats, sixty E-boats and the same number of R-boats, and 130 submarines.[15] The paper also highlighted the risk of reinforcements from the Baltic and Norway, including additional submarines and light surface craft, six cruisers, the pocket battleships *Admiral Scheer* and *Lützow*, and even the Kriegsmarine's pair of ancient and barely seaworthy pre-dreadnoughts, *Schlesien* and *Schleswig-Holstein*.[16] For all the irritation displayed by some American commentators about British fears of another Jutland, 'the possibility of heavy units being able to evade the covering force and to reach the Channel' was clearly recognised as a legitimate threat by US planners.[17]

The last lines of defence against the Allied fleet were mines, coastal batteries and beach obstacles, the construction of which Rommel threw himself into with his customary energy when he arrived in the West in November 1943. Although the Pas-de-Calais and the main naval bases were strongly fortified, Normandy and the Seine Bay were, according to Hans Speidel, his Chief of Staff, 'practically unfortified'. There were only thirty-seven heavy coastal defence guns grouped into eleven batteries along 600 miles of coast between Dieppe and Saint-Nazaire; in comparison, there were thirty-eight guns in the Channel Islands, which Hitler had singled out as an area of particular concern.[18] According to Hitler's tactically illiterate Directive 40, heavy batteries were operated by the Kriegsmarine, which was responsible for 'fighting the enemy on the water', whereas smaller-calibre batteries were operated by the Army, which was responsible for the land campaign. 'At first glance this gave the impression of a clear solution', commented Rommel's naval adviser, Vizeadmiral Friedrich Ruge, 'but ... who was to determine the moment of transition? What happened if the enemy landed at several points while his ships were still approaching the coast at other points? Who decided if it was more important for a coastal battery to fire on those companies already ashore or at landing craft that could considerably reinforce these companies?'[19]

The batteries were armed with a miscellany of odd weapons, many of them captured, and were often sited in open emplacements, partly because the Army were concerned about restricting their fields of fire and partly because of a shortage of concrete. This left both guns and crews unprotected from bombardment. Responsibility for constructing most of the fixed defences had rested with the Nazi civilian labour force, the *Organization Todt*, which according to Speidel 'had … no experience of co-operation with the armed forces'.[20]

There was little time for Rommel to build more batteries, or find the guns with which to equip them, but he had more success with mines and obstacles. Just under 2 million land mines had been laid in France prior to the end of 1943; Rommel had an additional 4 million laid in 1944, and had he been given more time, he had a target of 50 million in mind, although many were laid in the wrong place.[21]

The Germans also strengthened the Channel sea mine barriers. The standard sea mine used by all nations during the Second World War was the horned contact mine beloved of cartoonists, tethered to an anchor on the sea bed to keep it at a set position and depth, and detonated when a lead horn struck the hull of a ship and bent, breaking a glass vial inside which released sulphuric acid, completed an electrical circuit and detonated the explosive. In addition, closer inshore the Germans added 'ground' or 'influence' mines which had no tether. Instead, they sat on the sea bed and detonated in response to either the change in the earth's magnetic field caused by a passing ship (magnetic mines) or the sound waves of a ship's engines passing through the water (acoustic mines), the resultant shock wave being sufficiently powerful to break a ship's back.[22]

The oldest German minefields in the Channel had been laid as early as 1942, but in the challenging environment of the Channel, sea mines only had a life expectancy of one to two years and in addition *Marinegruppenkommando West* did not want to obstruct its own coastal shipping lanes, so many had been allowed to become inoperative.[23] Sixteen new mixed fields of ground mines and contact mines interspersed with explosive sweep cutters were laid between Boulogne and Cherbourg over the winter of 1943/4. This mine barrier ran from about latitude 50° North to between 7 and 10 miles from the French coast.[24] It included the Seine Bay as 'the enemy had always bypassed [it], an observation that strengthened our suspicion that they would land there', but most of these were also due to render themselves inoperative by the end of May.[25] The fields were due to be refreshed again, but in the event all the supplies were diverted to protect Italy's long, vulnerable coast – further evidence of the extensive indirect benefits deriving from the Mediterranean campaign. No mines arrived until 15 May, and efforts to lay them were interdicted by Allied air and sea forces.[26] *Marinegruppenkommando West* also prepared a system of rapid minelaying known as *Blitzsperren* (lightning barrages), which would be laid by all available ships as soon as the invasion was believed to be imminent, but this ridiculously optimistic notion came to nothing as the Allied navies moved into the key area – the Seine Bay – before they could be laid. *Blitzsperren* were essentially laid everywhere except in the most vital place.[27]

Construction of beach obstacles began in January, with the aim of producing four belts, sited at various different depths of water, although only two had been completed by 6 June 1944. There were some 517,000 in total along the Channel coast, of which 31,000 had been tipped with mines or obsolete artillery shells. 'The object of these new underwater obstructions', Rommel wrote, 'is not only to halt the enemy's approach to the beaches ... but also to destroy his landing equipment and troops.'[28] They took many forms, from simple wooden stakes and steel or concrete tetrahedra transferred from central European border defences, known as 'Czech Hedgehogs', to complex ramp structures designed to force a landing craft up until a mine or shell blew out its bottom, and the huge gatelike structures known as 'Element C', the largest obstacles found in Normandy, which were sometimes as high as 2.4m, and could weigh 1.5 tons.[29] The obstacles were reinforced by a variety of what would today be called 'improvised explosive devices', including a new Coastal Mine,

Type A. Type A mines were cheap and easy to produce. They consisted of a concrete block filled with explosives and detonated using a lead horn similar to that fitted to a moored naval contact mine. A variation on this was the 'snag mine', which lay on the seabed with a long wire attached, sometimes disguised with seaweed. Ships passing over the mine would snag the wire, which would get tangled in the propeller, eventually pulling on the line and detonating the mine.[30] Several types of lever-operated 'nutcracker mines' were also produced using land mines, old shells and other readily available devices. All of this frenzied work meant that the defences the Allies had to assault in 1944 were far stronger than those anticipated by Morgan when he drew up the COSSAC Plan in 1943.[31]

The obstacles were undoubtedly unpleasant for Allied sailors to negotiate, and a genuine impediment to the landings and subsequent operations. One post-Neptune report, compiled by a Royal Engineer officer who assessed German beach defences immediately after the invasion, concluded 'that these obstacles were our greatest enemy . . . no one will deny. It was . . . the combination of weather and obstacles which inflicted such a heavy loss on landing craft, and thus materially affected the LCT availability during the build-up'.[32] The same report, however, pointed out that the obstacles had rather less effect on the initial assault waves, as 'few LCTs were prevented by obstacles from reaching the beach and disembarking their loads [and] although a number of craft received damage from mined obstacles, the damage was seldom sufficient to prevent the load being disembarked'.[33]

If the Kriegsmarine was catastrophically outnumbered in the Seine Bay in June 1944, the Luftwaffe was even more depleted. As commander of the Allied Expeditionary Air Force, Leigh-Mallory had access to 2,434 operational fighter aircraft and 700 light and medium bombers in the Allied Tactical Air Forces, which would fly 5,276 sorties during the 24 hours of 6 June 1944.[34] Following a long political struggle with the so-called 'Bomber Barons', Eisenhower could also call upon the strategic bombers of the United States 8th Air Force and Royal Air Force Bomber Command if he needed them. Against this, Generalfeldmarschall Hugo Sperrle, commanding *Luftflotte 3* in France, could deploy just 198 bombers and 125 fighters.[35]

Allied estimates of Luftwaffe capabilities seem to have been exaggerated. The same US briefing paper warned of 850 aircraft of all types 'available for close support in the OVERLORD area'.[36] Ultra had provided the actual strength of *Luftflotte 3* as 891 aircraft, so the headline number was broadly accurate. However, many were unserviceable, and Ultra had also showed that 'the enemy's bomber arm and his potentially formidable anti-shipping force had been seriously weakened' and the Luftwaffe 'was suffering from inadequate training and shortage of pilots'.[37] The air threat was much diminished, but Allied planners were undoubtedly scarred by the mauling they had received at the hands of this potent foe in earlier campaigns.

Strategically, this tiny force would have little impact, but the threat could not be entirely ignored by the sailors who would be taking their ships into the Seine Bay: being strategically irrelevant would be of small comfort to any man who found himself struggling in the water as a result of a late night mine drop or tip-and-run bombing raid. The Tiger tragedy had graphically illustrated what even these outnumbered German air and sea forces could achieve, if they were well led and enjoyed a little luck, and the loss of half a dozen loaded LSTs or troopships on the day of the invasion could be catastrophic.

The enormous Allied preparations could not be hidden and the Germans were perfectly aware that an invasion was coming in the summer of 1944, but they did not know where or when. Rommel, according to Ruge, had his suspicions about the Seine Bay, as did Hitler, although his opinion fluctuated wildly from week to week, but OKW myopically focused its pre-invasion planning on the shortest sea crossing across the Strait of Dover, essentially because it was dominated by sea-blind soldiers who saw the invasion as some sort of grandiose river crossing, and utterly failed to understand Allied maritime capability in 1944. The Kriegsmarine was perfectly capable of interpreting tidal data to identify the most promising times, and as well as highlighting the strength of the defences around the Pas-de-Calais, German Naval Intelligence had also flagged the strong current and the limited capacity of the relevant British ports, primarily Dover and Folkestone, but in the end, the soldiers' views prevailed.[38]

On the other side of the Channel, it is hard to imagine that the Allied invasion forces could have been any better prepared, after months or in some cases years of practice. Each Assault Force, Assault Group, Squadron, Flotilla and many individual ships had practised each and every movement, rehearsed every last manoeuvre, timed to the last minute. So had the minesweepers, the bombardment forces, the follow-up waves and build-up forces. Although some US ships did not arrive until May, missing all the big exercises, most of the Seine Bay fleet was trained to perfection. But no training exercise, however comprehensive or even hazardous it might be, could ever entirely replicate the hazards of combat.

Operations in the Seine Bay would be the final, and deadliest, classroom.

By the end of May 1944, the emphasis had shifted from training to preparations for what even the least perceptive sailors recognised as the 'real thing'. On 15 May, the final plans were presented to senior commanders at Montgomery's 21st Army Group Headquarters, St Paul's School in Hammersmith, West London. Rear-Admiral Carleton Bryant flew over from Belfast for the occasion, recalling wryly that 'a German bomb, dropped on that particular building on that day, would certainly have upset things'.[39] Rear-Admiral Frederick Dalrymple-Hamilton, commanding Bombardment Force E and the Royal Navy's 10th Cruiser Squadron from the cruiser HMS *Belfast*, travelled south in rather greater comfort, accompanying King George VI in the Royal Train, the monarch having just completed a three-day inspection of the fleet at Scapa Flow.[40]

Ramsay held his final naval briefing at his headquarters at Southwick Park on 20 May. The pace was exhausting. Dalrymple-Hamilton, having returned to Scapa Flow after the London briefing, went south again on the 19th, this time by air. Lieutenant Michael Chichester, one of his staff officers, was stunned by the scale of the preparations. 'We found Hampshire an armed camp with troops in every village, tanks, vehicles and guns in fields and on roadsides, and traffic jams wherever we went', he wrote after the war; 'the final Naval briefing . . . left us astonished by the huge scale of the opera-tion and the complexity of the plan . . . we became aware that we were about to play a modest part in one of the most decisive operations of the war, in short that we would be making history.' The briefing ended with a short but moving presentation from Eisenhower, who 'radiated confidence', inspiring all present with a simple but sincere exhortation to do their best.[41]

Now, everything depended on the sailors who would take the fight into the Seine Bay. Commanding officers of every type of warship, from 30,000-ton battleships to 300-ton landing craft with crews of twelve, opened their voluminous sealed orders on 25 May. Sub-Lieutenant Phillip Stephens, aged 19, was First Lieutenant of *LCT-7074*, a Landing Craft (Tank) in the 17th LCT Flotilla, assigned to Force L, the first follow-up wave. He opened his orders on 2 June, recording in his diary that 'The CO and I spent a hectic weekend coping with an avalanche of secret operational orders and charts.' Stephens's CO was John Baggott, also 19, and a trainee solicitor from Swindon.[42] Roger Hill, CO of the destroyer HMS *Jervis*, was older, more experienced, and blessed with a bigger command team than Baggott and Stephens:

> Tuesday 30 May was very hot with a clear blue sky; and from this clear sky dropped on us two large sacks of books, which were the orders for the invasion ... the majority of the books were to be read by me only and passed to the relevant officers on 4 June. Then came an officer, requesting signatures for another 'Most Secret' sack of books ... these were the amendments to the books in the other two sacks, pages and pages of them.[43]

Like many experienced officers, Hill bent the security rules for the sake of operational efficiency. 'There was only one thing to do', he recalled. 'I sent for all the officers to my cabin, sat them down and swore them to secrecy. Put a bottle of whisky on the table, and a bottle of gin, told Charley [his steward] to fix sandwiches, and then dealt round the books. We married the amendments to the books and got to work.' It took until 1 June.[44]

The assault forces learned who they would embark, from where, and where they were to take them. The first assault waves were broken up between landing craft, so that no entire unit would be destroyed if a ship was sunk. 'Movement Control was responsible for this arrangement', remembered war correspondent Gordon Holman; 'a Unit Sheet showed the battalion, battery or squadron commander exactly how to split his unit into parties for embarkation. A Ship Sheet showed the craft load commander [i.e., the senior Army officer on the craft] exactly what unit parties went to make up his whole command.'[45] For the naval side, each ship was listed on a Landing Table, which itemised for each CO precisely what his craft should be embarking. He was also provided with a temporary 'Landing Table Index Number', cross-referenced with the military documents. This was hung in a prominent position and was detachable, so that in the event of a breakdown, the number could be transferred to another craft without wrecking the whole complicated jigsaw.

John Baggott's load in *LCT-7074* (LTIN 3517) was relatively straightforward, although it did involve three distinct units, all from the 7th Armoured Division, Montgomery's famous 'Desert Rats': seven Stuart light tanks from the Reconnaissance Troop of 5th Royal Tank Regiment, a pair of unarmed M4 Sherman 'Observation Post' tanks from 5th Royal Horse Artillery (a self-propelled gun regiment), and a single Cromwell tank from the headquarters of 22nd Armoured Brigade. Sometimes, however, these combat loads could be utterly bewildering, as the complex Landing Table for LTIN 1510, the Mark IV *LCT-672*, which was bound for Nan White Beach in Juno Area, shows:[46]

'A' Squadron, 10th Canadian Armoured Regiment (The Fort Garry Horse)
- One Sherman VC Firefly tank with 4 crew
- Four Sherman Mk III tank with 20 crew

La Régiment de la Chaudière (the assault infantry)
- Three Carriers, Universal (a small, armoured vehicle)
- One Carrier towing a 6-pounder (57mm) Anti-Tank gun
- One Jeep
- One Carrier, Mortar
- Twenty men

Plus
- Two men – Headquarters 8th Canadian Infantry Brigade (CIB)
- Two men – Headquarters 8th CIB Defence Platoon (Lorne Scots)
- One Jeep with two crew – 7th CIB Liaison Officer
- Sixteen men and four handcarts – 'K' Section (8 CIB), 3rd Canadian Infantry Division Signals
- One Jeep with two crew – 'K' Section (8 CIB), 3rd Canadian Infantry Division

Signals
- One Carrier with two crew – 'K' Section (8 CIB), 3rd Canadian Infantry Division Signals
- One Jeep with two crew – 184 Field Company, Royal Engineers
- Two men with a balloon – 52 Beach Balloon Unit, RA

This extraordinarily intricate jigsaw was repeated for thousands of craft, across every assault group. Making it work from the naval side was the responsibility of staff officers like Colin Madden of Assault Group J1. 'It really boils down to, where do the military want the one soldier, the one vehicle, the one tank, a particular amount of food, etc on a certain day', he recalled; 'it has to be worked and planned back in reverse for days ... loading, the passage and the timing. It really was a terrible problem and it was a very worrying one.' On the basis that two heads were better than one, Madden and his opposite number in J2, Lieutenant Peter Wyatt, got together and worked it out.[47]

Every CO's approach to briefing was different: aboard the Royal Marines-manned *LCF-32*, the Commanding Officer brought out a map of the European coast from Norway to the South of France and held a sweepstake on where the invasion would take place.[48] As the Assault Forces and Follow-Up Forces began to embark troops, the Bombardment Forces prepared to slip anchor and head south from distant Scottish and Northern Irish anchorages; aboard the cruiser HMS *Mauritius*, part of Bombardment Force D, 18-year-old Midshipman John Carlill was very aware of what was riding on this huge operation. 'I had been one of the last ashore before sailing and had been surprised and a bit disturbed because many of the young Wrens in the Greenock base had been in tears as I and others handed in the personnel records of our ships', he recalled. 'This was the Big One. On the outcome of the battle we were going to fight the next day, the war could be lost; it was as simple and as stark as that . . . the tension was electric.'[49] The Battle of the Seine Bay was entering its climactic phase.

For Force J, embarking three brigades of infantry accompanied by commandos from Southampton, Portsmouth and around the Solent, this sense of impending departure probably began on 24 May when King George VI visited a representative group of 600 officers and men at HMS *Vectis* in Cowes, after which he inspected the force at anchor in the Solent. By the time the force started to embark its troops on 1 June, Commodore Oliver was understatedly reporting the 'very creditable figure' of 100 per cent serviceability among his landing craft thanks to the efforts of his engineering team, 'who worked indefatigably in spite of difficulties experienced from berthing arrangements, shortage of spares and last minute break-downs'. The benefits of the months of training were readily apparent, with accidents and collisions during the difficult manoeuvring in congested anchorages being kept to a minimum and 'the knowledge that they were really off at last' acting as a great incentive. Loading was not without delays, but the 'high spirits' of the embarked Canadians were reported as 'outstanding'. 'Their enthusiasm', wrote Oliver warmly, 'suffused itself throughout the fleet.' Once the troops were embarked, all ships were sealed until the force sailed. Oliver reported very few cases of 'Channel Fever', apparently a euphemism for desertion.[50]

Some loads were distinctly unimpressive. 2nd Lieutenant Tony Lowndes and his LCVP crew from the 802nd Flotilla, now part of Build-Up Squadron A in Force J at Hayling Island, were ordered up the Beaulieu River to Bucklers Hard to pick up 'stores' on 3 June. They were greeted by an elderly Chief Petty Officer who 'took me over to six very long scaffolding poles which were lying on the deck. "There you are Sir," he said. I replied, "What are they for?" He replied,

'Don't ask me, Sir, but we shall be glad to get rid of them, we keep tripping over them.'[51] Lowndes and his marines returned to Hayling Island, the scaffold poles hanging humiliatingly over the LCVP's ramp as they were too long to fit in the well deck. They arrived to find the camp locked down and the guard on the gate doubled. At a briefing the following day, they learned that this extraordinarily unwarlike load would be the one they would take to France and deliver to the Beachmaster at Nan Red Beach near Saint-Aubin-sur-Mer, who would use them to mark safe exits off the beach.

Talbot, reporting on Force S, was less sanguine about his colleagues in 3rd (British) Division, embarking at Portsmouth, Newhaven and Shoreham. The Army's three brigades were 'very slow' with reported delays of three hours caused by military vehicles arriving late. Overloading was also a significant challenge: 'Vehicles were inevitably crammed full of boxes of provisions, pots and pans and other personal gear of considerable aggregate weight', the Rear-Admiral wrote wearily, 'for which no allowance had been made in the loading tables.'[52] Ramsay met his doubtless exhausted subordinate at Gosport on 3 June and was privately less diplomatic, writing in his diary that the situation 'was the fault of the Army, whose one idea was to cram as many vehicles into each ship and craft and as much into each vehicle as possible without regard to the disastrous results'.[53]

Talbot's report singled out the AVREs as a particular problem; they were, he wrote, 'so fully loaded with flails, bridges, ploughs and petards that the watertight door just abaft the LCT bridge would not close'.[54] Possibly the planners had allowed for the weight of the huge cumbersome machines, but not for the increased size and shape of vehicles with odd bits of kit projecting from their sides. 21-year-old Sub-Lieutenant Dennis Till, another Y Scheme entrant who had spent two hazardous years at sea as a DEMS gunner aboard merchant ships in the North Atlantic, was First Lieutenant of *LCT-1094* in the 45th Flotilla, part of Assault Group S3, and took on AVREs over newly constructed hards at Stokes Bay, near Gosport:

They had to reverse on so that they were facing forward when they got on the beach ... they had all sorts of gadgets on their tanks, such as a great big roll of material that they could roll out over soft sand, and they had explosive devices on the end of spars that could blow up obstacles, and they had flails on their tanks to set off any mines that had been buried ... They had great big things that they could plonk over to bridge any craters.[55]

Away to the west, the Americans were also embarking. Force U, which had already experienced the setback at Slapton Sands, and had been granted the shortest preparation time, also had the furthest distance to travel and so embarkation began early. To add to the US Navy's challenges, Force U was the only assault force without access to a major port, so it was forced to embark its three RCTs from nine small harbours widely spread across the West Country.[56] Several American embarkation ports were bombed by the Luftwaffe, proving as the E-boats had at Slapton that the German air and sea threat was still present. Portland was hit on 28 May in the midst of embarkation, which was going on around the clock. At 0100, the attack transport USS *Thomas Jefferson* reported five twin-engine bombers speeding across the harbour. *Thomas Jefferson* and the destroyer USS *Frankford* were both shaken by near misses, and a pair of mine explosions damaged *LCT-30*, wrecking the galley and causing several injuries.[57] Approximately twenty German raiders took part, dropping a mix of mines and bombs; the raid, along with attacks on other invasion ports, including Torquay, Weymouth, Falmouth and Portsmouth, marked the end of a bombing offensive codenamed *Steinbock*, often nicknamed 'the baby blitz', which had been underway since the start of the year. It cost the Luftwaffe more than 500 aircraft from its dwindling inventory and had very little impact on the invasion preparations.[58]

Sub-Lieutenant Jimmy Green, now second-in-command of an LCA Flotilla embarked aboard the LCI(L) *Empire Javelin*, came into Portland a few days after the raid to take on board soldiers from A Company, 1st Battalion, 116th Infantry Regiment. Some of them would go down in history as 'the Bedford Boys' when they landed in Omaha Area in the first wave on 6 June, as many hailed from the same small town in Virginia:[59]

They were a friendly but shy bunch of fresh-faced country lads. The officer commanding ... was Captain Taylor Fellers ... he was a very serious, thoughtful officer who seemed a lot older than our sailors who were in their late teens or early twenties ... [He] spoke to me of his concern that this would be the first time that he and his Company would see action and asked me to give them every support.[60]

Most of the American preparations were completed on schedule by 1 June, which had been designated as Y Day, the date when all commands had to be ready.[61] The veteran Force O completed loading four RCTs plus supporting Rangers at Portland and Weymouth in just three days, reporting the process complete by 31 May.[62]

Despite its relatively short preparation time and Douglas-Pennant's earlier lament about making 'bricks without straw', Force G's embarkation of three assault brigades passed largely without incident, most of it taking place in Southampton. Marshalling such extraordinary numbers of ships in the congested waters of the Solent required exceptional patience and skill. Norman Yates was a naval officer and a qualified marine pilot who was brought down from the Humber in April 1944 and seconded to Trinity House, the civilian body responsible for lighthouses and other navigational aids around the English coast, to try to bring order to the chaos and prevent accidental damage to urgently needed shipping. Yates and other pilots rushed in from around the UK and even, in one case, from West Africa and received a crash course in what in 1944 was probably the most congested body of water in the world (see Map 3).

They made a few trips with an experienced Solent pilot, took some notes, and were hastily examined by a pair of Trinity House Sub-Commissioners, 'elderly retired men of the sea', who 'in a formal, dignified manner ... found each and every one qualified to pilot ships of any tonnage and granted [them] a temporary licence'. Yates went to Sea View on the Isle of Wight, where the last twelve days of May saw him personally pilot a ship every day, a process which involved going out to collect it in a small launch, climbing aboard in open water, and then navigating it successfully to its berth. June was

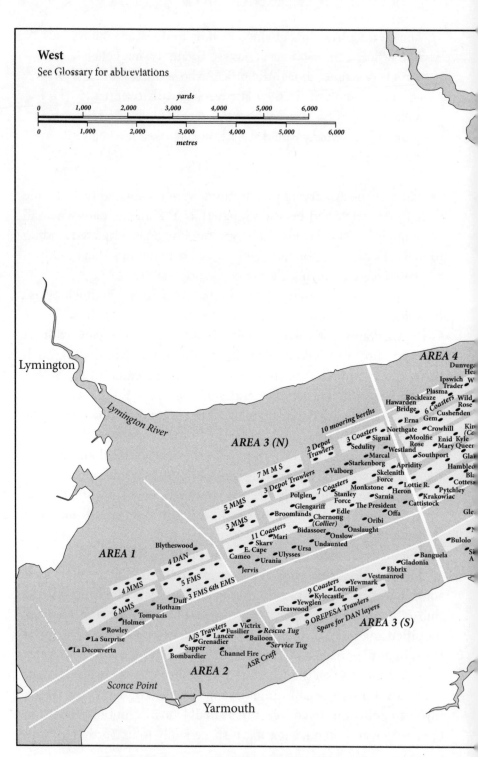

West

See Glossary for abbreviations

yards

| 0 | 1,000 | 2,000 | 3,000 | 4,000 | 5,000 | 6,000 |

| 0 | 1,000 | 2,000 | 3,000 | 4,000 | 5,000 | 6,000 |

metres

Lymington

Lymington River

AREA 4

Dunvega
Hea
Ipswich W
Trader
Plasma
Rockleaze Wild
Hawarden 6 Coasters Rose
Bridge Cushenden
Erna Gem
10 mooring berths Northgate Crowhill Kin
AREA 3 (N) 3 Coasters Signal Moolfie Enid Kyle (Co
2 Depot Sedulity Rose Mary Queer
Trawlers Westland Southport
Marcal Gla
7 M M S Starkenborg Apridity Hambled
3 Depot Trawlers Valborg Skelenith Bl
Force Lottie R. Cottes
5 MMS Polglen 7 Coasters Monkstone Heron Pytchley
Stanley Sarnia Krakowiac
Glengariff Force The President Cattistock
3 MMS Edle Offa
Broomlands Chernong Oribi Gle
(Collier)
11 Coasters Bidassoer Onslow
Mari Onslaught
Blytheswood Skarv Undaunted Bulolo
AREA 1 4 DAN Cameo E. Cape Ursa Banguela Si
Urania Ulysses Gladonia A
Jervis Ebbrix
5 FMS Vestmanrod
4 MMS 3 FMS 6th EMS 9 Coasters Yewmark Looville
Duff Kylecastle
6 MMS Hotham Yewglen 9 OREPESA Trawlers
Tompazis Teaswood Spare for DAN layers AREA 3 (S)
Holmes A/S Trawlers Victrix
Rowley Fusilier Rescue Tug
La Surprise Lancer Bailoon
Grenadier Service Tug
La Decouverta Sapper Channel Fire ASR Craft
Bombardier
AREA 2
Sconce Point

Yarmouth

Map 3. Final assembly anchorages in the Solent, June 1944.

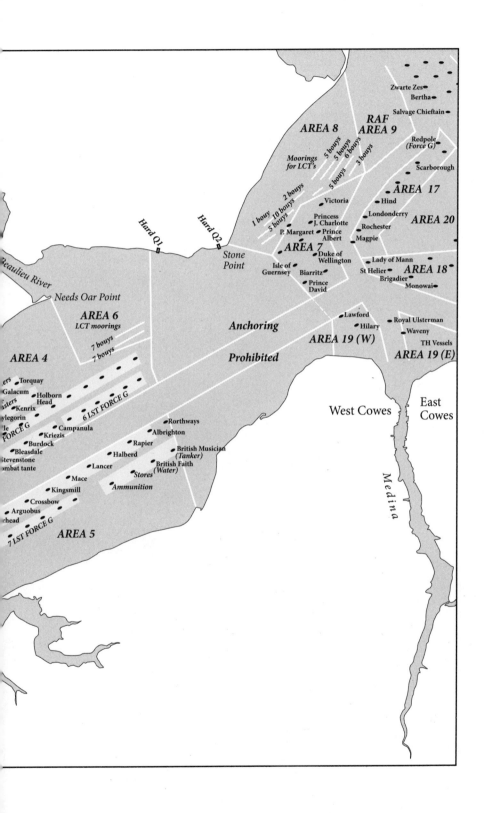

Zwarte Zes
Bertha
Salvage Chieftain

AREA 8

**RAF
AREA 9**

Redpole
(Force G)

Scarborough

Moorings
for LCT's

5 bouys
5 bouys
6 bouys
3 bouys

5 bouys

AREA 17

Hind

2 bouys
10 bouys
5 bouys

Victoria

Princess
J. Charlotte
P. Margaret
Prince
Albert

Londonderry

Rochester

Magpie

AREA 20

1 bouy

Hard Q1

Hard Q2

*Stone
Point*

Isle of
Guernsey

AREA 7

Duke of
Wellington

Biarritz

Lady of Mann

St Helier

Brigadier

AREA 18

Monowai

Beaulieu River

Needs Oar Point

Prince
David

AREA 6
LCT moorings

Anchoring

Lawford

Hilary

Royal Ulsterman

Waveny

TH Vessels

7 bouys
7 bouys

AREA 4

Prohibited

AREA 19 (W)

AREA 19 (E)

ers
Torquay
Galacum
asters
Holborn
Head
Kenrix
ylegorin
le
FORCE G
Burdock
Bleasdale
Stevenstone
ombat tante

Campanula
Kriezis

6 LST FORCE G

Rorthways

Albrighton

Rapier

British Musician
(Tanker)

West Cowes

East
Cowes

Halberd

Lancer

British Faith
(Water)

Mace

Kingsmill

Crossbow

Stores

Ammunition

Medina

Arguobus
rhead

7 LST FORCE G

AREA 5

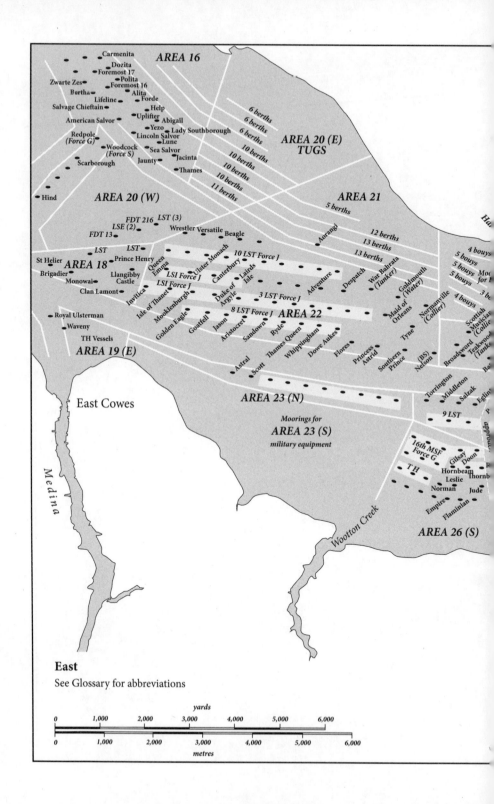

AREA 16

Carmenita
Dozita
Foremost 17
Polita
Foremost 16
Zwarte Zes
Bortha
Alita
Lifeline
Forde
Salvage Chieftain
Help
Uplifter
American Salvor
Abigail
Yezo
Lady Southborough
Redpole
Lincoln Salvor
(Force G)
Lune
Woodcock
Sea Salvor
(Force S)
Jacinta
Scarborough
Jaunty
Thames

6 berths
6 berths
6 berths
10 berths

AREA 20 (E)
TUGS

10 berths
10 berths
10 berths
11 berths

Hind

AREA 20 (W)

AREA 21

5 berths

FDT 216
LST (3)
LSE (2)
Wrestler Versatile
FDT 13
Beagle

Aorangi

12 berths
13 berths
13 berths

4 bouys
5 bouys
5 bouys
Moc
for I
5 bouys

St Helier
LST
LST
Prince Henry
Queen
Emgua
Ulster Monach
10 LST Force J
AREA 18
Canterbury
Lairds
Brigadier
Llangibby
LSI Force J
Duke of
Isle
Despatch
War Bahrata
(Tanker)
Goldmouth
(Water)
Monowai
Castle
LSI Force J
Argyle
3 LST Force J
Adventure
4 bouys
Clan Lamont
Invicta
Isle of Thanet
Mooklenburgh
8 LST Force J
AREA 22
Maid of
Orleans
Normanville
(Collier)
Scottish
Musician
(Collie
3 bo
Royal Ulsterman
Golden Eagle
Goatfell
Jason
Aristocret
Sandown
Ryde
Thames Queen
Tyne
(BS)
Teatswoo
(Tanke
Waveny
Southern
Broadsword
Ba
TH Vessels
Astral
Scott
Whippingham
Dowe Antes
Flores
Princess
Astrid
Prince
Nelson

AREA 19 (E)

East Cowes

AREA 23 (N)

Torrington
Middleton
Salzak
Eglin
P
approa

9 LST

16th MSF
Force G
Gilsay
Doon
R
Hornbeam
Leslie
Thornb
TH
Norman
Jude
Empire
Flaminian

Moorings for
AREA 23 (S)
military equipment

AREA 26 (S)

Medina

Wootton Creek

East

See Glossary for abbreviations

yards
0   1,000   2,000   3,000   4,000   5,000   6,000

0   1,000   2,000   3,000   4,000   5,000   6,000
metres

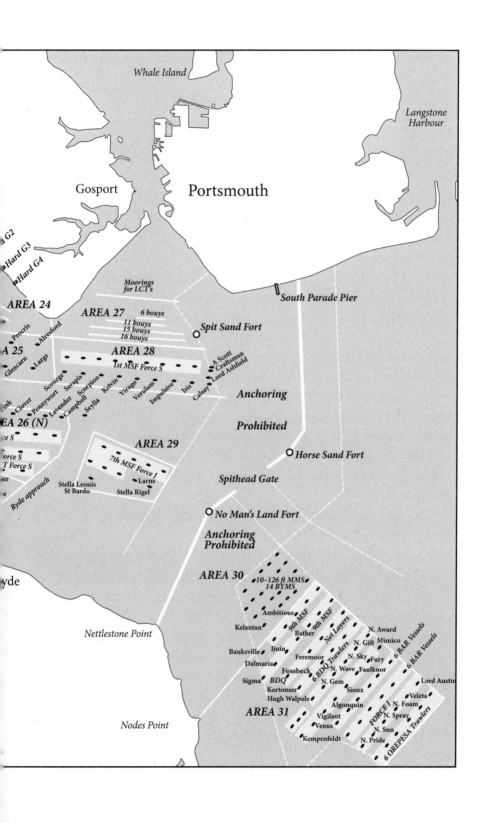

Whale Island

Langstone
Harbour

Gosport

Portsmouth

a G2
Hard G3
Hard G4

*Moorings
for LCT's*

South Parade Pier

AREA 24

AREA 27   *6 bouys*

*11 bouys
15 bouys
16 bouys*

O Spit Sand Fort

Procris   Alresford

A 25   AREA 28

Glencarn   Largs   *1st MSF Force S*

A Scott
Craftsman
Lord Ashfield

ink   Clover   Pennywort   Lavender   Scorpion   Kelvin   Virago   Verulam   Impulsive   Isis   Calsay

Scourge   Serapis   Seylla   Campbell

Anchoring

EA 26 (N)

Prohibited

ce S

AREA 29

O Horse Sand Fort

orce S
T Force S

7th MSF Force I

er

Larne

Spithead Gate

Stella Leonis
St Bardo   Stella Rigel

Ryde approach

O No Man's Land Fort

Anchoring
Prohibited

yde

AREA 30   10–126 ft MMS
14 BYMS

Nettlestone Point

Ambitious

Kelantan   9th MSF   9th MSF

Bather   Net Layers   N. Award

N. Gift   Mimico

Banksville   Ijuin

Dalmaria

Feremoor   6 BDQ Trawlers   N. Sky   Fury

N. Wave   Faulknor

6 BAR Vessels
6 BAR Vessels

Sigma   BDQ   Fossbeck

N. Gem   Sioux   Lord Austin

Kortonser

Hugh Walpole   Algonquin   Veleta

AREA 31   Vigilant   FORCE J   N. Foam

Venus   N. Spray

Kempenfeldt   N. Pride   N. Sun   6 OREPESA Trawlers

Nodes Point

even busier. 'Just before D Day almost every berth had a ship anchored in it', Yates related, 'leaving only a narrow navigable channel from East to West. I cannot recall ever seeing so many merchant ships anchored in such close formation.'[63]

Yates was part of a large group of sailors who helped to win the Battle of the Seine Bay without going to Normandy. Not all were men. Wren Freda Flowers was coxswain of a former pleasure launch called *Ocelot*. Operating out of Newhaven, as D-Day approached they were tasked with delivering kite balloons to the invasion fleet. These small barrage balloons were intended to deter German dive bombers, whose pilots were wary of becoming entangled in the cables. The attention given to anti-aircraft defences during Neptune is significant: hindsight seduces us into a simplistic assumption that everyone knew the Luftwaffe was a spent force in June 1944. But less than a year before, Allied warships had been relentlessly bombed by German aircraft off Salerno and in Churchill's disastrous attempt to liberate the Dodecanese Islands. Nobody could know for sure what would happen in the Seine Bay. Nevertheless, the balloons were not universally popular, some captains believing they would make them an easy target. Flowers recalled crews conveniently 'forgetting' them as they set out into the Channel with *Ocelot* in hot pursuit, the insistent Wrens desperately trying to get the balloon aboard before they left.[64]

The first two follow-up waves embarked at the same time, Force L for the British Eastern Task Force taking on three brigades at Tilbury and Felixstowe on the east coast, and Force B for the US Western Task Force loading two RCTs at Plymouth, Falmouth and Fowey.

On Sunday 28 May, as many commanding officers as possible crowded into Southampton's Civic Centre for a collective briefing, then broke into smaller groups for more detailed sessions. Three days later, preceding Eisenhower's more celebrated message, Ramsay issued his carefully crafted Order of the Day. It was only now, on the eve of what was undoubtedly the high point of his distinguished wartime career, that Ramsay was finally restored to the Royal Navy's Active List, his previous successes at Dunkirk and in the Mediterranean having been achieved as a notionally 'retired' officer:

It is to be our privilege to take part in the greatest amphibious operation in history – a necessary preliminary to the opening of the Western Front in Europe which in conjunction with the great Russian advance, will crush the fighting power of Germany ... the hopes and prayers of the free world and of the enslaved peoples of Europe will be with us and we cannot fail them. I count on every man to do his utmost to ensure the success of this great enterprise which is the climax of the European war. Good luck to you all and God speed.[65]

Douglas-Pennant boarded his headquarters ship, the converted liner HMS *Bulolo*, at 1500 on 3 June, after which he was unexpectedly visited by Churchill and Field Marshal Jan Smuts, the feisty septuagenarian Prime Minister of South Africa and a key adviser.[66] By this point, both men were harbouring grave concerns about the worsening weather, as were Ramsay and the rest of the Allied command team. 'The violence of the enemy' could be met and matched, but there was little that could be done to defeat the 'dangers of the sea'.

The poor weather which delayed Neptune has been well documented. Eisenhower and his commanders met daily to review the forecasts in minute detail. D-Day was provisionally set for 5 June but by 3 June the reports were worsening by the hour. Eisenhower was understandably reluctant to postpone, but by the conference at 0415 on 4 June, even though the weather over Hampshire was beautiful, the forecast was dreadful: strong to gale force winds, heavy cloud and rain. The Supreme Commander postponed D-Day by twenty-four hours. The big ships of the bombardment forces like HMS *Belfast* could simply ride out the storm. The cruiser was off the Bristol Channel at the time, and simply turned back north for twelve hours, steaming back and forth near Lundy Island. Sailors aboard a 10,000-ton cruiser, who had endured far worse weather on the Arctic Convoys, phlegmatically took the setback in their stride, Ron Jesse facetiously describing how *Belfast* 'sailed round and round Lundy Island ... first of all we went twice round one way and then turned round and went twice round the other way because we were getting giddy!'[67]

For those on smaller ships, and particularly the landing craft crews and embarked troops, the experience was less amusing, even though most never sailed or put back to port as soon as the postponement was announced. Royal Marine Dennis Small was now serving aboard an LCM operating out of HMS *Cricket*, a base on the River Hamble. After their final briefing – 'hit the beach as hard as you can!' – they went out into the Solent at 0700 on 4 June, where the sea began to get rough and most of the crew became seasick, including the coxswain, who became so ill that he asked 19-year-old Small to take over. The tiny LCM tied up alongside a larger ship but when the operation was postponed, the crew were dismayed to be told that they had to stay there for the next twenty-four hours. 'At this point I must admit to a feeling of apprehension and foreboding', Small recalled. 'We had a terrible night being tossed around and we now began to realise that our craft was not designed for anything other than ship to shore operations.'[68]

The most serious consequences of the postponement once again fell to Force U, which as it had the furthest distance to travel was some way out to sea when the order came. One large convoy was forced to put into Weymouth Bay and Portland Harbour, which were already packed with the ships of O2 Assault Group. Worse still, Convoy U2A was well on its way to France and far outside of the secure short-wave radio system known as TBS, or 'talk between ships'. Moon was unwilling to risk a conventional wireless message, which could have jeopardised the security of the entire operation if it had been intercepted by the Germans, so the destroyer USS *Forrest* was sent through the gale at more than 30 knots to turn it back.[69]

All this meant that the sailors were that much more tired and apprehensive when the invasion finally came, and their military passengers were uncomfortable and often severely seasick. Nobody could know for sure whether an alert German E-boat commander or pilot might have glimpsed the convoys at sea and guessed their destination. Only hindsight allows us to consider Neptune a foregone conclusion – nobody in June 1944 was in a position to take success in the Seine Bay for granted.

At 2100 on 4 June, Eisenhower and his command team again reviewed the weather with RAF Group Captain James Stagg, his senior meteorologist: it was not perfect, but the wind was due to drop and visibility would improve through 6 June. They agreed to reconvene at 0415 on the 5th to make the final decision. 'This time the prophets came in smiling', Ramsay wrote, 'conditions having shown a considerable improvement.'[70] Ultimately, of course, the responsibility lay with Eisenhower. Famously, according to almost every account of the meeting, he paused briefly and then simply said, 'OK. We'll go.'

As well as the thousands of ships preparing to cross to the Seine Bay, these three short words had implications for other naval forces all around the British coast. Far to the north, the Home Fleet maintained its watch on German surface units in Norway and the Baltic. Sailors like Paddy Vincent in the battleship HMS *Duke of York* understood their contribution, for sure, even though the work was far removed from the action. 'We were at sea off the coast of Northern Norway, marking the *Tirpitz* and ensuring she did not break out and interfere with the invasion. But it was frustrating to know that the Second Front was going on and we were not there.'[71]

Veteran anti-submarine escort Groups and Support Groups brought in from the North Atlantic and the Arctic swept in to guard the southern flank against attack by the *Landwirt* U-boats. Closer to home, the deception operation rolled into action. Alongside the very well-known dummy paratroop drops which accompanied the invasion (codenamed Titanic 1–4), aircraft and ships set forth to keep the Germans convinced for as long as possible that the threat lay everywhere but the Seine Bay. 'The Deceivers' believed that with enough effort, even after the invasion the Germans could be persuaded that Neptune was just a feint preceding the main event. Pilot Officer Malcolm Lenox-Hamilton was flying Lancaster bombers of the RAF's 617 Squadron, the famous 'Dambusters'. On D-Day he was assigned to Operation Taxable, off Cap d'Antifer, north of Le Havre. Instead of bombs, the Lancasters 'had to fly carefully for about four hours, dropping window [aluminium foil, known as 'chaff' today] and simulating a task force coming in at about eight knots'. The bombers were equipped with the RAF's Gee navigation system, developed for precision bombing. It worked by measuring time intervals between radio pulses received from three shore-based transmitters, which gave an accurate measurement of distance and allowed the operator to plot a precise cross-bearing:

> The Navigator had to work out exact courses and we did it with stopwatches. We'd go down towards Calais and each time we'd go eight seconds further than the last time. And then you'd go round and you'd go back up your course ... dropping Window in the alternative configurations ... each time you extended the leg a little bit further.[72]

Taxable was one of a pair of deception operations executed off northern France in the early hours of 6 June. The second, Glimmer, took place off the Pas-de-Calais. Below the formations of aircraft, warships were hard at work adding to the illusion. David Repard was First Lieutenant of the frigate HMS *Byron*. 'Having been preparing for the invasion ... *Byron* took part ... as a decoy', he remembered. 'We were given a whole set of instructions as to what we were to broadcast and when, and we went out into the North Sea and squawked loudly to suggest to the enemy that we were preparing for further landings in the Pas-de-Calais.'[73]

Harbour Defence Motor Launch *HDML-1410* was part of the deception operation, working with five other launches 5 miles off Boulogne Harbour, some flying balloons and others broadcasting electronic clutter through a pair of huge aerials, resembling goalposts, which had been erected forward of the bridge. Later, incredibly, they were expected to close to within half a mile of the shore and then run along parallel to it playing the sounds of a large fleet at sea through a loud hailer system. When this last element was cancelled, the MLs simply wallowed uncomfortably offshore for hours before speeding gratefully home 'at probably the best speed ever obtained by 1410'.[74]

Further south in another smaller operation, Big Drum, MLs and aircraft distracted German radar stations and coastal batteries in the north of the Cotentin Peninsula around Cherbourg. The deception operations, supported by other jamming from ground stations in the UK, were extraordinarily successful, according to at least one impeccable source: Baron Hiroshi Oshima, the Japanese Ambassador to Nazi Germany, whose regular and detailed reports back to Tokyo were being intercepted and read by US intelligence in a code-breaking operation codenamed Magic. Oshima had access to the highest levels of the German government, including Hitler himself. On 8 June 1944 he triumphantly signalled his government that 'it is uncertain whether the enemy will try to land in the Calais-Dunkirk area; however, an enemy squadron which had been operating off that coast has now withdrawn'. A few days later he reported that landings near Le Havre had been defeated.[75]

'The Deceivers' and the flank guards made a huge contribution to Neptune but ultimately, the fate of the entire operation, and of Nazi-occupied Europe, depended on the gigantic fleet which was about to enter the Seine Bay, and then operate in this dangerous and exposed body of water for months.

7
Crossing to the Bay
5/6 June 1944

> Minesweeping was the keystone of the arch in this operation.
>
> British Naval Staff History[1]

Minesweepers went ahead to clear the way for the assault and bombardment forces, but some sailors went across even earlier to mark the way for the sweepers, illustrating the complicated interdependencies which characterised Neptune.

In Operation Enthrone, three Fairmile B Motor Launches from Force J went out on the night of 31 May/1 June and laid ten FH830 ASDIC beacons to mark the entrances to the swept channels, indicating where the minesweepers were to start work. These were timed to transmit a distinctive underwater signal which could be picked up by ASDIC operators aboard the approaching warships, between 1400 and 2200 on six successive days, starting on 4 June.[2]

At 2135 on 2 June, towed by a pair of trawlers, the miniature submarines *X-23* and *X-20* left HMS *Dolphin*, the submarine base in Gosport, escorted by *ML-196*. Each boat carried three crew and two COPPists, and their job was to mark the eastern and western ends of the British and Canadian assault areas, a similar service having been offered to the Americans but declined. Early on 3 June they cast off their tows and the two tiny boats proceeded submerged towards France, surfacing periodically to ventilate their cramped craft, charge their batteries, pass over enemy minefields or check their location. The operation was codenamed Gambit, which in chess usually involves the sacrifice of a piece to gain a tactical advantage; undoubtedly this afforded those taking part a wry smile.[3]

X-23, commanded by Lieutenant George Honour with Lieutenant Lionel Lyne of COPP 9 as Senior Officer, arrived off Ouistreham at the eastern end of Sword Area at 0400, surfacing to periscope depth four hours later so the two officers could confirm their location using church towers and other prominent buildings. 'One of the main things we saw', Honour recalled, 'was a lorry load of Germans ... playing beach ball and swimming! At the back of my mind, I thought "I hope there are no Olympic swimmers here and they don't swim out a mile offshore and find where we are!"'[4] *X-20* (Lieutenant-Commander Paul Clark of COPP 1, and Lieutenant Ken Hudspeth, CO) arrived on station off Arromanches at 0455, surfacing at 0730 to perform the same checks, Clark's markers including the churches at Saint-Aubin-sur-Mer and Bernières-sur-Mer, and the lighthouse at La Rivière.

Incredibly, there the two submarines remained, mostly on the bottom, for the next thirty-six hours, the crews sleeping and conserving energy when they were not on watch, while Eisenhower and Ramsay mulled over dreadful weather forecasts and eventually opted to postpone. Food was dismal and in short supply, Clark reporting a diet of 'nutty' (chocolate), bread and jam, chocolate biscuits, orange juice, 'hyoscine' (a strong motion-sickness drug) and pure oxygen supplied in bottles salvaged from crashed Luftwaffe bombers, the lightest design available at the time. *X-20*'s crew had only two hot meals during the entire period, as the 'smell and oxygen used when heating made more undesirable'.[5]

Both boats surfaced to maintain a radio listening watch during a prearranged window between 0100 and 0130 on 5 June, so received notification of the change.[6] Early on 6 June they surfaced for the last time and erected a 5.5m-high pole mast which showed a green light to seawards; at dawn this was replaced by a large letter D signal flag. The wait for the invasion forces was long and uncomfortable, members of both crews being repeatedly swept overboard from their submarines' low casing in the rough seas. Each submarine was also supposed to deploy a small dinghy to mark the boundary further inshore but the weather prevented this, much to the frustration of the two young COPP dinghy officers, Lieutenant Jim Booth (*X-23*) and Sub-Lieutenant Robin Harbud (*X-20*), the former working 'hard and cheerfully' on other tasks and the latter apparently offering 'many convincing arguments' as to why he should be allowed to go![7] Honour also flew a huge White Ensign; in part this was undoubtedly service pride but it also served a practical purpose, helping ensure the tiny submarine would not be run over by one of the hundreds of ships which would shortly be passing. As additional insurance, each X-Craft also deployed a radar beacon and a 'rod sounder' transmitting an underwater pulse which could be picked up by ASDIC operators aboard the navigational leader motor launches that would follow.

The first of these, ten Harbour Defence Motor Launches, departed at 1800 on 5 June to take up position near the FH830 buoys as additional markers.[8] Equipped with QH and other navigational aids to ensure they maintained their position, they signalled the number of their channel on a shielded blue lamp at thirty-second intervals, and transmitted the letter D from a Type 78T radio beacon.[9] *HDML-1383* and *HDML-1387*, the Channel Identification Group for Channels Three and Four, marking the route into Omaha Assault Area, were also fitted with experimental Decca radio-navigation equipment.[10] Lieutenant-Commander Oliver Dawkins, the specialist Navigation Officer in a minesweeping flotilla, who also had access to the Decca system, described it as 'uncanny – it seemed as if we had some overhead cable which not only showed us the direction but also our speed through the water'.[11]

Other navigational leaders went further afield. Much has been written about the airborne landings which guarded Overlord's flanks, the British 6th Airborne Division to the east around the River Orne and the US 82nd and 101st Airborne Divisions on the Cotentin Peninsula, but the sailors – actually seagoing airmen – who marked their way in Royal Air Force High Speed Launches rarely get a mention. Norman Eastmead served in *HSL-2513*, one of four boats from the Air/Sea rescue base at RAF Mount Batten near Plymouth which quietly slipped their moorings on the afternoon of 5 June and made their way south with a strong Coastal Forces escort. Only the commanding officers knew precisely what they were doing, although the wireless operators were given call signs, radio frequencies and codes. At 1130 they reached their stations, switched on powerful light beacons and waited for another seven hours, drifting uncomfortably in the heavy seas and periodically starting their engines to get themselves back in position. 'It was a real filthy night', according to Eastmead, 'choppy seas, squally showers, really overcast, and we got there and formed up in a diamond formation, facing west, so that our lights could be seen.' Once the airborne forces had passed over, the launches resumed their air/sea rescue work, remaining at sea until their fuel was almost exhausted. 'When we got back to Plymouth, I'd been at sea on duty for thirty hours without a break', Eastmead remembered. 'They called it the Longest Day. It was for me.'[12]

Other navigational leaders were stationed closer inshore, and followed the sweepers in. Sub-Lieutenant Graham Rouse, from Barry, was First Lieutenant of the Fairmile B *ML-197*, a marker for Force S. The small launches were packed with so much navigational equipment that they had to be reconstructed, their funnels removed to make way for an oversized lattice mast 'like a small pylon' on which was mounted a large dome and numerous aerials.[13] Below decks, the wheelhouse was altered to accommodate two additional radar operators and their screens. After working up on the Cromarty Firth with Force S, Rouse's boat came south to HMS *Hornet*, the Coastal Forces base at Gosport, and the crew were given their briefing, which included a robust pep talk from Vian, who 'stressed to us that it was "your job to keep the men under your command alive and afloat". We were warned to expect exhaustion such as we had not known before', Rouse remembered, 'and were advised to try sleep in short snatches if the circumstances permitted. However, we were alerted to the dangers of drifting off into a really deep sleep (which he called "80 fathoms down"). To prevent this, we were told to order a rating to shake us periodically every fifteen minutes.' In the event, like many sailors who went to war in the Seine Bay, they were given Benzedrine amphetamines to keep them awake, which gave the user 'a lovely rosy complexion – you all looked terribly well!'[14] They were then sealed inside *197* until mid-morning on the 5th, when the ML left for Normandy.

There was a brief but heart-stopping moment when *197*'s comprehensive navigational array was jammed by the Germans, but Rouse had been warned that this might happen and went through a methodical process to change the frequencies, at the end of which the signals returned.[15] Otherwise, the trip passed without incident, although Rouse recalled being subject to what he called 'DMS' – dry mouth syndrome – all the way over: 'this is caused by the fear of making a navigational mistake resulting in the ship – or, in this case, the whole of S Force – ending up somewhere different from where they are supposed to be'.[16] At daybreak they sighted George Honour's tiny green light and took up their allocated position off Sword area.[17]

The minesweepers, many of them veterans of years of hazardous and often unrecognised service, left port with confidence and *esprit de corps*. According to one seaman in HMS *Seagull*, the veteran Halcyon Class fleet sweepers of the 1st Flotilla left Portsmouth with brooms pre-emptively lashed to their masts, the traditional markers of a successful sweep.[18] When the Algerine Class fleet sweepers of the 7th Flotilla left Portsmouth to clear the way for Force J, the HQ Ship *Hilary* signalled them dramatically to 'sweep on relentlessly'; not to be outdone, the illustriously named Senior Officer, Acting Commander George Nelson (no relation) replied, 'Aye aye Sir, with Nelson in the van!'[19]

There were potentially thousands of mines to deal with. As well as the German fields, 7,000 new British mines had been laid in Operation Maple, although in theory their 'sterilisation clocks' had rendered them harmless.[20] Contact mines were swept using the 'Oropesa' method, which used an arrangement of floats to hold a serrated sweep wire out to the side of the ship. As the mines' tether cable caught in the sweep wire, it would be dragged through the cutters until it parted, the mine would bob up to the surface, and be sunk or detonated using small arms fire. Additional equipment was carried to deal with ground mines. The 'Double L' sweep consisted of two thick electrical cables towed astern of a wooden minesweeper, which passed a current through the water, created a magnetic field, and detonated magnetic mines. Acoustic mines were dealt with using noisemakers.

The Germans had developed a new influence mine, 'oyster' mines, which were ground mines fitted with fuses triggered by the change in water pressure caused by a passing ship. Their early use had been prohibited by Dönitz, who was concerned that if they were captured and replicated by the Allies they would seriously disrupt supply traffic in the Baltic. Hitler agreed, instructing Göring in May 1944 'that under no condition [should] mines of this type fall into the hands of the enemy'.[21] They were not in fact any great surprise, confidential discussions about pressure mines having begun in the Admiralty as early as September 1941, but they presented, in the words of one report, 'an insoluble sweeping problem'. For this reason, the British had decided not to develop the technology themselves, for much the same reason as Dönitz had banned their use.[22]

Each Allied invasion force would initially pass along the shipping channels running along England's south coast, which were already swept regularly. This would help maintain security as the Germans were accustomed to heavy traffic along these routes.[23] Then they would turn out into the Channel, some formations passing through a large, buoyed patch of water 30km south-east of the Isle of Wight. Predictably nicknamed 'Piccadilly Circus', it was known more formally as Area Z and is often incorrectly called an 'Assembly Area', which misleadingly implies the entire fleet occupied it at the same time. The convoys then made their way down ten carefully marked, mine-swept approach channels to their Assault Areas – 'The Spout'. Force U, coming from the far west, bypassed Area Z entirely and made its way down a specially swept channel running from Portland Bill. All areas were assumed to be mined until the convoys reached the German coastal shipping channel, which could reasonably be assumed to be clear. The lowering positions for the assault forces, where the big LSIs would drop their assault craft, were therefore located in this area. Sweeping and marking this huge stretch of sea was an enormous undertaking.

'Minesweeping', the Naval Staff History records, was an 'unspectacular role [and] its importance is apt to be somewhat overlooked; it nevertheless called for careful and continuous planning, and a high degree of seamanship, courage and constant hard work in execution.' The plan was divided into four phases. The first was to sweep and mark two channels for each assault force, so ten in all. The second was to identify or clear swept areas closer inshore in which the bombarding forces could manoeuvre and the larger transports could anchor. Later, after the landings, the minesweeping forces would work on Phase Three, to widen these channels, until eventually they merged into one single, huge swept channel joining the assault area to the embarkation ports in the UK.[24] After this, in Phase Four, the minesweepers would work continuously to keep these swept areas clear of mines which the Germans might lay at night using aircraft or small surface ships. Phases One and Three involved close co-ordination across the assault forces and were planned in minute detail by Ramsay's staff but planning Phases Two and Four were left to the Assault Force Commanders.[25]

Ramsay called the Neptune minesweeping operation 'the largest single minesweeping operation ever undertaken in war'.[26] The number of minesweepers required was enormous. The British Naval Staff History cites 255, other sources claim as many as 306 sweepers were involved in all aspects of mine countermeasures connected to the invasion.[27] They were gathered together from everywhere, and some crews were only partially trained. They ranged from big, purpose-built fleet sweepers, through mass-produced wartime designs like the Royal Navy's ubiquitous Bangor Class and the US Navy's Auk Class, down to the simple US-built Yard (or British Yard) Minesweepers, MLs, converted trawlers and the coastal Motor Mine Sweepers, nicknamed 'Mickey Mouse Boats'. The 4th Minesweeping Flotilla (MSF) consisted primarily of ancient coal-burning Hunt Class sweepers dating back to the First World War, derisively nick-named 'Smoky Joes'. The grim reality was that sweepers were expendable. Richard Cooper served on the 'Mickey Mouse' *MMS-44*:

When a Mickey Mouse explodes a mine – when the sweeper explodes the mine, not the sweeping gear – is something to behold. One second there's a boat with a crew of twenty, some of whom you know reasonably well, and then there's nothing, except a big pall of very black smoke and a tiny bit of debris floating on the sea . . . What happens next is the 'coffin ship', who has been trailing two miles astern, comes up and takes the place of the departed and you carry on as if nothing had happened . . . Mickey Mouse sweepers were very dispensable.[28]

According to Richard Michell, Squadron Navigating Officer with the 9th MSF in HMS *Sidmouth*, the highly trained squadron staff were the exception to this general rule. Bizarrely, in the 9th Flotilla at least, these men were all issued with brightly coloured bathing hats, to ensure that if the worst happened, they could be recovered quickly from the water and resume their work aboard another ship.[29]

Able Seaman William Gostling was serving aboard *ML-206*, a Fairmile B motor launch which had been adapted for minesweeping. Fairmile Bs were assigned to each flotilla, to clear the way ahead of the bigger ships and, if necessary, 'take one for the team'; they were, it was widely understood, even more 'dispensable' than the 'Mickey Mouses'. *ML-206* and three sisters were sweeping ahead of the 6th MSF, clearing the path into Gold Area. Lieutenant-Commander Harry Leslie, *206*'s CO and the Senior Officer of the 1st ML Flotilla, issued a grim warning that 'nobody's going to stop for you. If you go in the water, they're not going to put the whole invasion at risk to stop to pick YOU up.'

As far as possible the sweepers took part in many of the large-scale pre-invasion exercises, although as one report commented acidly, 'some of the value of these practices was lost through lack of mine-sweeping knowledge among the Staffs of the Assault Force Commanders who planned them'. This deficit was later partially remedied by introducing a Captain Minesweeping to co-ordinate flotilla training, but the same report was in no doubt that the under-lying reason for the ultimate success of the minesweeping element of Neptune was the skill and professionalism of the Flotilla Commanders, not the training.[30]

The configuration of the 7th MSF's stablemate in Force J, Commander Roger Thomson's 9th Flotilla, can be taken as reasonably illustrative of the minesweeping flotillas, although there were some variations. The 9th MSF comprised eight Bangor Class fleet sweepers, six of which would sweep in a standard formation devised to ensure each ship was covered by the outside portion of the next ship ahead's sweep wire. Two Bangors would act as reserves – Richard Cooper's 'coffin ships'.

A pair of Fairmile Bs were assigned to clear the way ahead of the bigger and more valuable Bangors and had to keep station on the flotilla leader astern of them, which was fitted with Gee and/or Decca and was the guide for the entire force. One of the officers in the Bangors commented admiringly:

> I think any naval officer will readily appreciate their problem to keep station on a ship in one's rear, and to steer so as to keep her always covered by one's own sweep wire in a tide of varying strength ... and to do so at night, called for skill of a high order ... as severe a station-keeping test as could be imagined was surmounted. It was, of course, impossible for the M.L.s to have any notion of what the tide was actually doing, and information had constantly to be passed to them by the flotilla leader, so that they could work out the correct course to steer to keep her covered. This information was passed by loud hailer, as no light could be shown ahead, and such a method worked surprisingly well.[31]

This 'severe test', it should be remembered, was often 'surmounted' by young reservists with little or no previous seagoing experience; one of the MLs supporting the 9th MSF, for example, was apparently commanded by the celebrated Shakespearean actor Paul Rogers.[32]

A reserve ML in case of casualties and four Dan Layers – often adapted trawlers, which were used to lay large 'Dan Buoys' indicating the margins of the swept channel – made up the balance of the force. The work of the Dan Layers has if anything been even more overlooked than that of the sweepers, although this apparently simplest of tasks was complex and vital. One pair followed the lead ship, marking one side of the channel, and the other followed the rear ship, marking the opposite side, the two sides being marked by different coloured lights and flags. Only the lead ship laid buoys, and the first buoy displayed flags and lights which were unique to each channel; in total, eighty-one were used to mark each channel. Every effort was made to locate the Dan Buoys as precisely as possible, ideally using Gee. If the Dan Layers were not fitted with it, then the locations were double checked by Gee-equipped reserve sweepers as they passed up the channel.[33]

Aboard HMS *Pique*, a sweeper assigned to Dan-laying in the 40th MSF, the intersecting radio beams were nicknamed 'Christ and the two thieves'.[34] Sub-Lieutenant Leslie Hasker in HMS *Chamois*, the 40th MSF's other Dan Layer, remembered giving a blast on the siren each time a buoy was laid, to indicate that *Pique* should drop its buoy as well, recalling how 'the awful noise of the siren made us wonder if the Germans wouldn't hear us coming'.[35] Commander Roger Thomson, Senior Officer of the 9th Flotilla, took care to recognise the performance of his Dan Layers after the operation, noting that their work was 'consistently first class [and] precisely and efficiently carried out'.[36]

As if the huge size of the operation and the very poor prevailing weather were not challenge enough, the sweepers had to deal with an added level of complexity. The late discovery of Rommel's additional beach obstacles and the resultant shift in H-Hour to allow a longer window of low water for the LCOCU and NCDU teams to clear them meant that the tide would change halfway through the sweep. The precise time varied depending on the route being followed but for all flotillas it would happen in the middle of the night. In order to avoid sweeping against the tide, all flotillas would therefore have to alter the side on which they streamed their Oropesa sweeps. This was a far more complex manoeuvre than this one simple sentence might imply. Brendan Maher, Navigating Officer of *ML-137*, which led the 1st MSF into Sword Area, described the challenge it presented:

> It was necessary to proceed slowly or stop altogether ... the plan called for us to turn around and head back north slowly ... and then, once the sweeps had been changed, to turn around

southward and resume the approach . . . no signals were permitted on the radio. The signal to make the turns was given by the brief exposure of a small light on the masthead of the [flotilla leader] Harrier.[37]

This tiny light, only briefly visible, had to be seen by every ship, Maher recalling the 'immense strain' of watching until it finally appeared at 0026. The manoeuvre took well over an hour to complete.[38] Ramsay noted that, as it had been added into the plan so late, 'some flotillas had no opportunity to rehearse this manoeuvre at all. The fact that all successfully achieved it', he continued with typical understatement, 'is considered most satisfactory.'[39]

Changing over the sweeps produced some heart-stopping moments for the 9th Flotilla, which had to carry out the manoeuvre just as they entered the mine barrier. Ten minutes before changing over the Flotilla Leader, HMS *Sidmouth*, detonated a mine, followed almost immediately by the ship behind her. *Sidmouth* then reported a stray mine, apparently cut by an ML, drifting down the starboard side, and then there was a huge explosion from ahead. Minutes later, *ML-185* came limping back along the column, 'reporting by loud hailer that her sweep had been blown to the skies and her port engine put out of action'.[40] As the flotilla changed over sweeps, HMS *Tenby* caught a mine in its wire, forcing the CO to sheer away and cut loose his gear, and as the flotilla started to sweep again with their gear streamed on the other side, *Bangor* and *Eastbourne* both detonated more mines.[41]

Most of the minesweepers clearing the way for Kirk's Western Naval Task Force were also British or Canadian but two squadrons of US Navy-manned Yard Mine Sweepers took part, as did a full squadron of Auk Class fleet sweepers. These 'Bird Boats' were versatile 67m long, 890-ton warships capable of anti-submarine and convoy escort work as well as minesweeping. There were eleven ships in 'Minesweeper Squadron A', the US Navy's Mine Squadron 7 re-titled for Neptune, which set out for Utah Assault Area under Commander Henry Plander in USS *Pheasant*. The Squadron had been tasked with sweeping a channel for the Bombardment Force, forming a dog leg down the eastern side of the Cherbourg Peninsula and then across the estuary of the River Vire near Carentan. The Squadron left Tor Bay early on the 5th and proceeded without incident until they were south of the Isle of Wight, when they had to pass a large assault convoy, Convoy U2A1, and also became entangled with British ships emerging from Portsmouth and Southampton. It was during this complicated manoeuvre that USS *Osprey*, which was one of two flotilla Dan Layers, struck a mine which had apparently broken adrift during the earlier gale.

The mine exploded in the forward engine room at 1759. It knocked down or threw into the air almost every member of the ship's company, started a serious fire amidships, and wrecked the minesweeper's steering gear. Observers on the USS *Raven* nearby reported that *Osprey* 'was seen to shudder violently and almost instantaneously a circle of orange flame girded her amidships ... a great volume of black smoke arose from her port side' and some twenty sailors were blown into the water. Damage control was excellent and the fire was put out after ten minutes, but the sweeper was a mess. 'Of course, the forward engine room was demolished', recalled Lieutenant Charles Swimm, *Osprey*'s Commanding Officer, which put the starboard engine room out of action, but in addition the overworked port engine 'burned up, the reduction gears were smoking and they had to secure it ... at 1816 we abandoned ..., the damage to the ship being so extensive that repairs could not be made, and she had taken a list and was in bad shape'.[42]

Lieutenant William D. Allen brought USS *Chickadee* alongside and, as the two sweepers pounded against each other in the rough seas, Swimm organised the transfer of 114 survivors, including 21 badly burned men. *Osprey* finally capsized and sank at 1945, the first vessel to be lost due to enemy action on D-Day, and the five sailors and one officer killed were Neptune's first official deaths in action. Minesweeper Squadron A completed their mission without any further problems.

There was one final hazard. As the minesweepers were generally going around 2½ knots (nearly 5km/h) faster than the landing craft following them and leaving the swept channels untended would risk

German minelayers slipping back in, the sweepers were forced to loiter at the end of the sweep, very close to the enemy-held shore, sometimes for hours. Incredibly, the mainly Canadian 14th MSF, clearing Channel 2 into Utah, arrived off Point Barfleur on the Cherbourg Peninsula at 1957 on 5 June, with the light still clear enough to distinguish houses ashore. The 14th then spent three hours on the day before D-Day patiently sweeping their way to the assault area, well within radar range of the French coast. Fortunately, they were, according to one junior officer, 'completely disregarded by the enemy . . . I credit it with the enemy assuming it was just a feint, another one of the routine sweeps that they had become accustomed to'.[43]

The 9th Flotilla completed its channel at about 0300, after which there was nothing to do but wait, observing the preliminary bombing of the shore defences which was starting to develop. 'No one ashore appeared to take the slightest interest in us, and we had a curious feeling of detachment from what almost seemed to be a private war being waged within a few miles of us', recalled one officer; 'there could be little doubt, however, that this bombardment from the air was giving the shore batteries such a pounding that they had little chance of transferring their attentions to anything afloat'.[44] William Gostling reached the French coast around 0120, and *206* finished sweeping then waited in silence. Gostling found the opportunity in the sudden inactivity for a little reflection. 'This is one of the most ridiculous things', he thought, 'there's one of those poor German soldiers there who's said to his French bird "I'll see you at six o'clock tomorrow night, darling", and he ain't gonna see her 'cos we're here!'[45]

Ultimately, of course, whether Gostling's imaginary *landser* would meet his paramour would not be up to the minesweepers. His fate would depend on the assault forces behind them, which had set out once more, leaving their harbours, ports and anchorages at their allocated times. The process took a long time. Assault Group S3, for example, with 8th Infantry Brigade and supporting formations embarked, began to leave at 0945 on 5 June and did not complete until 2200. Force S's Reserve Group took well over twenty-four hours to depart Spithead.[46] For hours, they passed along the coastal shipping lanes, then turned south through Area Z, and entered their designated channel through the 'Spout' to the assault area (see Map 4).

It is almost impossible to imagine the vast scale of this movement of shipping. Everything from clumsy barges and the barely seaworthy powered rafts known as Rhino ferries, through landing craft of all shapes and sizes and tiny harbour launches, up to the converted liners proudly masquerading as Landing Ships, the ubiquitous Tank Landing Ships and the battleships and cruisers of the Bombardment Force set out at their allocated time, as part of their allocated higher formation, following the detailed orders meticulously prepared by Ramsay and his staff. The sense of drama was palpable and the Navy rose to it: when Force S left Spithead, Talbot's HQ ship HMS *Largs* hoisted the signal 'Good Luck. Drive On', keeping it flying until the last ship left at the end of the day.[47] The 7th ML Flotilla played a popular song called 'We Don't Know Where We're Going (Until We're There)', made famous by Tommy Handley on the radio show *ITMA*, over loudspeakers as they left Southampton Water.[48] The attention to detail was extraordinary. Each ship in the British and Canadian sectors, for example, was marked with a coloured band around the funnel, providing a swift and easy indicator of where it was supposed to be: Force S was green, Force J was red, Force G was blue and Force L (first follow-up wave) was yellow.

Conditions were still marginal: wind speeds were around Force Five (25–30km/h) with strong gusts. 'Conditions on the day of sailing were in my appreciation unexpectedly severe for the launching of an operation of this type', Vian wrote in his report, 'and imposed a high test on the landing craft crews.' Not usually the most effusive of men, he went on to say that 'their spirit and seamanship alike rose to meet the greatness of the hour and they pressed forward and ashore ... in high heart and resolution'.[49] Remarkably, despite these difficulties, only a few landing craft were unable to sail, and in most cases every force left and arrived on time. Ramsay singled out the hard-working Force U for particular praise, commenting in his Despatch that 'by H Hour their Commanding Officers had been on their bridges for about 70 hours'.[50] Departure times were carefully orchestrated to ensure that each force arrived at its station off the enemy-held coast

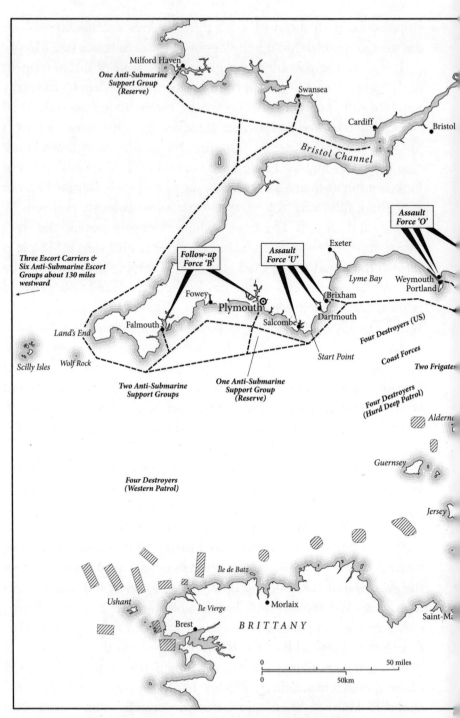

Map 4. *The Spout: routes to the bay, 5/6 June 1944.*

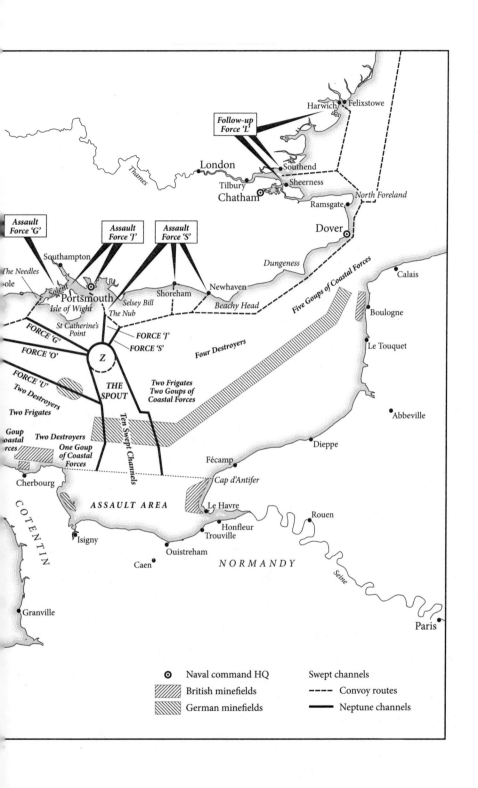

Follow-up Force 'L'

Harwich • Felixstowe

London
Thames
Southend
Tilbury • Sheerness
Chatham ⊙
Ramsgate •
North Foreland

Dover ⊙

Assault Force 'G'

Assault Force 'J'

Assault Force 'S'

Dungeness

Calais •

Southampton
The Needles
ole
Selsey Bill
Solent
Portsmouth ⊙
Isle of Wight
The Nub
St Catherine's Point

Newhaven
Shoreham
Beachy Head

Five Goups of Coastal Forces

Boulogne •
Le Touquet •

FORCE 'J'
FORCE 'S'

FORCE 'G'

FORCE 'O'

Four Destroyers

Abbeville •

Z

FORCE 'U'
Two Destroyers

THE SPOUT

Two Frigates
Two Goups of
Coastal Forces

Dieppe •

Two Frigates

Goup
oastal
rces

Two Destroyers

One Goup
of Coastal
Forces

Ten Swept Channels

Fécamp •

Cherbourg

Cap d'Antifer

ASSAULT AREA

Le Havre
Honfleur
Trouville

Rouen •

C O T E N T I N

Isigny •

Ouistreham

Caen •

NORMANDY

Seine

Granville •

Paris •

⊙	Naval command HQ
▨	British minefields
▨	German minefields

Swept channels
---- Convoy routes
—— Neptune channels

at the correct time, a requirement which was further complicated by the variations in H-Hour. The bigger Landing Ships would deploy their tiny assault landing craft at their assigned 'lowering position'. All were some miles offshore to keep the vulnerable transports out of range of German coastal defence guns, although the precise locations varied between 7–8 miles in the Eastern Task Force and 10–11 miles in the Western Task Force.

There are really only four distinct narratives for most of the hundreds of thousands of men who crossed the Channel to the Seine Bay on the night of 5/6 June 1944. The official reports describe the passage briefly. Talbot, reporting on Force S, conceded that 'the weather, set down in bald terms of Beaufort Scale, does not sound as bad as press reports have made it out to be, but ... any sea or wind over 3 [the wind was at Force 5, or 29–38km/h] is a lot to Landing Craft, and much more to seasick soldiers'.[51] Oliver of Force J reported 'weather conditions were most severe for loaded landing craft'.[52] For Force G, Douglas-Pennant simply referred to an 'unpleasant passage'.[53]

None of this does justice to the experience of the embarked soldiers, most of whose narratives were a kaleidoscope of misery encapsulated in the single word 'seasickness'. Like 19-year-old Leslie Perry of the Suffolk Regiment, they spent the journey folded over the rails or laying in a heap on the cold, wet steel decks. 'I was sick all the way over', he recalled, 'I was sitting on top of the stairs munching biscuits and sipping water because when you're retching and you haven't got anything to eat it just tears you to pieces.'[54]

The larger ships took the bad weather in their stride, and for most sailors aboard them the journey passed without incident. Those on watch below, in the machinery spaces and other compartments buried deep inside the battleships and cruisers of the Bombardment Forces, or the Landing Ships and other large assault craft, had little awareness of what was going on around them, but many of those fortunate enough to be off watch, or on duty on the upper decks, took a moment to see the sights and consider the momentous importance of the operation in which they were taking part. Some observed the streams of aircraft passing over, laden with paratroops or towing gliders. Some reflected uneasily on the danger from mines or the risk of U-boat attack. Others were more relaxed, utterly confident in the ultimate triumph of the vast, well-equipped fleet which surrounded them. Most simply recalled vast numbers of ships: 'the armada stretched for miles', HMS *Belfast*'s Senior Engineer, Charles Simpson, observed when he went on deck to look, 'miles and miles of small craft carrying soldiers. They sat or stood in the open air in utter silence . . . you could turn and look astern and see these lines disappearing over the horizon, it was so long.'[55]

For the often young and inexperienced sailors driving the smaller assault craft, the passage was a very different experience, one characterised by uncertainty, danger and occasionally outright terror. These sailors were putting themselves in harm's way from the very moment they left the safety of their anchorages.

After a chequered but adventurous career which included action at Salerno, service with the COPPs and, briefly, X-Craft training, until it was brought to a premature end following an unfortunate incident involving his commanding officer and a thousand smuggled duty-free cigarettes, Lieutenant Hugh Irwin went to the Seine Bay as second-in-command of the 591st LCA (Hedgerow) (LCA(HR)) Flotilla, seventeen flimsy wooden assault landing craft fitted with Hedgehog spigot mortars, which launched twenty-four mortar bombs in a pattern designed to blast a $91m^2$ area of beach, detonating mines and clearing barbed wire. The mortar, adapted from an anti-submarine weapon, proved very effective in its allocated role but did nothing to improve the already questionable stability of the LCAs, and prevented the small craft from being transported on davits, so the LCA(HR)s had to be towed across by larger landing craft; they were the smallest vessels to make the crossing.

The 591st Flotilla was bound for Gold, and the journey was a nightmare. There was no possibility of food, as the tiny, overloaded LCA(HR)s had no galley, and the weather was too rough to pass anything across from the LCF which was towing them. Irwin, at just twenty-four years old, an experienced sailor who had joined the RNVR before the war, realised that the tow lines were too taut for the prevailing weather conditions and lengthened the line from his own boat, *LCA(HR)-1110*, to ease the strain on the shackles. Other young commanding officers, less experienced or perhaps just less fortunate, were unable to prevent disaster. The *960*'s fragile wooden hull was so mangled by being towed alongside an LCT for four hours that by around 2100 it was going down by the bow; Sub-Lieutenant Duffin and his crew were taken aboard the LCT but his former command 'was last seen floating astern, half submerged'. Sub-Lieutenant Cole's *972* was also towed alongside an LCT and swamped; despite strenuous efforts by the crew to bail out with helmets and buckets, it filled with water above the Hedgehog mortar until at 0445 it abruptly turned over and sank, although the crew were saved.[56]

Sub-Lieutenant Barker and three of his crew were saved from *1108* when it shipped a heavy sea and immediately sank at 2100, although 26-year-old Able Seaman Alexander Milne was never seen again. Sub-Lieutenant Colin Knott had cast off his tow and *961* was proceeding under its own power when it, too, was swamped.[57] At 29, Knott, from Crantock in Cornwall, was in Irwin's opinion 'a bit too old to have gone on the job'; he had, chillingly, bought himself a new lifejacket in preparation for the assault but this wasn't enough to save his life in the exceptionally challenging conditions prevailing in the Channel that night. He left behind a young wife, Dorothy.[58]

The problems with the LCA(HR)s were not confined to Gold: according to Talbot's report, only one of the flimsy craft assigned to Force S survived the passage, commanded by Royal Marine Lieutenant F.H. Penfold. Five were known to have sunk and one broke its tow but was later recovered and towed back to base. 'Two which broke adrift have not been heard of since and are presumed to have foundered. The plain fact is', Talbot went on to note, 'these heavy craft are not suitable for towing in anything other than a flat calm.'[59]

Irwin considered himself lucky: the towing LCF broke down later in the night and he was forced to cast off and 'went on under my own steam'. Alone in the darkness with no navigational aids, *1110*'s crew had no idea where they were until they saw the start of the aerial bombardment and realised they were nearing the coast. Then they ran out of fuel and drifted until a passing destroyer passed over jerricans filled with petrol, a 'precarious operation' in the heavy seas, before finally reaching the lowering position and preparing to meet 'the violence of the enemy'.[60] Suddenly they were surrounded by warships. 'One then felt a bloody fool for having volunteered for this job', Irwin remembered, 'because, particularly having been in Salerno, I knew and felt there would be . . . murder. When they were cheering, I was really very frightened.'[61]

Theron Dosch was Quartermaster aboard the US Navy's *LST-345*; never before prone to seasickness, on the night of 5/6 June he was 'just sick as could be, I just could hardly do my job until we got into combat . . . I was sick most of the time, I was trying to do my job, but I wasn't very efficient, I'm sure.'[62] R.G. Watts was a Wireman aboard *LCT-2455*, a US-built Mk V carrying Centaur tanks of the Royal Marines Armoured Support Group into Juno. 'I remember looking down from the poop deck at those soldiers [*sic*]' he recalled, 'and thinking what a healthy lot they were, all that training for fitness, but now old Mother Nature was laughing at us.' The crossing was miserable, even the Marines were ill, and the cramped landing craft soon stank of diesel oil and vomit. By the time they reached the enemy-held coast, crew and passengers alike were filthy and exhausted.[63]

Tony Lowndes nearly lost his LCVP, thanks to their unwelcome cargo of scaffolding poles, which not only made the landing craft very bow-heavy but also punctured a hole in the tarpaulin stretched over the open well deck, causing it to fill with water every time a wave broke over the ramp. About six hours into the crossing Lowndes noticed that the craft was not coming back up from the troughs of the waves as quickly as it should and sent one of his crew under the tarpaulin to see what was going on. 'He disappeared for a couple of minutes', Lowndes remembered, 'and came back looking green and was immediately seasick over the side. He reported that the hold was half full of water.' The problem was partially solved by refuelling, which shifted weight from jerricans of spare petrol in the well deck to the fuel tanks aft, but even this apparently simple process was difficult and frightening in the heavy seas. Lowndes did it himself, lying on the aft deck and pouring the petrol through a funnel while his crew held on to his legs. Eventually, the bow lifted and the LCVP continued its journey, arriving off the French coast at about 1530.[64]

Dennis Small's concerns about his LCM's ability to make the crossing proved amply justified:

> Nothing had prepared us for being in a craft with a flat bottom, and a flat front, and being in such a sea as this. At this point we really felt that we would be lucky to make it. As we met each swell the craft would be lifted up like a cork, and as it got to the top of the swell the stern would come out of the water and the propellers would scream. The flat bottom would crash down on the water making the bottom plates shudder and boom. I did my best to keep the craft heading into the swell for fear of being caught broadside and turned over.[65]

At this point the LCM was still in sight of the Isle of Wight when the LCM in front broke down. Acting against orders Small tried to lash it alongside, but the two craft started to rip each other to pieces and eventually he was forced to cast off.

> Because of the propellers coming out of the water, one of the drive shaft couplings broke and one rudder dropped off, so now we had only the one rudder and one engine, but I still managed to keep up with the flotilla.[66]

After nervously skirting a drifting mine and taking pot shots at it with rifles until their escorting corvette signalled them bluntly to leave it alone, the weather calmed, and as darkness fell, Small took a break; leaving another Marine to follow the wake of the craft in front, he fell asleep. He awoke a little later to find the LCM lost in the pitch dark, and the crew 'in a high state of concern'.[67] Small calmed them, and they eventually made it to France. Analysing the performance of LCMs after the operation, the Admiralty concluded that they were ineffective and unsuitable, having been designed 'for a long sea voyage operation, to be carried to the assault in landing ships', which even had they been aware, would probably have been of limited comfort to Small and his shipmates.[68]

Royal Marine Lieutenant Frank Milton made the crossing in an even more fragile craft. Just 19 years old, he had been appointed – 'I was informed ... that I had "volunteered!"' – to command a tiny Landing Craft Personnel (Large), an early Higgins-designed boat which had been fitted with additional navigational aids and been assigned the important task of navigating DD tanks onto the beach as part of Assault Group G2, landing on beaches King, Red and Green opposite Ver-sur-Mer.[69] Captain Frank Balance, Senior Officer of G2, simply noted in his report that 'LCP(L) had difficulty in keeping up ... and it is reported that they did not arrive at the lowering position. Their movements after 0130 are not known.'[70] Actually participating in this journey was considerably more fraught.

Milton left HMS *Tormentor* on the Hamble at 1000 on 5 June, with a crew of two RN sailors and three Royal Marines. Convoy G4 consisted of eight LCTs carrying the tanks, a headquarters landing craft, six more LCPs and seven assorted armed support landing craft, escorted by an ML and the sloop HMS *Magpie*. Milton described his boat, *LCP(L) 4*, as 'one of the oldest involved in D-Day', believing it had taken part in the Dieppe raid. Battling heavy seas in mid-Channel was heavy going for the LCPs. 'Their passage would have been hair-raising to watch', Milton remembered, 'disappearing behind one wave and bursting out on top of the next, but they were a bit like seagulls on the surface in rough weather, and quite safe.'[71]

Eventually, the LCTs were ordered to take the smaller craft in tow, an easy instruction to give but rather harder to carry out. The first tow rope passed over to Milton's craft snapped, and the second immediately tore out the bollard it was tied to. The lines had been kept short, an understandable precaution because of the number of other ships around, but it meant that as the towing LCT rose on a wave the LCP was simultaneously plunging into a trough, and the pressure on the lines was irresistible. When the second rope parted, the LCT crew tried attaching a steel hawser to the main lifting ring in the LCP's deck, but this, too, failed. 'On the LCP it felt like being on the end of a whip', Milton recalled, 'we were all very sick – even the RN personnel.'[72]

The flimsy LCP was now taking in water through the hole which had been ripped in the foredeck. The flooding overwhelmed the pumps, the tiny craft started to fill with water, and eventually it slipped behind the rest of the group. Corporal P.J. Warren, Milton's Royal Marine Coxswain, clambered out onto the foredeck and tied a groundsheet over the hole, which helped a little, but it was clear that the LCP was doomed. Eventually, in defiance of orders and undoubtedly terrified, Marine Barton, the Signaller, began using his Aldis lamp to signal SOS. Milton gave him a half-hearted 'telling off' and then sensibly turned a Nelsonic blind eye to his actions: 'I suspect he decided to forget my words, God bless him, because the next thing happening was the approach of a destroyer out of the darkness. She drew up close giving us some shelter from the sea and a loud speaker demanded "Do you require assistance?" '[73]

Lieutenant-Commander Norman Murch, the experienced commanding officer of the destroyer HMS *Beagle*, sized up the situation swiftly and ordered the LCP evacuated; Milton and his crew climbed gratefully aboard and arrived in the Seine Bay in rather more comfort than they had left the Solent. *Beagle* was carrying a Reuters Correspondent, Desmond Tighe, who reported Milton's misfortune in the *Yorkshire Post* on 8 June:

> A faint light signalled SOS out of the darkness. We turned towards it and found a small Assault Landing Craft, manned by a Royal Marine 2nd Lieutenant, three Marine privates and three naval ratings [*sic*], tossing about in the sea. She was holed badly up forward. We pulled the crew aboard, one of the Marine privates had been so seasick that it took the ship's doctor some time to pull him around.[74]

Perhaps the most vulnerable of all the invasion craft were the converted Thames barges. Peter Bird left from Langstone Harbour near Portsmouth in *LBV-45*, part of the 2nd LBV Flotilla bound for Juno Area as part of the Build-Up Squadrons in Force J. The ungainly craft were now heavily overloaded and drawing a mere 450mm of freeboard, revealing a design flaw which had been overlooked during conversion and not picked up during training when loads were far smaller. When the stern ramps were fitted, two small holes had been cut in the narrow deck, through which the ramp wires passed forward to the winches which raised and lowered them. The holes were located directly over the barge's engines, and when *LBV-45* was 'shipping it green' on the passage over to the Seine Bay the water flooded inside the hull, swamping the engines and eventually causing them to fail.[75]

Lost and alone, Bird and his crew spent the night working the barge's single, inadequate hand pump in back-breaking twenty-minute shifts in a desperate effort to keep the water level down. Remarkably, they succeeded: *LBV-45* was still stubbornly afloat when Bird's Flotilla Officer, Lieutenant Arthur Prothero, appeared in a trawler – having 'declined to go over on any of his own barges' – and took them in tow. Not everyone was so lucky. Dozens of the ungainly barges were lost or damaged in the Seine Bay, mostly due to weather rather than enemy action. *LBV-42* crossed over as part of the 12th Flotilla on the 6th, bound for Omaha, but was never seen again; the body of Stoker Bernard Hayward was recovered in mid-Channel on the 7th, but the other three crew members were never found.[76]

Although the weather probably posed the greatest threat to those crossing to Normandy on the night of 5/6 June 1944, the enemy were not far away, and mines were a constant threat. At 0645 on D-Day, while escorting assault convoy J7, the veteran destroyer HMS *Wrestler* (launched in 1918) detonated a mine while attempting to assist a disabled LCT which had drifted outside the swept channels. The explosion blew a huge hole under *Wrestler*'s bow, killing two men and setting the ship on fire. The destroyer's damage control was excellent: Lieutenant Reginald Lacon's crew successfully fought the flames and made the hull watertight, after which his stricken command was towed back to Portsmouth. *Wrestler* was never repaired and was sold for scrap on 20 July.

And so 7,000 ships and hundreds of thousands of sailors crossed the Channel, generally defying the dangers of the sea and the violence of the enemy. 'The assault forces all drove on', wrote Ramsay admiringly in his Despatch, 'and almost without exception arrived off their beaches to time . . . as our forces approached the French coast without a murmur from the enemy from their own radio, the realisation that . . . almost complete tactical surprise had been achieved slowly dawned.'[77] Thanks to outstanding planning and training, good intelligence and the unprecedented success of the deception operations, coupled with some luck, notably weather so bad it discouraged the Germans from believing any invasion could take place, the fleet had arrived in the Seine Bay. Here it would operate, under the guns of the enemy and very much in harm's way, for the next three months.

'So ended D-Day', wrote Commander Duncan Irvine, Senior Officer of the 40th MSF in HMS *Grecian*, 'with no casualties at all. We had been lucky.'[78] For everyone else, it was just beginning.

Now, the sailors had to put the soldiers ashore.

✳ 8 ✳
Into the Fire: The Americans at Utah and Omaha
H-Hour 0630, 6 June 1944

The supporting destroyers and gun support craft stood in close inshore during the period of fiercest fighting on the beach and rendered great support to the troops.

Admiral Sir Bertram Ramsay[1]

In each assault area, the action began in similar fashion. Miles offshore, battleships and cruisers pounded the German defences as the assault troops climbed precariously down the sides of their landing ships on scrambling nets and boarded their assault craft or, in some fortunate cases, climbed in from the ship's deck and were swung into the water using davits. The assault craft circled offshore until each was in position and then made for the beaches, joining up with larger LCIs and LCTs, which made their own way over. As they approached, destroyers and support landing craft braved German shellfire to fire their final rounds of drenching fire just before the assault waves landed, in theory allowing the soldiers to cross what must have appeared to be a vast expanse of exposed beach before the stunned German defenders could recover.

However, as each beachhead battle unfolded, they started to take on very different characteristics. Ramsay wrote of the assault that 'in every main essential the plan was carried out as written'.[2] The British Naval Staff History went further, describing it as 'easier than expected' but continued 'it would be a great mistake to suppose on that account

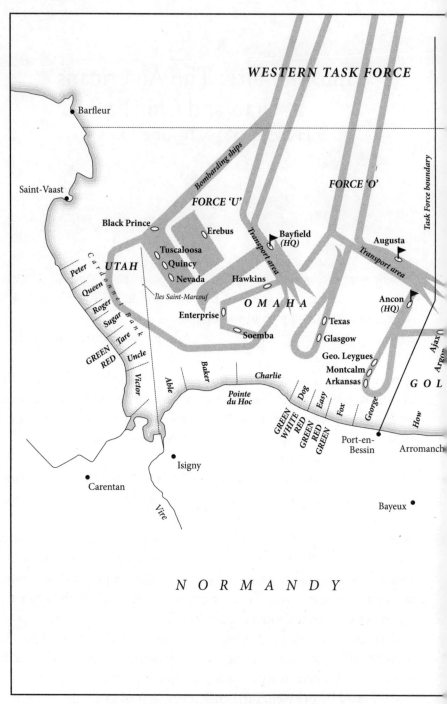

WESTERN TASK FORCE

Barfleur

Saint-Vaast

Bombarding ships

FORCE 'U'

FORCE 'O'

Black Prince

Erebus

Transport area

Bayfield
(HQ)

Augusta

Task Force boundary

Peter

Cardonnet Bank

UTAH

Tuscaloosa

Quincy

Nevada

Hawkins

Transport area

Ancon
(HQ)

Queen

Roger

Îles Saint-Marcouf

OMAHA

Sugar

Tare

Enterprise

Texas

GREEN

RED

Uncle

Soemba

Glasgow

Geo. Leygues

Ajax

Victor

Montcalm

Argo

Able

Baker

Charlie

Arkansas

GOL

Dog

Easy

Fox

George

How

Pointe
du Hoc

GREEN

WHITE

RED

GREEN

RED

GREEN

Port-en-
Bessin

Arromanch

Isigny

Bayeux

Carentan

Vire

N O R M A N D Y

Map 5. Beaches and bombardment areas.

EASTERN TASK FORCE

English Channel

Northern limit of assault area

FORCE 'G'   FORCE 'J'   FORCE 'S'

Bombarding ships

Le Havre

◗ Warspite

◗ Ramillies

Seine

◗ Roberts

Lowering positions

Lowering positions

◗ Flores
◗ Belfast
◗ Diadem

▶ *Lowering Position*

▶ ◗ Mauritius

Largs (HQ)

▶

Hilary (HQ)

Scylla
Danae ◗ ◗ Dragon
Frobisher

◗ Arethusa

J U N O

S W O R D

B A N D

• Trouville

King
Love
Mike
Nan
Oboe
Peter
Queen
Roger

GREEN
GREEN
RED
GREEN
WHITE
RED
GREEN
WHITE
RED
GREEN
WHITE
RED

• Ouistreham
Cabourg •

Caen Canal
Orne

Caen

| 0 | | | | 10 miles |
| 0 | | 10km | | |

that the assaults were easy or unopposed landings ... [the landings] called for endurance and seamanship of the highest order in the handling of the landing craft'.[3] 'Easier' does not mean 'easy'. Driving a landing craft on to any beach in Normandy on 6 June was exhausting, stressful and dangerous for all: for some sailors it ended with life-changing injuries, and for others it proved fatal.

There is only space here to give a flavour of the huge range of experiences which made up D-Day for sailors, taking each assault area in turn and beginning with Utah, in the west, the earliest H-Hour. 'Almost complete surprise appeared to be achieved in this sector', wrote Ramsay, 'assault waves were generally landed on time and against only slight enemy opposition.'[4] The Naval Staff History went further, referring to the 'comparative feebleness of the enemy opposition'.[5]

Compared to what happened elsewhere this was perhaps true, but Utah was no pushover. The assault actually began two hours before H-Hour, when a small US force occupied the Îles Saint-Marcouf, two tiny islands which were strategically placed 4 miles offshore on the flanks of the approaches to Utah and were believed to be occupied. In the event, no Germans were there and the islands were taken without fighting, although not without loss, as a number of GIs became casualties to mines.

The bombardment was supposed to open at H-40, with the battleship *Nevada*, four cruisers and the Dutch gunboat *Soemba* firing from 10,000m at their pre-assigned batteries and strongpoints and the cruiser HMS *Enterprise* and the destroyers drenching the beaches at the same time from 4,500m out, supported by the secondary batteries of *Nevada* and the US cruiser *Quincy*. Ten minutes before H-Hour, *Nevada* and *Quincy* would turn their big guns on to the beaches as well, then the accompanying LCT(R)s would discharge 5,000 rockets. Following a black smoke rocket fired by the commander of the first wave of landing craft, all ships would shift fire to the flanks.[6]

Allied planners estimated that there were twenty-eight German gun batteries threatening Utah, mounting 111 guns.[7] The most formidable was *Stützpunkt* (strongpoint) *135*, or *Marineküstenbatterie*

'Marcouf', a heavy naval battery sited inland near the village of Saint-Marcouf. *StP135* was armed with three powerful Czech 210mm siege guns, two enclosed in casemates, and a host of smaller guns. It was commanded by Oberleutnant-zur-See Walter Ohmsen, a decorated veteran who had joined the pre-Nazi Reichsmarine in April 1933 and worked his way up from the ranks. Ohmsen would turn 33 on 7 June 1944.[8] He and several other battery commanders pre-empted the carefully crafted Allied plan by opening fire on the invasion force at 0505, targeting the destroyers *Fitch* and *Corry*, and then the minesweepers. HMS *Black Prince* replied, the situation was in danger of spinning out of control, and so Admiral Deyo opted to bring his bombardment forward: at 0536, Force A opened fire.

At 0610, aircraft were supposed to lay smoke to screen the bombarding ships from flanking fire but the aircraft allocated to screen *Corry* was shot down; as the destroyer closed the beach, still accompanied by *Fitch*, both ships were fatally exposed and *Corry* came under further heavy, accurate fire. Violently manoeuvring at high speed in restricted waters, at 0633 the destroyer was torn apart by a huge explosion which flooded the engine rooms, fractured the keel and broke the ship in two across the main deck. Despite this, according to the commanding officer, Lieutenant-Commander George Hoffman, 'we tried to get her out by calling for flank speed but all power was lost and the ship started going in a high-speed circle because just prior to being hit, we had given full right rudder [and] increased speed'.[9]

Corry gradually slowed, water sluicing over the upper decks, and Hoffman launched his boats at 0637, signalling 'this ship needs help'. Just two minutes later it became clear that his ship could not be saved, so he ordered his men to abandon ship and, as German shells continued to fall around the stricken destroyer, stepped off into the water.[10] German gunners continued to shell the wreck for another hour and a half, apparently because *Corry* had sunk in shallow water and they still believed the ship was afloat, an illusion which one courageous but sadly unidentified sailor helped maintain by returning to the wreck, salvaging the ensign and tying it to the main mast. *Fitch* and another destroyer, USS *Hobson*, suppressed the batteries for two hours before they felt able to stop safely and rescue survivors. Ten members of *Corry*'s ship's company were killed and fourteen injured; dozens more were pulled from the water suffering from severe shock and exposure.[11]

Hoffman's initial report and a radio interview he gave to the CBS reporter Ed Murrow made it clear that his ship was struck by two heavy projectiles, pointing the finger clearly at Ohmsen's battery, and Ohmsen himself was awarded the Knight's Cross for sinking what was initially believed to be a cruiser.[12] This was borne out by reports from *Fitch* and the War Diary of Konteradmiral Walter Hennecke, in charge of German coastal defences in Normandy, but for some reason later reports attributed the explosion to a mine, and this was how the loss was recorded by the US Navy's official historian.[13]

Retribution was not long in coming, one of the 210mm guns at Saint-Marcouf apparently being put out of action by a 15-inch (380mm) shell from the monitor HMS *Erebus*, which according to the ship's log stopped at its firing point 7 miles off La Pointe de Saire at 0628, fired four rounds at its first target at 0635, shifted berth and fired another eleven rounds at 0745, and then another fifteen at 0855.[14]

Underneath the bombardment the young, hastily trained graduates of HMS *Lochailort* and the ATB at Solomons Island drove their tiny, flimsy landing craft full of seasick soldiers onto the beaches. For all the efforts of the bombarding warships to suppress the defenders, the experience was still terrifying, and deadly. Force U landed a single RCT on a two battalion front across Tare Green and Uncle Red beaches. The first two waves comprised assault infantry and DD tanks accompanied by conventional tanks in LCT(A), NCDUs and Army combat engineers.

The most significant setback at Utah turned out to be a blessing in disguise. As at Omaha, each beach was assigned a US Navy Patrol Craft (PC) as primary control vessel, with a radar-equipped Landing Craft Control as back up, to guide in the waves of landing craft. As the assault forces ran in, they crossed the Cardonnet bank, an area of shallow water just south of the Îles Saint-Marcouf and about 7,000m offshore, which had been mined. One of the support landing craft, *LCF-31*, either struck a mine or was hit by a shell and sank. Another shell then struck Lieutenant Rency Sewell's *PC-1261*, the control vessel for Red Beach, in the starboard side amidships, and the little vessel immediately took on a serious list, water sluicing over the fantail. At first Sewell, a former telephone engineer from Atlanta, tried to save his stricken ship, but two minutes later, *1261* rolled over 90 degrees: 'the order was given to abandon ship', Sewell reported, 'and all hands walked over the side as though you would walk over a treadmill'. The shocked and freezing sailors made for the life rafts, watching and some even finding the energy to cheer as the assault waves swept by. They remained there for three hours, many succumbing to the cold and their injuries; in the event, twenty-two of the crew of sixty-five were killed, posted missing or died of their wounds.[15] Mines also claimed three LCTs, including *LCT-597*, which was carrying four DD tanks.

The call went out for the back-up control boat, *LCC-80*, but the landing craft had fouled its propeller on a Dan Buoy and could not reach the beach. With no control boats available and the shoreline obscured by smoke and haze, the assault waves drifted off to the left and eventually landed just under 2,000m south-east of their intended landing area, famously prompting Brigadier-General Theodore Roosevelt, deputy commander of the 4th Division, to leap ashore, briefly survey the area, and proclaim 'we'll start the war from right here!'[16]

Twenty landing craft from the first wave touched down precisely at H-Hour, the assault infantry faced with a 100-yard wade but very little surf or opposing fire. Twenty-eight DD tanks got ashore, although twenty minutes later than planned. Eleven NCDUs landed and immediately started work blowing up obstacles, clearing 640m of beach by 0800 and another 800 in the afternoon.[17] Their work was not without incident. Gunners Mate First Class Jackson 'Tex' Modesett was part of an NCDU: after 'the worst boat ride I ever had' they landed under fire and prepared their first obstacle for demolition. Modesett ran back to grab a smoke grenade to warn the troops of the imminent explosion, he got about 30m down the beach when a shell landed in the middle of his comrades. Two men were literally blown to pieces, and the remainder catastrophically wounded:

I saw a couple of tops of human heads lying in the sand a few yards apart and almost a whole backbone with all the flesh and ribs torn away from it . . . Janowicz was dying with a hole as big as your fist in the left side of his chest. He only lived about five minutes.[18]

Above their heads, the bombarding warships continued to pound the German coastal batteries. *Erebus* fired what would turn out to be the monitor's final ten rounds at 1340. The relentless shock of repeated bombardments was hard on all ships, but especially the older ones, and *Erebus* had been launched in 1916, before the Battle of Jutland. At 1643 the monitor fired the first round of its next shoot, and the shell promptly exploded in the barrel of the right gun, splitting it down the middle.[19] 31-year-old Lieutenant Alan Miller was on the bridge at the time. 'When the gun fired', he recalled, 'I saw the shell come out in pieces and it had just disintegrated . . . [the barrel] tilted up in its turret . . . it was realised that the right gun was off its trunnions and the captain daren't fire the left gun because it would very likely have caused the right gun just to drop and it would have gone right through the bottom of the ship.'[20]

Erebus was towed out of the anchorage, a precaution against mines, and returned to Plymouth, where the remnants of the gun were removed on 20 June, which 'took thirty-six hours of continuous oxyacetylene cutting to get through the various layers that made up the gun barrel at the breech end'.[21] It really didn't matter. *Erebus* and the other bombarding ships had already made their contribution. If Utah really was 'easier' than other assault areas, this was due in no small part to 'abundant and accurate naval gunfire support'. USS *Nevada* alone fired 337 rounds of 14-inch (355mm) and 2,693 rounds of 5-inch (127mm) on 6 June.[22]

Captain James Arnold, Naval Officer in Charge (NOIC) for Utah, came ashore under fire and scraped himself a fox hole, before moving his command post to a former German strongpoint later in the afternoon. 'Plans were discussed in the candlelighted dugout', he remembered, 'where mooring charts and landing diagrams with their overlays were placed upon the bulkheads of the concrete stronghold

... at least two of the "master race" still lay sprawled on the steps leading down into the shelter ... they were awfully dead.'[23]

Once he was organised, Arnold jumped into an LCVP and reported to Moon aboard the attack transport USS *Bayfield*. 'He ... directed me to assume the duties of NOIC Utah at once', so Arnold returned to the beach to start establishing supply dumps and unloading transports in swift succession, all the while 'surrounded by milling army officers' anxious to get on with the war. Such was the life of an NOIC. Arnold managed the expectations of needy generals, while his staff methodically brought their commands ashore, and the 4th Division raced inland.[24]

By early afternoon the 4th Division had penetrated 6 miles and linked up with the paratroops of the 101st Airborne Division, for a cost of only 197 casualties, far fewer than those lost in Force U's principal rehearsal, Exercise Tiger.

This was not the case at Omaha.

Omaha: H-Hour 0630

More has been written about Omaha over the years than perhaps any other aspect of Neptune/Overlord. Its story has been told and retold in documentaries and in works of fiction, notably Spielberg's epic *Saving Private Ryan*. The almost total absence of sailors from these popular narratives is hard to justify. Omaha was undoubtedly saved from becoming a disaster by the determination of ordinary GIs and the inspiring leadership of their officers, but it was also saved by the courage and professionalism of US and British sailors. Naval bombardment was instrumental in ensuring Omaha was ultimately won.

The challenges at Omaha can be easily summarised. The beach was wide, exposed and backed by steep, thirty metre high sloping features referred to as 'bluffs', from which the defending Germans could pour down fire. The obvious exits were via five steep ravines which the Americans called 'draws', through four of which tracks or roads led up the bluffs to one of four villages: Vierville, Saint-Laurent, Colleville and Saint-Honorine-des-Pertes. These exits were equally obvious to the Germans and were heavily defended. The beach was thickly sown with obstacles, the German defenders had recently been reinforced with additional troops, and there were fourteen strongpoints, all constructed together as a coherent, interlocking defence system.[25] On the day, the assault landing craft carrying troops from the US 1st and 29th Infantry Divisions and their supporting elements were dropped 11 miles offshore, mainly to keep out of range of a partially completed German heavy coastal battery, *WN75*, to the west of Omaha and outside the assault area on top of the cliffs at Pointe du Hoc. Omaha suffered from an overly complex landing plan whose successes 'depended on every boat's beaching within fifty yards of the right spot ... too much to expect of landing craft sailors who had eleven miles of rough seas to cover before hitting the beach', and the assault troops were badly scattered by the time they arrived.[26] Finally, the weather remained marginal at best, with rough seas adding to the disruption of the assault forces, and the preliminary air bombardment failed dramatically. Heavy cloud meant more than a quarter of the attacking aircraft brought their bomb loads home because they could not see the target, and the remainder, bombing blind, delayed their drops by thirty seconds to avoid any chance of 'friendly fire' and bombed miles inland: 'soldiers and sailors alike watched the beach in amazement as H-Hour drew near and they saw no bombs exploding'.[27] The assaulting troops at Omaha arguably needed naval gunfire more than anyone else on D-Day.

As in other sectors, there were three phases to the naval bombardment at Omaha beginning with pre-planned shelling of assigned targets by Admiral Carleton Bryant's battleships and cruisers in advance of the landing, after which Admiral Hall's eleven British and US destroyers would close the shore to fire on beach front strongpoints, and then rocket landing craft and embarked artillery would drench the beach in the final minutes before H-Hour, scheduled for 0630. The Germans opened fire first, a light gun near Port-en-Bessin dropping a shell near the battleship *Arkansas* at 0530, but otherwise the planned bombardment went according to plan, Bryant recording how it was 'a noisy time and *awesome*' aboard his flagship *Texas*, which began to methodically pound the battery at Pointe du Hoc at 0550.[28] This was in preparation for an assault by US Army Rangers, who would have to climb the cliffs using grappling hooks and extendable ladders, commandeered from the London Fire Brigade and mounted in Ducks.

Felix Lloyd-Davies, Executive Officer of HMS *Glasgow*, remembered Bryant instructing the British cruiser to take the head of the line, a significant honour paid by the Americans to their allies. 'As we steamed down the line the padre said to me "shouldn't we say a prayer?"', he recalled. The Chaplain's words burst from the cruiser's main broadcast system just as *Glasgow* passed *Texas* and as Lloyd-Davies watched, the US Navy gunners at their action stations solemnly removed their helmets. Soon afterwards, the fire gongs rang out and the cruiser let fly her first salvoes: 'at long last the battle had started'.[29]

For the men aboard the Free French cruisers in Bryant's command it was a strange time. 'You may well imagine what emotion was aroused when we were ordered to bombard our homeland', Contreamiral Robert Jaujard wrote to the US Navy's Official Historian after the war, 'but it was part of the price we had to pay for defeat in 1940.'[30] Kenneth Howe, a 21-year-old Royal Navy Telegraphist from County Durham, was aboard the FFS *Georges Leygues* as part of a ten-man RN liaison team, and remembered the cruiser 'flying a very large tricolor French flag which they said was for morale purposes. I could never understand whose morale', he went on, 'because the French crew weren't particularly enchanted by it! It turned out it was for the morale of the people ashore.'[31]

Closer inshore, the destroyers blazed away, USS *Satterlee* and HMS *Talybont* firing on defences flanking Pointe du Hoc, and USS *Thompson* pummelling strongpoints on Pointe de la Percée, at the extreme western end of the assault area, with 163 5-inch (127mm) shells. Other destroyers, LCGs, and the secondary batteries on the battleships started to 'work over' German defences in the draws.[32] Finally, as the assault craft made their way in, the drenching fire began, 6,000 rockets flying towards France from US-manned LCT(R)s. Captain Lorenzo Sabin, commanding the 11th Amphibious Force's gunfire support craft and the close gunfire support group at Omaha, noted grimly that although the rocket fire was a significant morale boost for the assault troops, 'it was the last morale boost those troops, boat coxswains and beach personnel were going to get for hours, for the enemy finally let us know that he knew we were there, and that if we wanted Omaha Beach, we were going to have to pay for it'.[33]

The problem at Omaha was that the preliminary bombardment was just not long enough. The US Army had insisted, against naval advice, that the shelling not begin until after daybreak, which allowed just thirty-five minutes of bombardment before H-Hour.[34] As the warships lifted their fire and the landing craft hit the beach even Bryant, circling several kilometres off the beach in *Texas*, could see things were going badly: 'We knew instinctively that something was wrong', he recalled, 'the beach was a most alarming sight. Tanks were burning, ships were burning, and every so often a larger explosion would indicate a hit on an ammunition dump.'[35]

Assault Group O1, commanded by Captain Edward Fritzsche of the United States Coast Guard, landed the 16th Regimental Combat Team of the veteran 1st Infantry Division, the famous 'Big Red One', so named because of their divisional insignia, to the east on beaches Easy Red and Fox Green. To their west, the 116th RCT of the green 29th Infantry Division were landed by O2 (Captain Watson Bailey, USN) across Easy Green, and Dog Red, White and Green, supported by nine companies of Rangers from the 2nd and 5th Battalions; O3 and O4 would be bringing in the reserves, the 115th RCT from the 29th Division and the 18th RCT from the 1st.

Some 3½ miles west of Omaha, three companies of Rangers had been detailed to assault *WN75*, the battery at Pointe du Hoc, but arrived thirty-five minutes late because of a navigation error on the part of the RN Fairmile B, *ML-304*, which was leading them in. One LCA foundered with the loss of all aboard, two DUKWs were lost, and the ex-London Fire Brigade ladders they carried were unusable in the heavy swell; worse still, the German defenders had now recovered from the effects of the barrage and were on the cliff edge, firing and tossing down grenades. Supporting fire from the destroyer USS *Satterlee*, *ML-304* and a pair of RN support landing craft, *LCS-91* and *LCS-102*, cleared the cliff edge, then the Rangers managed to deploy their ropes and grappling hooks and ascend, only to find the battery empty as the guns had been moved back as a precaution against air attack. Isolated but supported by sustained and effective naval gunfire, and reinforced and resupplied from the sea, the Rangers defended their perimeter against repeated counterattacks until 8 June.

The main body of Force O crossed the Channel with almost no difficulty, but the problems started as soon as the assault troops started to board, Hall writing after the war that:

> The weather at this time was unfavourable . . . the sea was choppy with wind Force 5 from the south-west. The sky was partially overcast with visibility about ten miles. Due to the wind and sea, debarkation from transports into LCVPs was difficult . . . the trip of the LCVPs from the Transport Area ten miles off shore into the line of departure in the face of fresh wind and choppy sea was neither easy nor pleasant. Nevertheless, they arrived at the line of departure in fairly good order.[36]

The landing craft had a journey of more than 16km inshore from the transport area before they began to circle about 4,000m from the beach at the 'Line of Departure', marked by lines of small Submarine Chasers and Patrol Craft. Richard Crook was the executive officer of *PC-553*, off Easy Red at Omaha. 'They needed traffic cops to mark the route', he recalled, 'we had British QH gear installed . . . [which] was able to pick up radio signals that gave us lines of position. When we plotted the intersection of those lines, we had a navigation fix. So, we knew within fifty to one hundred yards where we were.'[37] *PC-553* flew a letter E signal flag and a red flag.

When everyone was assembled, the order to go was given, with the planned order of landing being: DD tanks between H-10 and H-5, LCT(A) carrying conventional tanks and armoured bulldozers for obstacle clearance at H-Hour; the first wave of infantry at H+1 and the NCDUs and military Combat Engineers at H+3.[38] Unfortunately these careful timings began to unravel almost immediately. The DD tanks were divided into two groups. Those in O2 heading for the western sector were landed directly on the beach, as the senior naval officer, Lieutenant Dean Rockwell, assessed the weather conditions and rightly concluded that the weather was too rough for the fragile DDs. After conferring with his Army opposite number, he made the call:

> I was the one responsible for making the decision ... naval regulations dictated that the senior naval commander was responsible for them until they went either into the water or on to the shore. Fortunately [he] agreed ... but if he had insisted on following the orders to launch offshore, we would have gone on to the beach anyway.[39]

Under heavy fire, Rockwell slowed to avoid landing too early, then ran in for the last 4,500m and beached alongside the LCTs carrying the conventional armour at H-Hour. Two LCTs were hit, taking casualties, but 'we lowered our bow ramp and the four tanks rolled off directly onto France ... the other seven LCTs in my group off-loaded their tanks within thirty seconds'.[40]

Unfortunately, in the eastern sector the DDs launched as planned, according to some accounts because the senior Army officer over-ruled the sailor, Lieutenant (jg) John Barry.[41] Most of the vehicles sank like stones, some immediately after launching. Only two made the crossing; three more survived because Ensign Henry Sullivan in *LCT-600* watched his first tank sink, pulled up his ramp on his own initiative, and landed them on the beach.[42] The DDs had been instructed to make for the steeple of Colleville church, and recent archaeological investigation of the wrecks suggest this is what they did. This meant that after launching in a line, most of the clumsy vehicles altered course, broached and were swamped. Average losses were one crewman per tank, most of the rest escaping exactly as they had practised in training.[43] Hall called the Army decision 'unsound' and went on to write that Barry 'acquiesced ... by his failure to take action to change the order', a brutal judgement on a young officer trying to deal with a very challenging situation, but an accurate one: at sea on 6 June 1944, the sailors were intended to be in command.[44]

As the DD tanks floundered, the US LCVPs and British LCAs carrying the assaulting infantry ran in past them. Richard Crook, the 'traffic cop', watched helplessly as many gradually veered off course as they passed *PC-553*, carried away by the strong current and then distracted by enemy fire. The SCs and the PCs were assigned to their roles as control vessels late in the day. They had no experience working with the landing craft crews, missed the big rehearsal exercises, and were not even in radio contact with them on the day. 'We didn't really see the LCVPs for all that long', Crook remembered, 'they quickly disappeared into the smoke and haze.'[45]

The assault craft beached on time, but were hopelessly confused thanks to the poor weather, with companies landing on the wrong part of their beach, or on the wrong beach entirely; only two out of eight were where they were supposed to be.[46] Many landing craft were smashed by shellfire or wrecked on obstacles. The experience of three ships from the Coast Guard's LCI(L) Division 58 gives some sense of the experience. Lieutenant (jg) Arand Vyn brought *LCI-91* into Dog White at 0740, landed over half of his troops, then moved his ship forward because of the rapidly rising tide. Detonating one mine as he retracted, Vyn then made a second beaching, and was starting to land his remaining sixty soldiers when a huge explosion ripped through the forepart and his ship burst into flames; unable to control the blaze, he ordered his men to abandon ship. Half an hour later *LCI-92* landed alongside, Lieutenant Robert Salmon trying to conceal his ship behind the smoke from its burning sister, but was devastated by a similarly catastrophic explosion and also caught fire; both ships burned for hours. *LCI-94* was hit three times in the pilot house just after the celebrated *Life Magazine* photographer Robert Capa came aboard, returning from the beach to get dry. Motor Machinist's Mate Clifford Lewis recalled 'a horrible sight with blood and flesh scattered over everything. [Seaman Jack] De Nunzio had both his legs blown off and part of his stomach but was still living. I helped the doc give him plasma but it was hopeless. He died fifteen minutes later. [Seaman August] Buncik was decapitated and only occupied half a stretcher. [Seaman Fletcher] Burton was still intact but was killed by the concussion.'[47]

Most of the unfortunate soldiers had to disembark into over a metre of water, then wade up to a hundred metres and run across the open beach all under heavy fire. Casualties were appalling, particularly among the officers and NCOs who were usually first off the landing craft. 19-year-old Royal Navy Sub-Lieutenant John Gaskin remembered that:

> We were under fire all the time ... it was torture watching the boys cut down from the top of the cliffs and not being able to do a thing to help them ... When I was seconded to the US Navy, I was pretty unhappy about it, but after a short time with the Americans I felt like an honorary Yank. They were all brave men.[48]

The presence of hundreds of British landing craft crews at Omaha Beach is often overlooked, particularly by American writers and film makers. Jimmy Green took Taylor Fellers and his 'Bedford Boys' from the 116th into the maelstrom of Dog Green. The landing was challenging from the outset, *LCA-911* fouling Green's own boat, *LCA-910*, during the process of lowering from the LCI *Empire Javelin*, and then slowly sinking on the way in. 'All the crew and soldiers had life jackets and I could only hope they would keep everyone afloat until I returned', Green remembered; 'it goes against the grain for a sailor to leave his comrades in the sea, but *LCA-910* had no room and our orders were explicit that we were to leave survivors in the sea to be picked up later.'[49]

Nearing the shore, Green started to notice the German defences and then watched in dismay as the rocket landing craft dropped their barrage 'woefully short'. Shortly afterwards he noticed that there were no craters from the preceding aerial bombardment, either. Shaking his fist in rage and frustration, Green formed his flotilla into a line abreast and ordered his crew to take cover as the LCAs made their final run to the beach, an LCG firing over their heads at a pillbox in the Vierville Draw. An LCA on the left flank was hit by an anti-tank round, the missile passing right through from one side to the other and badly wounding a GI on the way:

Now we were alone, at the right beach at the right time. Taylor Fellers wanted to be landed to the right of the pass and the other three boats in the port column just to the left of the pass. We went flat out and crunched to a halt some twenty or thirty yards from the shore line. The beach was so flat that we couldn't go any further so the troops had to go in single file up to their waists in water and wade to the shore through tidal runnels. Taylor Fellers was gone as soon as the ramp was lowered, before I could wish him luck, followed by the middle file, then the port file and the starboard file as practised and in good order. They all made the beach safely and formed a firing line at a slight rise.[50]

Green landed Company A in a lull; other than the occasional mortar round dropping in the sea and the irritating anti-tank gun, there was very little fire. After collecting some stranded sailors from other landing craft, Green retracted *LCA-910* from the beach, 'sent a signal to the effect of "Landed against light opposition"', and headed back out to collect the shipwrecked crew and passengers from *911*.[51] Returning to the LCI, Green handed over his survivors. The German defenders came to life soon after his departure: Captain Taylor Fellers and 102 men from Company A, 1st Battalion, 116th Infantry Regiment, died on Dog Green, including nineteen young men from Bedford, Virginia; 'in a matter of minutes', the British author Alex Kershaw has written, 'a couple of German machine-gunners had broken the town's heart'.[52]

20-year-old Sub-Lieutenant Hilaire Benbow, an ex-clerk from Balham who had been commissioned under the CW scheme, landed Rangers on Dog Green from the LSI *Prince Charles*, another ex-Belgian ferry. He ran them in through rough seas, the seasick GIs bailing out with their steel helmets to keep his LCA afloat:

The craft on my port side hit one of these poles with a mine on the top ... in a twinkling of an eye I looked to my left side and there were all these bodies like statues in a shop window in various poses, they were jet black, on ... what was left of the bows of this landing craft. It must have been one of the craft from our ship but

I never quite worked out who it was. I didn't really know the names of the fellows; I'd only been on that ship about six days.[53]

Benbow grounded on a sandbar, and as the Rangers rushed ashore, the bow tilted into the sea and water swept along the troop deck into the tiny engine room, flooding the machinery. With his little craft helpless, Benbow took his crew over the side into the water, under a hail of mortar and machine gun fire. The sailors spent an hour up to their necks in cold water before struggling ashore and digging out shallow scrapes in the shingle under a grassy bank, gratefully accepting food from the GIs who were sharing their refuge.[54]

From Benbow's perspective it felt like 'the whole invasion had failed, and I was going to be a prisoner of war'. Crouched in the dirt, barefoot as he had lost his boots in the water, he watched as the carnage unfolded around him. 'The day dragged on and I saw some very badly wounded men', he recalled:

I saw a chap with his chin just off staggering along, he was an officer and he had no chin . . . I couldn't spend the day on shingle in bare feet so because there was a lull I crawled back to the water's edge and there was literally a wall, about two foot I'd say, of dead bodies all along the surf line.

Steeling himself, he recovered a pair of boots and put them on, then found another pair for one of his young seamen.[55]

The strong German resistance in the draws meant that the assault troops piled up on the beaches, sheltering under a concrete sea wall at the foot of the bluffs or hiding behind obstacles. Sailors detailed ashore were caught up in the maelstrom. The NCDU plan was a fiasco and casualties in the demolition parties were appalling: 52 per cent of them were killed, wounded or missing.[56] Those who made it ashore were often lost, and without much of their equipment. The rising tide covered the obstacles before much could be achieved. Chief Aviation Ordnanceman Loran Barbour was about to fire the charges set by his team when a German shell detonated one of the packs: it killed five sailors and wounded the rest, including Barbour, along with fifteen Army engineers.[57] Only five poorly marked gaps through the obstacles were cleared. Orval Wakefield was there with NCDU 132 and described the chaos, as he tried to attach explosives to the beach obstacles: 'Soldiers of the first wave were coming in ... dodging around us and sometimes taking cover behind those giant pretzels ... we had to keep chasing the GIs away because they didn't realise how hazardous those obstacles had become.'[58]

Wakefield at least managed to destroy some obstacles. Signalman Paul Fauks was part of the US Navy's 7th Beach Battalion, and really could not do his job at all:

I thought I had a pretty good idea what I was supposed to do on the beach ... but once I got there it was turmoil ... my only job at that point was trying to stay alive ... I was terribly frightened. I joined the men with me in digging a hole in the sand and that was it ... for the remainder of 6 June and probably a good part of the next day as well, I don't remember getting out of that hole.[59]

Without the Beach Battalions to bring order, the chaos spread out to sea. Eventually the landing craft started milling around offshore, circling either under orders or on the initiative of individual coxswains because there was no room to land. 'This soon resulted in a mass of craft in which all semblance of wave organization was lost, until the Deputy Assault Group Commanders arrived on the scene, took charge of the situation, moved the craft to seaward to give them more room, and reformed the waves as best they could.'[60] Ramsay under-statedly wrote that 'the order of landing was somewhat mixed'.[61]

The situation remained touch and go all morning, and at one point Bradley seriously considered shutting Omaha down and diverting subsequent forces to Utah and the British beaches.[62] Hilaire Benbow was still stranded on the beach, making his way slowly along the shore:

One quite large ship had somehow been beached and grounded, bows on to the beach ... and we came around the bows and that was a shock because all these ... stretcher cases [were] laid out in the shelter of this great ship ... that sort of brought you up with a shudder. All these lorries were being landed and they couldn't get off the beach, whole packs of lorries with canvas covers and of course the fire from the Germans set them alight, and the flames spread from one lorry to the other and there were whole packs of lorries burning away, black smoke ... the beach was very smoky.[63]

Eventually, having collected sixteen stranded British sailors, Benbow managed to hitch a ride offshore on an American LCT, they were transferred to a troopship and taken to Tilbury, where they were debriefed. He finally found his way back to the *Prince Charles* ten days later.

At 0800, destroyer skippers began to take action on their own initiative to fire on targets of opportunity and break the deadlock.[64] Lieutenant-Commander Edgar Powell's USS *Baldwin* began a brutal duel with a German battery to the east of Port-en-Bessin, on the eastern edge of the assault area. The German gunners hit the destroyer twice at 0820, smashing the port whaleboat, blowing a huge hole in the main deck, and riddling the ship with splinter holes, though miraculously nobody aboard was hurt. Two minutes later Powell's command struck back, battering the enemy gun position with 5-inch (127mm) guns and 40mm Bofors until 0839, by which point the German gunners had ceased firing, and *Baldwin* 'resumed lookout for targets of opportunity'.[65]

At 0900, Captain Harry Sanders, commanding the US Navy's Destroyer Squadron 18 and a veteran of landings at Salerno and Anzio, ordered all his destroyers to move in to support the troops; fifty minutes later Bryant called all the gunfire support ships over the TBS exhorting them to 'Get on them men! Get on them! They are raising hell with the men on the beach and we can't have any more of that. We must stop it!'[66]

Gradually the warships turned the tide. Initially they were severely hampered by the absence of their Shore Fire Control Parties (SFCPs), who at first were caught up in the general chaos on the beaches, struggling ashore under heavy fire and taking casualties, their radios in some cases wrecked by the water. Lieutenant (jg) Coit Coker commanded SFCP No. 3. Scheduled for the third wave, because of the backlog on the beaches his first section, the Forward Observer Group, came ashore with the first wave, under heavy fire. '[Technician 5th Grade Burt] Krogstad and [Private William] Holmes were hit while still in the water', he wrote a few days after the assault, 'Krogstad succumbing after the fifth bullet wound. Holmes received two hits in the leg and one in the abdomen; though seriously wounded he managed to crawl onto the beach ... Captain [John] Easter received a bullet in the hip as he attempted to drag Krogstad out of the water. [Sergeant Beverley] Wren was killed while attempting to cross the beach.'[67]

Coker himself came ashore with the second section at about 0740, a mile east of their allocated landing position. The ramp of their LCVP stuck, two soldiers of 1st Battalion, 116th RCT, getting stuck and a third getting his leg crushed between their craft and the one alongside. Despite these challenges, remarkably Coker and his men 'jumped over the side, swam to shallow water and made it across the beach ... with neither casualties nor loss of vital equipment'. By 0830 they had their SCR 609 radio working and had made contact with the destroyer USS *McCook*, but 'the beach situation at that time was so obscure and confused that it was unwise to designate a target'.[68]

The frustration was repeated everywhere. 'It was most galling and depressing', wrote Commander William Marshall, CO of Destroyer Division 36 in USS *Satterlee*, in his after action report, 'to lie idly a few hundred yards off the beaches and watch our troops ... being heavily shelled and not be able to fire a shot to help them just because we had no information on what to shoot at.'[69] *Satterlee*, supporting the Rangers at Pointe du Hoc, was actually the exception, as their SFCP established contact by signal lamp at 0728, and this continued excellent fire control allowed the destroyer to help repel a series of German counterattacks, enabling the Rangers to hold their ground.[70]

Elsewhere, the destroyer skippers improvised. USS *Carmick* relied on friendly troops acting as improvised spotters, watching for them firing repeatedly on certain spots as they struggled painstakingly up the Vierville Draw, and then hitting the same areas with devastating effect. USS *Emmons* acted as a spotter for *Arkansas*, directing the battleship's 12-inch (304mm) fire on to the troublesome battery east of Port-en-Bessin, which had come back to life shortly after noon.[71]

Air spotters and additional SFCPs began to function effectively after 1300, dramatically improving the precision of the naval gunnery. The warships began to focus their attention on the German defences in the draws, blasting ahead of the troops as they worked their way off the beach. Coit Coker worked his way up the Vierville Draw, codenamed Dog-1, with soldiers from the 116th RCT, calling in fire from *McCook* as the fighting opened out on the plateau above which was so heavy and accurate it eventually prompted a group of German soldiers to stagger from their bunker waving a white flag. Even the battleships got in on the act, Bryant bringing his flagship *Texas* in close between 1223 and 1230 to slam six 14-inch (355mm) shells into the Vierville Draw.[72]

Commander Robert Beer of USS *Carmick* gives a flavour of just how tricky it was working with observers ashore in the confused circumstances which prevailed at Omaha. At 1710, his SFCP asked for help dealing with a strongpoint in exit Easy-1, the Saint-Laurent Draw. 'Considerable time was lost because the target ... was in an area believed to be occupied by our own troops', Beer wrote; 'the ship opened fire shortly afterwards after the SFCP had repeated the target coordinates twice. Repeated spots ... were given.'

> The SFCP said finally that they could not see the target clearly and they were more or less guessing with regard to the spots. The ship was able to fire on the target directly and the SFCP furnished ... an accurate description of it. After a few salvoes of direct fire ... rapid fire was requested and delivered for two minutes. Cease fire was given by the SFCP and they signalled that they were closing down and moving forward.[73]

By 1100 determined bands of soldiers had managed to work their way up the bluffs, and reports started to come in that the German defenders were surrendering. Colleville fell at 1300, and half an hour later a general advance up from Easy Red and Fox Green began. Although the perimeter at Omaha was perilously shallow, and the area was still under accurate artillery fire, the first follow-up, Commodore Campbell Edgar's Force B, arrived at 1430 and began to unload from about 1630, assisted by whatever battered minor landing craft remained from the assault.

General Clarence Huebner, commanding 1st Infantry Division, and Major General Charles Gerhardt, commanding the 29th, came ashore just after 1700 to establish their command posts, confirmation if it were needed that the beach was secure. The efforts of the destroyers had been prodigious. USS *Doyle* reported expending 2,359 rounds of 5-inch (127mm) in twenty-four hours, as well as 558 rounds of anti-aircraft ammunition and 156 shells filled with coloured dye and used for reporting the fall of shot; it is hard to imagine there was much left in the magazines.[74]

Everyone concerned acknowledged the astonishing bravery of the assault troops in forcing their way off the beach at Omaha, Ramsay writing that 'all naval personnel were unanimous in paying tribute to their determination and gallantry'.[75] However, General Omar Bradley, commanding US First Army, generously acknowledged in his memoir what had marked the difference between success and failure at Omaha. 'The Navy saved our hides', he wrote. 'Twelve destroyers moved in close to the beach, heedless of shallow water, mines, enemy fire and other obstacles, to give us close support. The main batteries of these gallant ships became our sole artillery.'[76]

* 9 *
Resolute and Seamanlike: The Anglo-Canadians at Gold and Juno
6 June 1944

Endurance and seamanship of the highest order.

British Naval Staff History[1]

Gold: H-Hour 0725

HMS *Belfast* went to Action Stations at 0400 and dropped anchor an hour later alongside the buoy which marked the cruiser's precisely allocated bombardment position opposite Gold Assault Area, where the 50th (Northumberland) Division would land between Le Hamel in the west and La Rivière in the east. At first, Captain Frederick Parham and his Gunnery Officer, Lieutenant-Commander Rex Mountifield, struggled to identify the cruiser's primary target, *WN32* or *Batterie Vera*, four partially encased ex-Czech 100mm field guns at La Marefontaine, behind the village of Ver-sur-Mer. While the two senior officers pondered, their junior colleagues were 'seething with impatience'. Peter Brooke Smith, a young RNVR officer in charge of one of the ship's secondary gun directors, wrote in his diary 'What the hell's the delay? Let's get cracking, for God's sake!'[2]

In the meantime, the cruiser *Orion*, away to the west, opened fire at 0523, increasing frustration levels until *Belfast*'s 6-inch (152mm) guns finally opened up four minutes later. 20-year-old Gordon 'Putty' Painter was a gunlayer in B Turret:

We were firing broadsides, which means that all the guns were firing together – the whole lot! You get ... twelve 6-inch guns firing, it rocks the ship backwards and forwards, and this continually going on. I think we did have ... something to put in your ears, if you didn't, you'd soon go deaf. The only time we could leave [the turret] was if nature called![3]

WN32 had already been heavily bombed by the RAF on 28 May, and then again for twenty-five minutes before H-Hour. Despite this, and *Belfast*'s prolonged and accurate bombardment, which went on until 0716 and placed 224 rounds inside the battery area, the guns inside were undamaged and managed to fire off 87 rounds.[4] However, the gunners were suppressed during the crucial period of the assault, which was what really mattered. *WN32* was eventually overrun by 7th Battalion the Green Howards, advancing up from the beach through Ver-sur-Mer, and the fifty or so demoralised gunners were taken prisoner. Despite the absence of direct hits 'the guns' crews must have had a very unpleasant time from blast from shells and bombs', recorded one report, 'both through the gun aperture and open back to the casemates'.[5]

Other than briefly blind firing at a German machine gun position for twenty minutes from 0955, *Belfast* made no further contribution in Gold area before being ordered to move to Juno. Douglas-Pennant chose to delegate much of the subsequent impromptu support to Captain James Gornell's *Orion*, a veteran ship with an extraordinary record in the Mediterranean – only *Warspite* had acquired more battle honours, and the battleship's service had begun in the First World War.

As the number of targets only justified the use of one spotting aircraft, and as it was politic to shoot one ship out of ammunition at a time, most of the bombardments ... were carried out by HMS *Orion* ... the promptness and accuracy with which targets were engaged was beyond praise and reflects very great credit on her fighting efficiency.[6]

WN48 at Longues-sur-Mer proved a more formidable foe. Despite being heavily bombed prior to D-Day and then bombarded by HMS *Ajax*, the battery opened fire on Omaha at 0537 and then switched to the ships off Gold just after 0600, narrowly missing the headquarters ship HMS *Bulolo*. Thomas Bartlett was a Radar Operator aboard. 'They got a bead on us', he remembered, 'we didn't know the damn thing was there, and they fired a salvo and it dropped in the water just by the side of us and we had to shift a bit quick!'[7] The battery went on to duel with *Ajax* and the French cruisers *Georges Leygues* and *Montcalm* for twenty minutes before it was silenced. Even then, the German gunners opened up intermittently throughout the day.

The pattern of bombardment at Gold was identical to those at the other beaches, with larger warships engaging their pre-arranged targets before destroyers and support landing craft closed the beach to saturate the defences with 'drenching fire' just before the assault. Roger Hill's HMS *Jervis* was one of them. 'The bombardment reached a crescendo as we all increased to rapid fire for ten minutes from 0712 to 0722', he remembered; 'we watched in awe as the shore and low hills around the beach leaped and rocked in the hailstorm of shells ... coming in from the big ships were the flotillas of the landing craft and as we watched ... they formed in line abreast and were rushing for the surf line.' Hill described banging the bridge with his fist, exulting that 'by God, we're ashore in France, we're back in France again!'[8] Lieutenant-Commander William Donald remembered a brief moment of calm, lost in thoughts of home and family as his destroyer HMS *Ulster* rocked gently off the Normandy coast, guns loaded and ready, until he gave the order to open fire and 'for one hour and ten minutes we fired without ceasing, in one long, magnificent and exhilarating roar'. At one point his smiling signalman handed him a naval message form, on which was written the old Nelsonic signal 'Engage the Enemy More Closely'.[9]

Once again, LCGs were highly effective at drenching fire, even though some of those assigned to Force G were the oldest and earliest improvisations hastily converted for Husky back in 1943.[10] Douglas-Pennant also praised the performance of the Army's self-propelled guns firing on the approach from landing craft, though he was more doubtful about the swimming DD tanks, which in Gold Area were taken into the beaches in their landing craft rather than swimming ashore from 6,400m out to sea as originally intended.

Hugh Irwin and the eight remaining Hedgerow-equipped LCA(HR)s of the 591st Flotilla formed part of Douglas-Pennant's drenching force; like Talbot, the Commodore concluded that the tiny craft were 'not suitable for a long passage in anything but fine weather', although he described the performance of the eight survivors as 'most creditable'.[11] After shaking themselves out into some sort of formation, they headed into the beach in line abreast with the LCTs carrying the DD tanks behind them: 'we had to put our spigot bombs onto the beach, quick turn to port, and clear the way for the tanks to go in'.

At 1 mile out, Irwin ducked down into his tiny, armoured cockpit. The depleted flotilla suffered its next loss 100 yards from the firing point when LCA(HR)-1106, commanded by 23-year-old Bruce Ashton from Kingsford, New South Wales, was lost: 'Bruce and his crew were hit by an LCT, it turned over and as the water was very shallow, they were drowned ... which was a bit shattering to me.' Ashton had apparently been due for a posting back home to Australia but had been determined to take part in Neptune; his stoker was the only survivor.[12]

At 30 yards out the LCA(HR)s fired their spigot mortars, two craft failing due to electrical faults, and then lurched hard to port to get out of the way of the incoming LCTs. Irwin and his crew were now observers, watching with horror as two tanks were knocked out by a gun in one of the deadly enfilading bunkers, trying and failing to place explosive 'sticky bombs' on the mined beach obstacles, and then finally witnessing the assault troops from 5th Battalion, The East Yorkshire Regiment, storm ashore. Irwin recalled:

By then we thought 'well our job was done'. It took us something like four hours to get back seven miles [to the Landing Ships]. In that time, we lost two craft, no casualties, they sank because of the bad weather ... I got on board this Empire ship and turned in ...

at probably eleven in the morning ... and slept till the early hours of the following morning.[13]

Royal Marine Lieutenant Richard Hill was serving in an even smaller support craft, a Landing Craft Support (Medium), a modified LCA equipped for close support with a 101mm smoke mortar, Lewis machine-guns dating back to the First World War, and a twin 0.5-inch (12.7mm) Vickers machine-gun mount. Sixteen were allocated to Gold Area, formed into the 904th Flotilla. Assigned to the extreme western end of Gold – there was nobody else between him and the Americans at Omaha – Hill's voluminous orders had been pithily summarised for him at a briefing in Southampton just before D-Day:

> Get as close as you can and attack them with all that you've got ... as soon as the main Landing Craft Assault, LCA, wave makes for the beach ... get the hell out of it and go straight to the right flank ... there will undoubtedly be pillboxes and machine gun emplacements firing into the beach. Get there and attack those.

Hill was left in no doubt that the LCS(M)s were thoroughly expendable. 'The more fire you attract', he was told, 'the greater is your value to the people on the beach because if they're not firing at you, they're going to be firing on the beach and the most important thing we've got to do is to get the Army ashore.'[14]

Hill was dropped from the *Empire Arquebus* at 0515 and took his craft, *LCS(M)-117*, in as planned, his machine gunners blazing away at their first target, a machine gun position on the beach, no easy task in the rough seas. As instructed, when he saw the assault craft begin their final run, he lurched to starboard to get out of the way, heading west and discharging smoke dischargers as he went. The tiny LCS(M) passed close under the guns of a German battery, fortunately so close that the German gunners were apparently unable to depress their weapons low enough to target it. Beyond that, Hill and his men spotted a pair of sandbagged machine-gun emplacements in the village of Le Hamel: 'We proceeded to attack those machine guns with everything we had . . . this is where one loses sense of time, but it seemed to be going on for about half an hour.'[15]

Inevitably, the aggressive little LCS(M) soon attracted the attention of heavier artillery. Miraculously the Marines avoided being hit but water spouts erupted all around them and the landing craft was soaked with spray and peppered with shell splinters. Improbably, Hill found himself shouting to his coxswain to 'make straight for where that shell landed, they never strike twice in the same place'.[16]

By now *117* was riddled with splinter holes and was shipping more water than the pumps could deal with; worse still, the twin Vickers had jammed. Wisely, Hill decided to put out to sea, where they frantically began to throw stores over the side to stop the craft from sinking. 'The gunwales were almost awash at one stage', he recalled, 'and it really became a choice now of chucking all the ammunition overboard and getting everybody down to the bilge pumps.' Just as the situation seemed beyond recovery, a passing destroyer hailed them and offered assistance. Hill made fast alongside, and the destroyer's crew put a giant hose over the side and into *117*'s engine room, drying it out within seconds. The hose was followed by an even more welcome pot of piping hot soup. Hill and his men eventually made their way back to Gold Area. With no immediate task, they were ordered back out to sea, where they tied up alongside an LCG for the night. The next day they were reunited with the *Empire Arquebus* and returned to Southampton.[17]

The extraordinary efforts of men like Hill and his Marines in providing close support on the beaches were summarised in a few lines in Douglas-Pennant's report. 'The LCS(M)', he wrote, 'were able . . . to give useful close support to the LCG by firing at machine-guns engaging the latter from the flanks.'[18] 'You've no idea how proud we were to have come back and come out alive', Hill recorded in an interview given years after the war.[19]

Gold Area extended roughly from Ver-sur-Mer in the east to Port-en-Bessin in the west, adjoining the US WTF at Omaha, although only the two eastern beaches, Jig and King, were used for the assault, and the Americans did not use their eastern sector, George, so there was a significant gap between the US troops and the British

50th (Northumberland) Division. To further complicate things, H-Hour fell fifty-five minutes after the Americans landed, but ten minutes before the Canadians at Juno. Captain John Farquhar, commanding Assault Group G1 from the converted frigate HMS *Nith*, landed 231st Infantry Brigade and 47 (Royal Marines) Commando at Jig. G2 under Captain F A Balance in HMS *Kingsmill* put the 69th Brigade ashore at King, Captain George Dolphin following up with G3 and two reserve brigades. Despite delays on the passage, everything ran close to time, Douglas-Pennant commenting that 'great credit must be given to those officers in charge of the various groups that, after such a difficult passage, they all touched down at the right place and at the right time'.[20] Again, the weather was too rough for the DD tanks, which were put directly ashore alongside the AVREs, after the assaulting infantry, and under heavy fire from both the Germans and the supporting warships, some of whose shells were dropping short.[21]

Beach obstacles were more thickly sown than the intelligence had indicated and were more robust; this, coupled with the higher than anticipated tide which rapidly covered them, meant that the work of the LCOCUs was inhibited. Douglas-Pennant commented that 'their work is deserving of the highest praise', but in the end, all the LCOCU commanders reported that they were unable to clear gaps.[22] Sub-Lieutenant John Taylor of LCOCU 4 at King Red only managed to clear five obstacles and prepare six more before the tide and enemy fire stopped work; the team moved a few more with the help of a tank but then had to wait until the tide went out again. As elsewhere, Taylor was careful to credit his colleagues from the Royal Engineers, who were really instrumental in clearing obstacles: 'It was a privilege and an honour to serve with 280 Field Company RE', he wrote, 'who gave us every assistance and support at all times.'[23] Taylor was a bank clerk from Middlesex and was just 22 – it was not only landing craft crews who had a steep learning curve at Normandy.[24]

The failure of the LCOCU plan, coupled with the heavy surf and an apparent reluctance of crews to deploy their kedge anchors, meant that many landing craft were damaged, some broaching on to the beach and filling with water. The FOB teams also suffered from delays, at least two were noted as becoming casualties (FOB54 at 1435 and FOB53 at 1855) and generally they proved ineffective in the confused close-quarters fighting which followed the assault. Air observation, on the other hand, was 'invaluable ... not only did the spotting aircraft invariably find prearranged targets but on occasion ... they looked for and found targets themselves, often under AA fire'.[25]

When 47 (Royal Marine) Commando landed at Jig at 0930, they lost all but two of their LCAs, along with much of their equipment and all their radios. Their objective was to head west along the coast, take Port-en-Bessin and make contact with the Americans, which they eventually did with the aid of captured German weaponry, but they remained out of contact until 1400 on D+1. The severe loss of LCAs had a serious knock-on effect as they were not available to go back out and ferry in subsequent waves, which slowed down the landings.

Resistance at Jig was intense; as elsewhere, German strongpoints which had been suppressed but not destroyed by the bombardment came back to life during the assault. *WN38*, a pair of emplaced anti-tank guns and a mortar enfilading the beach at Le Hamel, was particularly troublesome. D LCT Squadron, carrying the AVREs, landed in the teeth of its fire. Lieutenant-Commander Arnold Nyberg was Flotilla Officer of the 28th Flotilla, embarked in *LCT-886*. Wisely he had allowed his force to drift slightly to the east, away from *WN38*, having noticed that the strongpoint 'was not receiving the attention it was entitled to and that we may be running into a lot of trouble'.[26] *LCT-886* beached, dropped its ramp and the first AVRE started to rumble ashore, only to get stuck. Efforts to shift it were in vain and the German gunners in *WN38*, noticing that they were in difficulties, started to pour fire into the stranded craft. A shell hit the bridge, knocking Nyberg out, killing two soldiers and wounding several more men. In swift succession more 50mm shells exploded in *886*'s engine room, wardroom and forward winch shelter, causing more casualties and completely disabling the landing craft. 'Two ensigns were shot away', Nyberg wrote later with a sangfroid worthy of Nelson, 'which justified the three we flew.'[27] Helpless, *886* drifted broadside on to the beach, was holed by mines, and only managed to offload its tanks at 1400. *LCT-749* was also hit several times. 'Our cargo was disembarked without serious problems', recalled the Commanding Officer, Lieutenant Jack Booker, 'due largely to our anchor winch controller, Stoker Mountain. He stood by his winch, totally unprotected from bullets and shrapnel, slowly easing 749 up to the beach during the half hour or so it took to offload our tanks.'[28] The remainder of the squadron beached with less drama, as did the LCTs carrying the Army's self-propelled artillery, which landed 'safely and without loss and many of them practically dryshod'.[29]

The stubborn resistance of *WN38* meant that the western end of Jig Green was unusable, and subsequent waves, including the Reserve Brigade, were switched to Jig Red, further to the east, which caused congestion and slowed things down. The strongpoint held out until 1600; it was eventually suppressed by gunfire from destroyers and LCGs, and stormed by the 1st Battalion, the Hampshire Regiment, who outflanked it from the west. (The Hampshires also cleared *WN36*, or Sofa, at Asnelles, subject of Bombardment Serial 14.)

At King, German resistance centred on *WN33*, a strongpoint containing a 50mm gun enfilading the beach at Ver-sur-Mer (referred to as La Rivière in many accounts) and commanded by Oberleutnant Hans-Gerhard Lilloch. Despite being pounded in the opening bombardment, when William Donald's HMS *Ulster* apparently killed his gunlayer, Lilloch's 50mm inflicted a great deal of damage on the approaching landing craft, which perhaps accounts for it being consistently misidentified as one of the Wehrmacht's much-feared 88mm dual purpose weapons.[30] Compensating for the delayed DDs, the LCG and LCS of the 332nd Support Flotilla 'closed the beach at maximum speed ... in order to get well in front of the AVREs and smash as many as possible of the beach defences before the AVREs touched down'. From about 2,700m, 'accurate, rapid and concentrated fire was put down by all ships' on a range of pillboxes and fortified buildings along the sea front.[31] They included *WN33*, which was engaged by *LCG(S) 2*, but continued to resist until it was finally knocked out by a Sherman Flail tank commanded by

Captain Roger Bell of C Squadron, Westminster Dragoons, who put two 75mm rounds directly through the narrow embrasure.[32]

LCA losses at King were high. In the 540th Flotilla, which landed from SS *Empire Lance*, every LCA in two out of the three flights was sunk or disabled, the Flotilla Officer reporting that this 'had a most unfortunate disrupting effect on the organisation for Ferry Service'.[33] More than half of the LCAs in the 542nd Flotilla from SS *Empire Rapier* were lost or unusable by the end of D-Day, and casualties in the 541st Flotilla (*Empire Mace*) were also high. 'The work of the small landing craft', wrote Douglas-Pennant admiringly on 15 July, 'exceeded my highest expectations.'[34]

In the 539th Flotilla, Royal Marine Corporal George Tandy, Coxswain of *LCA-786*, was commended and later decorated for steering his craft into the beach under fire by precariously perching on the stern, clinging to a metal cleat, and pushing the rudder with his feet, after the landing craft's wheel and engine room telegraph were smashed as it was dropped into the water. 'At one moment he was high out of the water', one of his officers related, 'and the next he was plunged into the sea up to his armpits. How his leg was not broken against the rudder rail was a mystery.' As if that were not enough, he then repeated the exercise for nearly three hours, battling the incoming tide and a headwind across seven miles of water, to get *786* back to its parent ship, the LCI *Empire Halberd*. As the former mechanic's frozen feet were carefully immersed in tepid water, which felt scalding after his long immersion, he simply said 'there were thirty-two soldiers' lives at stake ... any one of them would have done the same as I did'.[35]

Dolphin's G3 landed the reserve brigades at 1050 and 1120, some disembarking from US Navy LCI(L) of Lieutenant-Commander Willard Patrick's Group 31, and Major-General Douglas Graham, commanding 50th (Northumberland) Division, came ashore at 1205, followed in the evening by Lieutenant-General Gerard Bucknell, commanding XXX Corps. By this time the fighting had moved inland and follow-up troops from Force L were starting to arrive.

Gold, like Utah, has often been described as an 'easy' beach, as the casualties were far fewer than anticipated. Recent scholarship has done much to refute this.[36] There was hard fighting at Gold; its success and low body count were attributable to the training and skill of both the assault troops and the sailors who put them ashore and provided them with superlative fire support throughout the day.

Juno: H-Hour 0745–0755

According to Commodore Oliver, the bombardment in Juno Area, supporting the landings of 3rd Canadian Division around Courseulles-sur-Mer, Bernières-sur-Mer and Saint-Aubin-sur-Mer, was 'carried out exactly according to plan and successfully achieved its object'. With eleven destroyers and just one dedicated cruiser, HMS *Diadem*, Force E was the smallest bombarding force. Oliver could also call upon Dalrymple-Hamilton's flagship, HMS *Belfast*, once the big cruiser had moved across to Juno from Gold Area at 1132. As at Sword, bombarding fire was controlled from Oliver's headquarters ship, HMS *Hilary*, and like Talbot, Oliver found that the actual physical damage inflicted proved disappointing, although 'the neutralising effect appeared to have been excellent [and] it was gratifying to observe that practically every visible concrete pill box and possible OP [Observation Post] had been hit'.[37]

Shore bombardment, while undoubtedly a necessary prerequisite for invasion, came at a cost for the unfortunate French communities on the receiving end. Oliver estimated that 'less than a dozen French civilians were killed', but he also noted that almost every building in the small seaside towns of Bernières-sur-Mer and Courseulles-sur-Mer had been hit. Liberation it undoubtedly was, but D-Day was a terrifying and potentially fatal experience for the liberated.[38]

Diadem, commanded by Captain Eric Clifford, was a sister to the unfortunate *Charybdis*. Clifford's prearranged priority target was *WN28a*, an unprotected battery of four 1914–18 vintage 100mm howitzers near Bény-sur-Mer. The cruiser took up its bombarding position at 0500, established radio contact fifteen minutes later with a spotter aircraft (codenamed Khaki III) and opened fire at 0552, firing twelve salvoes of 5.25-inch (133mm) for effect and silencing the battery during the initial assault. The German gunners

1. Dead Canadian soldiers with wrecked landing craft and tanks on the beach after Operation Jubilee, the disastrous raid on Dieppe on 19 August 1942. Vital lessons were arguably learned, but they came at a very high price in men and materiel. Losses like this could not be repeated in the Seine Bay.

2. Quadrant, the Quebec Conference of 17–24 August 1943, where Churchill, Roosevelt and the Combined Chiefs of Staff endorsed the COSSAC plan, confirming that the Allied landings would take place in Normandy. Standing behind Canadian Prime Minister Mackenzie King, Roosevelt and Churchill are (left to right): General H.H. Arnold; Air Chief Marshal Sir Charles Portal; General Sir Alan Brooke; Admiral Ernest J. King; Field Marshal Sir John Dill; General George C. Marshall; Sir Dudley Pound; and Admiral W.D. Leahy, Chief of Staff to the Commander in Chief of the Navy.

3. Admiral Sir Bertram Ramsay, Allied Naval Commander-in-Chief (centre) with Air Marshal Arthur Tedder, Eisenhower's Deputy Supreme Commander (left), and Rear-Admiral Sir Philip Vian, Commander Eastern Naval Task Force (right). Retired in 1939, Ramsay was recalled in time to mastermind the Dunkirk evacuation. Vian shot to fame when in command of the destroyer *Cossack*. Both officers had then distinguished themselves in the Mediterranean.

4. Rear-Admiral Alan Kirk, USN (Commander Western Naval Task Force), chats to gunners aboard his flagship USS *Augusta*. A former Director of the Office of Naval Intelligence, Kirk had already commanded amphibious forces in the Mediterranean.

5. Sailors pose aboard a completed Phoenix caisson in Portsmouth Dockyard, March 1944. They would be far less content crossing the Channel on one after the invasion – a grim crawl along under tow at 4 knots (7.5kph) on a giant slab-sided monster with a blunt bow and the seakeeping qualities of a house brick.

6. German soldiers erecting beach obstacles run for cover as an Allied reconnaissance aircraft makes a low-level pass. Rommel's drive to strengthen the beach defences following his appointment as General Inspector of Western Defences in November 1943 posed a late and significant challenge to the Neptune planners.

7. *LCT-1169*, a Mark 4 Landing Craft Tank, is commissioned at Alloa in 1943, cheered on by the women from Arrol and Company who built it. Like many yards, Arrol's at Alloa had been derelict for decades but was reactivated during the Second World War. 60 per cent of the workers were women.

8. US troops wade ashore from LCVPs during an invasion training exercise at Slapton Sands, Devon, in 1944. Although every effort was made to make the training realistic, their calm faces and relaxed demeanour clearly show how hard it was to truly replicate the strain and tension of combat.

9. USS *LST-289* limps into Dartmouth Harbour, its stern blown off during a torpedo attack by German E-boats during Exercise Tiger, the invasion rehearsal off Slapton Sands on 28 April 1944. *289* reported four crew lost, eight missing and twenty-two wounded.

10. Royal Marines from 45 (Royal Marine) Commando embark on Landing Craft Infantry (Small) from Lieutenant-Commander Jack Deslandes's 514th Flotilla at Warsash, near the entrance to the Solent. They were bound for Queen Red Beach, west of Ouistreham in Sword Area.

11. The greatest invasion fleet in history, seen from the air near the French coast. 'The armada stretched for miles', HMS *Belfast*'s Charles Simpson observed when he went on deck to look; 'you could turn and look astern and see these lines disappearing over the horizon, it was so long'.

12. US troops crouch inside a 'Higgins Boat' LCVP on their way into Omaha Beach, 6 June 1944. The very marginal weather conditions on D-Day are obvious and conditions in this little craft must have been indescribable.

13. With Operation Gambit successfully completed, HM midget submarine *X-23* comes alongside the Headquarters Ship HMS *Largs*, a weary Lieutenant George Honour on the casing. 'Once the tanks and commandos had landed, our job was done,' Honour recalled in 1993, 'we cut the anchor rope (we were too exhausted to put it up) and reported to ... *Largs* at 0935.'

14. Clinging to lifelines and complete with bicycles, troops of 9th Canadian Infantry Brigade disembark through heavy surf from *LCI(L)-199* at Bernières-sur-Mer, on Nan White Beach, Juno Area, at around noon on 6 June. Ashore, others move methodically inland through the burning, shell-torn waterfront houses.

15. Commodore Cyril Douglas-Pennant, Naval Commander Force G (standing, centre), chats to weary-looking Royal Marines from a Landing Craft Obstacle Clearance Unit on Jig Green, near Asnelles. *Widerstandnest 36*, the German strongpoint codenamed 'Sofa', is off left, and the National Museum of the Royal Navy's preserved *LCT-7074* is among the beached craft in the background.

16. The veteran battleship HMS *Warspite* bombards German batteries around Le Havre on 6 June 1944. Worn out after years of action, X Turret remains out of action following a catastrophic hit by a German glider bomb off Salerno in September 1943.

17. Laden with trucks, jeeps and a military ambulance, US Rhino ferry *RHF-3* approaches the invasion beaches on 6 June 1944, towed by Rhino tug *RHT-3*, nicknamed 'Hell's Angels'. In the far distance is one of the invaluable 83-foot US Coast Guard rescue boats.

18. 'Jesse James', a US Army DUKW amphibious truck, brings supplies ashore on 11 June 1944. Eisenhower described the ubiquitous 'Ducks' as one of the five most valuable pieces of US-produced equipment, the others being the bulldozer, jeep, 2½-ton truck and C-47 Dakota transport aircraft. Logistics were the secret to the liberation of Nazi-occupied Europe.

19. Unloading supplies from the US Navy's *LCT-583* at low tide on 15 June 1944. Despite the Mulberry Harbours and the efforts made to use the small ports captured during the assault, directly unloading assault craft on to the beaches was the key to logistics during the first days after the invasion.

20. The extraordinary activity on Omaha Beach in the immediate aftermath of the invasion, as the 'Battle of the Build-Up' begins. Ferry craft shuttle backwards and forwards from freighters lying offshore, while LSTs 'dry out' and unload on the beach. Columns of trucks and halftracks towing anti-tank guns are moving inland.

21. A jumble of smashed Royal Navy Landing Craft and Mulberry Harbour components piled up after the 'Great Gale' of 19–22 June. 800 ferry craft were driven ashore, many of them badly damaged, and the discharge of the stores and equipment needed so desperately by the troops fighting inland virtually ceased.

22. The minesweeper USS *Tide* sinking off Utah Beach after striking a mine near the Îles Saint-Marcouf at 0940 on 7 June. The explosion blew the ship 5 feet into the air and the wreck broke in two and sank minutes later. Twenty-seven men died. USS *PT-509* and USS *Pheasant* are standing by.

23. A German *Schnellboot* at speed earlier in the war. Nicknamed E-boats (short for 'Enemy boats') by the Allies, these fast, well-armed and robust motor torpedo boats were, apart from mines, arguably the most significant threat posed by the Kriegsmarine in the Seine Bay.

24. Royal Navy Motor Torpedo Boats returning from a dawn patrol off Cherbourg. The pressure and pace of activity for the Coastal Forces crews patrolling the flanks of the Seine Bay were relentlessly intense.

25. Men on a US Rhino ferry drop to the deck as a German aircraft passes over, 11 June. Behind them, *LCT-522* is backing away. The sunken 'Corncob' blockships of the Gooseberry breakwater can be seen in the background. Daylight attacks were rare but nighttime bombing, torpedo or mine-laying runs were a constant threat.

26. The *Charles Morgan* partially sunk off Utah Beach, 10 June 1944, with US *LCT-474* alongside. German aircraft hit the Liberty Ship with a glider bomb, starting fires and blowing out the ship's bottom. The tug USS *Kiowa* attempted to recover the freighter but its broken stern was embedded in the seabed.

27. A German shell falls between USS *Texas* (background) and USS *Arkansas* (foreground) while the two battleships duel with *Batterie Hamburg* during the bombardment of Cherbourg, 25 June 1944. At around 1315 a shell hit *Texas* in the conning tower, smashing the bridge above, killing the helmsman and wounding several others.

28. Royal Navy minesweepers detonate German mines in the Grande Rade, Cherbourg, 2 July 1944, with *Fort l'Ouest* in the background. Cherbourg had been lavishly seeded with contact, magnetic, acoustic and pressure mines, as well as concrete shallow-water Anti-Invasion Type A mines. Three sweepers were lost clearing the port.

29. One of Lieutenant-Commander Robert Bulkeley's PT boats manoeuvring at high speed around German-occupied forts on the *digue*, Cherbourg's outer breakwater, spraying them with machine-gun fire. Bulkeley withdrew when *PT-521* was shaken by two near misses which stopped the engines, loosened the decks and shook a torpedo out of its rack.

30. The shattered remains of Cherbourg's formerly opulent Gare Maritime, built for the transatlantic liners and once the second-largest building in France after the Palace of Versailles, on 17 July 1944. The Germans comprehensively destroyed almost every useful facility in the port long before it was finally captured.

31. Hoisting a German *Neger*-type human torpedo into the water, probably during training given the calm conditions and relaxed demeanour of the shore party. The attrition rate amongst the often very young and poorly trained operators of the *Kleinkampfverbände* ('small battle units') was dreadfully high.

came briefly back to life at 0915 and the FOB called up the cruiser again. *Diadem* resumed fire and scored six more direct hits. *WN28a* played no further part in D-Day, and neither did the cruiser: 'Although *Diadem* was in communication with various spotting aircraft, no further targets could be found [and] no further calls from Forward Observation Officers were received.'[39] The only other battery in the area consisted of three 105mm howitzers behind Nan White Beach, assigned to the destroyer HMS *Kempenfelt*, flagship of the 26th Flotilla, which opened fire at 0619 directed by a spotter aircraft. When the aircraft had to leave, *Kempenfelt* continued to fire blind on the target until 1250, when the destroyer was ordered to cease fire shortly before Canadian troops captured the site.[40]

The remaining destroyers steamed perilously near to the shore, some closing to well under 300m to engage their targets and eventually having to withdraw stern first. The entire flotilla opened fire at 0655. The veteran Free French destroyer *La Combattante* came in for particular praise, engaging a battery hidden inside a house near Courseulles Pier and destroying it with six salvoes before Capitaine de Corvette André Patou signalled that his ship had touched the beach and he was moving back out to seaward. 'I am sure you were glad to be on your native soil again!' replied Commander John Richardson in HMS *Venus*.[41]

Frank Holmes was part of Richardson's ship's company in *Venus*. Although the actual physical damage eventually proved to be limited, from his perspective the bombardment was nothing short of apocalyptic and it is easy to understand why the effect on the morale of the German defenders was so catastrophic: 'Hell was certainly being let loose', he wrote home in a letter, 'not a building was left untouched, everything was razed to the ground . . . the bombardment from the naval guns plus the bombing from the RAF can only be described as "TERRIFIC"!'[42]

Closer inshore, the shallow-draught support landing craft poured their drenching fire onto the beach defences during the last vital minutes before the assault craft hit the beach. The Royal Marines-manned Landing Craft Gun (Large) (LCG(L)) were singled out for particular praise, although these improvised ships still had no sophisticated fire control equipment and fired over open sites, which made it hard to distinguish targets 'owing to the general dust and smoke of battle'. Royal Marine William Cockburn of *LCG(L)-764*, for example, recalled firing on seafront houses at Juno using the 'unique' commands 'move next door – through the door – shoot – through the window – shoot'.[43] Despite upgrades drawing on experience gained since Dieppe, the inshore fire support craft remained crude, slow and poorly protected considering how close inshore they had to go.[44]

One LCG(L) at Juno was carrying a pair of unexpected additions to the crew: US Marine Corps (USMC) Captain Herbert Merillat, a veteran of the brutal fighting on Guadalcanal in the South Pacific, and his assistant, Technical Sergeant R.T. Wright, both of whom embarked aboard Lieutenant Hugh Ashworth's *LCG-1007* a few days before D-Day. Although no USMC formations took part in Neptune, a number of their personnel were present as observers and liaison officers, and others served aboard US Navy battleships and cruisers. Wright left an account of just how dangerous life could be on an LCG, which also confirmed that United States Marines never went into battle as passive observers. 'Corporal James Easton of Glasgow, Scotland, and I headed for the twin Oerlikon gun on the port side of the bridge', he wrote at the end of June; 'he fired two magazines and then loaded for me and I squeezed a few off.' At this point things got interesting:

> A 3-inch shell hit the water not more than four yards from the ship ... I saw two [Royal] Marines coming down from a gun platform dripping blood from hand wounds. One kept holding his hip. Corporal Easton ripped his pants down and we found a piece of shrapnel. We bandaged them as best we could. The Marine with a gaping wound in his hand insisted on going back to the gun.[45]

In an account clearly written for public consumption – Merillat was a combat correspondent – Wright goes on to describe vividly how one Royal Marine was concerned only for the fate of his ring, a gift from his girlfriend – 'if those blokes smashed my ring I'll kill 'em all!' – another had left his false teeth out in case they were damaged in action and a third had been 'chased around the mess deck' by a German shell which failed to explode and 'dropped to the deck, spent – not more than five feet from the magazine'. Merillat, clearly briefed to emphasise inter-Allied fraternity, concluded his brief report by saying that 'I know of two US Marines who are full of admiration for the fighting spirit and skill of the Royal Marines and Royal Navy. We have a new understanding of the tradition of the "Royals", whom we are proud to claim as a brother Corps.'[46]

Oliver noted the effectiveness of the LCT(R)s in 'drenching' the beaches just before the assault. He also noted in passing one of the most unfortunate 'blue on blue' incidents of 6 June 1944, which many veterans recall, although the precise location and aircraft type are often confused: 'It was very unfortunate that one Typhoon fighter flew into the salvo fired by *LCT(R)-378* and was destroyed.'[47]

There was a lull once primary and beachhead targets had been neutralised, as the risk of hitting the fast moving assault troops was too great. Force J attacked across a two brigade front stretching from Saint-Aubin in the east to Courseulles in the west, Captain Tony Pugsley's Assault Group J1 landing the 7th Canadian Infantry Brigade across Mike Green and Red beaches, and Captain Robert Otway-Ruthven's J2 landing 8th Brigade at Nan White and Red, with J3 bringing in the reserves. Juno had staggered H-Hours (0735 for J1 and 0745 for J2) to ensure the landing craft could clear rocks in Nan Sector, and these were then postponed by another ten minutes because of delays in the passage.[48] DD tanks and AVREs accompanied the first waves.

As the bombardment began 'with clockwork precision' the LSIs reached the lowering position and offloaded their LCAs, which formed up and headed inland in what Oliver called 'a resolute and seamanlike manner'.[49] Both groups of infantry arrived late, threading their way through obstacles under fire. Almost all the LCAs were damaged by fire or holed by obstacles, and extraordinary efforts were made to get the troops ashore safely and then save the craft; the Flotilla Officer of the 526th Flotilla in J1 singled out one Able

Seaman Thomas for particular praise, as he 'sat in a hole in the bows ... all the way back and his action undoubtedly saved the boat'.[50] Fourteen out of eighteen LCAs in the 557th Flotilla were lost, either on the beach or on the way back.[51]

36-year-old Royal Marine Sergeant Fred Turner was sub-division leader with 556th Assault Flotilla, which crossed to Normandy on the 'Red Ensign' LSI SS *Monowai*; the fact that many of the Neptune assault ships were operated by the Merchant Navy is often forgotten. The 556th Flotilla landed the Queen's Own Rifles of Canada opposite Bernières-sur-Mer. Some 7 miles offshore the LCAs were lowered into the choppy sea and headed inshore, forming up in divisions and following a US Coast Guard cutter, until 'they left us with a compass bearing and the assurance that it was right ahead – as if we did not know!'[52]

The flotilla ploughed in to the beach under the bombardment:

> At a signal from the flotilla officer we increased speed and turned into an extended line to hit the beach. The buildings on the seafront at Bernières appeared intact and a replica of the panoramic photographs we had been shown earlier. Strangely we met little opposition until, after negotiating the beach obstacles, we struck the beach simultaneously, then the enemy let loose and my craft's starboard gunwale was raked with machine-gun and small-arms fire. Tanks landed ahead of us had been unable to clear the beach, and with no cover the infantry had to dash ahead supported by firing from the tanks behind them.[53]

Sergeant Jack Hunter had to abandon his LCA but was later decorated for passing messages between the beleaguered Canadian infantry and their supporting tanks. Marine Earnshaw took over his LCA when his Coxswain was wounded; he successfully landed his troops but was then wounded when the landing craft blew up on a mined obstacle while retracting, a common story for LCAs – he was awarded the Distinguished Service Medal. Turner's Flotilla Officer, Captain Geoffrey Clelland, apparently stood on the gunwales of his LCA under fire, fending off obstacles with a sounding pole as if he were punting on the River Cam, while his second-in-command, Lieutenant Johns, lost his LCA but remained on the beach, collecting up and organising stranded crews. In total, sixteen of twenty-four LCAs from the 556th and 557th Assault Flotillas attached to the *Monowai* were lost.[54]

There was more confusion and drama among the DD tanks and the AVREs. At first the LCT Flotilla Commanders were instructed to take the tanks onto the beach because of the poor weather, but the Flotilla Officer of the 4th Flotilla in J2 stated he had authority to make a judgement call if the weather improved, and he duly did so, offloading his tanks to swim in from about 1,300m off the beach, so J2's DD tanks arrived behind the infantry.

Gerald Ashcroft commanded *LCT-517*, part of the 20th Flotilla, which carried AVREs into J1. As an 18-year-old Sea Cadet in 1940 he had helped Charles Lightoller, former Second Officer of the *Titanic*, when he took his yacht *Sundowner* across to Dunkirk. 'Having brought the men out of France I wished to take them back again', he remembered, '[so] I applied for a transfer to Combined Operations.'[55] *LCT-517* was one of three LCT Mk 4s carrying tanks of C Squadron, 6th Canadian Armoured Regiment (1st Hussars): six Sherman IIIs and two Fireflies fitted with the more powerful 17-pounder gun.[56]

LCT-517 landed near Courseulles at around 0820 under heavy fire, to find the beaches congested and the exits still closed.

> We were constantly under fire from approximately half a mile off the beach ... shellfire, gunfire and as we got nearer to the beach, shrapnel and of course mortar fire ... Being the port wing ship of the Flotilla we had no cover ourselves on the port side and we came under mortar fire.[57]

Seaman Allan Thompson, a 32-year-old from County Durham, was killed on the approach and a number of other men from *517* were injured. Ashcroft threaded his big LCT between the beach obstacles, knocking mines off with his steel bow ramp until a pair of mines on stakes jammed between the ramp extensions, forcing him to pull off the beach and dislodge them, before returning to beach again at full speed.

Ashcroft landed his tanks under the guns of a German pillbox on the harbour wall at Courseulles with a pair of embrasures; as he watched, aghast, the German gunners hastily hauled their gun back in from the slit facing westwards along the beach and all aboard knew it would only be a matter of seconds before it reappeared, pointing menacingly from the one immediately in front of them. Major Marks of the 1st Hussars brought his lead tank up close behind *517*'s watertight doors, and Ashcroft ordered his ramp dropped and the doors opened. The Sherman 'did a large jump and came to rest, training his gun' and put a solid armour-piercing shell straight into the strongpoint, which silenced it immediately.[58]

Ashcroft offloaded the rest of his tanks without incident, moved in closer to land his jeeps, and then acted as a causeway allowing smaller assault craft to come alongside and land their troops dryshod, until eventually *517* unbeached, Ashcroft transferred his wounded to a destroyer offshore and returned to Southampton. Before he left, he was unable to resist taking a look in the pillbox. 'It was really an astonishing sight', he recalled; 'it showed how effective a solid shot inside of a concrete pillbox can be. There was literally nothing left but skin, blood, bits of flesh . . . all mixed up, tossed about like a load of mincemeat where the solid shot had simply ricocheted . . . round in it.'[59]

At 0830, 48 (Royal Marine) Commando arrived in LCIs at Nan Red off Saint-Aubin to find that the assaulting Canadian infantry in front of them had fought through the stunned German defenders and moved inland, leaving several strongpoints uncleared; they came under fire and took heavy casualties. Dennis Newman was a Wireman on *LCI(S)-536*. At 0800, the ship's company were called to beaching stations and he took up his position at the side of the ramp, lying flat as the landing craft approached Saint-Aubin: 'Looking ahead I could see a row of houses badly damaged, a shingle beach and a sea wall. A tank up by the wall with a few soldiers up against the wall.'[60]

As *536* crunched into the shingle, the Commando officer and the chaplain ran onto the beach. Shortly afterwards a German rifleman in one of the house targeted them, wounding a Marine in the next group to run ashore, and mortar bombs started to fall around. 'We couldn't move a thing', Newman remembered; 'every time someone approached the top of the ramp they were shot at. A marine officer shouted, "Come on you matelots come and hold this ramp for us", but we weren't going to move because of the sniper. I said my prayers and laid flat on the deck.' Several more Marines were wounded and all unloading stopped, crew and Commandos alike taking cover until another landing craft grounded alongside and opened up on the house with its guns, silencing the marksman. A process which had taken three minutes in training took over half an hour.[61]

Tony Lowndes' eventual arrival at Nan Red Beach was fairly undignified: 'we followed the drill and threw the kedge anchor over the stern; the anchor took hold and because of our speed the rope parted and whipped back knocking me overboard. The craft then broached to in the surf and overturned on to its side throwing the rest of the crew overboard.' The scaffold poles were in Normandy. Soaking wet, Lowndes reported to the Beachmaster and asked him what to do with them. 'His reply was unprintable, indicating that not only had he not expected to receive any poles but that he had quite enough already. If I were you', the understandably harassed Beachmaster continued, 'I'd f— off and get dry.'[62]

A number of the wooden LCIs were wrecked on beach obstacles which had not been cleared. Unfortunately, as at Sword, the LCOCU teams were almost entirely ineffective during the assault phase as most of the obstacles were covered by the incoming tide by the time they arrived. The trials and tribulations of LCOCU 12, commanded by Royal Marine Sergeant Keith Briggs, which landed on Nan Red, provide an interesting illustration of just how challenging this work was. Briggs beached at 0900 – nearly an hour after the assault infantry – by which time the stakes and Element C were completely covered. The team tried to place charges but the sea was too rough and they would not stay in place. Briggs considered blowing the exposed Hedgehog obstacles closer inshore, but in the end decided this was a risk to the troops on the beach. He was then ordered to suspend operations until the tide turned. At 1030, Briggs and his men tried to tow the Hedgehogs out of the way with bulldozers but were again ordered to stop because of the mass of inbound landing craft and heavy enemy fire. At 1220 he boarded his survey landing craft to carry out an ASDIC sweep of the harbour but holed it in four places on the beach obstacles and had to beach it. At this point the team were ordered to walk along to Nan White and start work there. They arrived at 1345 and, alongside the Royal Engineers, finally became effective, clearing 360 explosive devices by 1930. The commitment and courage of the LCOCU teams is without question – Briggs was ultimately awarded the Distinguished Service Medal, and another team was commended for their efforts in helping troops disembark under fire – but as Lieutenant Robert Bellington, commanding the LCOCU teams at Juno, wrote a few days later, 'the employment of LCOC Units in their designed role i.e., diving and hand placing of charges, is not a practicable proposition'.[63]

Ninety landing craft were lost or damaged at Juno, including forty-five of the valuable 'major landing craft', most of them 'by striking mined beach obstacles when retracting'.[64] This dramatically refuted a report from 20 May 1944 – written well after evidence of Rommel's reinforcement of the beach obstacles had first come to light – which rather smugly concluded that 'the obstructions as they exist at present should not be a formidable obstacle to the assault'.[65] Every lost hull would impact on the subsequent build-up, a fact of which the crews were only too aware, and they made extraordinary efforts to get their battered ships home. Lieutenant D.S. Hawkey's *LCT-513* returned from Juno with a mine stuck in its ramp extensions. Telegraphist George Humphries had to report the unwelcome news, signalling '"request instructions, we have live mine on door". So, they sent back "keep away from shipping as far as possible".' The unwanted LCT circled the assault area for some time until Hawkey was instructed to return to the UK; on arriving at Portsmouth, they were prevented from entering harbour until they had disposed of their unwelcome appendage off Stokes Bay near Gosport. The story made the national press, as did another landing craft which was mined and blown in half, but apparently returned home after the crew made temporary repairs and used the stern to tow the bow.[66]

German fire was still intense when the 30th LCT Flotilla arrived at H+85, so around 0910. *LCT-707*, commanded by 29-year-old Lieutenant Alfred Hollands, beached, and then immediately broached side-on to the shore as German mortar bombs started to drop alongside her. When a bomb landed on the deck, the appropriately named Leading Stoker James Gamble, 'with utter disregard for his own safety', picked it up and threw it overboard, while his comrades blazed away at the German defenders with their anti-aircraft guns, and Hollands took on the Atlantic Wall with a 9mm Lanchester sub-machine gun. When he was eventually killed by a mortar bomb his 19-year-old Liverpudlian First Lieutenant, Midshipman Charles Fowler, took over. Fowler ran along the beach and commandeered a bulldozer to shove *707* back into the water. The battered LCT was heading back to the UK by 1305, the young officer steering using engines as both rudders had been lost on the beach. Fowler, his Flotilla Commander noted, 'displayed a high degree of courage and initiative, his display of seamanship being of very high order bearing in mind that this Officer had never in his life been to sea prior to joining *LCT 707*', an extraordinary testament to the courage and skill of the civilians in uniform who manned landing craft in the Seine Bay.[67]

The impact of naval gunfire depended to a great extent on the FOB teams struggling ashore. At Juno, all ships with initial attachments reported that they had made contact with their FOBs by noon apart from the destroyer HMS *Fury*, whose FOB had damaged his wireless set. However, they were handicapped by the delayed arrival of the jeeps carrying more powerful Type 22 Wireless Sets due to congestion on the beach. Ralph Dye of the Royal Artillery, from Great Yarmouth, was responsible for bringing over the Type 22 belonging to FOB Party 73. As well as Dye there were three naval telegraphists, all commanded by Captain James Tyrer of the Royal Artillery. 'I had just turned 21', he remembered, 'and I was the old man of the party, the officer was about two years older than I.'[68] FOB 73 was assigned to support 48 (Royal Marine) Commando and was assigned a Bombardment Liaison Officer (BLO) aboard the Canadian destroyer HMCS *Sioux*.

Tyrer and the telegraphists were due to land at H+45, with Dye following between fifteen and thirty minutes later with the jeep and the 22 Set at Nan Red Beach, but unexpectedly fierce resistance badly delayed the Canadian assault battalion, the North Shore (New Brunswick) Regiment, and Dye's landing craft was 'waved off'. Eventually he landed, on a beach which was still very much a battlefield:

> There were three huge explosions as we hit the mines which were in the water. We came in at high tide [onto] a very narrow beach. [People asked me] afterwards 'what was it like?' and I said 'well it was all in technicolour'. I was right in the middle of a battlefield and everything we'd seen about the war so far had always been black and white photographs . . . and it was all in technicolour![69]

Dye drove his jeep ashore, following a bulldozer and leaning out of the side as he had a trailer strapped to his bonnet and couldn't see where he was going. In front was a burning DD tank. Halting alongside it, he enlisted the help of two infantrymen to remove the trailer; the three men had just lifted it free when they had to throw themselves to the ground as a German machine gun opened up. Dye crawled back inside his jeep, started the engine and lurched off the beach with his head below the dashboard. Remarkably, when he arrived at his assigned rendezvous point, Tyrer and the telegraphists were waiting for him, exactly according to plan. 'I just sort of got out the jeep and slapped him up a salute, said "good morning", and that's where we started from!'[70] The FOB party hastily embarked and set off along the road through the battered seaside town of Saint-Aubin-sur-Mer, following the Commandos to their next objective, a German strongpoint along the coast in Langrune-sur-Mer. Dye established contact with *Sioux* at 0913, but the fighting was at close quarters and nobody wanted to take the risk of calling in naval gunfire so close to friendly troops, so no fire missions were called that day.[71] As night fell, the FOB team formed a defensive perimeter with the Commandos in and around a large walled villa a few hundred metres from the Germans. Dye spent the night in the attic.

That kind of experience simply could not be replicated in training. Vian, in his final report, echoed Talbot and Oliver in saying that FOB parties 'need not be landed with assault brigades . . . as the situation is too fluid and confused to allow naval fire to be used in direct support of the military'.[72] Ralph Dye would surely have agreed.

Despite the setbacks, Juno saw rapid success. Captain Colin Maude, the legendary NOIC and Principal Beachmaster made famous by his portrayal by Kenneth More in the 1962 movie *The Longest Day* (complete with dog and blackthorn stick), landed at 1140 and had his headquarters functioning two hours later; by this time the Canadians were advancing well inland and 48 Commando had cleared the coast as far as Langrune-sur-Mer. The first of the LSTs in J3 started to offload the reserve brigade by Rhino ferry at 1150, and Alan Villiers arrived with his war-weary LCI(L)s early in the afternoon, carrying troops from the first follow-up wave, Force L. Enemy fire might have quietened down, but conditions were still dreadful, 'the worst any officer in the squadron had ever experienced', he wrote, and these were not inexperienced new entrants but men who had experienced almost all of the Mediterranean landings. He went on:

A freshening north-east was bringing in an increasing sea which broke upon the hundred wrecks and tanks with which the Juno beaches were littered . . . the greater part of the beach obstructions were still there, and the cleared portions of the beach were so littered with wrecks and stranded LCT waiting to refloat on the tide that there was extremely little room. An explosion under the bow of LCI(L) 268 soon indicated that there were still mines.[73]

Major-General Rod Keller, commanding the 3rd Canadian Division, came ashore at 1310, and at 1710 Vian arrived in HMS *Scylla* to hold a conference of Flag Officers on board at 1800.[74] By this time the battle for Juno had essentially ended except for tip-and-run air raids and random outbreaks of sniping.

✳ IO ✳
Sword and the Follow-Up Waves
H-Hour 0725 6 June 1944

There were craft which were beached. There were bodies lying about ... one just had to start to establish some kind of organisation.

Lieutenant-Commander Teddy Gueritz, Principal Beachmaster,
Fox Commando[1]

According to the ship's log, *Warspite* stopped in her 'bombardment billet' at 0525, and opened fire with three salvoes on her primary target, the battery at Villerville, between 0545 and 0558.[2] Sword, stretching from Ouistreham in the east to Saint-Aubin-sur-Mer in the west, formed the extreme eastern flank of the invasion area, close to the strongly defended German naval base at Le Havre, and Force D had to provide support to three division-sized formations: 6th Airborne, 3rd British and the reinforced Special Service (Commando) Brigade. Consequently, Force D was the strongest bombardment force, and the bombardment programme at Sword the most complex of the invasion. To further complicate things Sword was also subjected to Hoffmann's torpedo boat attack, although this did little to slow the overall momentum of the assault.

The nerve centre of the bombardment was the Support Control Position in the headquarters ship HMS *Largs*, a rather grandiose description for 'a desk six feet by four feet [and] a certain amount of wall space for maps, not very conveniently arranged'.[3] Here the Staff

Gunnery Officer, Commander Dan Duff, worked alongside his military colleagues the Senior Bombardment Liaison Officer and a liaison officer from 3rd (British) Division to plot the movements of the army ashore and the location and status of German batteries, while an RAF Deputy Controller organised the arrival of spotter aircraft from Lee-on-Solent. Three naval telegraphists, 'first class operators', managed the staggering volume of radio traffic coming across the dedicated frequency, the Bombardment Calling Wave (3,500 kilocycles per second).[4]

The two battleships and the monitor HMS *Roberts* were tasked with neutralising the heavy batteries to the east of the invasion area, towards Le Havre. *Warspite*'s log records how, throughout the day, the battleship methodically suppressed Villerville and a heavy army coastal battery at Mont Canisy near Benerville, *WNVill013*, every time they opened fire. Although German gunners straddled the veteran battleship early on, causing minor splinter damage and forcing *Warspite* to shift berth, they scored no direct hits. In exchange, *Warspite* fired seventy-three rounds of 15-inch (380mm) at Villerville on 6 June, scoring nine direct hits.[5] This accuracy and notable shot-to-hit ratio was attributed to a great extent to 'the excellent observation provided by the fast Aircraft Spotters [who] kept the ammunition expenditure on these tasks down to a much lower level than had been expected'.[6]

Mike Crosley was one of them. Rising at 0500, he and his wingman, Don Keen, made three sorties over France spotting for *Warspite*. Once over the target, the spotters called up the battleship, codenamed 'Spunyarn', and went to work, balancing military maps precariously on their knees, plotting grid references and reporting the fall of shot, while simultaneously watching for hostile fighters and controlling their own aircraft. The cloud was still heavy, so Crosley and his fellow aviators had to fly uncomfortably low, and as a consequence their casualties were high: four Seafires were lost, with two pilots killed. Another airman successfully force landed in France and the fourth managed to nurse his stricken aircraft as far as the Isle of Wight before baling out; he survived with a broken arm.[7]

Crosley attributed the high casualties to so-called friendly fire or 'blue on blue' incidents, recalling hair-raising close encounters with

Allied fighter pilots on overhead Combat Air Patrol. 'They could see us, in twos, circling over the beachhead ... they could see we had square wing tips. They naturally thought, therefore, that we were [German Messerschmitt] 109s. In spite of huge white stripes on our wings and round our fuselages they leaped on us in large numbers.' Allied anti-aircraft gunners with state-of-the art gunsights and new proximity fuses which did not even require a direct hit to cause damage were even more trigger-happy: 'the Army and the Navy shot off at anything that flew anywhere near them'.[8] Despite these challenges, the use of single seat fighters for observation was extraordinarily effective, Vian noting afterwards that 'this form of observation proved reliable and accurate throughout the operation'.[9]

Captain Gervase Middleton's *Ramillies* was also working to suppress *WNVill013*, the battery of captured French 155m guns at Mont Canisy, which had taken advantage of Hoffmann's attack to enjoy a few moments of uninterrupted shooting at the old battleship. Middleton noted shells falling about, 'gradually getting closer, but never menacing', and swiftly called up his allocated spotting aircraft. Their 15-inch shells began to fall rapidly on target, the fourth registering as a direct hit, and the German gunners ceased firing, while *Ramillies* pounded them for fifteen minutes. Middleton's account provides a vivid illustration of the importance of aerial spotting; when his aircraft returned home *Ramillies* was forced to cease fire until it was replaced. The German gunners took advantage of the peace and quiet to resume firing, 'and it was at this time that he missed my cabin by 12 feet!' *Ramillies* re-engaged and kept the battery quiet for the rest of the day. The guns were fully enclosed in concrete casemates and only direct hits stood a real chance of doing any damage, but heavy shells falling on the battery area dramatically reduced their effectiveness.[10] Contingency plans had been drawn up to capture both batteries, and a third at Houlgate (*WNVill032*), by landing 46 (Royal Marine) Commando in Operations Frog and Deer but ultimately Commander Thomas Bell, the Force Commander, aborted both operations, writing in his report that 'in view of the damage to the batteries ... by air and sea bombardment (all were silenced) it was decided that Operations Deer and Frog were unnecessary'. The Commandos later landed on Juno White Beach.[11]

Not everything went according to plan. The cruisers were intended to neutralise batteries on the assaulting 3rd Division front, but the target allocated to HMS *Frobisher* turned out to be a dummy, and *Danae* and *Dragon* failed to make contact with their spotting aircraft, so were forced to resort to much less effective 'blind firing'. HMS *Arethusa* had been instructed to engage the Merville Battery, on the edge of the assault area, if the 9th Parachute Battalion failed to capture it. Although the cruiser never received the required success signal from the paratroops – the codeword 'Hammer' – her spotter aircraft reported that the battery was silent and so *Arethusa* refrained from firing, a fortunate decision as the paratroops had in fact seized the battery but had lost their wireless sets and their FOB party in the drop, along with most of their force and nearly all their heavy equipment.[12]

Bombardment was hard on both ships and men. Conventional naval actions tended to be shorter in duration and often had lulls in the firing while the opposing sides manoeuvred for position or visibility deteriorated, which provided an opportunity to rest ships' companies and maintain complex and sensitive machinery. Bombardment work, on the other hand, went on non-stop for hours. There was no rest for the gun crews, whose meals took the form of 'action messing', a quick corned beef sandwich and a cup of tea in the gun turrets, and their ships could on occasion simply break, often in unexpected ways. Patrick Bayly was First Lieutenant of the cruiser HMS *Mauritius*, responsible among other things for the electrically powered machinery in the fo'c'sle which operated the forward anchor. Instructed to prepare for anchoring later on D-Day, he went below to find that 'the shells firing flat over the fo'c'sle had absolutely wrecked the cable machinery. If you remember those Tom and Jerry pictures where somebody gets hits in the face and all their teeth fall out, that was exactly what it looked like.'[13]

Ahead of the battleships and cruisers, support landing craft and destroyers closed inshore 'to engage the landing beach defence with direct fire right up to the touch down and the flank beach defences until they were silenced or over-run by our own troops'.[14] They engaged their targets effectively and in some cases with considerable verve, the commanding officer of *LCG(L) 1* apparently blowing a hunting horn as his ungainly craft went into action.[15] The German strongpoint at La Brèche d'Hermanville, a complex of bunkers, pillboxes and gun positions codenamed Cod by the planners, was especially hard hit, although post-battle analysis confirmed that naval gunfire was only temporarily effective in suppressing defenders, casualties were often limited, and in this case, Hauptmann Heinrich Kuhtz's riflemen continued to resist once the fire had lifted:

> It is thought that the great weight of fire concentrated on the La Brèche strongpoint ... effectively stunned and paralysed the defenders, because the assault companies' casualties were comparatively light. It was found later that little material damage was done to the strong points. Stronger opposition was encountered by the reserve companies and later arrivals, confirming the theory that the defenders had by then somewhat recovered.[16]

The very limited physical damage was mainly attributable to the fact that, as on all the beaches, most of the defences were sited with their firing embrasures facing along the beach rather than directly out to sea. This meant that the side which faced the warships was solid concrete. The experience of being inside a concrete box being repeatedly pummelled by large calibre naval shells was thus unspeakably grim, but the risk to life and limb – and to weapons and equipment – was much reduced.

There was then a lull in the bombardment while the FOB teams struggled ashore with the assault troops and set up their equipment, a process which was far faster and more efficient in training than in reality. Some FOB teams experienced casualties, others just frustration, and in the aftermath of the landing it was rightly concluded that there was absolutely no merit in landing these valuable specialists with the first assault waves.[17] The parachuting sailors of the airborne FOB teams went through some particularly hair-raising experiences. The Staff Officer Bombardment, 34-year-old Captain Robert Hunter, vanished in a glider with his entire team. Several other teams were badly scattered, with members being killed or captured. One naval telegraphist was dropped miles behind the German lines with a Royal Artillery Bombardier. The two men spent eleven weeks evading capture; linking up after a while with two more lost paratroops and a pair of shot-down airmen, the group finally made it to safety thanks to help from the FFI – the Forces françaises de l'intérieur, better known as the French Resistance. 'Travelling across country with two of the FFI and dressed as civilians', recalled Bombardier Luggar, 'we were stopped one night by a German patrol ... they asked for the papers of the two FFI but they did not ask for Telegraphist Peters' or mine. We were very lucky to get away with it as the curfew was on. We finished up by all shaking hands with the patrol!'[18]

A few calls for fire from FOBs ashore came through in the morning – Captain Vere Hodge with 5th Parachute Brigade and Captain Heard with 8th Infantry Brigade were singled out for praise – but most did not begin until around noon. Lieutenant Derek Plummer of the destroyer *Impulsive* described the experience as understood by junior naval officers:

> We got an Army officer on board ... he was a BLO, and that stood for Bombardment Liaison Officer. Sounds marvellous, [but] all it was, was that he was going to interpret Army jargon for us ... after the first fall of shot, he'd say 'up 500' so we'd increase the range of our gun by 500 yards, and 'left 15' so we'd turn our guns fifteen degrees, and by doing this from time to time we could get on to whatever we were firing at. We never knew what we were firing at, we couldn't see, just, 'boom!' And the BLO ... was in contact with the ... [FOB] at the other end. Between them, they controlled our guns.[19]

The limited ammunition supply in smaller warships was a challenge for the military, who were used to army artillery with vast dumps of shells behind the lines. 'Destroyers particularly were inclined to let the FOB run away with them', grumbled a post-battle report, 'firing sixty to eighty rounds on targets which would have been equally well neutralised with twenty rounds.'[20]

Force S was divided into two assault groups but was unique in that the entire 3rd (British) Division was landing on a narrow, single brigade front, with assault Group S3 under Captain Eric Bush landing 8th Infantry Brigade on Queen White and Queen Red beaches, near Ouistreham, and S2, under Captain Renfrew Gotto, following behind with 185th Brigade. Group S1 was in reserve. To make matters worse an exceptionally high tide, in part the result of the marginal weather, made the area of beach between the water and the shelter of the seafront buildings much shallower than anticipated, which soon led to congestion and slowed the advance inland.[21] Thankfully, the bombardment was effective in keeping the Germans' heads down until the assault; Talbot described German fire as 'desultory' and although Hoffmann's attack gave the force what he lightly described as '*a mauvaise quart d'heure*', generally things went well.[22] S3 crossed the Channel in six convoys. The heavy seas made station-keeping difficult and meant arrival at the Lowering Position was delayed for some formations. Some craft broke down. Despite this, Bush commented that 'in nearly all cases lost time was made up before touch down'.[23]

Number 5 Beach Group were also 'conspicuous by their absence', so unloading was slow and there was congestion. The LCOCUs and the Army's Royal Engineers were ineffective at Sword, Bush commenting sympathetically that the former struggled because 'to clear armed beach obstacles under water in rough weather is not a practical proposition' and the latter were simply 'very slow in starting'; on White Beach, their commanding officer had been wounded and they had suffered heavy casualties.[24] This meant casualties to landing craft were heavy from the outset and steadily mounted throughout the day; the time and energy Rommel had invested in beach obstacles had been well spent.

Most of the DDs made it to the beach, ably guided by COPPists in LCPs, although one deployed from *LCT-444* was swamped, and another was rammed and sunk by an LCT. They were, however, so slow that they were passed by the LCTs from Lieutenant-Commander 'Jimmy' James' 45th Flotilla carrying the AVREs, which arrived before them. *LCT-947*, James's craft, unloaded one of its Sherman flail tanks but as the second drove over the ramp it was hit by two mortar bombs, slewed around and blocked the ramp. The explosion ignited explosive Bangalore torpedoes strapped to the third tank in line causing a huge secondary explosion which killed 39-year-old Lieutenant-Colonel Arthur Cocks, commanding officer of 5th Assault Regiment Royal Engineers, who was standing on the lead tank directing the disembarkation, and two of his men; a further seven were wounded, and the two Churchill tanks which were next in line were damaged. *LCT-947* was carrying a war correspondent, Lambton Burn, who published a graphic account of the incident after the war:

> There is a call for morphia, and I climb into the tank hold and discover a grim tale of dead and wounded. Bob Brotherton has been dragged from Dunbar with his back smashed. He dies quickly. I stoop to squeeze morphia into the sweat-covered arm of Trooper Raby. Barbarian's crew are unhurt, although they received a shell fore and aft. Troop-Sergeant Jock Wingate, commanding the 'plough' tank, is dead by a stray rocket. His driver Winstanley lies pitted with shrapnel in his back. Fred Linsell, of the 'bobbin' tank, has a thigh wound. He acts bravely: tries to walk unassisted: collapses. Jock Charlton, commanding the assault bridge, has a face wound.[25]

LCT-947 was a sitting target on the beach and was soon hit again; efforts to clear the wrecks were in vain and eventually James ordered the commanding officer, Lieutenant Lionel Watson, to unbeach and return to the UK. All the other 45th Flotilla LCTs unloaded but Bush's report is a litany of shell and mortar hits and other damage; the operation was by no means easy and Bush took care to commend James for the conduct of his flotilla, commenting that 'all craft were handled with skill and resolution'.[26] The AVREs and DDs were invaluable in knocking out German guns in the defiladed bunkers which had proved invulnerable to the naval bombardment.[27]

Casualties were worse in the 100th Flotilla, which arrived at H+5. These were support craft, LCT (Armoured) carrying Centaur tanks of the Royal Marines Armoured Support Squadron and LCT (Concrete Buster) carrying Sherman Firefly tanks with high velocity 17-pounder (77mm) guns. *LCT(A)-2191* was repeatedly hit and all three officers aboard were killed, along with two ratings; not one of the men was out of their twenties, and Able Seaman Robert Bryson from County Durham was just 19. Bush considered that 24-year-old Sub-Lieutenant Julian Roney, *2191*'s Commanding Officer, 'did remarkably well before he met his death'.[28]

The first assault infantry landed at the same time as the 100th Flotilla. 535th Assault Flotilla departed from their LCI, HMS *Glenearn*, and headed inland to White Beach from the lowering position, their embarked troops from A and C Companies, 1st Battalion, South Lancashire Regiment, 'singing songs in chorus' to keep up their spirits; all ten LCAs beached successfully, landed their troops and withdrew without casualties. 536th Flotilla, landing from SS *Empire Cutlass*, was less fortunate: two LCAs had to be abandoned on Red Beach and two were so badly damaged they sank on the way back.[29]

At H+20 Group V, elements of the 536th and 537th Flotillas, landed on White Beach without casualties although two LCAs sank. On Red Beach, twenty-two LCAs from the 543rd and 538th Flotillas landed the 2nd Battalion East Yorkshire Regiment without serious incident; as they ran into the beach 'the battalion Bugler played the general salute and other tunes ... and this did much to keep the troops cheerful'. Generally, the small, manoeuvrable LCAs found it easier to avoid the obstacles, which was fortunate as, if the flimsy plywood craft did trigger a mine or were hit by German fire, it meant total destruction. The next wave of LCIs and LCAs carrying the Commandos arrived between 0750 (H+25) and 0800; again numerous craft were lost, either on the beach or when trying to return to their parent craft with holes in their hulls. They were followed by a group of eight of the larger LCMs from the 653rd Flotilla, of which only two returned to the UK, the remainder having been lost on the beaches or had sunk on the way home, although only two men were lost. The determination of the landing craft crews to get their battered, leaking vessels back was again remarkable: the Commanding Officer of the LSI HMS *Prinses Astrid*, one of a number of converted Belgian ferries in Assault Group J4, the Commando and Ranger lifts for Forces S, J, G and O, singled out the 'outstanding' Leading Seaman Mills, who had his crew bailing out his craft with their steel helmets in a desperate attempt to keep it afloat, giving up only when the engine room flooded.[30]

George Kirkby was coxswain of another of *Prinses Astrid's* LCAs and described a beach

strewn with dead and wounded bodies, the air thick with smoke and the water around us spraying up into the craft through concentrated mortar and machine gun fire. I can't remember being scared though . . . it's a funny thing but as a young man of twenty-one it never crossed my mind, I could be killed . . . I did feel sorry for the fellows that had wives and families back home, I think I would have felt different in their shoes.[31]

Maid of Orleans lost one LCA on an obstacle and another to 'enemy action', the briefest of notes in the ship's report. Jim Froggatt was a Royal Observer Corps aircraft spotter on the LSI who watched as it was 'hit by a mortar shell which killed three soldiers and wounded several others. These included the Padre whose pack of bandages and dressings on his back was hit by the mortar. The pack took the brunt of it and saved his life but he had a terrible hole in his back.'[32]

Only one landing craft came in for extended criticism. When it beached at H+60 (0825) the senior army officer aboard was apparently incapable of command because of seasickness, and not one of the twenty-three other Army officers aboard got a grip: as a consequence the ship's decks were obstructed by soldiers milling about and getting in the way. At this point the naval officers aboard should have asserted their authority but apparently failed to do so, and it was over an hour before the soldiers were finally disembarked. 'This is not an inspiring story', Bush wrote acidly; 'the Army appear to have behaved very badly.' He goes on to comment that he had 'never been in the least impressed' with the senior naval officer aboard.[33] In studying these events comfortably, decades later, the extraordinary thing about D-Day is not, however, these rare instances of failure, but the determination and skill of almost everyone else in incredibly challenging circumstances, despite in many cases their youth and inexperience.

At H+75 (0840), the eighteen LCTs of Group IV arrived carrying Royal Artillery self-propelled guns, which blasted the German defences as they ran into the beach. One, *LCT-532*, was hit by mortar fire on the way in and the army's reserve petrol supplies caught fire, as did three SP guns at the back of the tank deck. It beached in flames, but despite this the crew, inspiringly led by the Flotilla Commander of the 38th Flotilla, Lieutenant-Commander T.G.S. Unite, managed to extinguish the blaze, land all of the undamaged SP guns and assist two other LCTs in difficulty on the beach. *LCT-750* detonated a German mine, which blew a huge hole in the ramp; despite this two SP guns managed to creep past and land before a pair of half-tracks got stuck and flooded. Sub-Lieutenant Cash, the CO, started to take his battered craft off the beach but by this point it had become a tempting target for German gunners; hit in the engine room *750* was eventually left wrecked on the beach. *LCT-859*, the Flotilla Commander's ship for the 32nd Flotilla, triggered at least two mines which broke its back. Almost every craft in the group was damaged by German fire, beach obstacles, mines or accidents.[34]

One minute later Commander Rupert Curtis, Senior Officer of Convoy S9, brought in his twenty-four Landing Craft Infantry (Small) of the 200th and 201st Flotillas, fast Fairmile boats developed from motor launch hulls carrying the 1st Special Service Brigade, the Commandos led by Brigadier The Lord Lovat. Lovat's Commandos were tasked with landing on Queen Beach, leapfrogging through the assault battalions and rushing inland to link up with the paratroops of the 6th Airborne Division. As Curtis ran in, he passed a grinning matelot on the deck of an outbound LCT who 'informed us with great gusto that it was a piece of cake. Judging from the reception accorded to us', Curtis went on to note in his report, 'this LCT had beached before the enemy had recovered from the initial softening of the soft underbelly!'[35]

Just as we touched down my craft was hit twice by armour piercing shells which fortunately went clean through their gun shields without hitting any sailors or commandos. 502, the craft close on my port hand, commanded by an Australian Lieutenant, John Seymour, was hit by shells in her port engine and four of her petrol tanks were pierced. By some miracle she did not blow up. Had she exploded we should have been engulfed in flames and Lord Lovat and most of his headquarters troops would not have got ashore.[36]

The laden Commandos waded ashore under heavy fire into a smoke-shrouded chaos of damaged and wrecked armoured vehicles, bodies and wounded men calling out for help. Curtis's LCIs then began the tricky process of unbeaching under fire. *LCT-519*, his own craft, narrowly missed a mine and lost its port engine. '*LCI(S)-518* commanded by Lieutenant-Commander Jack Deslandes, leader of our follow-up wave, had her ramp crew beheaded by an 88mm shell, and mortar bombs exploded amidships, killing more sailors and commandos. In his words, his deck looked like a butcher's shop.' The mortar bombs apparently touched off Commando ammunition on the deck, in total *518* lost seven Commandos and sailors killed and nine injured. *LCT-509* struck a mine as it closed the beach and the explosion under the troop space killed a number of commandos.[37]

After unbeaching, *LCI(S)-524* was closing the headquarters ship HMS *Dacres* at 0925 to take the brigadier commanding 185 Brigade ashore when it exploded in flames and sank, apparently after the fuel tank was hit. Lieutenant George Clark from New York, commanding one of the invaluable US Coast Guard cutters, took his ship into the flames to rescue a few survivors, including the badly wounded CO, Lieutenant Nigel Cromar, but nine officers and men died.[38] In total Curtis lost five craft sunk and most of the rest were badly damaged, two arrived in the Solent in near-sinking condition. He reported that '49 sailors and commandos were killed in the craft and twenty-one wounded, but the job was done.'[39]

Sub-Lieutenant Frank Hayes was First Lieutenant of *LCT-1126*, part of the 43rd Flotilla which arrived in S3. It was carrying vehicles and equipment from the Royal Army Medical Corps, and beached at H+120, so around 0925, still under heavy fire; reports note that the LCT was hit by anti-tank fire which damaged a DUKW and wounded an RAMC corporal.[40] Hayes recalled the event vividly. *LCT-1126* was hit eight times on the port side:

> One of them came straight through and it came through the side of . . . an army jeep which belonged to the ambulance people. There was a corporal sitting with his legs dangling over the side of the vehicle ready for manoeuvring off and apparently this shell entered the gear box, went straight through that and went straight through . . . the fleshy part of his legs and there was profuse blood oozing out all over the place. I can remember that we got a sheet and tore it in pieces and stuffed it into the hole and wound it round whilst we tried to get proper medical attention for him. I never know to this day whether he survived.[41]

So it continued. Talbot went ashore from HMS *Largs* at 1535 to find the beach still under fire and an air raid by German Junkers 88s in full force; 'people were still rather dazed and shaken', he noted, before returning to his ship and arranging for working parties to go ashore and start clearing the beaches.[42] Shortly afterwards Derek Plummer nervously landed a pair of distinguished passengers from the destroyer HMS *Impulsive*, Lieutenant-General Miles Dempsey, General Officer Commanding British 2nd Army – 'an extremely quiet man' – and Lieutenant-General Frederick 'Boy' Browning, commander of 1st Allied Airborne Corps, who 'never stopped talking – you couldn't get a word in'. Plummer ran them ashore in a motor-boat through heavy surf, praying he wouldn't capsize.[43]

By now the Beachmasters with F and R Beach Commandos were ashore and attempting to organise the landing. Ken Oakley was with Fox Commando on Queen Red. 'LCAs, LCTs and LCIs were landing, one after the other and in some cases one on top of the other when LCTs got a bit impatient and dropped their ramps hither and thither without enough care', he remembered, and the troops often had to be encouraged to move off: 'the chaos of the water's edge had to be sorted because craft were coming in all the time and without someone there to continually move them and push them to go, groups would form and block the exits. Difficult, but we managed it.'[44]

Landing with the first waves, the skilled specialists of the Beach Groups were exposed to the same risks as the assault infantry. In Sword Area, one officer and two ratings were injured, along with the Deputy NOIC, Commander Hugh Nicholl, who was seriously wounded in the shoulder shortly after coming ashore; 'Their job', the NOIC subsequently noted in his report, 'was made considerably more difficult as a result.' Nicholl continued to work until the Principal Beachmaster of Fox Commando, Lieutenant-Commander Teddy Gueritz, landed at H+30. 'With guile', Gueritz persuaded him to head for the Beach Dressing Station and took over his duties.[45] 'We didn't beach very well', Gueritz recalled, 'because we jumped off the ramp of the craft . . . we shook ourselves and looked around.'

> There were craft which were beached. There were bodies lying about. The general impression I have is one of greyness, a result of smoke and the weather and spray . . . There was some small arms fire but I think most of the activity was from mortars and field artillery, and one just had to start to establish some kind of organisation.[46]

Beach Groups were built around an infantry battalion, with added Engineer, Transport, RAF and naval components, and their job was to receive men and vehicles from landing craft and clear them through the beach exits into transit areas, from where they would go on to the front or to depots. The RN Beach Commandos and the USN Beach Battalions set up navigational marks, cleared obstacles, marked obstructions like sunken landing craft or drowned tanks, and helped organise unloading:

> It's never straightforward . . . it doesn't help when you're being shot at as well . . . we had considerable difficulty in clearing the vehicles off the beach in our area, partly because of mining by the Germans and partly simply because we were victims of our own success in getting a large amount of stuff ashore and the exits were ill-suited to the volume of traffic we could provide . . . We had to close our beach for a period.[47]

The very shallow, restricted beach area at Sword added to the challenge Gueritz faced.

Being a Beachmaster required discretion combined with authority. Leaving the beach for the uncertain hazards inshore required courage and determination on the part of the soldiers and sometimes this understandably failed. Gueritz recalled a group of military policeman who refused to leave the shelter of an armoured vehicle, and two men who were 'blue with fear'. All were eventually moved on. Captain William Leggatt, the NOIC for Sword, came ashore a few hours later, with his large staff, specialising in everything from Signals and Motor Transport to Landing Craft Recovery and Bomb Safety.[48]

The reserve brigade finally landed at 1550, several hours late, but it was not until just before 2100, when 300 troop-carrying aircraft and gliders swept over the beach to reinforce the 6th Airborne Division inland, that everyone began to breathe a little easier. 'As far as the eye can see there is one continual flow of aircraft ... what a sight, everyone has stopped breathing', one sailor on the headquarters ship HMS *Largs* recorded in his diary.[49] The landing was not without incident. Lewis Goodwin was also watching from *Largs* when 'one Stirling, having released its glider, with its engines on fire, was heading straight for us as we lay broadside onto the beach. It crashed in flames no more than 100 yards away from us. It was an awesome sight seeing so many planes and gliders in the sky.'[50]

Although air attacks and alarms continued through the night, Sword was secure.

Force B and Force L

At the end of the day, the first follow-up waves arrived. These formations were combat loaded into assault shipping and formed up into Force L for Vian's British Eastern Task Force (ETF) and Force B for Kirk's US Western Task Force (WTF). They landed across the beaches just like the assault waves, and sometimes under fire. The two 19-year-old Sub-Lieutenants, John Baggott and Philip Stephens, respectively CO and First Lieutenant of *LCT-7074*, brought their ship down from Felixstowe through the Dover Straits and over to

Normandy as part of Force L. They arrived near midnight on D-Day, accompanied by the flash of anti-aircraft fire and the rumble of guns ashore. 'With daylight we saw the Bay of the Seine packed with ships as densely as traffic in Piccadilly Circus', Stephens wrote in his diary, 'Cruisers, destroyers, troopships, LSTs, LCTs, MGBs, every type of ship in the Navy was there.'[51]

Congestion on the beaches meant *7074* did not actually beach on Jig Green at Asnelles, in Gold Area, until 0930 on 7 June. The LCT collided with another ship on the way in, ripping off the port guard-rails, and then one of seven 7th Armoured Division M5 Stuart light tanks drowned in the surf, the crew being collected by a Duck. Immediately after unloading, *7074* was swept into a tangle with two other landing craft and 'we proceeded to chew each other to pieces', wrecking the bow ramp, before they drove hard onto the beach near 'Sofa', or *WN36*, the now somewhat battered 50mm gun emplacement, and dried out alongside the shell-scarred wreck of Arnold Nyberg's *LCT-886*, now emblazoned with the stark message: 'ALL LOOTERS WILL BE SHOT'. 'In a pool left by the receding tide', wrote Stephens eloquently, 'there floated the body of a soldier – mute witness to the battle which had raged to secure the beachhead.'[52]

Over at Omaha, when the first personnel convoy of Force B arrived off Utah early on D+1, the 16,000-ton transport *Susan B Anthony* struck a mine while approaching the assault area. The former ocean liner was loaded with more than 2,500 soldiers from the 90th Infantry Division, including rifle company commander Captain Orwin Talbott, who was leaning casually against a bunk on the upper deck, watching events ashore while waiting to land. At 0800 he heard an explosion and was thrown violently up in the air. Landing on his face, the 24-year-old Californian was immediately battered by the tumbling bodies of his fellow soldiers, complete with weapons and equipment, as they fell on top of him. At first there was shocked silence, then instant hubbub, until Talbott shouted 'at ease' and 'discipline took over totally. I was very proud of how well they responded.' Opening a door on to the deck, he watched, aghast, as a mass of dirty black water fell over the doomed ship.[53]

Within five minutes, two holds had flooded and the big troopship took on a starboard list, corrected by the commanding officer,

Commander T.L. Gray, USNR, by moving the soldiers to the port side as they came on deck. Remarkably, although there were a number of serious injuries – one of Talbott's men had a badly fractured leg – not one man was killed. At first, it seemed the *Susan B Anthony* could be saved and the US Navy fleet tug *Pinto* came alongside at 0822 to take the troopship in tow, but then a fire broke out in the engine room and Gray reluctantly ordered abandon ship. The troops calmly scrambled down nets onto the *Pinto* and two British frigates, HMS *Rupert* and HMS *Narborough*, most carrying their personal weapons and equipment; 'Even though I was leaving a sinking ship', Talbott recalled, 'I managed to be rescued without even getting my feet wet.'[54] Gray and his crew jumped into the water at 1000 hours, as the *Susan B Anthony*'s bow lifted out of the water in preparation for the final plunge, and the troopship sank ten minutes later. Coder Don Hitchcock watched the ship's final plunge from the deck of *Narborough*:

> By this time smoke was issuing along with flame out of the hull. It was going down by the stern and the last rights were being performed. It rose out of the water, the bow stuck up, and with very little ceremony the *Susan B Anthony* disappeared, rather like a dart going into the Bull's Eye because ripples came out from the remnants . . . as she disappeared forever.[55]

Narborough headed inshore, packed with 700 soldiers, including Orwin Talbott. Remarkably he was put ashore in Utah Area with half his company, marched inland and started his war on the same day.

By the end of the day, the Allied navies had fulfilled their first challenge: 'the breaking of the strong initial crust of the coastal defences by assault together with the landing of the fighting army formations'.[56] The armies were ashore and established in each assault area; the beachhead at Omaha was smaller than intended but it was strongly defended. Some 57,500 US and 75,215 British and Canadian troops were ashore, supported by heavy weapons and vehicles.[57] 'By the end of D-Day', Ramsay wrote, 'immediate anxiety was felt on only one count – whether the weather would improve sufficiently quickly to enable the start of the build-up as planned.'[58]

The next phase of the Battle of the Seine Bay, the Battle of the Build-Up, would be just as important as anything which had gone before.

✳ II ✳
The Battle of the Build-Up:
Logistics and the Great Storm
6–25 June 1944

What we need is a permanent bridge, not a bridgehead.

Admiral Sir Bertram Ramsay[1]

Neptune's second key task, as summarised in the British Naval Staff History, began as soon as the soldiers were ashore: to 'commence, and continue without pause ... their reinforcement at as high a rate as possible'.[2] The objective was deceptively simple: to ensure that the army was 'built up' in strength and numbers faster than the German forces opposing them. The challenge presented by its practical delivery cannot be overstated, although it has often with the benefit of hindsight been made to look simple. It was not.

The Germans had access to the entire road and rail network of Europe to rush reinforcements to Normandy. Admittedly, this network was under constant assault from the air and by the FFI, and many potentially useful combat formations were retained elsewhere for weeks, notably around Calais, because of the success of Fortitude. However, despite all this, it should have been easier for the Germans to reinforce by land than for the Allies to reinforce by sea. Success required extraordinary efforts, by hundreds of thousands of men and women, afloat and ashore, and the efficient use of ships and landing craft on a vast, unprecedented scale. Like a conveyor belt, at least eight convoys a day crossed the Channel, loading, sailing, unloading, returning and then doing it again, carrying tanks, guns, men, ammunition, food and fuel, only to have it used up within days or even hours in the relentless attrition of the Normandy land campaign.

It was now that the work of the British Beach Groups and the US Navy Beach Battalions became important, ensuring this flow of men and materiel landed in the right place and got off the beach quickly to make way for the next arrivals. In the British sector, the Beachmasters folded into a much larger staff under an NOIC, as soon as possible; the Americans preferred to replace their Beach Battalions with a completely separate NOIC staff a few days later.[3] Captain George 'Fish' Dolphin, commanding G3, which brought the reserve brigades into Gold, became NOIC for Gold Area immediately afterwards.

> I put on my other 'hat' of NOIC Gold and the Sub-Area Commander and I, plus our own operational staffs, landed – but not dry-shod! There were two- to three-foot waves. The time was about 0830, and it was half-tide. There was a bit of sniping going on ... in my HQ staff I had included two Royal Marines, one as batman and one as car driver. These two spent D-Day digging a slit trench for me in the soft sand above high water mark.[4]

There were three routes into the beachhead, all of which were used for months after D-Day. It is all too easy, sometimes, to become distracted by the debate about which made the most significant contribution to victory in Normandy. In the end they all mattered. The first was bringing materiel over the beaches using the same assault shipping which had put the army ashore: this was why every hull lost on D-Day impacted on the vital work which followed. This process began with the arrival of Forces B and L on 6 June. The second was new technology: to boost capacity, the Allied navies helped transport, build and operate the two Mulberry Harbours off Saint-Laurent in Omaha Area and Arromanches in Gold. Later, sailors helped transport and build PLUTO – actually several pipes – bringing fuel from the UK. The third, often ignored, involved making use of the small harbours which were captured in the landings, places which few outside Normandy knew of before 1944, like Port-en-Bessin, Courseulles, Ouistreham and Arromanches (see Map 6).

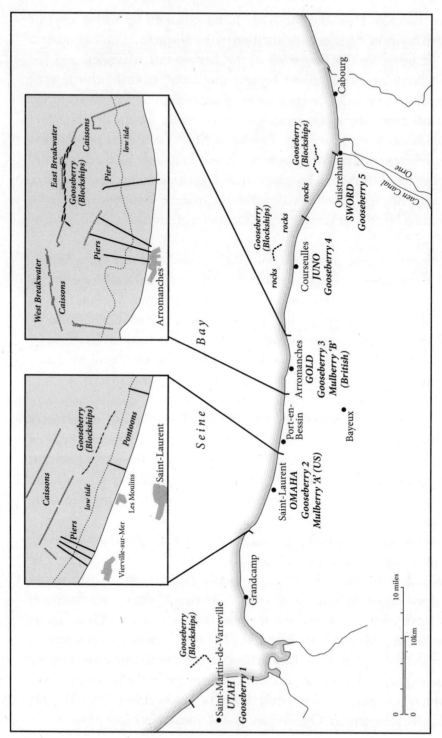

Map 6. *Mulberries, Gooseberries and ports.*

In the British ETF Area, a daily meeting chaired by Vian determined discharge priorities, and the NOIC and senior Beachmasters issued the necessary orders to the Beach Groups. For the first three days, the plan was simply to push every hull across the Channel as quickly as possible, and until D+7 most of the ships had been preloaded.[5] During this period, much of the burden fell on the LSTs and the larger landing craft: on D+1 and D+2 LCTs made up more than 50 per cent of the total arrivals.[6] There was inevitably some confusion, a risk Ramsay had accepted in order to maximise discharge rates during the army's time of greatest vulnerability, when a strong German counter-attack could have jeopardised the entire operation. Sorting out this extraordinary mass of shipping in the ETF area of the Seine Bay was the responsibility of two officers, both of whom had already carried out difficult and demanding jobs during the assault: Captain Renfrew Gotto in HMS *Dacres*, formerly Senior Officer of Assault Group S2, became Captain, Northbound Sailings, on the evening of D-Day, and Captain Aubrey Fanshawe, former SOAG J3, became Captain, Southbound Sailings, on 11 June after his predecessor was seriously wounded. Between them they were responsible for sorting out what Gotto called 'the seething mob', passing new arrivals onto the right beach into the care of the NOICs, and sending empty hulls back to the UK as quickly and efficiently as possible.[7] A similar system was introduced in the WTF sector on D+6.

Fanshawe noted in his report that in those first hectic days 'LST and LCT did not know for which area they were bound', going on to comment wryly that 'the Commanding Officers understood that Captain, Southbound Sailings, would know, which was not the case.' The only solution was for Fanshawe to hail each arrival from his headquarters ship, the frigate HMS *Nith*, and establish precisely which military units were embarked. To make himself more visible and speed up this tortuous process, Fanshawe ordered *Nith*'s bridge and upperworks to be painted bright red.[8] Even when they knew where to go, the shore was often obscured by ships and landing craft, making it difficult for inexperienced skippers to get navigational fixes.

All of this, coupled with the rough weather and general chaos of the assault, meant that by the morning of D+1 there were a hundred LSTs waiting to be unloaded in the British sector alone. The original plan had been to discharge LSTs afloat by dropping their ramps onto the clumsy but invaluable army-operated Rhino ferries, which were huge rafts with powerful outboard engines attached, there being concern that the LSTs might break their backs if they were left to 'dry out' on the beach for long periods, but it meant that their most useful characteristic – their ability to discharge onto the beach – was nullified. Ramsay therefore gave approval to beach them. The process passed without incident and 'drying out' became the standard method for discharging LSTs and small coasters, the latter being unloaded by gangs of military stevedores from the Royal Engineers' Port Operating Companies.

Commander Thomas Brunton, Principal Ferry Control Officer in Juno Area, reported a 'formidable' challenge on D+1, with fifty-three LSTs, twenty-seven coasters and six big MT ships lying offshore, and only forty-three landing craft available to clear them. By D+3 'the majority of the troubles had been overcome and the work was going well. The decision to beach . . . was in great measure responsible for the clearing of arrears.' Brunton recorded discharging an average of 2,877 tons of stores and 2,011 vehicles on D-Day and over the seven days that followed; in passing, he also commented that the personnel of the ferry craft became 'somewhat exhausted'.[9]

Many LSTs returned to the UK filled with wounded or German POWs, which introduced further delays at the UK end as they had to be offloaded before a new cargo could be brought aboard. 20-year-old Liverpudlian Sick Berth Attendant (SBA) William Fry was drafted to *LST-409*, which had been adapted as a medical LST, just before D-Day. Medical LSTs carried a pair of naval surgeons and a group of SBAs like Fry. They carried combat troops across but, once they had been discharged, were rapidly converted into makeshift floating field hospitals. Fry remembered:

At the rear bulkhead we had a folded operating theatre which folded back [on] scaffolding poles', 'behind it [were] . . . the operating table, sterilising units, all the instruments ... and while we were rigging it up, the steriliser was being boiled. The rest of us used to go round ... the tank space [and] together we pulled out the brackets on the wall in three tiers ... each set of two brackets took a stretcher, so you had stretchers in three tiers. By the time we'd call all that ready, the whole place smelled like a hospital![10]

Medical LSTs also carried supplies of blood, and the new 'wonder drug', penicillin.

While other LSTs were refloated and went back as soon as possible, the medical craft waited until they were full, on average embarking 400 stretcher cases and 250 walking wounded, and then returned, Fry and the other SBAs cleaning up and treating filthy, traumatised casualties as they went: 'some that were coming in, you wouldn't think anything was wrong with them till you released their clothing ... you'd probably just rip their sleeves and you'd find their blinking arm just hanging off inside the sleeve'. In total he made eleven numbingly exhausting trips to both the British and the US sectors; by the end of it all the medics were functioning like automata:

You never got any sleep ... We used to get Benzedrine tablets [amphetamines] to keep us awake. Everyone was dropping on their feet. We got back here, discharged the ship of all patients and turned the tank space back to the military again, and the whole procedure started all over again.

On leave after it was all over, Fry found that 'for the first ten days I'd wake up in the middle of the night screaming sometimes, going through my mind, and my father would be sitting across me holding me down ... to stop me struggling. It was terrible.'[11]

By D+3 a steady stream of LSTs carrying casualties were arriving back in the UK; they were not always clearly identified as 'medical' and often were unsure precisely how many wounded they carried, complicating things for those who ran the bases. 'Loading LSTs at the Hards was taking longer than scheduled and thus the time necessary for disembarkation of casualties could ill be spared', Rear-Admiral

Frederick Buckley, the Commodore, Landing Craft Bases, wrote in a subsequent report.[12] Portland was not prepared to receive casualties at all, and when the 'flood' of US wounded from Omaha began on 9 June the local authorities had to improvise, unloading LSTs offshore using paddle steamers and a pair of adapted drifters until US Navy landing craft became available.[13]

Ramsay had established two organisations to minimise delay or wasted capacity. The Build-Up Control Organisation, or BUCO, was strategic: it co-ordinated available shipping and matched it to the Army's ever-shifting priorities. TURCO, the Turn Round Control Organisation, was more tactical, organising the movement of ships between ports in the UK where berths were available and the correct cargos were waiting and then, with the NOICs, ensuring valuable hulls were emptied and left Normandy as soon as possible. Like any administrative body, TURCO had its critics among the fighting sailors, but Colin Madden, the overworked staff officer in J1, was a fan. 'They had the most difficult job', he remembered. 'They took hold of every craft coming in and ... they put it into the best place possible at the time to do the best job available for the follow up. They did a very great job.'[14] Certainly the Admiralty agreed, concluding in a post-Neptune report that 'the need for an organisa-tion of this type is conclusively proved'.[15]

Derek Whitehorn, a veteran Beachmaster who had been badly wounded in Sicily, was posted to TURCO at Fort Southwick when he returned from sick leave. The pace was frenetic as they stripped out damaged craft from those returning from Normandy, formed the remainder into convoys to return to the far shore, and matched them up to appropriate loads provided by Whitehorn's military opposite number. 'Keep them going, keep them going' was the refrain.[16]

The damaged and otherwise unserviceable ships rejected by Whitehorn passed into the care of another new organisation, designed to improve the efficiency of the repair and maintenance process: COREP, the Control Repair Organisation, with local COREP Committees ensuring that every facility in their area, whether state or privately operated, worked as efficiently as possible to repair damaged ships and return them to service as quickly as possible.[17] On

Ramsay's instruction, the LCTs and LSTs, often commanded by inexperienced COs with limited formal navigation training, would stick to the same ports and hards to build familiarity, with the more experienced merchant skippers going where they were sent.

Allowing for loading, the voyage, unloading and return, any convoy or individual ship voyage could be repeated on every fourth day, so convoys sailed on a recurring three day cycle, which began on D+4, once enough of the preloaded shipping had been emptied and returned to the UK.[18] Ramsay's aim was to build a bridge to France, with regular northbound and southbound 'traffic' flowing over it. In addition to landing craft groups, at least eight full convoys of merchant ships a day sailed for the Seine Bay, each given an alphanumerical code, where the first letter was the country of origin, the second the area of departure in the UK, and the third the type of convoy, as follows:

Country: E (England) or F (France)
Area: T (Thames), X (Newhaven, Sussex), W (Isle of Wight), P (Portland), C (Cornwall and Devon), B (Bristol Channel), M (Miscellaneous)
Type: P (Personnel), M (Motor Transport), L (LST), C (Coasters)

So, convoy ETM5 was the fifth convoy in a southbound sequence leaving England from the Thames carrying motor transport. Every ship displayed a large blackboard displaying these codes so convoys could be assembled quickly and efficiently; one commentor wrote that 'it would be impossible to guess at the amount of paperwork, signalling and time that was saved by this system'.[19] More whimsically, for wider communications and planning purposes landing craft convoys sailing at night were codenamed 'Starlight' and those in daylight 'Bluesky'. The system was not perfect: as with everything else, battle teased out wrinkles in systems which had worked flawlessly in training. Fanshawe noted in his report, for example, that 'the boards ... were, in nearly every case ... hidden by the wings of the bridge when approaching'.[20]

The first build-up convoy, ETM1, consisted of fourteen motor transport ships sailing from the Thames through the Strait of Dover, a perilous route which had been closed to all but the long-suffering coasters for much of the war. German coastal gunners at Cap Gris-Nez had hit the 7,219 ton Liberty ship *Sambut* twice, holing the freighter on the port side and setting alight cased fuel and lorries with full fuel tanks. At 1215, a lorryload of gelignite exploded and fifteen minutes later Captain Mark Willis ordered the ship abandoned: 130 soldiers were killed, many from 92nd Light Anti-Aircraft Regiment, apparently due to an understandable reluctance to jump into the sea.[21] ETM1 was to be followed by ETP1, a far more precious and vulnerable convoy of personnel ships, but despite the loss of *Sambut*, Ramsay decided that 'the risk of a daylight passage must be accepted' and the nine troopships slipped through the Strait without loss at 1700, protected by smokescreens laid by motor launches and aircraft. No more personnel ships were passed through the Strait of Dover; although the likelihood of another loss was low, the consequences were simply too serious.[22]

On average, in the first week 25 Liberty ships, 38 coasters, 9 troopships and 135 assorted landing craft arrived in the assault area every day, and until a port was available, bigger ships carrying stores and vehicles had to unload into ferry craft: the invaluable Ducks, along with landing craft, LBVs and Rhino ferries.[23] Tony Lowndes and his LCVP crew were transferred to ferry duty after dropping off their scaffolding poles, following a night on the beach – Lowndes slept in a wrecked LCT – and a few grim days awaiting instructions while refloating their flooded craft and watching burial parties carry away dead Canadian soldiers.[24]

Ferry craft and in particular the much-maligned landing barges were absolutely essential and the pace was brutal. 'IT IS VITAL THAT CRAFT SHOULD BE *"ON TIME"*' exhorted the orders given to *LBF-310* before sailing to France. 'STRAGGLERS CANNOT BE WAITED FOR.'[25] Dennis Maxted's *LBV-327* was one of them:

We just took ... our barge alongside, these merchant people loaded it and the Pioneer Corps stacked it ... they just came down in those nets, those slings, dropped them on the deck and they were soon stacked . . . we had shells and bombs . . . strapped and put onto pallets along the deck . . . We also took petrol in those jerrycan things. They were all carried on, one in each hand, two at a time.

More attractive cargoes included military rations, rum and cigarettes, which occasionally 'disappeared'.[26]

The LBOs, LBWs, LBK, and LBE, were formed into Supply and Repair Flotillas to provide floating bases for the Ferry Craft.[27] Perhaps the most welcome sight to the hard-pressed ferry crews was one of the ungainly Landing Barge Kitchens (LBKs). Louis Gray in the launch *HDML-1383* certainly took heart from them, feeling that 'if this degree of attention could be paid to such mundane provision, it must surely be reflected across the entire operation, and the war must inevitably be won!'[28] Frank Douglas served in an LBK:

There were two big ranges in there that were capable of producing enough food to feed 2,500 men every day . . . the landing craft and the support craft used to come alongside and we had what you called 'Hay Boxes' . . . about 18 inches cubed. Inside there was an empty circle and it was insulated around the outside and we had four containers in there. We put the food in and then we had big thermos flasks called Safari Jars that held a gallon, and in those we put the liquid, soup or tea.[29]

If food from the LBKs was not available, Ferry Craft sailors supplemented it by salvaging cases of military 'compo' rations from the water. Some of the sailors serving ashore fell outside the supply organisation of the army units they were serving alongside, and if food was short they too were forced to resort to roaming the beaches searching for waterlogged 'compo', washed up from wrecks offshore or lost during the assault. One member of René Le Roy's LCOCU 5 became adept at boarding military supply trucks and 'ditching' boxes of food off the back while they were picking up speed.[30]

Ferrying was a dreadfully slow process, made worse by the fact that many ferry craft had been lost or damaged during the assault, or delayed by the bad weather. Military interference also played its part, notably at Omaha, where the army at first tried to insist on a process of 'selective unloading', which meant trying to identify specific cargoes (notably ammunition) among the floating armada offshore, sometimes without having access to cargo manifests or even names of ships, rather than simply unloading every ship as it arrived as quickly as possible.[31] 'The beachmaster on Omaha Beach was a man who'd not had my confidence even when I was back on the amphibious command at Chesapeake Bay', Kirk recalled. 'I had to displace him by a man called Captain Sabin of the regular Navy . . . I put him onshore and he took charge.'[32]

The capable Captain Lorenzo Sabin had formerly commanded the Omaha gunfire support group – multitasking was a given for naval officers in the Seine Bay. Sabin reported back to Hall, Hall told Ramsay, Ramsay took the matter up with 1st US Army and insisted on the immediate unloading of ships regardless of cargo.[33] More generally, the situation eased once the decision had been taken to dry out LSTs and coasters, which freed up more ferry craft to offload the larger ships. Rarely mentioned in general histories of the Normandy campaign, the Ferry Service was a huge operation in itself, involving thousands of personnel, eleven depot ships to accommodate them, a Flag Officer in both the ETF and WTF areas to run it, and a Senior Officer Ferry Craft in each beach area reporting to them.

The Rhino ferries were particularly useful, although they had been hastily built and hard use in the Seine Bay wore them out quickly: the Royal Engineers' 3 Inland Water Transport Group reported that by 27 June they had given up using Rhinos as self-propelled ferries and were towing them using LCT and LCM and soon afterwards they gave up altogether, choosing instead to recycle the fragile rafts: 'As the Rhino Ferries became unserviceable to the point where they were not worth repairing they were handed over to Port Maintenance and Port Construction and Repair units who used the components, minus the bow and stern sections with motors and ramps, to construct jetties.'[34] Leonard Fifield arrived in the Seine Bay with convoy ETM3 as Third Officer of the US-built freighter *Ocean Volga*, anchoring off Juno on 9 June, and discharging his cargo of trucks onto a Rhino, 'a thing that we got to know very well', he recalled:

> A Rhino was simply a whole mass of tanks sort of connected together, a floating square, which could hold about twenty-four trucks. It was just a flat top with a row of outboard motors at the back end and they were working simultaneously, and they drove this wretched float from the ship to the shore, and back and forth again. You got rid of twenty-four [trucks] at one go then . . . they'd just come up alongside, we furnished them with ropes to tie up, and then we had to work our own derricks, there were no stevedores. Everybody from Captain to Galley Boy was working.[35]

The back-breaking process took most of the day, and was repeated across the assault area, while back in the UK vital cargoes piled up at the docks and frustrated soldiers sat in queues. Even when the backlog of shipping was cleared, the resultant mass of hulls returning to the UK at the same time had a knock-on effect in the UK ports, causing a similar backlog in the loading process. Ramsay highlighted particular challenges in the Isle of Wight and Southampton, where an extraordinary volume of shipping had to pass through the restricted waters of the Solent.[36] Again, Norman Yates and his fellow pilots really made a difference. 'During the month of June', he recalled, 'forty pilots worked at top pressure and averaged forty-three ships per man for the month. We took snatches of sleep when and where we would, having most of our meals on board the ships.'[37]

As the situation stabilised a procession of senior figures made their way over to the Assault Area, bringing with them their attendant security and bureaucratic headaches: perfectly naturally, Ramsay and Eisenhower came over in the cruiser HMS *Apollo* on 7 June – the assault area was their command responsibility – but they were followed in rapid succession by Churchill, Brooke and Smuts on 12 June, de Gaulle on the 14th and King George VI and the British Chiefs of Staff on the 16th.[38] Over in the WTF Area, Lieutenant William Snelling, commanding the diminutive *PT-71*, 'claimed the all-time record for carrying gold braid' when he ferried five US admirals and five generals around, including Admiral King, General Marshall and Eisenhower.[39]

Port capacity was the solution to the build-up, but it would be many weeks before Cherbourg, the nearest large deep water port, could be captured and brought into use, followed, it was hoped, by the big Biscay ports of Brest, Lorient, Saint-Nazaire and Nantes, supported by an artificial port at Quiberon Bay, south-east of Lorient, although the latter was never used. In the meantime, the only local ports were the tiny harbours captured during the invasion. Ouistreham, in the east, was almost immediately available but essentially useless as it was built to service the city of Caen, which remained in German hands for weeks, and was still under enemy fire. Port-en-Bessin, between Gold and Omaha, was captured in the afternoon of D+1 and opened for business the following day under the formidable Commander William Cowley Thomas, a 45-year-old retired submariner, as NOIC. Cowley Thomas was awarded an OBE for his skill in opening up Port-en-Bessin, which 'greatly exceeded expectations', averaging over 1,000 tons a day of stores by D+8 and becoming particularly useful as a base for the vulnerable LBVs.[40]

Courseulles, in Juno Area, was more challenging. Commander Alfred Wilmott, the newly arrived Resident Naval Officer, reported the general condition as 'very poor' and the facilities as 'very neglected'; in particular he singled out the town's swing bridge and lock gates which had 'apparently not been maintained since 1876, when they were constructed'. The harbour basin and entrance were silted up, the piers had been cut down by the Germans to give them a clear field of fire and, to make matters worse, the port had been badly damaged during the assault. It was also liberally sown with mines, booby traps and unexploded ordnance, and had been prepared for demolition, although this had not been carried out, apparently because 'the neglected condition of the Port had probably led the enemy to believe it would be useless for our immediate purpose'.[41]

Wilmott landed at 1600 on 7 June. By 2100, he had moved his team, Naval Party 1502B, into a temporary camp in the town, and they set to work on the decrepit swing bridge, lock gates and sluice. By 2300 they were welcoming their first LBV into the inner basin, accompanied by a heavy German air raid which put the sailors right in the firing line. 'Two buildings close to the bridge were on fire', Wilmott recorded, 'and a DUKW was blown into the inner basin by a near bomb miss. Anti-personnel bombs were dropped along the East Quay and phosphorous [incendiary] bombs on the west side near wooden buildings.' Sporadic bombing and shelling continued until dawn, the Germans apparently trying to make up for their mistake in leaving Courseulles undamaged. To make matters worse, enemy snipers were still active. Despite this, Naval Party 1502B had Courseulles working by D+2, and once the harbour had been cleared of silt by bulldozers at low tide, it too was handling 1,000 tons a day, mainly arriving in LBVs. A few days later a pair of 700ft LCT pontoons were installed, further increasing capacity.[42]

The two tiny ports in the US Assault Area, Grandcamp and Isigny, were not developed until the end of the month and were of limited use, but the US Navy's famous Construction Battalions, or 'Seabees', had other fish to fry, using Rhino ferries and innovative pontoon causeways to maximise the discharge capacity of the beaches: one such causeway alone, Easterly Causeway Number 1 at Omaha, discharged 746 vehicles, 3,500 tons of bulk cargo and 8,695 personnel from 12 LSTs, 14 Rhino ferries and 95 miscellaneous craft between 11 and 17 June.[43]

In the end, the beaches would always remain vulnerable to weather and the tiny Normandy fishing ports could never process the vast quantities of men and materiel required. By D+11, discharge of men and vehicles was about 50 per cent behind the ambitious targets set during planning.[44] As soon as the assault areas were secure, no effort was spared to expedite the construction of the third pillar of Neptune logistics: the Mulberry Harbours.

Force Mulberry was commanded by Rear-Admiral Bill Tennant, who had distinguished himself as Senior Naval Officer Ashore at Dunkirk in 1940, and then narrowly survived the loss of HMS *Repulse* off Singapore the following year, with Captain Christopher Petrie as NOIC for Mulberry B and Captain Augustus Clark, USN, NOIC for Mulberry A. Petrie was belatedly gifted HMS *Despatch* as his flagship, saving the old cruiser from the breaker's yard where she had been moored, stripped of guns and stores. So few sailors were available at this point that *Despatch* sailed for Normandy armed with military anti-aircraft guns, manned entirely by soldiers.[45]

The first components to arrive were the Corncob blockships which would form the Gooseberry breakwaters. Scuttling old but serviceable merchant ships when every hull was desperately needed had been controversial but in the end sixty were provided, mostly British and American. Among them were two former battleships, the British *Centurion* and the French *Courbet*, which was scuttled flying a huge tricolour and repeatedly targeted in the weeks that followed by the Germans, who were convinced the old ship was operational – they were encouraged in this by Allied bombarding ships, which would anchor behind *Courbet*'s bulk and fire over the top. Conceived as landing craft shelters before any plans had been finalised for the rest of the harbour complex, there was a Gooseberry at each beach.

The Corncobs and the first Mulberry components – Bombardons and Phoenix – left the UK late on D-Day, travelling along specially allocated channels and arriving on D+1. As the blockships were carefully manoeuvred into place by tug crews, then planted and scuttled by blowing out their bottoms with explosive charges so that they dropped straight to the seabed, their Merchant Navy crews were taken off. The embarked anti-aircraft gunners were not so lucky: 'RN officer begin to plant the Gooseberry', recorded a Royal Artillery Lieutenant named Holladay assigned to the blockship *Empire Bunting* in his diary; 'we stay on and they blow us all up. Ship settles smoothly but main deck almost entirely awash. Life is to be very uncomfortable. Sleep in crowded wireless cabin.'[46]

Mulberry was a complicated inter-Allied and joint service project, with demarcation lines which did not always aid collaboration. For example, the Royal Navy was responsible for providing the blockships and bombardons, assembling all the equipment and transporting it to Normandy, and sailors were in charge of laying out or 'planting' the breakwaters, but soldiers operated the valves which sank them in place.[47] The entire operation required huge amounts of shipping: each Mulberry had a Royal Navy mooring force of boom carriers, net layers, boom defence vessels and trawlers; sixty-two more trawlers were assigned to smoke-making duties to help conceal them, and still more ships acted as control ships back in the UK.[48]

More than 200 tugs were committed to the build-up, including British naval and mercantile, US Army and Navy, and a few Dutch, and nearly all had to be used in support of the Mulberry project. They were co-ordinated by another new organisation, COTUG, with the US Navy's Captain Edward Moran, a reservist who had before the war run the largest tug company in New York, as Tug Controller.[49] Many British tug crews signed onto a T124T agreement, where they continued to receive higher Merchant Navy pay scales but wore Royal Navy uniform and were subject to RN discipline. Albert Barnes was Quartermaster aboard HM Tug *Storm King*, which had towed Phoenix units round to Selsey Bill for sinking and then took them over to the Seine Bay in 'one of the worst tows we ever had. People's idea of towing is the tug ahead [but] there were times when the block was abeam because they were showing such a wide side to the gale.' On the way back they found an abandoned, drifting Phoenix and Barnes and a sailor called Harry Skinner boarded it, waiting until the little tug and the giant concrete monolith were roughly level in the heaving seas and making a perilous jump across to a small platform for the towing bollards, set low down at the back. 'It's just something that you learned being a Tuggie', he recalled, 'when to jump and when not to jump!'[50]

Each Phoenix unit had a small crew, a pair of sailors and a pair of soldiers manning a Bofors anti-aircraft gun mounted precariously on the top. It was a grim experience, crawling along at 4 knots on a giant slab-sided monster with a blunt bow and the seakeeping qualities of a house brick, feeling naked and vulnerable in the middle of a hostile Channel. 'If we were hit with a torpedo that would be the end', remembered Able Seaman Kenneth Bungard, who took over several; 'we were sixty feet up in the air, it was all concrete [and] it would just disintegrate!' The routine was punishing: once they got to France, the Phoenix would be 'planted', then Royal Engineers would come aboard, hurry down deep inside and open the sluices, and as the monster settled in position, Bungard and his mates would be sent home to fetch another one. On one occasion, their Phoenix leaked so badly it nearly sank, and conditions aboard were indescribable:

> Most of the time we were frozen stiff. We didn't wash, we were absolutely filthy and very tired . . . At one end you could go down a small ladder and there was a hole . . . no windows, nothing, very claustrophobic, which over a period of time seems to have been used as a toilet for a good many . . . inside there you would be absolutely trapped if you were hit with a torpedo, you'd [have] no chance at all . . . nobody ever went in there.[51]

The only consolation was the rations, which included the ubiquitous self-heating soup and were 'extremely good'.

Whale units followed on D+2 and Mulberry convoys sailed daily after that. Enemy action destroyed two Phoenixes but the effect of the weather was worse: 40 per cent of the roadway components failed to survive the crossing. Despite these setbacks, Mulberry B at Arromanches was discharging cargo by D+7, and by D+10, 16 June, the provision of sheltered water was 50 per cent complete. The Americans moved even faster and Mulberry A at Saint-Laurent was essentially fully operational by D+10, by which point a staggering 557,000 men, 81,000 vehicles and 183,000 tons of stores had been landed.[52] Captain John Hutchings, Senior Officer of Force Pluto, arrived in his flagship, the corvette HMS *Campanula*, to reconnoitre the proposed sites on D+1, and work began at Port-en-Bessin in the British sector and Saint-Honorine-des-Pertes in the US sector to install Tombola, the first stage of PLUTO. Tombola consisted of four flexible pipelines, buoyed so they could be connected to tankers offshore, and became operational on D+18 (24 June).[53]

Such extraordinary pace required some compromises: the Americans only moored alternate spans of their roadways, and left an extra entrance in the breakwater to speed up arrivals. In their defence, the sailors and Seabees were building their harbour under fire and the situation at Omaha was fragile. This was not mere braggadocio: there was an urgent need to get troops and armour ashore at Saint-Laurent as fast possible. The US harbour was also more exposed, and the seabed less stable. Unfortunately, the consequences of this calculated gamble would be felt sooner than expected: in responding to the threat posed by the 'violence of the enemy', the Americans had left themselves terribly exposed to the 'dangers of the sea'.

If Eisenhower had chosen to postpone D-Day again, it would not have been possible to reschedule the landings for 7 June, the last window of that particular low tide, as the landing craft and other smaller ships would have had to refuel. His next opportunity would have been 19 June, D+13. This was the day that the worst summer storm in living memory swept through the Seine Bay. Although the forecasts had been reassuring, it was obvious to everyone afloat that the weather had been deteriorating steadily from the 14th, swamping the precious Mulberry components as they were towed across the Channel and hampering discharge over the beaches. After a brief lull on the night of 17/18 June, it turned ferociously on the night of 18/19, the wind sweeping down from the northeast at speeds which rose dramatically, from Force 4 to Force 6 and finally Force 7, or 56km/h.

For thirty-six hours, wave heights in the Seine Bay averaged 8ft, or 2.43m.[54] Unloading ceased, and the ferry craft fled for shelter behind the Gooseberries, larger ships returning to the UK or trying to ride out the storm in deep water. The performance of the coaster crews, who had distinguished themselves since the start of the war, battling to carry coal and other vital but unimpressive cargoes around the British coast, continued to be exemplary. Civilians all, many were far too old for military service; the Master of the MV *Dawlish* was apparently 70.[55] Renfrew Gotto singled out the 632-ton coaster *Wallace Rose* for particular praise, commenting in his report that despite losing both his anchors the Master, Captain Patrick McCourt, from Newry in County Down, remained off the beach for three days until he could discharge. 'The conduct of this little vessel in refusing to be turned from her purpose ... is I think most noteworthy ... in this operation these fine little ships have won the admiration of all concerned here.'[56]

Shuttle convoys were suspended. At Saint-Laurent, US Navy Captain Edward Ellsberg recalled, 'all traffic ashore over the floating roadways, undulating violently now on their heaving pontoons like writhing pythons, was suspended altogether'.[57] The gale persisted until late on 22 June. In Gold Area, discharge rates plummeted from nearly 2,000 tons of stores, over 1,200 vehicles and nearly 10,000 men on the 18th to 271 tons of stores and no vehicles or personnel at all on the 21st, prompting the usually phlegmatic Ramsay to note with concern in his diary that 'this is a damnable spell we are going through'.[58] 'We realised halfway through the night that this was something quite special,' recalled Sub-Lieutenant Bertie Male of *LCT-628*. 'By daylight, the ensign was cracking up on the mast and all the halyards were thrumming and it looked abominable.' *LCT-628* ran out to sea and barely survived the experience: 'we went astern as best we could to get the anchor up and ... at full ahead and emergency full ahead she finally pumped slowly round into the wind'.[59]

Seven of twelve LCTs which arrived at Juno on the morning of the 19th, running ahead of the storm into the shelter of the Gooseberry, were driven ashore, six breaking their backs.[60] Hundreds more landing craft were wrecked, the bigger steel Rhino ferries and LCTs driving into the smaller assault craft and 'pounding them to matchwood'. A staggering 800 of the vital ferry craft of all types were stranded, many of them badly damaged or total losses. *LCT-737* lost its First Lieutenant, 20-year-old Sub-Lieutenant Brian Gee, a New Zealander originally from Cheltenham, who while struggling to manage his unwieldy craft at the height of the gale was tragically crushed between his LCT and another, dying eleven days later.[61]

Predictably, the landing barges proved vulnerable. Sub-Lieutenant Eric Simpson's LBV dragged its anchor and was driven ashore at Omaha: Simpson was found face down on the beach and awoke hours later in a US hospital being treated for exposure.[62] Albert Rogers' *LBV-121* sank off Utah and Rogers was in the water for hours, hanging onto a Carley Float; after being discharged from a US Army field hospital, he remained ashore in Normandy until 5 July, helping US engineers to clear mines.[63]

A number of larger ships were also damaged, including the cruiser HMS *Diadem*, which was hit by a drifting Rhino and holed in several places: the flooding was stopped using the time honoured naval damage control technique of stuffing the breaches with duffel coats and hammocks.[64] At both Mulberries, the Bombardon floating breakwaters

were a disaster, many breaking free and turning into gigantic navigational hazards, threatening harbour and ships alike. Mulberry B at
Arromanches escaped relatively unscathed, losing five Phoenixes and
sustaining some damage to its pier, but Mulberry A was completely
wrecked, Tennant reporting that this was partly because of its exposed
location, but also putting the damage down to gaps in the breakwaters.
The blockships had settled down, reducing their effectiveness, and the
open-topped Phoenix caissons had become swamped because they had
been 'planted in excessively deep water'. At Arromanches, most of the
drifting Bombardons were carried clear of the harbour, but at Saint-
Laurent they were not. Finally, the hastily anchored Whales were
smashed by drifting landing craft which had anchored to windward
but too close to the pier.[65] Clark, the NOIC for Mulberry A, desperately tried to fend them off 'shrieking orders through loudspeaker and
megaphone into the teeth of the gale' and when that failed, threatening
to fire on them, but there was really nothing he could do: 'the man who
for a year had lived for nothing save to make a working reality of
Mulberry had to stand impotently by and watch more and more of
those fouled up landing craft battering his priceless roadways to
destruction'.[66]

According to one eyewitness, the strain and anxiety of the storm
was the last straw for Clark, by all accounts a devoted and hard-
working officer who had driven himself relentlessly for months and
had, it should be recalled, been obliged to build his harbour under
fire. Exhausted, he was transferred to a staff job soon afterwards and
retired from the Navy in 1945.[67] Major Alan Beckett, a Royal
Engineer who had worked on the artificial harbours project since
1942, was sympathetic to the Americans, who he said, 'really did
know their stuff'. For Beckett, the main trouble was that 'at Mulberry
A the Phoenix units were founded on sand which could be eroded
away and result in the breakwaters being gradually lower in the sea
... once the breakwaters were overtopped in storm conditions there
was little hope for vessels inside'. Beckett was horrified by the devastation when he arrived in Normandy after the gale. 'For as far as the
eye could see in each direction down the coast it was ... wreckage on
top of wreckage without any gaps in between ... that they were able

to clear this up and make some use of the beach is very great credit to the American Seabees.'[68] Additional resources were rushed out from the UK, including extra repair ships, and the Home Fleet was stripped of shipwrights: 'all hands set to work to clear up the mess' and, by 8 July, 600 of the wrecks had been patched and refloated.[69] A hundred more were back in the water two weeks later, but the remainder were total losses.

A fleet of fifty-five salvage vessels had been assembled for operations in the Seine Bay, including lifting lighters, wreck dispersal vessels and Rescue and Salvage Tugs, as well as shore-based workshops for repairing small craft, and two fully equipped repair ships, the converted Australian seaplane carrier HMS *Albatross* and the former minelaying cruiser HMS *Adventure*.[70] In Kirk's WTF area, salvage was led by Commodore William Sullivan, the US Navy's Chief Salvage Officer, and in the ETF by Commodore Thomas McKenzie as Principal Salvage Officer. McKenzie, a reservist, had learned his craft as a senior salvage expert between the wars, recovering sunken German battleships from the bottom of Scapa Flow in Orkney for first Cox and Danks and then Metal Industries Limited. It was now that they earned their keep. Between 8 and 28 June, Captain Donald McGrath's *Albatross* patched up seventy-four landing craft, thirty Coastal Forces craft and another twenty-one ships of various shapes and sizes. Inevitably operating close inshore and mostly off Sword Area, *Albatross* was for weeks 'the man-o-war anchored closest to the enemy batteries' and was shot at repeatedly, losing two sailors killed and another seventeen wounded, as well as two more men 'invalided for mental derangement'. In between salvage tasks, the pugnacious McGrath even found time to shoot back.[71]

As well as putting right the damage caused by the storm, the salvage crews had to deal with the ongoing impact of enemy action, and the work must at times have seemed never-ending. On the same day that McGrath was trading shots with German coastal guns, another German battery hit the freighter *Empire Lough*, which was passing through the Dover Straits bound for Gold Area carrying a cargo of cased petrol and other stores. *Empire Lough* burst into flames and the crew abandoned ship but Lieutenant Victor Nichols placed his salvage tug *Lady Brassey* alongside the inferno without hesitation, fighting the fire for half an hour before Ordinary Seaman Victor Brockman, 'entirely of his own initiative ... climbed on board the burning vessel' and attached a towing wire. While the freighter continued to burn fiercely and ammunition cooked off and exploded, showering *Lady Brassey* with red-hot splinters, Nichols patiently towed this lethal floating bomb out of the busy shipping lanes, eventually putting the hulk ashore near Folkestone. Four days later, with Lieutenant George Holman in the tug *Lady Duncannon*, Nichol repeated the feat when the freighter *Dalegarth Force* was hit and set on fire in similar circumstances. Both officers were recommended for the MBE, and several of their crew, including Brockman, for the British Empire Medal, Admiral Sir Henry Pridham-Wippell, commanding at Dover, noting that 'it is difficult to speak too highly of the conduct and bearing of the crews'.[72]

Thanks to the hard work and dedication of the salvage teams, which would continue largely unrecognised throughout the Battle of the Seine Bay, the recovery after the storm was extraordinary. In Gold Area discharge rates of motor vehicles were back to pre-storm levels by the end of the 22nd, and by the 23rd the beaches and Mulberry Harbour hit the staggering totals of 3,343 tons of stores, 2,966 vehicles and 14,012 men, more than 4,000 more men than the previous most productive day.[73] At Omaha, 10,000 tons of stores were unloaded over the beaches on 23 June, rising to 12,000 tons in July and August, and 10,000 tons remained the average right through to September even without the aid of the Mulberry. In total, by 30 June (D+24), 861,838 personnel, 157,633 vehicles and 501,834 tons of stores had been brought into the assault area.[74]

Although behind schedule, the build-up was back on track. Some sense of the pace and scale is provided by the record of Commander Christopher Dalrymple-Hay's *LST-425*, which made its seventh crossing on 24 June – it would eventually make twenty which, according to London's *Evening Standard* at least, made it the record holder for crossings to the Seine Bay. By this date *425* had carried across 429 vehicles and 1,558 men from the British, Canadian and

US Armies to Gold, Juno, Utah and Omaha, returning with casualties on every occasion and, on 20 June, bringing back 1,100 German POWs.[75] This was how the 'Battle of the Build-Up' was won.

The Neptune plan had the quite staggering ambition of landing on average one and one third army divisions per day after the initial assault, a division containing somewhere between 10,000 and 15,000 men.[76] The daily passages made by landing craft crews and merchant mariners, working around the clock to bring the army what it needed, would continue until the end of the Battle of the Seine Bay and well beyond, and while this narrative could never hope to capture every exhausting, tedious, and often uneventful journey by ships like *LST-425*, it is important to remember that they were taking place: maritime logistics, in the end, would enable the military to win the Battle of Normandy.

But to ensure the safe and timely arrival of every precious cargo, other sailors put themselves in harm's way every night to try to protect the convoys from German warships and submarines, the almost constant threat of mines, tip-and-run air raids by Luftwaffe aircraft and continued shelling from the shore, especially at Sword, which was targeted by heavy batteries around Le Havre and by German forces on the eastern bank of the River Orne, firing small arms and mortars from less than 3,000m away. Once again, it was the 'violence of the enemy' with which the Allied navies had to contend.

✳ 12 ✳
Guarding the Bay: Action on the Trout Line
6–25 June 1944

In attacking enemy supply lines, our Air Force must concentrate on mines, torpedoes and guided missiles; the Navy on mines, torpedoes and small battle units ... we have got to lay more mines and still more mines in the Seine Bay with the tenacity of a bulldog!

                    Adolf Hitler, 29 June 1944[1]

Only hindsight allows us to conclude that the Battle of the Seine Bay was a foregone conclusion. That the Bay and the vital routes to and from it were taken and then held is a tribute to the skill and professionalism of the Allied sailors, as well as the quality of their training, equipment and leadership. There is no better illustration of this than the brutal fighting at sea which immediately followed D-Day against a foe which, although outnumbered, remained brave, determined and ruthless.

Thanks to the weather, the Germans were caught entirely by surprise on 6 June; even the regular *Sicherungsdivisionen* patrols had been cancelled, Dönitz and Rommel were on leave, and many of the local senior military commanders had been summoned to a wargame in Rennes. On 4 June, Krancke at *Marinegruppenkommando West* had submitted a report concluding that 'in the present strategic situation the enemy does not see any strategic reason for an invasion'.[2] He then reviewed the latest forecasts, concluded there was nothing to be concerned about, and headed south to Bordeaux on an inspection trip; he was asleep when his Chief of Staff passed on the first reports of landings sometime after 0230.[3]

Concluding that this was the real thing, Krancke sent out the codeword *Grosslandung*, summoning all available naval forces, and called Dönitz, who endorsed his assessment and began a futile campaign to persuade Hitler and von Rundstedt to do the same.[4] Other than Hoffmann's attack and an abortive sortie by the two E-boat flotillas at Cherbourg, the only other Kriegsmarine operation in the assault area on D-Day itself was a bizarre incident on the eastern flank, when a pair of *Vorpostenboote* came up the Caen Canal from Ouistreham and engaged the British paratroops defending the bridge taken by a glider-born *coup de main* and now famously known as Pegasus Bridge. One boat was driven off, but the other was disabled by a paratrooper using a PIAT portable anti-tank weapon and its crew taken prisoner.[5] However, Ramsay and his subordinates were well aware that this could change in hours. The Neptune plan envisaged a layered defence of the Seine Bay against the principal threats: air attack and attack by small surface craft, mostly at night; minelaying; and attack from the shore by military forces, coastal guns, miniature submarines, motor boats and human torpedoes.

Furthest out were the Home Fleet at Scapa Flow, still watching for any indications that the German surface fleet intended to steam south or, more likely, northwards out into the Atlantic, and air and surface anti-submarine patrols sweeping the North Sea, Western Channel and Bay of Biscay; these forces were controlled by the Commanders-in-Chief at Portsmouth and Plymouth, and the Vice-Admiral, Dover. With the anti-submarine warfare (ASW) groups deployed in the Western Approaches were the only aircraft carriers directly involved in Operation Neptune: the small ASW escort carriers HMS *Emperor*, HMS *Pursuer* and HMS *Tracker*.[6] The last piece of the puzzle outside the assault area was the Home Command Coastal Forces, mostly controlled by the Captain, Coastal Forces (Channel) at Portsmouth, the experienced Captain Patrick McLaughlin, and his staff.

The UK-based forces would soon have work to do. Following receipt of Krancke's signal three large destroyers, *Z32*, *Z24* and the ex-Dutch *ZH1* – the last major German surface units in the Channel – left the Gironde at 0348 on the 6th bound for Brest and operations in the Seine Bay. ULTRA provided their course, speed and destination, and Coastal Command aircraft sighted the ships at 1230 in the Bay of Biscay: 40 miles west of Saint-Nazaire they were subjected to intense air attacks, though they survived and made port.[7]

Late on the 6th, the *Landwirt* U-boats also put to sea, doubtless inspired by an standing order from Dönitz exhorting that 'every boat that inflicts losses on the enemy while he is landing has fulfilled its primary function even though it perishes in so doing'.[8] Herbert Werner, commanding the war-weary and obsolete *U-415*, recalled a subsequent order delivered verbally by his flotilla commander in May, which took this one stage further: if necessary, U-boats were to ram their targets in 'a German version of the Japanese Kamikaze sacrifice'. At 2130 on D-Day, *U-415* and fourteen other boats slipped out of Brest. Seven modernised, schnorkel-equipped submarines submerged and headed off at regular intervals. Werner and the other COs of non-schnorkel boats, chillingly, had been ordered to proceed at top speed on the surface 'at a time when the sky was black with thousands of aircraft and the sea swarmed with hundreds of destroyers and corvettes. 'Clearly', he grimly recorded, 'we would not survive long enough to commit suicide by ramming cargo ships.'[9]

Thirty-six boats sailed from various bases and, thanks to ULTRA, their precise dispositions were known to the Allies, including whether or not they were fitted with schnorkel; by 7 June the codebreakers were even passing on Dönitz's various exhortations.[10] Precisely vectored Allied aircraft and surface ships sighted fourteen of them on the night of 6/7 June and attacked eight: *U-629* and *U-970* were sunk, along with a bonus boat, *U-955*, homeward bound from a weather patrol in the Atlantic.[11] From 6 June until 10 July, eleven Escort Groups were hard at work in the western English Channel, guarding the Seine Bay against U-boat attack. They spent 67 per cent of this time actually at sea, investigating thirty-two possible contacts, many provided by aircraft, which were in turn often acting on ULTRA intelligence or direction-finding. One report estimated that the Escort Groups swept their entire operating area a remarkable twenty-eight times. Only a small number of the most determined German submariners got anywhere near the vulnerable traffic crossing backwards and forwards from Britain to the Seine Bay.[12]

Herbert Werner was not one of them. From 2310, when the first radar impulses were picked up by the U-boats' detector sets, the eight submarines were relentlessly attacked from the air. Four bombs straddled *U-415* at 0220, stopping the submarine's engines and rupturing the fuel tanks. Werner ordered his crew on deck and prepared to abandon, but eventually managed to submerge, against orders, and nurse his battered command back to base. *U-415* was leaking badly and devastated inside, with both driveshafts bent, the batteries cracked and leaking acid, and the compass, depth gauge, compressors and periscopes all unserviceable. One diesel engine had been shaken from its mount.[13] The schnorkel-equipped boats fared little better. Fourteen sailed, and three were sunk over the next few weeks, in exchange for some limited successes. U-boats would remain a threat to the traffic in and out of the Seine Bay for months, but the devastating, near-suicidal offensive which Dönitz had envisaged was an anti-climax thanks to ULTRA intelligence and highly effective ASW measures.

The defence system in the immediate neighbourhood of the assault area was complex (see Map 7). In the ETF area, attack from seaward was managed directly by an officer designated as Captain (Patrols), at sea in a frigate and initially reporting directly to Vian in HMS *Scylla*, and attack from land by the relevant Assault Force Commander. Captain Tony Pugsley, formerly commanding Assault Group J1 in the frigate HMS *Lawford*, became Captain (Patrols), the role he had unexpectedly been given during exercise Gold Braid back in March. To reduce the risk of friendly fire and collisions, the defence was largely static. Defence Line A, consisting of anchored minesweepers, ran along the assault area 6 miles offshore between Ouistreham and Port-en-Bessin to guard against any threat from the north, a loosely demarcated area of water codenamed Pike. At the end of this line on the eastern flank, a line of LCGs and LCFs supported by Coastal Forces craft, the Trout Line, ran south to the shore, watching area Tunny to the north-east, which was seen as the greatest threat as it faced Le Havre. 'Night after night we spent in the gun pits', wrote one Marine from *LCF-32*, 'staring apprehensively into the darkness for signs of enemy vessels, alternating with colleagues in snatching half an hour's rest lying on the ribbed steel deck ... the knowledge that we could suffer instant fatal damage from an unseen enemy was ever present.'[14]

Tunny was also patrolled by destroyers, apparently nicknamed 'pouncers', and more MTBs. At first the entire assault area was obscured by smokescreens laid by LCPs and MLs at dusk and dawn, but this was discontinued as it caused problems for anti-aircraft defence and mine watching: 'an absolute curse', Royal Observer Corps seaborne observer H.R. Uridge of the depot ship SS *Thysville* called it: 'The entire area was blotted out by thick rolling banks of evil smelling artificial fog. The stink used to penetrate everywhere below deck.'[15]

Kirk divided the WTF area into eight defence areas: Mountain, Hickory and Elder seaward to the north, and Prairie, Vermont, Kansas, Oregon and Ohio to the south, around the assault beaches. Destroyers, Patrol Craft and Royal Navy Steam Gunboats patrolled the Dixie Line, which started just west of the Îles Saint-Marcouf and ran along the coast 6 miles offshore, joining the British Line A at Port-en-Bessin. South of this patrolled a duty division of four destroyers and a pair of Radar Picket destroyers to provide early warning of aircraft, a lesson learned in the Pacific. MTBs and PT Boats watched the Mason Line, which ran north from the Îles Saint-Marcouf to the northern edge of Utah Area. Kirk controlled the seaward defence from USS *Augusta*, with the Assault Force Commanders managing landward defence and local patrolling. Peter Scott, who joined Captain Maclaughlin's staff at the end of June, wrote that 'the areas bounded by these imaginary lines became ... separate stages, on each of which the fighting developed in its own characteristic pattern'.[16]

Twenty-four fighter squadrons provided air defence during the periods of maximum vulnerability at dusk and dawn, while six squadrons of Mosquito night fighters covered the assault area during the

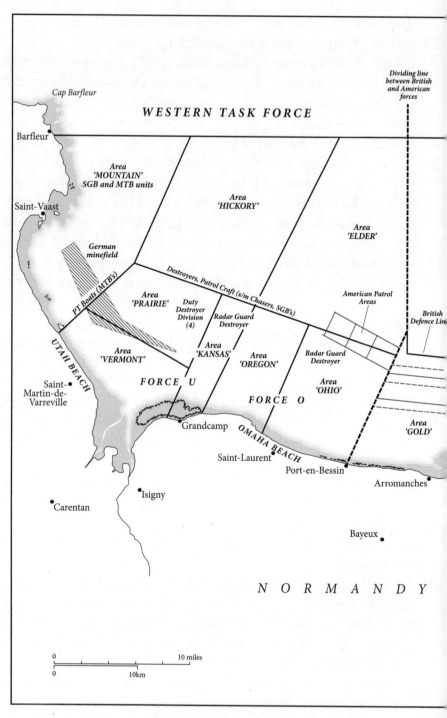

Map 7. *Guarding the bay.*

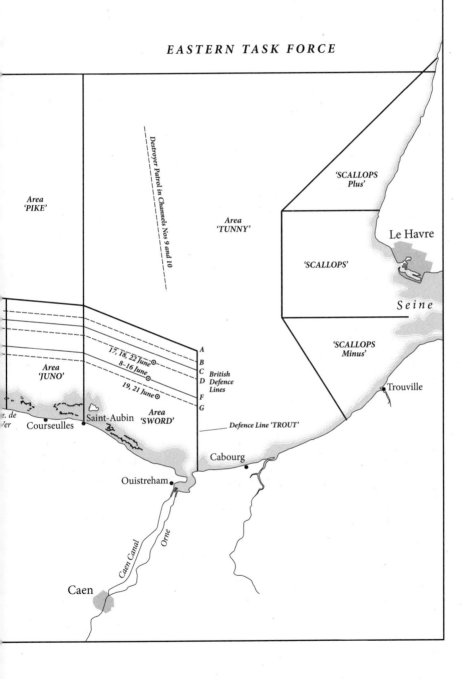

English Channel

EASTERN TASK FORCE

Destroyer Patrol in Channels Nos 9 and 10

Area 'PIKE'

Area 'TUNNY'

'SCALLOPS Plus'

Le Havre

'SCALLOPS'

Seine

'SCALLOPS Minus'

Trouville

A
B
17, 18, 22 June
C
8–16 June
D
British Defence Lines
F
19, 21 June
G

Area 'JUNO'

Area 'SWORD'

Defence Line 'TROUT'

e. de
/er
Courseulles
Saint-Aubin

Cabourg

Ouistreham

Caen Canal
Orne

Caen

hours of darkness. The fighters were controlled from three Fighter Direction Tenders, converted LSTs manned by joint RAF and Royal Navy crews with an 'Operations Block' fitted with RAF radar and multiple wireless sets. Despite reservations about their hasty and improvised design, 'thanks to the work of a first class operation team, the results obtained have been highly satisfactory'. *FDT-217* operated over the British ETF Area and *FDT-216* over the Americans; the third, *FDT-13*, operated in mid-Channel on convoy protection duties. As was so often the case, the sailors afloat were often unaware of just how much the FDTs and the night fighters did to protect them, one contemporary report lamenting that:

> it was probably not appreciated by the fleet how many raids were broken up and turned away before reaching a position which would have necessitated the promulgation of air raid warnings ... our strong fighter cover acted as a deterrent to the enemy. 'Y' [wireless intercept personnel, also present on the FDTs] reported that many of the enemy were distinctly 'jumpy'.[17]

Below, the fleet's anti-aircraft guns and Army batteries ashore put up a devastating explosive shield over the Bay every time a German aircraft appeared, although the tendency of inexperienced or battle-weary sailors to shoot at anything which flew meant this was not always helpful: 'we fired at our own planes as usual this morning', one sailor aboard the cruiser HMS *Diadem* recorded casually in his diary on 10 June.[18] To offset this, friendly aircraft fired coloured recognition flares, the pattern changing every day, and radar and naval lookouts were supplemented by experienced civilian Royal Observer Corps spotters like Uridge, whose routines were as punishing as any sailor's.

The first raids began on the night of 6/7 June. One bomber attacked the cruiser *Emerald*, one officer recalling how:

> we very nearly were expended at 2300 on 6 June when a Ju88 made a low level attack on us and dropped three bombs, one short, one a direct hit and one over. Fortunately, they were delay fused,

and the bomb bounced off our deck, demolished a couple of stanchions and continued into the water, where it exploded almost simultaneously with its companions. The ship was badly shaken (as was this observer); but its operational capabilities were not affected.[19]

The odds were stacked against the attackers. One group of Ju88s from *Kampfgeschwader 26* flew 900km from Montpellier to the Seine Bay that night, only to find an impenetrable barrier of anti-aircraft fire and barrage balloons which thwarted all attempts at torpedo attack. Flying low to avoid night fighters, the German bombers were forced further out into the Channel to make their attacks, before returning home pursued by night fighters. 'Hellish anti-aircraft fire greeted us', reported Major Ernst Thomsen of III Gruppe, KG26; 'in no time we were right in the middle of it. It flashed from all sides. The blast clouds lay thick around us, and the red-coloured tracers that covered us looked the worst. We didn't spot a target . . . through this firestorm. We weren't even in a position to make a target run.'[20]

Air raids continued every night until 30 June. On sixteen occasions the Luftwaffe even attacked in daylight, Vian recording that 'the air superiority exercised by our air forces made the attacks of decreasing frequency and of purely nuisance value', although, despite this overwhelming strength, Allied fighters and anti-aircraft gunners struggled to shoot them down.[21] Perhaps the most famous of the day raids was the sortie by Major Josef 'Pips' Priller of *Jagdgeschwader 26* and his wingman, whose strafing run over Sword Beach in their Fw190 fighters on 6 June was first described in Cornelius Ryan's 1959 book *The Longest Day*, and immortalised in the feature film of the same name three years later.[22]

The night attacks were a different matter. Every night and all night, as many as fifty lone aircraft would fly in low across the beaches bombing or, more frequently, minelaying, a form of attack which, according to Vian, 'presented a problem to the defence which was never solved'. The Bay was a huge area to defend, and the Germans tended to keep to seaward, out of range of shore-based anti-aircraft batteries, or use the high ground around Le Havre to screen their final approach. To make matters worse, the use of three different variants of Oyster pressure mines – over 200 were laid between 11 and 14 June – restricted the movements of warships on AA defence, and at any given time the skies were cluttered with hundreds of Allied aircraft.[23] Maintaining a constant watch against these nuisance raids was exhausting, and the risk of friendly fire was high: on the first night, a German air raid coincided with the arrival of the airborne reinforcements, and at least one RAF transport was shot down as a consequence. The AA gunners aboard the merchant ships were particularly suspect, Vian commenting that 'the guns' crews of close range weapons in merchant ships and some landing craft showed a lamentable lack of fire discipline ... and aircraft recognition'. On D+4, all efforts to impose workable restrictions having failed, a blanket ban on merchant ships opening fire at night was imposed.[24]

Like air defence, minesweeping was a constant responsibility as small German surface craft and aircraft slipped into the swept areas every night, reseeding them with ground mines. Fortunately, the first Oyster mines, described by Vian as the Germans' 'one tactical surprise', did not appear for a week.[25] Bizarrely most had been returned to a depot in Magdeburg when the invasion had not materialised in May.[26] Mining began in Sword Area around the mouth of the Orne, and was gradually extended westwards, and northwards into the main convoy route. Warships were detailed to watch for mines, but this was incredibly hard, particularly as the Luftwaffe tended to combine minelaying with bombing.

The final element of the defence of the Seine Bay is often overlooked: shore bombardment in support of the Army, which continued for weeks after the initial assault, particularly for the big-gunned battleships, monitors and cruisers, which could hit targets miles inland. It would be impossible to attempt to describe every fire mission: HMS *Belfast*, for example, fired her guns almost every day in June, apart from two brief trips back to Portsmouth to replenish its ammunition and the days of the great storm, and the same was true for many warships in the Bay.[27] German accounts can be justly accused of overstating the power and destructiveness of both naval gunnery and air power to build a pernicious myth that the 'superior' German soldier might have won the day had the playing field been level, but there is little doubt that the big guns were instrumental in breaking up German counter-attacks and helping Allied troops to expand their precarious beachheads, beginning with 21st Panzer Division's attack on the afternoon of D-Day itself. One battlegroup reached the coast but in the end the attack was broken up by 'heavy fire from the navy [and] relays of attacks by fighter-bombers', as well as a spirited defence by British tanks on Perriers Ridge and the threat posed by more airborne troops landing behind them.[28] Defensive fire missions were arguably as important to the defence of the Bay as any U-boat hunt or action on the Trout Line. 'The panzer divisions are being decimated by naval gunfire', wrote the notorious SS officer Kurt Meyer, describing events on 11 June, 'it can't go on like this!'[29] The point was rammed home to him three days later when naval gunfire killed his commanding officer, Brigadeführer Fritz Witt of the 12th SS Panzer Division, at his command post near Venoix, several kilometres back from the coast.[30] Naval gunnery continued to be effectively controlled by spotter aircraft and FOB parties ashore, joined over time by Royal Artillery Air Observation Post pilots flying tiny, vulnerable Austers and Piper Cubs from improvised airstrips ashore. Ian Neilson flew with 652 Squadron from a former French military airfield near the village of Plumetot and carried out 800 'shoots' in the first few weeks of the campaign, operating with both the Army and the warships: 'We were always of course delighted to be shooting with the Navy because they were so accurate!'[31]

Like the Luftwaffe the Kriegsmarine came out at night. Hoffmann's big fleet torpedo boats sortied four times between 6 and 30 June, and the E-boats and R-boats at Le Havre came out eight times. Hoffmann described penetrating the Allied escort screen during the night of 6/7 June, slipping in from the north and operating with impunity among the Allied escorts for hours before torpedoing three destroyers and making his escape, but there is absolutely no evidence in the official record for this extravagant claim.[32] The Kriegsmarine's coastal craft, however, were active on the night of the 6th, mostly attempting to lay mines. The legendary Lieutenant-Commander Don Bradford and four MTBs of the 55th Flotilla fought a short, violent action against an armed landing craft and eight R-boats in Area Scallop, towards Le Havre, between 0350 and around 0420. Bradford raked the German craft and closed the range at high speed until 'four mines exploded in rapid succession, four around R-boats and one fifty yards ahead of unit'. Realising the risk to his own boats if he pursued the Germans into a minefield, Bradford wisely withdrew, claiming one R-boat blown up on mines.[33] Shortly afterwards, the Canadian 29th Flotilla engaged six R-boats in Area Tunny, claiming three damaged and one sunk; all four of the Canadian MTBs were damaged and four men were wounded. To the west, E-boats from Cherbourg made repeated attempts to reach the Spout, at times showing Allied recognition signals, but were driven off every time; in the chaos of these high-speed night actions *S-139* and *S-140* were mined in a British defensive field codenamed Greengage with the loss of thirty-seven men.[34]

HMS *Bulolo*, headquarters ship for Force G, was an early victim of the Luftwaffe's tip-and-run strategy. Hit by an incendiary bomb just after dawn on 7 June, the former liner caught fire and two RAF officers were killed, along with Sub-Lieutenant Cyril Oaker and 23-year-old Able Seaman George Young, a gunlayer on one of the ship's Oerlikons. On the same night the hospital ships *St Julien* and *Dinard*, both former train ferries, were mined, the latter being nursed back to the UK by two naval trawlers. German bombers narrowly missed Hall's flagship *Ancon* in Omaha Area, the command ship retaliating by shooting down one of the raiders, and the minesweeper USS *Tide* was mined near the Îles Saint-Marcouf at 0940: the explosion blew the entire ship five feet into the air and the wreck broke in two and sank minutes later just after the last survivors were taken off. Twenty-seven men died and many of the survivors were catastrophically wounded.[35]

Seven separate actions with E-boats took place on the night of 7/8 June off Pointe de Barfleur as the Cherbourg-based *5.Sfltl* and *9.Sfltl* tried to interfere with invasion traffic running down the Spout.[36] By now Coastal Forces were practising innovative new tactics, largely developed by two young RNVR officers, Guy Hudson and Philip Lee, in which radar-equipped Captain Class frigates were used as control ships to vector the MTBs onto their targets.[37] 'We were quite active, we were always on the go', recalled seaman Tom Barker of HMS *Duff*, '*Duff* again, *Duff* do this, *Duff* do that! ... We never had no sleep ... we didn't even get an extra tot!'[38] Telegraphist George Lester, just 19 but a veteran of Torch, Husky and Avalanche, was part of the MTB control team aboard the frigate HMS *Kingsmill*, formerly HQ ship for Assault Group G2. The Control Officer was a highly decorated Coastal Forces veteran, Lieutenant Herbert Hollings MBE, DSC and Bar, RN, formerly Senior Officer of the 6th MGB Flotilla. 'He knew all the skippers of all the boats ... personally', Lester recalled; 'We used to operate on the table and we built up quite a rapport between ourselves.' The atmosphere was one of quiet contemplation, more like an academic study or a laboratory rather than the hyperactive frenzy beloved of Hollywood plot rooms:

He wanted it quiet, so therefore I had to receive all the things via headphones. Anything that came through I would jot down ... with my green chinagraph pencil and when he saw it and actioned it, he used to wipe it off. If he wanted a signal to go, to move one group of MTBs from another position, he would just give me the call sign of the group that he wanted to go – he just put V270 2.5. That meant he wanted to go vector 270 degrees, two and half miles. The call signs were changed every night ... they were just two letter call signs, George-Mike, George-Love, that would be the controlling ship ... usually began with a G. The [groups of] boats, they'd be ... George-Love 4, and then the individual boats in those would be 4-1 or 4-2 or 4-3, so you could pick up one particular boat if you wanted.[39]

The Control Ships went out every night. The work was so exhausting that the decision was taken to rotate the ships to rest the crews, but there was no respite for the specialised Control teams: as *Kingsmill* entered Portsmouth, an MTB came alongside and 'I had to throw some shaving gear and a towel ... into an attaché case and jump on the MTB with a few others, and we were immediately whipped back by MTB to the beachhead to board HMS *Retalick* to carry on the patrols that night.'[40]

This extraordinary tactical advantage, provided on the night of 8/9 June by the frigates HMS *Stayner* and HMS *Retalick*, allowed the British to drive off the Germans on almost every occasion. The raiders did enjoy one significant success, finding and attacking a convoy of landing craft from Q LCT Flotilla. Despite what was described as a 'spirited defence' by the escorting ML, Lieutenant J.C. Lewis's *ML-903*, there were simply too many torpedoes in the water for everyone to escape. One blew off the stern of *LCT-875*, which sank in seconds taking all twelve officers and men aboard down with her, another LCT and an LCI were damaged, one sinking on the way back to the UK.[41]

8 June was a terrible day. In Utah Area, Rear-Admiral Don Moon was shocked to lose three warships in swift succession. First to go was the USS *Meredith*, which detonated a mine at 0152. The explosion occurred shortly after the destroyer's Recognition Officer reported a pair of Heinkel 177 bombers streaking low across the water nearby, giving rise to incorrect reports that *Meredith* had been hit by a glider bomb. 'The ship gave a tremendous lurch forward and upward and everybody on the topside was thrown to their knees and we were all drenched with a huge cloud of water', Commander George Knuepler reported:

> This water just seemed to fall for minutes until it appeared as if we were going down under the sea, suddenly all abated, flying debris had stopped falling and we stirred around to find out the extent of damage. All communications had been lost and power was off the ship ... the mine had struck on the port side of the keel right under No. 2 Fireroom and had wiped out both No. 1 Fireroom, No. 1 Engine Room and No. 2 Engine Room, killing most of the men in that area including those that were in the repair parties on topside just above that area. The explosion blew a hole about 65 feet outward in this area, completely wiped out the main deck, the forward boat davit, the motor whaleboat, the super structure deck and half of No. 2 stack.[42]

Meredith was flooding steadily, listing, and there was every possibility of the destroyer's back breaking, as Knuepler believed all that was holding his stricken ship together was the starboard propeller shaft. Prioritising his crew, he called two PCs alongside to take off his wounded, and then the destroyer USS *Bates* took off everyone else. Within an hour and a half, *Meredith* was abandoned and drifting towards Cherbourg, Knuepler and his key team keeping pace aboard *Bates*. Although *Meredith* was eventually towed into the Transport Area, the ship's battered seams were further stressed when a bomb exploded nearby, and the destroyer broke in two and sank at around 1000 on the 9th. Thirty-five men were recorded as dead or missing. Chief Machinist's Mate Bryan Lawson was recommended for the Navy Cross for returning to his engine room when he realised none of the twelve men on watch with him had escaped: 'He obtained a flashlight and at the risk of his own life, he went down into the totally dark and shattered after engine room', Knuepler wrote, 'which at that time was flooded to within four feet of the overhead, and displayed extraordinary heroism and devotion to duty with his total disregard to danger ... he saved four injured men.'[43]

The destroyer USS *Glennon* was mined at 0803 while under fire from German shore guns: the huge explosion effectively blew off the stern, killing all power, launching a 150lb cement Dan Buoy 125ft along the deck, and blowing sixteen sailors into the water, including two unfortunate men standing on the fantail who were thrown 40ft into the air. As the destroyer escort (DE) *Rich* manoeuvred to assist, it too detonated a pair of mines in swift succession. *Glennon*'s dazed and seriously wounded CO, 32-year-old Lieutenant-Commander Edward Michel of Meadville, Pennsylvania, described looking aft 'through the weird green, yellow haze of smoke and water' to see 'a large section of the ship's stern floating away'. Two minutes later the DE triggered a third mine, Michel ordered the ship abandoned and *Rich* sank shortly afterwards: ninety-one men were killed or died of their wounds.[44] *Glennon* stayed afloat, her broken stern jammed into the seabed. Efforts were made to salvage the destroyer but on 10 June German shore guns found the range: *Glennon* was hit three times by heavy shells and sank at 2145.

The British did not escape 8 June unscathed. Early in the morning Captain (Patrols) Tony Pugsley in HMS *Lawford* was returning from a sweep for E-boats in murky weather when lookouts heard an aircraft approaching rapidly from the port side. Lieutenant-Commander Malcom Morris's command was at second-degree readiness with all guns manned and six signalmen posted as lookouts, but this was not enough to save *Lawford* from a sudden strike in terrible visibility. Nobody saw the aircraft, which raked the frigate's bridge and flag deck with cannon fire: immediately afterwards there was a huge explosion amidships, rupturing both pairs of engine and motor rooms, and blowing a hole in the port side. Her back broken, *Lawford* lost way and began to heel over to starboard. Within ten minutes the midships section was under water: it was clear the frigate had broken in two and both sections were sinking fast. Morris ordered abandon ship, and 237 of his crew and Pugsley's staff swam to safety aboard nearby minesweepers from the 40th MSF. Colin Madden was among them:

> Oil fuel . . . was extremely difficult and tiresome to swim through and indeed when one finally arrived at the ship which was going to rescue one, one couldn't hold on to anything because everything was so slippery . . . even though it was in the middle of the summer, everybody was frightfully cold and there was a great problem in getting warm . . . there were some people who were very badly burned.[45]

Twenty-four men died, mostly in the engine rooms.[46] Pugsley returned to the UK with the other survivors, his duties as Captain (Patrols) being taken up by Captain Peter Cazalet, Captain (D) of the 23rd Destroyer Flotilla, but, incredibly, by 1800 the same evening he had returned to the Seine Bay and resumed his command, initially from HMS *Waveney* and later from HMS *Retalick*.[47]

To complete a truly terrible day, the netlayer HMS *Minster*, a former train ferry, was mined and sunk off Utah while laying out coaster moorings for Gooseberry 1, sinking close to the wreck of the *Meredith* with the loss of fifty-eight men, and a Luftwaffe raider hit an ammunition and petrol dump in Sword with a single bomb, causing a huge fire and a series of secondary explosions which destroyed all the petrol landed to date, and half the ammunition.[48] Against these losses the Allies could set three more U-boats, *U-629*, *U-373* and, probably, *U-441*, all sunk by aircraft as the massacre of the *Landwirt* submarines continued; a fourth, *U-740*, was sunk the following day.[49]

E-boats got into the congested, target-rich Spout again on the night of 8/9 June, torpedoing US Navy LSTs *314* and *376* in Convoy ECM1P 18 miles east of Cap Barfleur, with heavy loss of life: Lieutenant-Commander Alvin Tutt of *314* reported that only 53 per cent of his crew survived, many dying from exposure after two and a half hours in the bitterly cold water. Sixty-four of his men lost their lives, along with another forty-six from *376*; the latter was so catastrophically holed that some of the survivors had to abandon their raft because it was about to be sucked back inside the ship. As the shaken sailors fought for their lives in the sea, their attackers cruised threateningly nearby.[50] After drifting into a minefield and spending several hours in the water, *314*'s survivors were rescued by Norman Murch's destroyer HMS *Beagle*, saviour of Giles Milton and his crew in *LCP(L) 4* on 6 June, and still carrying Reuters correspondent Desmond Tighe, who described the scene for the *Evening News* as 'the most courageous and cold-blooded rescue venture I have seen at sea'.[51]

Elsewhere, E-boats fought a running battle with the Canadian 29th MTB Flotilla and sank the Royal Navy's *LCT-875* with all hands. All of this proved one thing: the Allied warships in the Seine Bay could, and did, stop the Kriegsmarine's night hunters time and again, but the E-boats remained almost as hard to catch as they had been at the start of the war, and if luck was with them just once the results could be catastrophic. It was, perhaps, fortunate that the two LSTs were mainly loaded with equipment, which was relatively easily replaced, rather than men, who were not.

Elsewhere, in one of the most dramatic actions to be fought in defence of the Seine Bay, things went rather better for the Allies. Enigma decrypts on 8 June reported that the three German destroyers, *Z-24*, *Z-32* and *ZH-1*, would be leaving Brest for Cherbourg, accompanied by the torpedo boat *T-24*, to operate on the flanks of the invasion. The eight destroyers of 10th Destroyer Flotilla (DF), under Commander Basil Jones in HMS *Tartar*, were despatched to intercept. The 10th DF was a truly Allied formation, comprising three more British destroyers (*Ashanti*, *Eskimo* and *Javelin*), two Canadian (*Huron* and *Haida*) and the Polish *Blyskawica* and *Piorun*. Jones formed a patrol line in two divisions, running east to west, about 15 miles off Île de Batz. The sea was calm, visibility was good, and the Allied warships were equipped with excellent radar. *Tartar* picked up the Germans at 0114, and Jones closed in undetected, Kapitän zur See Theodor von Bechtolsheim remaining unaware of their presence until 0122, when, horrified, he ordered his ships to turn hard to port, firing off a salvo of torpedoes as they did so.[52] The Allied destroyers fired starshell and closed in for the kill, Jones having decided in advance to bring about a close-range gun action as 'It was . . . best to press on into the enemy during his own turn away to bring about a decisive result . . . the forward gun armament of the Tribals was powerful and ammunition for blind fire was plentiful with a Home Port under their lee.'[53] This aggressive response to what had become identified as a standard German tactic was the final outcome of years of bitter fighting in the Channel, a series of hard lessons which had begun with the Tunnel disaster back in October 1943.

Jones's destroyers set *Z-32* on fire, hit *ZH-1* repeatedly, severing steam lines and leaving the destroyer stopped, and smashed *Z-24*'s forward superstructure. The outnumbered Germans scattered, the badly damaged *Z-24* and *T-24* running to the south-west. Von Bechtolsheim in *Z-32* was suddenly alone, under the guns of the 20th Division, the two Polish destroyers with *Eskimo* and *Javelin*. Although hit multiple times, von Bechtolsheim fired torpedoes and escaped, the 20th Division having turned away, counter to Jones's orders. Turning east, just after 0200 the beleaguered von Bechtolsheim ran into Jones himself in *Tartar*, with *Ashanti* in company, and desperately opened fire, hitting *Tartar* hard. 'Four shells burst about *Tartar*'s bridge', Jones recalled, 'starting a fire abaft her bridge, cutting leads to her Directors, bringing down the trellis foremast and all Radar, and cutting Torpedo communications to aft.' Shells smashed into the bridge and wheelhouse killing four of *Tartar's* crew, knocking out all electronics and wounding Jones.[54] In exchange, *Ashanti* hit *Z-32* three times, starting a fire in a magazine which had to be flooded, and von Bechtolsheim broke away to the north-west, turning north-east at 0215. Following *Z-32* at speed, Lieutenant-Commander John Barnes in *Ashanti* came upon *ZH-1*, stopped and wreathed in clouds of steam. When the outgunned Germans opened fire, Barnes torpedoed *ZH-1*, blowing off the bows. Korvettenkapitän Klaus Barkow fired scuttling charges and the ex-Dutch destroyer blew up and sank at 0240 with the loss of thirty-nine officers and men.[55]

Von Bechtolsheim's ordeal was not over. Pursued and intermittently engaged by the Canadian destroyers *Haida* and *Huron*, at 0420 he gave permission for *T-24* and the badly damaged *Z-24* to return to Brest and ten minutes later he turned west to join them, writing later that 'with a heavy heart, I must therefore decide to break off the mission'.[56] The tenacious Canadians regained contact for the final time at 0445, joined by the Polish *Blyskawica*. At 0517, critically damaged and out of ammunition after fighting multiple gun actions against superior opponents all through the night, the determined and courageous von Bechtolsheim ran his battered ship aground on Île de Batz. As von Bechtolsheim and his crew clambered ashore, leaving thirty dead sailors behind them, the Canadians bombarded the wreck for ten minutes until it was well ablaze; the following day, *Z-32* was finished off by RAF Beaufighters which bombed and rocketed the destroyer into scrap metal.[57] 'The menace from the west was now liquidated,' Jones wrote dramatically after the war.[58] Ramsay was less happy, recording in his diary that 'It was disappointing in its result . . . I wanted all to be sunk.'[59]

The Luftwaffe and the E-boats continued to cause havoc every night. On 9/10 June Cherbourg-based boats torpedoed the ammunition coasters *Dungrange* and *Brackenfield* in Convoy ETC4W passing down the Spout. Soon after, Oberleutnant zur See Kurt Neugebauer's *S-179* torpedoed the small coaster *Ashanti*, which was carrying cased petrol and blew up and disintegrated almost immediately. Soon afterwards, the Allies stopped sending convoys south from the Isle of Wight after dark, a small but significant alteration to the build-up programme and a sinister portent of the E-boats' potential to disrupt.[60]

At 0400 the following morning bombers damaged the MT ship *Fort Pic* and hit the Liberty ship *Charles Morgan* with a glider bomb off Utah, starting fires and blowing out the ship's bottom. The salvage tug USS *Kiowa* attempted to recover the freighter but was eventually forced to report 'unable to tow as ship's stern was resting too heavily on the bottom. Removed dead and survivors and declared ship a derelict.'[61] Later on the 10th, German coastal guns damaged the Free French destroyer *Mistral*, which was declared a total constructive loss.

At 0220 on the 10th, in a joint attack with Hoffmann's torpedo boats *Möwe* and *Jaguar*, E-boats torpedoed the frigate HMS *Halsted*, blowing off the bows. Thirty-four of the frigate's crew were killed or posted missing and although the hulk was towed back to the UK, *Halsted* was declared a total constructive loss and broken up for spares. At 2111 on the same day, US *LST-496*, an Exercise Tiger survivor, was mined 6 miles off Omaha Area on the way in to Dog Red; the explosion blew a 40ft hole in the ship's bottom, the blast ripping up through the ship to wreck parts of the superstructure. The engine room flooded immediately, the ship lost all power and light, and fully 75 per cent of the officers and men were killed or wounded, including nine out of ten survivors from *507*, which had gone down in Lyme Bay.[62] Although efforts were made to take the ship in tow, the damage was catastrophic and at 2218 *496* rolled over and sank carrying a full load of tanks and other vehicles, which would have taken the Germans far more time and effort to destroy on the battlefield; successes of this kind in sufficient numbers could have started to have a significant impact on the campaign.[63]

The following night, 10/11 June, E-boats sank the old minesweeper USS *Partridge* and the Admiralty tug *Sesame*. Both were towing Whale units at the time and both sank with heavy loss of life. Albert Barnes's tug *Storm King* found the drifting Whale, and the veteran tug men immediately knew something was amiss. 'When we looked the tow was bar-tight', he recalled, 'so we knew there was something on the end of it! We had to board her and we had to chop the ... [tow links] and we towed her over. When we got back to

Pompey . . . we found out that it was our sister ship that was on the end of the tow, she'd been sunk by an E-boat.'[64] Elsewhere, just after midnight MTBs from the 55th Flotilla drove off a German force of two E-boats and five R-boats, Lieutenant G.W. Claydon claiming one destroyed and two severely damaged.[65]

ROC seaborne observer A.P. Dearden was serving on the US Liberty ship *Lucy Stone*, which returned to the UK in convoy FCM1 on the same night. His diary gives a vivid sense of the tension and drama at sea during this challenging period, when every journey to and from the Bay was fraught with danger. The day had begun in a lively fashion, with an exchange of fire between the bombarding warships and German shore batteries and later a heavy air raid by Allied medium bombers: 'it was as if a major volcanic eruption had split the earth open', Dearden wrote, 'an immense pall of brown smoke and dust shot skywards'.[66] At the end of the day, *Lucy Stone* was forced to move to avoid more German shelling, before 'orders were received to up-anchor and scram' at 2200, in the middle of an air raid. Passing up the Spout, they were subjected to an E-boat attack:

> On the port bow, starshells suddenly lifted the semi-darkness. They flared incessantly, gradually shifting ahead and round to starboard. The action was taken up by the starboard escort. More stars appeared astern, yellow and green . . . the gun crew were tense, the loader had a shell and cartridge in his arms – it looked sinister in the glare. It was obvious that E-boats were all around us.[67]

The cat-and-mouse action between escorts and E-boats went on for three and a half hours, a tumult of starshell, smokescreens and sudden outbreaks of gunfire; 'once, a pillar of red flame rose into the air, stood for a second, then flickered out'. The E-boats finally slipped away at daybreak, and FCM1's twelve freighters slipped gratefully into Falmouth on the 12th without loss, 'by the grace of God (Loud Amen)', Dearden wrote.[68]

The pendulum swung the other way the following night when the control frigate HMS *Duff* vectored Lieutenant Rod Sykes in *MTB-448* and *MTB-453* onto a group of five E-boats. In an action which typifies the extraordinary risks run by these young men, Sykes in *448* broke the German line in Nelsonic style, dropping a depth charge specially modified to explode at shallow depth alongside the second E-boat in line before turning to run up the starboard side of the leader, Kapitänleutnant Jurgen Meyer's *S-136*, until both boats were riddled and sinking.[69] *MTB-448*'s only fatality was Arthur Thorpe, a 42-year-old war correspondent from the *Exchange Telegraph* travelling as an observer. 'Suddenly a body fell though the doorway from the bridge on to the charthouse floor', recalled Rodney Timms, Sykes's First Lieutenant; 'I turned him over ... it was Thorpe the reporter sailing with us. I could see no blood or head wounds so I tried to find a heartbeat but the gunfire was deafening, I couldn't hear or feel a pulse.' Despite Timms's best effort to plug *448*'s gaping wound with blankets, it was clear the MTB was going down and Sykes abandoned ship, the crew transferring to *453* with as much useful equipment as they could carry.[70] *S-136* also went down, taking Meyer and eighteen of his men with it. Tom Barker aboard HMS *Duff* saw the aftermath as dawn started to break: 'there was about five or six men sitting on the front of the MTB', he recalled; 'they were trying to get their man out of the gun turret and he'd had his legs blown ... he was in a bad state'.[71]

The Battle of the Seine Bay was still very much in the balance. On 12 June, E-boats torpedoed the destroyer USS *Nelson*, blowing off the stern, and giving rise to rumours on the German side that they had damaged the British battleship of the same name. On the same day, Dönitz finally recognised in the face of catastrophic losses that U-boats without schnorkels simply could not operate in these heavily defended waters. Twenty-eight of the boats taking part in the initial *Landwirt* sorties were not equipped with schnorkel. Of these five had been sunk by 10 June, and five more driven back with heavy damage. On the 12th, Dönitz ordered the remainder back to a static defence line in the Bay of Biscay, ruling them out of any further attempt to interfere with Neptune, and a few days later they were recalled to their bases.[72]

That night the Luftwaffe launched one of their largest strikes against invasion traffic. Ninety-one Junkers 88 bombers from

2.Fliegerdivision attacked the 14th Escort Group in Lyme Bay and hit a convoy off Portland Bill, sinking one of the escorts, HMS *Boadicea*, with either a glider bomb or a torpedo.[73] Whatever the cause, the result was horrific: the explosion detonated the *Boadicea's* magazine and the old destroyer sank in minutes with the loss of all but 12 of the crew of 182. Brian Haskell-Thomas was the Gunnery Officer of a nearby escort, HMS *Magpie*. 'We were about 400 yards from HMS *Boadicea* ... it was so quick; nobody could have done anything. We were told not to stop under any circumstances.'[74]

On the night of 14/15 June, the redoubtable Commander John Barnes of HMS *Ashanti* was in action again when his ship and Komandor podporucznik Tadeusz Gorazdowski's Polish destroyer ORP *Piorun* surprised a group of four German minesweepers south-west of Jersey. The Allied destroyers picked up the German ships on radar at 0023 and closed at speed. At 0038, they sighted the enemy, opened up their gunnery arcs to bring every weapon to bear and opened fire. 'A very fine close action fight followed', reported *Piorun's* Royal Navy Liaison Officer, Lieutenant Charles Bain; 'many hits were observed on the enemy and one ship appeared to be suffering badly.'[75] Although significantly outgunned, the German sweepers fought back to the best of their ability. Heavy and accurate shellfire landed all around the Allied ships, and *Piorun* had a scary moment when a shell exploded in a ready use magazine, starting a fire which could have caused a catastrophic explosion, although it was soon extinguished. 'As the target seemed inviting', Barnes continued, 'it was decided to attack with torpedoes.' Gorazdowski fired a salvo of five, one blowing off the bows of *M-83*, his 'Headache' wireless intercept operator subsequently picking up a message that the German minesweeper was sinking. Barnes did not consider minesweepers to be 'suitable torpedo targets' and did not fire. The action continued until 0232, by which time the Germans had lost another sweeper, *M-343*, the remainder having reached the shelter of the coastal batteries on Jersey. The Admiralty were quite damning of the whole affair, believing the destroyers were 'overwhelmingly superior in gun power' and should have sunk more of the German sweepers. They were particularly scathing about Barnes's decision not to fire torpedoes, condemning 'an unfortunate lack of torpedo-mindedness for which Plymouth is notorious'.[76]

In the meantime, the decision had been taken to do something about the ongoing threat posed by the E-boats.[77] Exhaustion and maintenance issues coupled with the deteriorating weather as the great storm approached led to a tactical misjudgement by the Germans: by the morning of 14 June, Allied intelligence had learned that well over half of the available E-boats in the Seine Bay were concentrated at Le Havre; this was confirmed later that day by a photo-reconnaissance Spitfire, which brought crystal-clear images showing not only E-boats, but R-boats, minesweepers, patrol boats and Hoffmann's torpedo boats.[78] Ramsay considered the intelligence carefully and reached a decision: 'At my request', he wrote in his despatch, 'Bomber Command carried out a heavy attack on the port just before dusk.'[79]

The bombers went over in two waves. The first wave hit at 2232 and included 221 aircraft from several squadrons, including Lancasters from the famous 'Dambusters' of 617 Squadron. Among the fearsome weapons they dropped were 'Tallboys', huge 12,000lb bombs designed to penetrate the thick concrete of the E-boats' protective bunkers and cause an earthquake effect by penetrating deep into the ground before exploding, or if they exploded in water, send a tidal wave sweeping inside the open entrances. The entire raid was over in less than twenty minutes. The second wave of 119 Lancasters, arrived at 0115. They were almost unopposed, the Luftwaffe having ordered its anti-aircraft gunners to hold their fire as friendly aircraft were operating in the area – according to Ruge, 'a desperate Krancke had telephoned in all directions to have the order rescinded, but to no avail' – and they left behind absolute chaos.[80] In total, the bombers dropped twenty-two Tallboys, along with around three tons of high explosive on each acre.[81] The port was devastated, its basins choked with wreckage, its warehouses and stores ablaze and its cranes and other equipment smashed. Three torpedo boats were sunk and the remaining two damaged; ten E-boats had also been destroyed and three more crippled. Dozens more small warships were destroyed, and the raid also eliminated the Kriegsmarine's precious stocks of torpedo warheads and mines, which in turn caused massive secondary detonations.[82] Over 200 officers and men were killed. Sub-Lieutenant Sam Popham watched the raid from the minesweeper HMS *Recruit*, remembering

> a solid mass of white flame standing one inch high on the horizon and accompanied by flashes that lit the heavens and turned night into day ... when I went off watch at 4 o'clock, the fires were still unconquered and their flames illuminated the clouds of steam and smoke that hung over the town.[83]

The following night, Bomber Command followed up with a raid on Boulogne. Only eleven Tallboys were dropped, and 1–1.5 tons of HE per acre, but the bombers still sank between thirty and forty craft.[84]

E-boat attacks did not come to an end, as over time the Germans reinforced the flotillas threatening the Bay with new boats from elsewhere, but the raids drastically limited the Kriegsmarine's efforts to have a strategic impact on the build-up traffic during this critical period.[85] The 29th and 55th MTB Flotillas and 1st Coastal Forces Flotilla, all patrolling in the Seine Bay, reported no actions between 12/13 June and 23/24 June.[86]

Battle for Cherbourg
13 June–5 July 1944

Considering the hornet's nest that was encountered, it is probable
we should have done better if we had used more ammunition.

Rear-Admiral Moreton Deyo, USN[1]

The E-boats might have been temporarily silenced, but there
were plenty of other threats. The veteran battleship *Warspite*
detonated a mine off Harwich on 13 June while returning to Rosyth
to replace worn-out gun barrels. Having become the first Allied
capital ship to negotiate the Strait of Dover since 1940, the thoroughly worn-out grand old lady of the fleet now had all four propeller
shafts bent and a 6-degree list to port.[2]

Out in the Western Approaches, U-boats continued to try to
break through the escort screen. On 15 June, they scored two significant successes, Oberleutnant Walter Dankleff's schnorkel-equipped
U-767 torpedoing HMS *Mourne*, and Oberleutnant von Bremen's
U-764 HMS *Blackwood*, both frigates. Dankleff hit *Mourne* at 1345
with a G7es (T5) *Zaunkönig* acoustic homing torpedo, nicknamed a
GNAT (German Navy Acoustic Torpedo) by the British. It hit just
under the bridge, detonating the forward magazine, and the frigate
rolled over and sank in precisely sixty-four seconds, taking 111 men
with her. There were just 27 survivors. Seaman Eric Pickering of
HMS *Aylmer* helped rescue them:

They couldn't open their eyes for diesel oil and their throats, a lot of them had swallowed the water ... after they'd had a shower and a drink and what have you, they were OK [but] about half an hour afterwards they were all dropping down, delayed shock.[3]

'There is absolutely no hope of anyone being a prisoner-of-war', wrote the Admiralty bluntly to one grieving relative; 'there was a very violent explosion ... which killed or stunned all those who were in the fore part of the ship, and the majority were drowned having been stunned by the force of the explosion, in which case they suffered nothing.'[4] In the bitter see-saw fighting which typified this period, *U-767* was herself depth-charged into oblivion three days later off Guernsey; Dankleff and all but one of his crew of forty-nine died.

Blackwood lost fifty-seven officers and men when von Bremen blew off the bow just after 1900 with another *Zaunkönig*. Surgeon-Lieutenant M.J. Brosnan, who with spectacular poor luck had only transferred to *Blackwood* from another ship the day before, described a calm, ordinary night, the ship's officers relaxing in the Wardroom or doing routine administration. 'There was a blinding flash, a bang and the sound of tearing metal', he wrote later; 'on coming to I was lying under a piece of the Wardroom table in the corner.' Water was pouring down from the deck above, and the ship was full of white smoke and reeked of cordite. There was a sinister silence except for the sound of running water – the ever-present throb of the ship's engines had stopped. As Brosnan came to, he realised with horror that the forward bulkhead and port side of the wardroom were open to the elements and everything forward of this compartment had vanished.

Brosnan climbed up to the deck above through the twisted port side, passing 'two bodies ... hanging over these plates with blood pouring out of them [and] obviously dead'. Reaching the upper deck and finding a complete shambles, he started staggering aft, a nightmare journey with the smoke occasionally parting to reveal a terrible vignette of destruction and suffering. Eventually, Brosnan formed a working party and started to bring the wounded on deck. 'Most of the injuries were either head injuries or broken limbs,' he recalled in a report which was later praised for its clarity; 'they were all cold, shocked and soaking wet and thoroughly miserable.' Many needed morphine.[5] The Captain and most of the other officers were wounded or incapacitated.

> I saw Sub-Lieutenant Rennie standing on the deck and asked him if he was all right. He did not reply but stared vacantly in front of him. His face and clothes were black and filthy . . . he did not appear to recognise me or be capable of thinking.[6]

In the absence of anyone else to take command, Brosnan gave the order to abandon ship, worked tirelessly to evacuate the wounded and repeatedly searched the ship to ensure nobody was left behind. He finally left at 2100. At no point in his report did he mention that he was himself badly injured, 'badly shaken with a face like chalk and what appeared to be an enormous bruise across his face'. The salvage tug *Miss Elaine* arrived from Plymouth to take the wounded frigate in tow, but the conditions were considered too dangerous, and at 0413 *Blackwood* slipped away.[7] *Blackwood*'s loss warranted two lines in the British Official History.[8] It was a good day for the U-boats as *U-621* also torpedoed and damaged *LST-280* off Saint-Malo. Elsewhere, the veteran Trinity House tender *Alert* was mined and sunk, although fortunately without casualties. Six Trinity House tenders took part in Neptune; their part in the operation is rarely acknowledged. Mainly buoy laying, they also placed the light vessels marking the Mulberry Harbours: *LV-72 Juno* at Arromanches and *LV-68 Kansas* at Saint-Laurent.[9]

In Sword Area, it was German artillery which was causing the most problems. 'Shelling of the beach commenced again on D+9', reported Captain William Leggatt, NOIC Sword Area, when five out of seven US LSTs were hit and damaged while beached.[10] The culprit was apparently a mobile 105mm battery near the River Orne, and the shelling went on throughout the 15th, from 1100 until 1630, forcing the crews to take shelter ashore until the tide came back in, when they successfully retracted their ships and left. There were six fatalities among the crews, three British soldiers also died and there were multiple wounded, mostly aboard *LST-307*.[11] The shelling continued on the 16th, when ferry craft and the gunboat HMS *Locust* were hit, and as a precaution the drying out of LSTs was prohibited at Sword. The issue was not restricted to Sword: German batteries at Cherbourg hit HMS *Talybont* on 17 June, when the destroyer was steaming provocatively close inshore, 'able to see washing hanging out'. The shell knocked out one of *Talybont*'s engines and the destroyer limped back to port. There was just one fatality, Ordinary Seaman Charles Rickett, from Lower Sydenham. He was only 17 years old. 'God takes our loved ones from our homes but never from our hearts' were the words his grieving parents Alfred and Norah had the Commonwealth War Graves Commission inscribe on his grave at Haslar Royal Naval Cemetery in Gosport.[12] 'He hadn't even a job on the ship', *Talybont*'s Able Seaman R.T. Scales remembered, 'so they gave him a rake to clear the empties away from the guns.'[13]

Air raids continued every night, both in the Bay and on the convoy routes across to Normandy. On 18 June, torpedo bombers attacked Convoy EBC14 south-west of the Needles, sinking the Canadian steamer *Albert C Field* with the loss of four men, and the destroyer *Onslow* was subjected to a concerted attack off Barfleur at twilight.

The worsening weather, which eventually culminated in the great northerly gale, largely halted surface and air operations for both sides, although it had an unpleasant and potentially lethal side effect as the churning water triggered the sensitive detonators on some Oyster mines, which blew up unexpectedly right across the assault area. *ML-292* probably triggered one just after leaving Mulberry B at 1930 on the 17th, Coxswain Albert Taylor recalling that 'there was an almighty bang and everything changed in a second'. Sometimes, the smaller craft fared better than the larger ships, with their delicate instruments and vulnerable machinery; *292* lifted right out of the water, then crashed back down, but nobody was hurt and the launch was eventually towed back to Gosport.[14] The Free French frigate *La Surprise* detonated another mine on the 20th while escorting convoy ECP12, the commanding officer reporting that 'the ship was shaken by a powerful explosion at 1142. The ship was felt to lift and take a list to starboard. A column of black muddy water about 200 feet high covered everything on deck and bridge.' The litany of destruction included a broken propeller shaft, water ingress into delicate condensers, bent bulkheads and damage to all manner of delicate equipment, including radar, gunsights, echo sounder and gyro compass, but *La Surprise* remained afloat and was towed back to the UK the following day, as the weather began to worsen.[15]

The destroyer HMS *Fury* fell victim to a mine on the morning of the 21st, lost all power, and was driven ashore despite repeated efforts to save her. Although the CO, Lieutenant-Commander Thomas Taylor, ordered his ship lightened by throwing everything possible overboard, including torpedoes and depth charges, the list worsened as the gale began to bite and night fell. Sydney Wagstaffe recalled that 'a message from ashore came which more or less said "you are on your own but the tide has turned which will bring you ashore"'. At 0130 on the 22nd the drifting destroyer hit the rocks, Taylor ordered the strongest swimmers ashore with survival lines, and his crew swam, staggered and clambered ashore, remarkably without loss of life. *Fury* was refloated and taken back to the UK but declared a total constructive loss.[16]

As the gale eased on 22 June, the German guns at Sword came to life again, hitting and destroying the ammunition coaster *Dunvegan Head*. Counter-battery fire failed to check them, and the beaches were closed to ammunition ships. On the 25th, Sword was closed to all remaining coasters and also to the vulnerable personnel ships: a single hit on one of these packed transports could have been catastrophic. It had become very clear that the risks of continuing to use Sword outweighed the advantages, and the ferry craft and depot ships were withdrawn shortly afterwards. On 1 July the NOIC, Leggatt, was withdrawn and the beaches at Sword were closed for good, Vian noting that 'the decision was not taken until it was clear that the other areas could accept the consequent increase in discharge of stores and personnel'.[17] Air attacks also began again, Ju88 bombers attacking nine patrol craft on the night of 22/23 June.[18]

Vian suffered a personal blow on 23 June when his flagship HMS *Scylla* touched off a ground mine at 2255 while 'moving, as I believe, rather faster than safety dictated . . . I was in the after cabin working with staff officers', he recorded in his memoir, 'and a large bracket fell on my head, sending my teeth through my lower lip.'[19] The cruiser retained watertight integrity but all four turbines were cracked, the starboard side hull plates were badly distorted, and the radar and 80 per cent of the communications gear were put out of action.[20] Vian transferred to the headquarters ship HMS *Hilary* and *Scylla* was towed back to the UK. The same night, the frigate HMS *Nith* fell victim to one of the Luftwaffe's more outlandish weapons: essentially a prototype drone, the *Mistel* (Mistletoe) combination consisted of a piloted fighter aircraft directing a radio-controlled explosive-filled bomber slung underneath. The frigate was towed back to Cowes; nine men died instantly and a tenth later from wounds.[21]

The following day, 24 June, Lieutenant-Commander John Gower's *Swift*, rescuer of the *Svenner* survivors on 6 June, fell victim to another mine which exploded under Number 1 Boiler Room, instantly breaking the destroyer's back; within minutes her midships section was under water as the bows and stern started to rise, eventually reaching a thirty degree angle. All the bridge personnel and many of those on the upper deck were thrown into the sea, although Gower himself laconically recorded that he 'was fortunate to land back on the bridge, from whence I was able to control operations'.[22] Seventeen of his crew were killed in the explosion. *Swift* started to list and swung alarmingly to port, risking collision with a nearby LCF, until Gower ordered the port anchor let go before ordering his men to abandon ship. Fortunately, *ML-197* and boats from numerous nearby warships were on hand to pick up survivors, including one from HMS *Belfast*. ASDIC Operator Bob 'Ping' Shrimpton went with it, recalling 'seeing the ship's crew just sort of stepping off. One chap had a Burberry [coat] over his arm and he just sort of stepped into the water . . . another lad had lost quite a lot of his upper body . . . that wasn't a very pleasant morning.'[23]

Gower was rescued by *197*, whose young CO, Graham Rouse, remembered him as 'a pretty urbane sort. I remember saying to him "sorry about your ship, Sir" and it was almost like a Noel Coward response: "C'est la guerre", he said "c'est la guerre!"'[24] An extraordinarily determined and professional officer, Gower later returned to his dying command to ensure that the confidential code and signal books had been thrown overboard in their weighted bag and 'to satisfy myself that there were no living trapped on board', before visiting every ship in the area to count the survivors.[25]

Sweepers were not immune. Sub-Lieutenant Sam Popham in the big fleet sweeper HMS *Recruit* watched the shockingly rapid destruction of the 'Mickey Mouse' *MMS-8* on 24 June, recalling that 'I saw something hurtle from the water ... disaster descended on her so quickly.'[26] The little ship had been vapourised, leaving just four survivors from the crew of eighteen. The sea did not give up 20-year-old Engineman Herbert Tredgett from Epping until 1 October, when he was recovered and buried by the Army at Tilly-sur-Seulles.[27]

Objectively speaking the 'Mickey Mouses' were, as Richard Cooper said, 'dispensable', and Ramsay had plenty of warships, but the SS *Derrycunihy* provided an object lesson on how bad it could be if the Germans got lucky or Allied sailors dropped their guard for an instant. *Derrycunihy* left Southend for the Seine Bay on 19 June as part of convoy ETM13. Aboard were the vehicles and 583 men of 43rd (Wessex) Reconnaissance Regiment, as well as forty crew, twenty-three gunners, a pair of ROC observers and a storeman.[28] *Derrycunihy* arrived safely off Sword on 20 June and anchored, but after a long delay the freighter was given orders to move to Juno for unloading on the 24th. As soon as the engines started, at around 0732, the freighter was rocked by a huge explosion and broke in two. The stern sank in seconds, the weakened deck giving way, and vehicles falling through onto men struggling to escape the holds below. Fires broke out on the foredeck and trucks loaded with small arms ammunition began to 'cook off'. Sub-Lieutenant John Symon-Moss put his motor launch *ML-204* alongside, under fire from German guns ashore, and started to take off shocked and wounded soldiers, eventually loading more than 200 on his narrow deck, which became slick with blood and oil. Stoker Len Bridge watched aghast from his engine room scuttle in *204* as half-naked, terribly wounded soldiers tried desperately to struggle free of the wreckage.[29] Twenty-four sailors and gunners, one ROC observer and 180 members of the

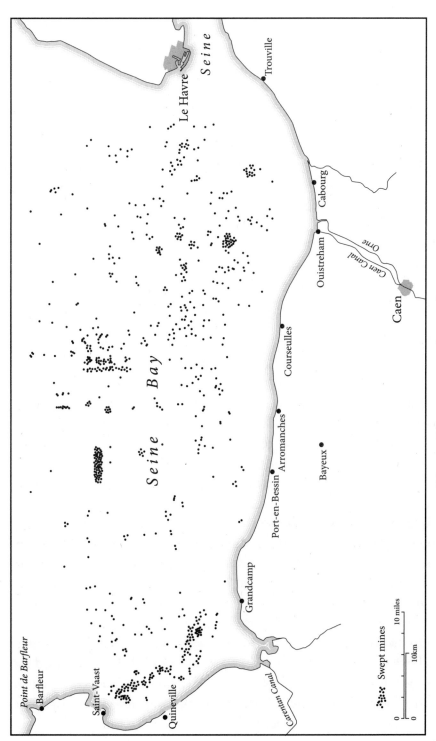

Map 8. Mines swept in the assault area.

Regiment died and over 100 more were injured. Remarkably, the salvage ship *Salvictor* kept the forepart afloat, recovering stores and 109 vehicles, but it was the end of July before 43rd Reconnaissance Regiment was rebuilt to full combat effectiveness.[30] One cheap mine had wrought the kind of havoc which might have taken days on the battlefield.

Mines were the most serious challenge faced by the Seine Bay fleet, with the Germans concentrating on the US assault area initially and then moving the main weight of their minelaying over to the British in the east after D+1 (see Map 8). Vian reported twenty-five ships sunk or damaged by mines in the British area by 25 June, including the battleship HMS *Nelson*, which was damaged on the 18th, and Kirk listed ten warships and twenty-four other craft lost in his WTF area by the 21st.[31] Rigorous sweeping took care of the more conventional mines, 261 being swept in the US sector and 291 in the British by 3 July, but by far the greatest threat was posed by the unsweepable Oyster varieties.[32] One was recovered intact on 20 June, but the only countermeasures remained keeping traffic in the Seine Bay to a minimum, not an easy thing to achieve given the rate of the build-up, and the rigorous enforcement of a 4 knot (less than 7km/h) speed limit.[33] Colin Madden, still on Pugsley's staff as Captain (Patrols) in HMS *Retalick*, remembered that 'to go ... from our patrol anchorage to the patrol position for the night which might be five miles would take almost two hours'.[34] Major units were also towed in and out of the assault area. The hard-worked minesweepers were also kept busy repeatedly sweeping the Spout and recovering wreckage and other drifting detritus, which all posed a hazard to navigation and could put an invaluable landing craft out of action for days. Pugsley apparently issued a reward of Mars bars to the ship which recovered the most flotsam on specified 'scavenging days'.[35]

Elsewhere, the battle to keep U-boats out of the Bay continued. On the 24th, HMS *Eskimo* and the legendary Canadian Commander Harry de Wolf's HMCS *Haida* despatched *U-971*, commanded by Oberleutnant Walter Zeplien, south of Land's End on its first patrol. 18-year-old Midshipman Eric Howarth was aboard Lieutenant-Commander Erroll Sinclair's *Eskimo*:

In the afternoon . . . a shout of 'she's surfaced' ran around the ship. Sure enough, there on our port side, perhaps 10 to 15 cables (1 to 1½ miles) away lay a sleek submarine . . . binoculars showed the gun crew running to their action stations. Canadian naval gunnery lived up to its high standards when their second and third salvo raised a puff of ominous smoke at the base of the conning tower. At the same time the Canadians had lowered their motorboat and set off at full speed towards the U-boat complete with an armed boarding party . . . the whole idea of boarding was to capture the U-boat, but well before the Canadians were able to reach her, she was scuttled and quickly disappeared.[36]

Eskimo collected forty-six soaked and apprehensive Germans, and *Haida* six; one man was killed. Howarth was handed a revolver and told to guard one group. 'They were mostly of my own age, in the 18–20 years old range, and were quite docile', he remembered; 'one of them asked me for "wasser", which I knew meant "water" so I let the steward who was watching from the wardroom pantry take it to him.'[37]

The Allied navies were of course fighting this gruelling and largely unrecognised battle at sea to win the battle of the build-up, ensuring that the soldiers of Montgomery's 21st Army Group received the reinforcements, supplies and equipment they desperately needed to win their equally demanding but much more widely acknowledged struggle ashore.[38] To the east, the Canadian 1st and British 2nd Armies were stalled in front of Caen, fighting a series of grim battles to take the city and the all-important plain beyond, perfect ground on which to build airfields and make use of superior Allied mobility. However, holding the British and Canadians back in front of Caen took a monumental effort on the part of the Germans, including the deployment of most of their armoured divisions: generally, there were around three times as many tanks facing the British and Canadians as there were facing the Americans. These key German formations sustained horrendous losses in men and machines, most of which were never replaced, whereas thanks to the extraordinary efforts of the Allied sailors, their opponents were reinforced, time and again. From 6 June until 23 July, the German Army lost 2,722 officers and 110,357 men in Normandy, receiving in exchange just 10,078 replacements.[39] The Allied armies had lost a total of 209,672 soldiers killed, wounded and missing by the end of August, but a staggering 958,536 replacements had been brought to Normandy by 4 July.[40] The sailors, along with the airmen who relentlessly battered the Wehrmacht's supply lines by day and night, had bought the soldiers a priceless advantage on the battlefield.

A few days after D-Day the German naval wireless intercept service, the *Funkbeobachtungdienst*, or *B-Dienst*, cracked the code used by the Allied Ferry Control Service, giving them daily updates on the rate of discharge in Normandy.[41] The intelligence brought little comfort, merely prompting Krancke to write glumly in the *Marinegruppe West* war diary on 25 June that 'the amounts quoted represent many times the reserves of materiel and men moved up to the front by us and offer a clear picture of the enemy's superiority and of the advantage of seaborne supplies, given sea and air superiority'.[42] Rommel's only hope was to withdraw to a shorter, more easily defensible line, out of range of Allied naval guns, a course of action forbidden by Hitler.

To the west, General Omar Bradley's 1st US Army took advantage of the German fixation with Caen to drive west from Utah Area across the Cotentin Peninsula, reaching the west coast late on 17 June. At this point, Bradley turned his newly arrived VIII Corps to the south to hold the line, while the VII Corps turned north for Cherbourg. Fighting their way up the peninsula, by 20 June Major-General 'Lightning Joe' Collins' men were 5 miles from the port. Collins attacked on the 22nd, as soon as the great storm had passed and his formations had closed up, after an attempt to persuade Generalleutnant Karl-Wilhelm von Schlieben's garrison to surrender met with no response: this was hardly surprising, given that on the 17th Hitler had ordered the fortress 'be held at all costs'.[43] After four days of bitter fighting, Collins broke through Cherbourg's outer defences, only to run up against an inner chain of strongpoints, including the citadel of Fort du Roule, which commanded both the city and its seaward approaches. 'Unwilling to waste time on a siege when we should have been getting underway', Bradley wrote after the war, 'I asked Kirk to attack the fort's coastal guns from the sea. Had Kirk told me to go soak my head in the Channel, I could not have held his prudence against him.'[44] Kirk looked at him and asked, 'is it worth that much to you?' When Bradley replied in the affirmative, Kirk did not hesitate.[45] Once again, the fleet was going into action against a defended shore.

Back on 15 June, Kirk had placed all the bombardment ships in the WTF sector into a single Task Force, TF129, under Rear-Admiral Morton Deyo in the cruiser USS *Tuscaloosa*. Deyo's ships had been badly scattered by the storm, but he reassembled them at Portland, drafting and distributing a plan by noon on 22 June. The earliest he could begin the operation would be sunrise on Sunday the 25th. Kirk's instructions were admirably clear:

Task 1. Support FUSA ASSAULT [First US Army] on Cherbourg by destruction shore batteries designated by CG [Commanding General] 7th Corps or as CG FUSA may direct ... Task 2: Clear and prepare Cherbourg for operation. Operate Cherbourg in conjunction with US Army.

Deyo's bombarding ships were the US battleships *Texas*, *Arkansas* and *Nevada* and the US cruisers *Tuscaloosa* and *Quincy*, screened by a strong force of US destroyers, with the British cruisers *Glasgow* and *Enterprise* representing the Royal Navy.[46]

Their task was a formidable one. Intelligence briefings indicated forty-nine distinct targets, ranging from light and heavy anti-aircraft guns to heavy coast defence artillery in concrete emplacements, although some were believed to be incomplete or damaged. The rapidly changing situation ashore made friendly fire a significant concern: 'SEVENTH Corps front lines will be signalled to all ships at the latest possible moment.' The original plan called for a long-range bombardment of the German heavy batteries, after which the bombarding ships would close the shore to fire on targets designated by aircraft or SFCP spotters with Collins's troops ashore. They would be swept in to their three designated Fire Support Areas by three flotillas of minesweepers, Henry Plander's squadron of US Navy

'Bird Boats' and the British 9th and 159th Flotillas, respectively Bangor Class coastal sweepers and British Yard Minesweepers.[47]

Close on the heels of TF129 would come the 'Salvage King', USN Commodore William Sullivan, and his Anglo-American Port Clearance Group of specialist salvage, mine clearance and hydrographic survey teams, whose job was to get Cherbourg operating as quickly as possible. Their task would be monumental, as the Germans had been hard at work methodically destroying Cherbourg for weeks, with intelligence reporting a litany of chaos, including demolished buildings, quays and equipment, scuttled ships and obvious signs of extensive mining.[48] The plan was thorough, running to dozens of pages, but for all its detail, it was not enough to reassure some participants. 'At the time I didn't believe the operation necessary', wrote Rear-Admiral Carleton Bryant of Battleship Division Five, still flying his flag in the veteran *Texas*, 'nor do I now.'[49]

Commander Roger Thomson in HMS *Sidmouth* weighed anchor and took the 9th and 159th MSFs out of St Helen's Roads off the Isle of Wight at 1611 on 24 June, to arrive off Cherbourg by H-Hour, 0600 on the 25th. Irritatingly, the operation was almost immediately cancelled and then reinstated, with a revised H-Hour of 1030, later adjusted again to 1200.[50] The confusion was caused by Bradley, who was concerned about the friendly fire risk and wanted a shorter bombardment, in daylight, and more directly controlled by the Army.[51] Thomson wrote, with weary patience:

> It will be evident that a certain handicap was imposed on the minesweeping forces by these changes of plan ... the whole of the minesweeping plan had to be changed from start to finish, the captains of twenty ships in company then informed, and this with all ships at sea in the gathering darkness where it was unwise to show many lights.[52]

The sweepers cleared their approach channels without incident, until 1155 when, as Thomson's ships approached the fire support areas closest to Cherbourg, they came under heavy fire. Eventually, unable to sweep because of poor visibility and repeated near misses, Thomson took his sweepers out of the way, signalling Deyo that although he had only been able to clear half of the intended area, no mines had been detonated, and the reasonable presumption was that none were present. HMS *Bridport* and HMS *Bangor* were both superficially damaged, without casualties.[53] The 9th Flotilla escaped largely unscathed thanks to their supporting MLs, which screened them with smoke as they made off. *ML-141* was singled out for particular praise. The Fairmile's young commanding officer, Lieutenant Anthony Barnard, was awarded the Distinguished Service Cross, and the operator of his smoke generator, Stoker Harry Pattinson, the Distinguished Service Medal for his 'coolness'. 'Working with no cover and under fire', his citation read, 'his prompt and effective operating of the CSA [smoke] gear made possible the laying of a complete screen around the 9th MSF before the enemy shore batteries could range properly.'[54]

The big ships opened fire when Germans shells started to fall around Thomson's sweepers. *Glasgow* and *Enterprise* led off for Bombardment Group 1, firing on *StP277*, or *Batterie Yorck*, four emplaced 170mm guns near Querqueville, aided by a Spitfire spotter flying low over the target. The duel was on, and the German fire was intense and effective. *Glasgow* was hit at 1251 and again a few minutes later, Captain Philip Clarke pulling the veteran cruiser briefly out of the line to assess damage before rejoining the fight. Commander Felix Lloyd-Davies recalled running into 'a very hot reception here . . . very different from D-Day'.

> *Glasgow* at times was on fire in three places, having been hit quite repeatedly by German shells . . . in a quarter of an hour we had all the fires under control and we steamed back into the line and started bombarding again. We were very fortunate in getting very few casualties, we had about fifteen men wounded but nobody killed, but a large hole was blown in the hangar side and there were several direct hits on the ship aft.[55]

Enterprise was extensively damaged by splinters, which also wounded both the cruiser's indomitable Canadian Captain, Harold Grant, and his Commander. 'I found [Grant] passing orders without a trace of excitement', war correspondent Gordon Holman recalled; 'he said "oh something bounced on my shoulder and knocked me over. It feels a bit bruised" . . . later I was in the Captain's cabin which had been turned into an emergency operating theatre and saw his tunic brought in by his steward. The sleeve . . . was soaked with blood.'[56]

Batterie Yorck was finally silenced at 1440, by which time more than 300 6-inch (152mm) shells had crashed down in and around the battery area, and even then the German gunners periodically came back to life throughout the afternoon.[57] *Nevada*, meanwhile, was supporting the troops, following directions given by an SFCP: 'you are hitting in there and digging in', the unnamed spotters called in at 1229, followed a few minutes later with 'nice firing. You are digging them out in nice big holes.'[58] The old battleship was repeatedly straddled but never hit, although the fire was intense enough to drive US Marine Irvin Airey and his fellow sightseers down from the upper deck: 'those of us on deck were saying "come on let's shag-ass out of here"', he remembered; 'we shagged out!'[59]

Carleton Bryant's Bombardment Group 2, *Texas*, *Arkansas* and five destroyers, engaged *StP234 Batterie Hamburg*, four 240mm guns at Fermanville, east of Cherbourg, which had carefully waited until the last minute before opening fire. *Texas* came under heavy fire from the outset, one shell penetrating under the port bow without exploding and coming to rest in a warrant officer's bunk. 'They had us pretty well pinpointed', Bryant recalled; 'having 11-inch shells fired at you is no fun. You can actually see those black specks when they pass over you. They have the most seductive sound – a soft swish, almost a caress. Then, when the salvo hits the water there is the most ungodly smack you ever heard.'[60] Around 1315 a shell hit the conning tower, smashing the bridge structure above, killing the helmsman and wounding several others. Bryant's destroyers came in for serious punishment, particularly after they adopted a tactic of closing the bigger ships when they were under heavy fire to distract the enemy gunners. *Laffey* and *Barton* were both hit but remarkably, both shells were duds; USS *O'Brien* was not so lucky, the shell that smashed into the Combat Information Centre exploded, killing thirteen men and wounding many more.[61]

So accurate and effective was the naval gunnery that, when Deyo came to the end of his prearranged ninety minutes, a reassured Collins permitted him to continue until 1500, when Deyo signalled TF129 to withdraw and the groups disengaged independently; *Nevada*, the Pearl Harbor survivor, kept firing until 1525, by which time the battleship had expended 112 rounds of 14-inch (355mm). By the time the action ended, all but one of the seven heavy ships taking part had been hit, along with the three destroyers. Collins and Eisenhower were effusive in their praise for the effectiveness of the bombardment, as were the Germans, Krancke recording that Cherbourg had fallen in part because of a 'naval bombardment of a hitherto unequalled fierceness'.[62] Others were less sure – Deyo wrote years later, 'I don't believe our venture advanced the surrender one hour!'[63] The bombarding ships returned to Portland, where Clarke invited Deyo and his fellow officers across from their teetotal commands for a celebratory 'captains' conference' aboard *Glasgow*, described by Felix Lloyd-Davies as 'quite a . . . party!'[64]

Von Schlieben surrendered on the following day, citing 'heavy fire from the sea' as the reason. Certainly, one of his battalion commanders described his men as 'completely worn out by the incessant naval bombardments', according to the German 7th Army's telephone logs, although as before this may in part have been a convenient excuse to justify handing over Hitler's 'fortress'; there is no doubt that Collins's soldiers had comprehensively defeated von Schlieben's troops as they fought their way through the city.[65]

Several of Cherbourg's forts and coastal batteries held out for longer, including those on the *digue*, Cherbourg's outer breakwater. The destroyer USS *Shubrick* and two of the US Navy's PT Boats, commanded by Lieutenant-Commander Robert Bulkeley, tried to distract them with typical flair, *PT-510* and *PT-521* manoeuvring at high speed around the breakwater at sunset spraying the forts with machine-gun fire until *521* was brought up short by two near misses from heavy-calibre shells which stopped the engines, loosened the decks and shook a torpedo out of its rack. After firing that weapon defiantly at the breakwater, Bulkeley withdrew, leaving fighter-bombers to pound the *digue* forts into submission.[66]

The last of the Cherbourg holdouts surrendered on 29 June, apart from 6,000 stubborn Germans who retreated east to Cap de la Hague, where they finally laid down their arms on 1 July. Seaman Helmut Lucke of the *Hafenschutzflotilla Kanalinseln* took part in an abortive attempt to try and extract key personnel – mostly senior officers – from this pocket. 'From Alderney we could see when they were fighting on Cap de la Hague', he recalled; 'there were so many generals [*sic*] . . . and we were going to fetch them back to Alderney. They asked for volunteers.' Lucke's ship approached within a few metres of the coast, waiting for the flash of a signal lamp, and stayed there until just before dawn, but nobody came and 'we couldn't wait any longer because . . . there were quite a few British ships in the vicinity'. When they returned, they were congratulated and decorated by Vizeadmiral Friedrich Huffmeier, the naval commander of the occupied Channel Islands.[67] Bizarrely even as Cherbourg fell the Germans, still dazzled by Fortitude, continued to believe a second landing was coming around Calais, and retained thousands of troops there to prevent it as the defence of Normandy was unravelling.

In the meantime, the legendary Sullivan – described by the usually restrained British Naval Staff History as a 'genius' – and his Anglo-American salvage teams prepared to enter the twisted wreckage of Cherbourg.[68] Some 95 per cent of the deep water quays had been ruined. At the Quai de Normandie, six huge cranes had been tipped into the water before over 15,000 cubic yards of masonry from the quay walls were blown down on top of them. The railway station had been demolished. The worst destruction was in the Arsenal and Naval Dockyard, where 'all drydock gates were wrecked, every bridge except one was demolished, including a retractable railway bridge, and all port cranes had been blown up. Where facilities remained standing, they had been prepared for demolition by 500-pound bombs. Only quay walls were intact in this entire area.'[69] All the basins were mined and blocked with dozens of scuttled ships of all shapes and sizes: the entrance to the Darse Transatlantique, for example, was completely blocked by an 8,000-ton whaler and an old coaster, and the entrance to the Avant Port was blocked by a naval auxiliary and two barges, one loaded with as many as seventy mines.

Most of the docks were choked with wrecks, rubble, cranes, vehicles and other debris. Everywhere was mined, with contact, magnetic, acoustic and pressure mines, as well as the concrete shallow-water Anti-Invasion Type A mines, nicknamed 'Kathys' or 'Kateys', and the buildings ashore were booby-trapped.

The first reconnaissance team, led by US Coast Guard Lieutenant-Commander Quentin Walsh, who had written the original plan for the occupation, clearance, and operation of Cherbourg, reached the waterfront late on 26 June, and on the 28th his team of Seabees, naval salvage experts and army engineers surveyed the port, still under occasional sniper fire. While his men got to work, Walsh took a team of armed Seabees into the Arsenal, clearing out pockets of stray German soldiers. On the 29th, Walsh's boss, Captain Norman Ives, took over command, and minesweeping began on the 30th.[70] The salvage crews moved in to lift wrecks and clear obstructions as each section was pronounced safe by clearance divers and mine-sweepers, which were required to carry out up to eight magnetic and eight acoustic sweeps every morning for days, as many mines had delayed-action fuses.[71] The entire operation involved nine salvage ships and dozens of minesweepers; three of the latter were sunk, along with another seven vessels.

Wireless Operator Claude Broomfield came into the harbour in the frigate HMS *Spragge* some days later and was given a vivid warning of just how dangerous the port remained. 'We had to go in slowly', he remembered; 'I heard a hell of a bang ... a British mine-sweeper was following us in, and hit a mine, and blew up ... there was just a bit of debris floating around.'[72] This may have been the 'Mickey Mouse' *MMS-1019*, which was mined and sunk in Cherbourg on 2 July with the loss of six officers and men out of a crew of twenty-one.

Brendan Maher arrived in in *ML-137* to help clear Cherbourg in early July. Among the many hazards were the lethal 'snag mines'. These were dealt with by a rating and an officer, who would row up to every floating oddity in a dinghy, and carefully pull it out of the water. If it revealed a line, they would secure a rope to it and detonate the mine from a safe distance. 'Mac and I rotated turns on this duty, as did the ratings,' Maher recalled; 'we got several mines, a lot of seaweed and no casualties. It was by far the most nerve-racking of the procedures that we used.'[73] There was no limit to the junk cluttering Cherbourg; another ML on an early sweep recovered the remains of a Heinkel bomber.[74]

Neptune planners aimed to have Cherbourg open within three days, which was wildly optimistic – clearing the port continued well beyond the end of this narrative.[75] In addition, work began to construct the facilities for the PLUTO fuel pipeline, codenamed Bambi, which would eventually connect the port to Sandown on the Isle of Wight, although the damage to the port was so extensive it was another month before any tankers could discharge, and PLUTO did not actually begin pumping until 12 August. Although the first Liberty ships were discharging using improvised facilities as early as 16 July, the port was still only 75 per cent operational by mid-September, and poor transport links down the Cotentin Peninsula meant that actually moving materiel out of the port remained challenging, which was why the beaches and Mulberry B remained vital well into the autumn. Cherbourg eventually more than doubled its predicted discharge rates, but by the time it reached full capacity, around November, it was so far away from the fighting front that its importance was diminishing.[76]

Cherbourg's capture meant the assault area's western flank was now essentially secure. With the exception of the sectors in front of Caen to the east, around Sword and the River Orne – Sword was closed down on the day Cherbourg fell – much of the fighting ashore was now well out of range. Ramsay had always responded cautiously to requests to give up his warships, but on 27 June he relinquished all the US battleships and cruisers, and eight British and Free French; four more RN cruisers would go just over a week later, leaving just one battleship, the two monitors and four cruisers, mostly older ships.[77] Most left for the southern France landings, Operation Dragoon (formerly Anvil), with others returning to the UK to be refitted for the Pacific. Vian returned to the UK on 30 June, along with all the assault force commanders, and Kirk left on 3 July, although he returned after a two-month break as Commander, US

Naval Forces, France. Operational command passed to Rear-Admiral James Rivett-Carnac RN as Flag Officer, British Assault Area (FOBAA), and Rear-Admiral John Wilkes USN as first Flag Officer West and after 14 July, Commander, United States Naval Bases, France. Both officers were based ashore, in Rivett-Carnac's case in the Maison Clos Charlotte at Courseulles, with his staff occupying a former German barracks nearby. 'The withdrawal of all these officers', Ramsay wrote, 'marked the stabilisation of the naval position in the assault area and the conclusion of the first phase in the capture of the lodgement area by our armies.'[78] Neptune was over. The Battle of the Seine Bay was not.

Far from the Bay, as the ground forces redeployed to prepare for the great American attempt to break out of the Normandy

Table 1. Neptune build-up, 11 June–4 July 1944.

Date	Personnel	Vehicles	Tons of Stores
11 June (D+5)	367,142	50,228	59,961
12 June (D+6)	395,798	56,659	79,485
13 June (D+7)	427,214	62,238	104,975
14 June (D+8)	477,047	68,923	126,724
15 June (D+9)	525,205	77,073	150,924
16 June (D+10)	535,494	83,357	175,496
17 June (D+11)	587,673	89,928	196,464
18 June (D+12)	621,936	95,750	217,624
19–29 June	Build-up and recording disrupted by Great Gale and subsequent salvage operations		
30 June (D+24)	861,838	157,633	501,834
1 July (D+25)	880,849	163,343	529,398
2 July (D+26)	905,072	171,339	564,644
3 July (D+27)	929,090	177,885	604,328
4 July (D+28)	958,536	183,540	649,568

Source: *Naval Staff Battle Summary No. 39 Operation 'Neptune': Landings in Normandy June 1944* (HMSO, London, 1944), Appendix H(3)

beachhead on the western flank, the battle went on to keep U-boats away from the convoys chugging along the Spout, continuing their unsung work to win the battle of the build-up (see Table 1). On the day of the bombardment, *U-269* was depth-charged to destruction south-east of Torquay by the RN frigate HMS *Bickerton*. Detecting U-boats in the shallow, wreck-cluttered channel was incredibly hard; unbelievably, *U-269*'s battered wreck was attacked again a few hours later by two British frigates, who claimed another kill, misidentifying it as *U-1191*. At 1514 on the same day Oberleutnant zur See Heinz Sieder in *U-984* blew the stern off the frigate HMS *Goodson* with a *Zaunkönig*: there was no loss of life and the ship was towed back to Portland but Lieutenant-Commander Jack Cooper's command was a total loss.[79]

On the 27th an unknown submarine torpedoed the Flower-Class corvette HMS *Pink*: again an acoustic homing torpedo unerringly made for the throbbing engines and blew off the stern. TURCO in Portsmouth reported that the corvette's outboard propellers and shaft were 'beyond repair', hardly surprising as they were, in fact, entirely missing. *Pink*'s machinery was wrecked, the upper deck aft had shifted by 2ft, and the shell plating and bulkheads were split and buckled. Lieutenant William Tadman's command, worn out after years of service in the Atlantic, was eventually scrapped.[80]

Coastal Forces, too, continued their unending vigil. The fall of Cherbourg prompted a reorganisation, with Peter Scott joining Rivett-Carnac's staff at Courseulles as Staff Officer (Coastal Forces). Scott took responsibility for a close blockade of Le Havre (where the E-boats had been reinforced and were active once more), patrols round the anchorage, and a new easterly defence line against German incursions from the north.[81] On the 27th, MTBs *673*, *676* and *677* fought an action off Jersey. *MGB-326* triggered a mine and sank within two minutes on the same night – the explosion ripped away more than half of the Fairmile C's hull but fortunately there was no loss of life, thanks to 'the regular practice in the past of Abandon Ship Stations' by the commanding officer, Lieutenant William Kempner.[82]

With Cherbourg captured, the Allied navies started to range along the coast of Brittany, neutralising what remained of the

Kriegsmarine in western France and the Channel Islands. HMS *Eskimo* and HMCS *Huron* intercepted the German minesweeper *M-4620* and a pair of *Vorpostenboote* off Saint-Malo on the night of the 28th. The destroyers set the sweeper ablaze within five minutes and after turning away to avoid fire from the Saint-Malo coastal batteries, returned to finish *VP-213*, but the third, *VP-209*, displayed an extraordinary will to survive. Emerging from smoke on the port side, *VP-209* raked *Eskimo* with 'unpleasantly accurate and rapid fire' from its puny deck gun and automatic weapons. Remarkably the German fire severed one of *Eskimo*'s steam pipes, filling the boiler room with steam and forcing the crew to evacuate. Seconds later a 20mm shell penetrated Number 3 Boiler. Steam pressure dropped dramatically, all power was lost to the forward guns and the 40mm Pom-Poms, and *Eskimo*'s speed dropped off to 6 knots (11km/h), a huge cloud of smoke and steam obscuring visibility for the after gunners. To make matters worse, the destroyer's 20mm Oerlikon jammed, leaving *Eskimo* 'almost outgunned by this determined and gallant trawler'.[83]

Having disabled one of the Royal Navy's most powerful destroyers the tiny trawler *VP-209* made off to the east bloodied but unbowed. Power restored, *Eskimo* attempted to finish off *VP-213* by dropping a depth charge under its bow, rather chillingly while passing through 'German survivors in the water who were shouting and blowing whistles', before shelling the stubborn trawler repeatedly with little effect. *Huron*, meanwhile, shelled the burning *M-4620* until the sweeper blew up and sank spectacularly, sped off on a futile hunt for *VP-209*, then returned to spare *Eskimo*'s blushes by finishing off *VP-213*. At 0205, Lieutenant-Commander Herbert Rayner signalled *Eskimo* to withdraw and both ships returned to Plymouth.[84] *VP-209* proved that the sailors defending the Seine Bay could never drop their guard, even if their enemy appeared to be outnumbered and beaten. The Kriegsmarine was down but not out, and its well-trained, highly motivated and in some cases undoubtedly fanatical personnel were far from giving up.

There was no better example of this devotion to a lost cause than Dönitz's U-boats, seventy-two of which were sunk between 16 May and 1 November 1944 trying to repel the invasion, with the loss of most of their 3,500 crew men.[85] On the same night as *VP-209*'s gallant action, the 'Red Ensign' LSI *Maid of Orleans*, a former ferry which had survived multiple trips to Dunkirk in 1940, was torpedoed and sunk by an unidentified submarine off the Isle of Wight while travelling back to the UK from Gold Area. The trip started badly, according to ROC spotter Jim Froggatt, as the LSI fouled its anchor and missed the convoy, so the Master, Herbert Payne, cracked on all available speed to catch up: 'twenty-two knots in a trail of smoke which could be seen for miles'. At 2130, with the convoy in sight, the torpedo slammed into the side:

> I had stepped down from the bridge and was talking to the Petty Officer in charge of our Bofors gun and the two Oerlikons, on the same deck as two of our LCAs ... When the explosion hit, it blew one of the LCAs into bits and the davits swung back embedding themselves in the super-structure and pinning me to the deck in my saturated and very heavy duffel coat. The other Petty Officer pulled me out from beneath the iron where I was trapped and helped me to my feet.[86]

Discarding his sodden duffel coat, Froggatt jumped to the deck below and helped lower the lifeboat. As the survivors rowed clear, *Maid of Orleans* slipped under. Fortunately, all but five men were saved, though many were dreadfully injured. Some were brought aboard Lieutenant Charles Fetherston-Dilke's destroyer HMS *Hotham*:

> We picked up one of the cooks and he had terribly burned hands because he'd been in the galley and when the [torpedo] struck his hands went down on the cooker ... of course he couldn't clamber up the side to get out of the water. Anyway, a couple of the sailors went over the side and got him up, but he was ... in tremendous pain. I jabbed him with morphia first of all when he got on board. Our Sick Berth Attendant was absolutely marvellous, he'd probably never met this sort of thing before, but he was absolutely calm as a cucumber [*sic*].[87]

The following night, 23-year-old Hans Sieder in *U–984* struck again, providing a grim lesson for the Allies about the consequences of letting even one U-boat into the Spout. Four days after blowing the stern off HMS *Goodson*, Sieder found himself perfectly lined up on convoy EMC17. His well-placed torpedo salvo hit four Liberty ships in the space of four minutes. All were brought back to the UK but only one, the SS *Edward M House*, could be repaired and used again. Seventy-six army personnel died aboard the Coast Guard-manned *H.G. Blasdel*.[88] Sieder was awarded the Knight's Cross for this thankfully rare success. A few hours later, an unidentified submarine torpedoed the SS *Empire Portia* off Selsey Bill in convoy FTM22.

Coastal Forces were in action again on 1/2 July. Three groups of MTBs were successfully vectored by the control frigates *Torrington* and *Trollope* throughout the night to harass German landing craft, R-boats and E-boats off Cap d'Antifer and Fécamp, claiming several hits. On the same night, forty-nine aircraft from the Luftwaffe's *Lehrgeschwader 1* hit the anchorage, gliding in to drop BM 1000 '*Monika*' aerial mines from 700m while dodging searchlights, Mosquitos and anti-aircraft fire.[89] The Luftwaffe still harassed the anchorage almost nightly, dropping mines and carrying out tip-and-run torpedo or bombing runs; another sixty-two *LG1* aircraft dropped mines over the Bay the following night. Two did not return, including Oberfeldwebel Alfred Soster's Junkers 88, which was shot down north of Ouistreham by a 504 Squadron Mosquito night fighter piloted by the highly experienced Wing Commander Michael Maxwell, who had claimed his first kills flying Hurricanes in the summer of 1940. Unteroffizier Helmut Knauf, the only survivor, bailed out into the Bay and was eventually rescued by the destroyer HMS *Goathland*:

I had suffered burns and was taken to the ship's hospital. I received exemplary care and was given a shot of morphine to calm me. My lips were burned, and I was asked if I had a wish. I asked for a cigarette. The officer lit one, wet it with his lips and let me draw on it. That was for me fair play![90]

*LG1*s were out again on a mining run on 3/4 July, before the unit switched to attacks on targets ashore. Once again two aircraft failed to return. On the same night, HMS *Stayner* vectored MTBs towards three groups of E-boats on minelaying missions around Cap d'Antifer. In a typically brief, chaotic sequence of actions, Units GA4 (MTBs *691* and *694*) and GA3 (MTBs *451* and *447*), supported by *Stayner* and the frigate *Thornborough*, intercepted two groups of E-boats from *2.Sfltl* after they had laid their mines and pursued them back into Le Havre, hitting *S-181*, setting the E-boat on fire and killing Maschinemaat Bernhard Häring. GA3 and GA6 (MTBs *611* and *615*) went on to engage a group from *8.Sfltl*, claiming one E-boat badly damaged, but the Germans returned to Dieppe unscathed.[91]

Remarkably, on 5 July the millionth man landed in France.[92] Each one owed his safe arrival to the efforts of sailors. In a reminder that this safety came at a cost, *U-390* torpedoed the minesweeping trawler HMS *Ganilly* off Utah with the loss of 26-year-old commanding officer Lieutenant Richard Beattie and thirty-eight of his officers and men; there were just four survivors. Beattie left behind a young wife, Rhoda, in his home town of Gateshead.[93] *U-390* was destroyed the following day by HMS *Wanderer* and HMS *Tavy* with the loss of all but one of the crew. Like Beattie, Leutnant Heinz Geissler, the commanding officer, was just 26. On the same day, Kapitänleutnant Ernst Cordes in *U-763* attacked convoy ETC26 near Selsey Bill and was then subjected to a thirty-six-hour-long depth-charge attack, during which the 31-year-old officer counted 550 separate explosions. Cordes, an experienced seaman who had joined the pre-Nazi Reichsmarine in 1934 as a rating, kept his cool and eventually extracted his battered command, bumping the submarine along the bottom and losing any sense of his position.[94]

In the first of a series of operations codenamed Dredger, the Royal Navy's 14th Escort Group and the all-Canadian 12th Escort Group, four older destroyers under Commander Alec McKillop in HMCS *Qu'Appelle*, struck at the approaches to Brest on the night of 5/6 July, trying to catch U-boats under escort on the surface as they left or approached their home port. EG12 picked up three small surface contacts on radar 9½ miles from their patrol position at 0113 and closed at high speed to try to get between the Germans and their base, then approach them from a friendly direction. As the Canadians closed, the confused Germans repeatedly flashed recognition signals. At 5½ miles two much smaller contacts appeared, presumably U-boats with only their conning towers above the surface. 'At 0137', Lieutenant-Commander Patrick Russell of HMCS *Skeena* wrote in his subsequent report, 'the target was illuminated and showed itself as three large trawler or flak ships in line ahead with a submarine on each quarter of the second ship from the rear.' The Canadians hammered three *Vorpostenboote* with 4.7-inch (120mm) shells and automatic weapon fire, leaving *VP-715* on fire and sinking, and damaged two others in a frenetic action initially fought at around 30 knots (55km/h), but the U-boats escaped to open water. The Canadians joined the British EG14 and left for home at 0236. Once again, the outgunned Kriegsmarine trawlers had fought back hard, *Qu'Appelle* was raked by German gunfire and McKillop himself was badly wounded: on putting his hand to his thigh, he found that he could put his finger though a large hole and touch bone. 'It is regrettable', he wrote in an understandably brief report written a week later, 'that my injuries, which turned out to be worse than I thought at first, prevented me from seeing to it that some ships at least ... remained in the area until daylight.'[95]

5 July also saw a new threat in the Seine Bay: the first of the *Kleinkampfverbände*.

* 14 *
Last Resort: The *Kleinkampfverbände*
5 July–3 August 1944

This weapon can be defeated by a high degree of alertness ... and
the liberal use of depth charges.

Naval Intelligence Department Report, 4 May 1944[1]

The Kriegsmarine had been working on small naval attack craft
since February 1943 when Dönitz, inspired by Italian, British
and Japanese successes, instructed Konteradmiral Hellmuth Heye to
become 'the Mountbatten of the German Navy'.[2]

The first weapons to arrive in Normandy were *Neger* human
torpedoes and *Linsen* explosive motor boats.[3] Each *Neger* unit
consisted of a standard G7e naval torpedo, slung beneath another
G7e, which had its warhead replaced by a tiny cockpit and basic
controls. It could not be submerged: instead the operator peered
through a Plexiglass dome and aimed using a rudimentary sight.
*Linsen*s worked in threes, a control boat and two more craft packed
with 300kg explosive charges, each with a single crewman. As they
neared their target the sailors in the armed boats jumped overboard,
the control boat operator guided them for the last few metres on
to their targets using radio control and then in theory picked up
the other two men and sped for home. It was rarely that easy. The
K-Verbände craft were built under difficult conditions and were crude
to the point of being dangerous. The crews were mostly very young
volunteers with limited training and sometimes no basic seamanship

skills. The first forty human torpedo crews were drawn from all branches of the Wehrmacht and the SS and went operational after just a few weeks; doubtless their confidence was heightened by the cocktail of cocaine and amphetamines they were given when they set out.[4] The first human torpedo sortie took place against the Anzio beachhead on 20 April 1944 and it was a fiasco. Of thirty-seven craft taking part, eleven failed to deploy, and only ten returned, accidents and Allied patrol boats accounting for the rest; the element of surprise was now totally lost. Admiral Sir John Cunningham, C-in-C Mediterranean, updated Ramsay as soon as his staff had collated the intelligence, following up with POWs and an intact *Neger*. POW interrogations revealed Heye's other devices, including 'one-man U-boats' and remote controlled 'invasion boats' (*Linsens*), as well as the inadequate training of the very young, drugged-up operators.[5]

On 19 June, twenty-four *Linsens* of *211.Kleinkampfverbändflotilla* deployed to Bolbec, east of Le Havre, and sixty *Negers* from *361.Kfltl* arrived in Normandy on the 28th after a hair-raising road journey, dodging Allied aircraft and the FFI. All were under the command of a veteran destroyer officer, Kapitän zur See Friedrich Böhme. They were hidden in woods near Villers-sur-Mer, 20km from the assault area, their vehicles disguised and the personnel wearing anonymous military uniforms. A second batch followed on 6 July.[6] It was a disastrous start for *211.Kfltl*: they lost so many of their volatile *Linsens* in accidents that they were never deployed operationally, but twenty-six *Negers* were wheeled into the water at Villers on the night of 5/6 July, bound for Sword Area, running with the ebb tide to boost their limited top speed and screened by an E-boat raid by *2.Sfltl*.[7] Despite the warnings, they enjoyed a relatively successful debut.

The first success of the night went to ex-clerk Walter Gerhold, who launched his torpedo just before 0130 and watched apprehensively as it 'porpoised' up and down before settling into its run. 'You had to measure the time with a stopwatch so that you could work out the running time,' he recalled; 'I was sweating loads and was quite nervous when the explosion came.'[8] At 0123, Gerhold's G7e ripped into the Coastal Forces Control frigate HMS *Trollope*, which had just disengaged from a fast-paced action with the *2.Sfltl* E-boats and a pair of minesweepers in Area Tunny. *Trollope* 'was beached to the west of Arromanches Harbour', according to Rivett-Carnac's melancholy report, 'from forward of funnel bows are missing and it is regretted ship must be considered total write-off'.[9] *Trollope's* bow was actually still drifting around the Seine Bay, until it was sunk as a hazard to navigation. The frigate's destruction was generally attributed to E-boats.[10]

Later that night, *Negers* found the 40th MSF, anchored north of Ouistreham supporting the Trout Line. The 40th consisted of Catherine Class minesweepers, US-built 'Bird Boats' transferred to the British under Lend-Lease. At 0353, Lieutenant-Commander Denys Richardson was huddled against the chill, chatting to his officer of the watch on the open bridge of HMS *Gorgon*, when his ASDIC operator reported an underwater explosion nearby. Simultaneously, at the eastern end of the patrol line, an apocalyptic smoke cloud boiled up around HMS *Magic*. 'I immediately weighed anchor and proceeded to the scene', Richardson reported, 'having slipped the motor boat to precede me and pick up survivors.' *Gorgon* reached the scene at 0420, by which time *Magic* had rolled over and sunk stern first. According to Lieutenant John Davies, the CO, the torpedo had slammed into the port side under the quarterdeck.[11]

Nearby, the sweepers *Catherine* and *Cato* had slipped their moorings and were searching the area for survivors and the attackers. *Cato* collected several soaked and shocked sailors, then, inexplicably, anchored again.[12] At 0508, another explosion reverberated around the anchorage, and as Richardson watched another smoke cloud swirled into the night sky, this time from *Cato*. At the same time, he was startled to observe a human torpedo collide with *Gorgon's* port quarter, then run up the sweeper's side and across the bow, by which time it was being 'riddled by machine gun and rifle fire at point-blank range' by *Gorgon's* gunners, until it eventually stopped moving.[13]

At 0515, Richardson took *Gorgon* alongside *Cato*, to find the stricken Bird Boat with a huge hole in each side and the back broken forward of the bridge, while the frigate HMS *Duff* roamed the anchorage, firing on other prowling human torpedoes. Lieutenant Robert Harris, *Cato's* CO, refused to leave his bridge until his wounded had been taken off. HMS *Chamois* tried to take *Cato* in tow, but the damage was catastrophic and at 0745 water rolled over the main deck; the sweeper sank in two minutes. Fifty-one men died aboard the two sweepers, tragically some of the *Magic* survivors got aboard *Cato* only to be killed when the latter ship was torpedoed.[14]

The *K-Verbände* paid a high price for sinking a pair of minesweepers and a frigate. Two *Negers* failed to deploy; of the remainder, ten were lost. Among the exaggerated claims of the survivors were a 'cruiser' – claimed by Gerhold – along with two destroyers, two LSTs and a 7,000 ton freighter. Gerhold was one of the lucky ones: after a perilous journey dodging alerted Allied patrols, he made it back to Villers and was awarded the Knight's Cross, the first member of the *K-Verbände* to be thus decorated. 'I've tormented myself for years,' he recalled; 'in the small hours of the morning I've thought about how many people must have gone down with that ship.'[15]

On 6 July, ULTRA decrypts indicated that *361.KFltl*, elated by their largely fictitious kills, were planning an attack on the crucial Allied-held bridges over the River Orne and the Caen Canal, including Pegasus Bridge. Aerial photos and ground reconnaissance were requested but the mission was eventually killed off by Heye, who signalled that 'after one successful attack enemy would probably adopt insurmountable defence measures'.[16]

At dawn on the 7th Ernst Cordes brought his battered submarine *U-763* to periscope depth expecting to see the friendly coast of the Channel Islands, only to find that, incredibly, he had slipped undetected into Spithead, the naval anchorage between the Isle of Wight and Portsmouth, which was perhaps the most heavily defended stretch of water in the world in July 1944. After lying on the bottom for twelve hours, Cordes skilfully extracted his command and brought *U-763* back to Brest on 14 July, his exploits unknown to the Royal Navy until after the war. 'One must give her captain and crew full credit for the endurance and resource displayed during what must have been a harrowing experience,' wrote the British Official Historian, although it was not enough to save Cordes, who was killed when his new command, *U-1195*, was sunk off the Isle of Wight a month before the war ended.[17]

Luftwaffe torpedo bombers scored a significant success on the night of 6/7 July when, probably unaware of the importance of their target, an unidentified Junkers 88 crew slammed a torpedo into the port side of the Fighter Direction Tender *FDT-216*, just aft of the bow doors and adjacent to a fuel tank and the paint store. Leading Aircraftsman Les Armitage was standing at his action station towards the stern when the former LST started to heel over, the grinding noise of 300 tons of pig iron ballast shifting across the deck providing a grim accompaniment. He climbed over the rail and lowered himself into the water using a convenient rope, then swam desperately away from the ship as it turned turtle: 'The water was covered in a thick film of heavy diesel oil and grey paint,' he recalled; 'eventually I found myself about sixty feet from 216 in the company of a few others. The little red lights attached to our lapels were shining merrily as we bobbed up and down in the swell.' Armitage was eventually rescued by HMS *Burdock*; hauling himself up a scrambling net while the corvette was underway, as Lieutenant Harold Collier had no intention of stopping with hostile torpedo bombers in the area, he lay down on the deck thoroughly exhausted and 'as black as coal'. *Burdock*'s seamen provided rudimentary treatment in the form of a rub down with a towel and a welcome tot of rum. Most of the 250 men aboard *216* were rescued, although five RAF men were lost.[18]

On the night of 7/8 July, the destroyers HMCS *Huron* and HMS *Tartar* sank a pair of German minesweepers off the Channel Islands in another Operation Dredger, and MTBs *451* and *447*, guided by the control frigate HMS *Thornborough*, fought an action off Cap d'Antifer in which both boats were badly damaged and the senior officer, 27-year-old Lieutenant John Collins, was killed. The same night the *K-Verbände* came out again, to score what was perhaps their greatest success.[19] Twenty-one *Neger*s sortied from Villers that night, bound once again for the eastern flank. Among their crew was 19-year-old Fähnrich-zur-See Karl-Heinz Potthast from Bethel in Nordrhein-Westfalen.

Potthast was one of the last to launch, the maintenance team wishing him good luck as they pushed him into the Seine Bay. After slipping through the patrols – 'I had no intention of wasting my torpedo on them' – he began to search for a suitable target. Sometime after 0400, Potthast spotted a line of warships crossing his course. As he watched, the ship at the end of the line, which appeared to be larger, slowed and anchored. Potthast manoeuvred to attack:

> When the range was a bare three hundred yards I pulled the firing lever then turned the *Neger* hard around. It seemed ages before an explosion rent the air, and in that moment my *Neger* was almost hurled out of the water. A sheet of flame shot upwards from the stricken ship.[20]

Potthast had found the Polish cruiser ORP *Dragon*. Formerly the Royal Navy cruiser of the same name, *Dragon* had been launched in 1917 and by 1944 was generally recognised as unfit for service.[21] But the Poles wanted a cruiser, with half an eye on their postwar Navy, and they also wanted it deployed against their main foe, Germany, so they firmly rejected a British compromise whereby *Dragon* could have ended her days in the Indian Ocean. After a protracted refit to work through a defect list of some sixty items, including most of the electrical systems, the old ship deployed to the Normandy gunline under the command of Komandor Stanislaw Dzienisiewicz, Vice-Admiral Sir Cecil Talbot, the Admiralty's Director of Dockyards, warning acidly that 'a 25-year-old ship cannot be turned into a new one in the course of a seven months' refit'.[22]

Dzienisiewicz had just brought his command back from a spell in Portsmouth, and after being given orders by Dalrymple-Hamilton aboard HMS *Belfast*, he was anchoring in an allocated morning bombardment position in Juno Area when Potthast's torpedo smashed into *Dragon*'s starboard side amidships at 0434. Smoke and flames erupted from the stricken cruiser, all the lights went out, and telephone communications with the after part of the ship and the engine rooms was lost. Dzienisiewicz ordered the magazines flooded and all hands on deck, except those needed for firefighting. One gallant sailor crawled through wreckage into the damaged compartments and extracted three wounded men, but the casualties in the engine room could not be rescued. The ship began to list to port and the Polish skipper ordered the guns trained to starboard to try and correct it. The fight to save *Dragon* was on.[23]

By 0450 the cruiser had a 9-degree list and was starting to settle by the stern, as most of the after end was flooded. Water was trickling inexorably into B Boiler Room through a distorted bulkhead, and Dzienisiewicz ordered his boats into the water as a precaution. Shortly after 0500 the Poles started to throw their ready-use ammunition overboard to reduce weight, later on they offloaded the ammunition from *Dragon's* magazines into an LCT as the corvette *Pennywort* prepared to take the cruiser in tow. At 0543, *Pennywort* started to tow *Dragon* back into Juno, attended by a flock of small craft and the tugs *Salveda* and *Thames*, the former a salvage tug able to help with pumping. At 0735, *Pennywort* cast off, the CO, Lieutenant Albert James, recording gratefully that 'the whole operation was carried out without any mishap whatsoever, and I have only praise for the way my crew responded to the urgency of the situation'.[24] A few minutes later *Dragon* touched bottom inside the Juno Gooseberry. Thirty-seven officers and men had been killed, ten of whom could not be recovered from the twisted wreckage, and the damage was catastrophic, Dzienisiewicz reporting a 35ft-long hole in the hull and a nightmarish catalogue of distorted or fractured bulkheads, twisted decks and burst plates.[25] Although some consideration was given to repairing *Dragon* the old ship was of such limited value that the hulk was eventually scuttled as part of the Gooseberry. *Dragon's* poor condition was an open secret in the Seine Bay fleet. *Belfast's* young Gunnery Lieutenant, Peter Brooke-Smith, recorded bitterly in his diary as his own ship left the gunline for the last time the following day that 'for what use that old thing is she might just as well have not been here. Is an insult to the Poles who have been given her to man and is just throwing away lives.'[26]

Dragon's assailant, Potthast, tried to steer his battered craft home but shortly after dawn, as the exhausted teenager was dozing off, he was fired on by the minesweeper HMS *Orestes*. Riddled with automatic weapons fire, the torpedo sank like a stone, but Potthast, despite being wounded in the arm, managed to extricate himself and was unceremoniously dragged aboard *Orestes* with a boathook. He was one of just a handful of survivors from the second *Neger* operation, all of them prisoners: not a single pilot returned to Villers that night.[27] HMS *Orestes* reported destroying four in less than an hour.[28]

Elsewhere, a pair of *Negers* torpedoed HMS *Pylades* in the space of a minute, lifting the minesweeper 3–4ft out of the water, buckling decks, straining frames and starting a fire in the engine room. Radar Operator Stan Parker called the bridge to report his set wrecked, only to receive the terse response 'wrecked the set be buggered, it's wrecked US!'[29] At first it seemed the Bird Boat could be saved, as it was only flooding slowly, but after a few minutes *Pylades* started to sink by the stern: 'About three minutes later', the CO, Lieutenant Montague James, reported, 'the ship heeled slowly but continuously over to port until she had completely turned turtle with her stern down.' Eleven officers and men went down with her.[30] Looking back from the water, Parker saw *Pylades* sitting almost vertically in the water. 'The noise was horrendous', he recalled, 'with everything breaking loose because of the position of it. Everything was crashing down inside and within a few minutes after that it started to slide. It just went down stern first and it virtually disappeared.'[31]

Navigating Officer Fred Bailey jumped off after throwing the confidential books overboard in their weighted bag. 'I swam away as quickly as I could,' he remembered; 'A fellow officer who had jumped into the water with me had lost his cap and asked me to retrieve it which I regretfully declined!!' After assisting a terrified seaman who was unable to swim, Bailey was rescued and transferred ashore. Commiserated with by some sympathetic soldiers while walking along the beach to find his transport home, he replied rather undiplomatically that 'we were going to England and they were not'. Thus were interservice relations cemented.[32] Most of the *Pylades* survivors were landed after being rescued and returned home on landing craft. Stan Parker was back in Portsmouth by the evening of the 8th, 'pretty well shaken … but it was over, it was all right. There was nothing drastic that I could say to myself, that I was a total wreck or anything like that … I was upset, of course.'[33]

So, the unrelenting efforts of the sailors to keep the vital supply lanes open beyond the formal end of Neptune continued. Responding to the new threats, on 8 July Ramsay approved the formation of a Support Squadron Eastern Flank, under the celebrated cricket and rugby player Commander Kenneth 'Monkey' Sellar, formerly commanding E LCT Squadron.[34] The Support Squadron pulled together around seventy MLs, LCGs, LCFs and LCT(R)s, to provide fire support to the army by day and anchor to form a double strength Trout Line by night, the LCGs and LCFs alternating every 640m with patrolling MLs behind. This punishing routine left just a few hours in the afternoon when they could rest. Working alongside Tony Pugsley's regular patrols, they lived in conditions of extreme hardship, surviving on army ration packs, with very few opportunities for a proper wash or a hot meal.[35]

Three days later, the Germans recognised their own naval commanders' desperate efforts to make a difference to the Normandy campaign in the face of overwhelming Allied superiority at sea by awarding Knight's Crosses to one of the most determined and successful E-boat officers, *Korvettenkapitän* Götz, Freiherr von Mirbach, CO of *9.Sfltl*, as well as Kommodore Rudolf Petersen, in overall command of the E-boat force, and the redoubtable Korvettenkapitän Heinrich Hoffmann of *5. Torpedobootflottille*. Outnumbered and outgunned, the Kriegsmarine had no intention of giving up.

On the night of 14/15 July, a third Operation Dredger was carried out by the destroyers HMS *Tartar*, HMCS *Haida* and ORP *Błyskawica*, in the area of the Île de Groix near Lorient. Learning from the unfortunate *Eskimo*, the three destroyers kept away from their opponents' unexpectedly punchy automatic weapons, and methodically destroyed the ex-Yugoslav submarine chasers *UJ-1420* and *UJ-1421* at long range.[36] MTBs directed by the frigate HMS *Thornborough* fought another high-speed action off Cap d'Antifer on the same night, engaging the enemy at just under 1,000m and driving them off. Petersen's crews came out again on the 17/18 and a force of R-boats took on *Stayner* and MTBs *415* and *416* on the 18/19, accurate German fire setting light to rockets on *415*, forcing the British to withdraw with five serious burns casualties.[37] Admiral Sir Charles Little, Commander-in-Chief, Portsmouth, pronounced himself satisfied with Coastal Forces' determined efforts to keep the

Kriegsmarine out of the Seine Bay, although he commented that the superior speed of the E-boats made them virtually impossible to catch and 'their heavy armament and concentration of numbers, together with the support of coast artillery and shore radar, has made them formidable targets'.[38] The Battle of the Seine Bay was far from over.

In a bizarre illustration of just how hard it was to find U-boats in the shallow, wreck-littered waters of the English Channel, on 18 July the frigate HMS *Cam* ran down and depth-charged a promising contact 22 miles from St Catherine's Point on the Isle of Wight. Sub-Lieutenant Herbert Southerst was the Depth Charge Officer. 'We dropped two', he recalled 'the first one at fifty feet and the next one at a hundred and fifty and then we fired the port thrower,' after which *Cam* was rocked by a huge explosion, water rising three times the height of the frigate's mast:

> The ship lurched and heaved heavily over to starboard, lying almost on her side, and I thought that she was going to go straight over ... we had something like forty-three injured and very heavily wounded men lying on the steel decks and also, we had shrapnel, sea bottom, sand, sea weed, lying all over our decks and then a tidal wave hit us, heeled the ship over and flattened everyone ... I was quite dumfounded for a minute; I couldn't understand what was happening.[39]

Cam was stopped and listing to starboard. Opening the hatch down to the tiller flat, Southerst was horrified to hear water pouring in through cracked plates. There was no power to operate the pumps, and fires had started in the engine and boiler rooms. The CO, Lieutenant-Commander John Smythe, had a broken back, and most of the other officers who had been on the bridge were critically hurt. Southerst, the only uninjured officer, recalled 'ratings with the calves of their legs hanging off where they'd split across the calf of their leg'. The young Sub-Lieutenant, just 21 years old, organised the evacuation of survivors from the shattered engine room and parties to fight the fires, before treating the wounded on the upper deck. *Cam* was towed to the Isle of Wight and declared a total constructive loss.[40] Small arms ammunition found littered across the buckled decks revealed that the frigate had attacked one of a pair of ammunition ships sunk on 8 July 1940. In a more successful attack on the same day, HMS *Balfour* sank *U-672* off Guernsey, Oberleutnant Ulf Lawaetz and his entire crew being taken prisoner.

On 20 July, the same day that a group of German Army officers and other conspirators attempted to end the war by planting a bomb under Hitler's conference table at his East Prussian headquarters, the Canadian frigate HMCS *Matane* was badly damaged while patrolling off Brest by a radio-controlled glider bomb launched from a Dornier 217. In the Bay, HMS *Isis* was carrying out a routine ASDIC sweep of Omaha Area when at 1802 the destroyer was rocked by three huge explosions in swift succession. Holed on both sides and with the bows almost severed, *Isis* sank in just a few minutes. 'No survivors interrogated made a statement regarding any attempt to save the ship,' read the report into the loss; 'in view of the damage they seem to have realised it would be hopeless.'[41] Many of the ship's company made it into rafts, but by the time a US Coast Guard cutter found them at 0615 the following morning, almost all had died of exposure; there were just 8 survivors from a crew of 145. Ken Davies was one of them. 'I remember the speed with which men died,' he recalled; 'the fellow next to me said he was feeling warm at last. This I knew was a sign of hypothermia. I tried to keep him awake by talking to him but failed. It seemed no time at all before he was stiff as a board and we tipped him over the side.'[42]

Once again, *Neger*s were the perpetrators, but this third operation proved equally costly to the operators: losses in *361.Kfltl* were now so high that the unit had been essentially wiped out. Reinforcements were arriving in theatre, in the form of another flotilla of *Neger*s, a flotilla of the marginally improved *Marder* (pine marten) human torpedoes, and more *Linsen*s, but for now the *K-Verbände* could only lick their wounds and regroup.[43]

As July drew to a close the fighting at sea showed no signs of abating. Another British Bird Boat, HMS *Chamois*, was mined on the 21st, Sub-Lieutenant Leslie Hasker recalling that 'it felt as though the ship had been struck underneath by an enormous rubber mallet — an extraordinary experience. The ship lifted right clear of the water, then dropped back on the sea with a shudder.'[44] South of Brighton, *U-212* was destroyed by HMS *Curzon* with the loss of all forty-nine crew. Geoffrey Cassidy was serving in the frigate and recorded the submarine's end in matter-of-fact style: 'it was a night action', he remembered; 'we just dropped the depth charges and it was reported sunk, we saw the oil and that was it'.[45]

Despite the continued German pressure from sea and air, the vital work of the build-up continued unabated throughout July, sailors working round the clock to bring the military the supplies and rein-forcements they needed. By the middle of August, the British were landing 17,000 tons every day, and the Americans an extraordinary 23,000 tons. Most of this was coming through Mulberry B, Juno and Omaha, so Gold was closed on 22 July.[46] By now, the greatest logis-tics challenge was moving everything from the beaches to the front, not getting everything to Normandy, and this was a conundrum which only the military could fix. Much depended on the famous 'Red Ball Express' of trucks, often driven by African Americans, which thundered to and from the front non-stop, day and night, on dedicated priority roads, their exhausted drivers swapping over on the move.[47]

On 25 July 1944, following weeks of bitter fighting in the Normandy *bocage* which cost 40,000 casualties, Bradley's US First Army began Operation Cobra, the breakout around Saint-Lô. With the Germans distracted by a simultaneous British offensive around Caen, Bradley's tanks smashed through the German lines following a pulverising aerial bombardment and raced out into Normandy and Brittany. The western flank of the assault area was now secure, and the warships switched to an aggressive forward defence posture, hunting U-boats and blockading what remained of the Kriegsmarine inside their increasingly isolated Biscay bases, as well as intercepting and destroying evacuation convoys and other coastal traffic. To the east, however, the tactical situation remained unchanged for some time: as the US armies in the west raced into Brittany, the British and Canadians remained locked in a bitter and far less mobile battle south of Caen, which had finally fallen during the difficult and costly Operation Goodwood between 18 and 20 July. Le Havre was still a German stronghold, and for the fleet, the requirement to defend the assault area against nightly incursions by German small craft and the *K-Verbände* remained unchanged. The most critical phase of the Battle of the Seine Bay had perhaps passed, but it was not yet over. To the east the fight against German forces based in and around Le Havre was unchanged, but to the west the fighting now stretched around the coast of Brittany and deep into the bay of Biscay (see Map 9).

On 25 July, the Admiralty resumed responsibility for the Channel, with Ramsay retaining operational authority over the former assault area but with a much reduced staff. Under him, Rivett-Carnac and Wilkes managed the former WTF and ETF areas. Ramsay respected Wilkes, describing him as efficient, but his private diary is peppered with concerns about Rivett-Carnac's lack of 'grip': 'He [Rivett-Carnac] is so obviously sleepy and willing to let anyone dictate and take charge,' he wrote on the 24th.[48] Rivett-Carnac ran an organisation which had been restructured to resemble the naval Home Commands in the UK, with sub-commands responsible for running the various ports, minesweeping, defence of the anchorage and other key elements.[49] The fleet was now much diminished. At its heart were the remaining bombarding ships, almost all very old or unsuitable for the new British Pacific Fleet. *Warspite* rejoined the fleet on 24 August after a makeshift refit to repair the mine damage from 13 June. The veteran battleship was clearly unfit for anything other than bombardment duties after decades of hard wear and action damage, returning to the gunline with 'one good [propeller] shaft, one fairly good one, and one very wobbly shaft', former Captain Marcel Kelsey wrote in September 1955; 'the fourth remained jammed solid'.[50]

With the Kriegsmarine a spent force, at least strategically, and political calls to restart the Arctic convoys to the Soviet Union and join the vast naval campaign in the Pacific growing, by the end of July 1944 the Seine Bay fleet was definitely the 'second eleven', but it still had work to do. With the Americans largely departed for the Mediterranean, the Royal Navy had to provide bombardment

Map 9. Western flank: the Bay of Biscay.

support to both armies. Dönitz's 'inshore' U-boat campaign was a significant challenge, not just in the Bay but on the convoy routes to it and the waters around every port of departure. E-boats and *K-Verbände* still tried to get into the former assault area almost every night, and mines remained a constant threat, even inside the Mulberry Harbour, where the Operation Taxable veteran *HDML-1410* was blown up after being ordered to 'dash around the anchorage' and round up a convoy.[51]

Until the Channel ports could be captured, Coastal Forces, the Fleet Air Arm and the RAF's Coastal Command remained fully occupied, as they had been since the invasion began, deterring German light coastal craft and preventing efforts to reinforce Le Havre, which was still the Kriegsmarine's main forward operating base. Air patrols were essential, but also exhausting and frequently dull. 848 Naval Air Squadron recorded 200 sorties (individual aircraft missions) during July alone. 854 Squadron's Avengers, flying out of RAF Hawkinge, spent the month 'divided between A/S Patrols from the Pas-de-Calais to the Isle of Wight and Night Rover Patrols along the French, Belgian and Dutch coasts'.[52]

Not a single submarine was sighted on the A/S patrols, a measure of just how hard it was to detect schnorkel-equipped submarines hiding among wrecks, although, equally, suppressed submarines found it very hard to attack targets. However, the 'Rover Patrols' led to thirty-six attacks on various small German naval craft. 'Although results are always difficult to observe at night, numerous hits, straddles and near-misses are claimed,' wrote Lieutenant-Commander William Mainprice, 854's CO; 'in view of the inexperience of most crews and the foulness of the weather . . . I consider this a very good effort on the part of all flying crews.' As an added bonus, Telegraphist/ Air Gunner Fred Shirman was Mentioned in Despatches for shooting down a V1 flying bomb on 9 July. V1s had been a common sight over the Seine Bay since the invasion, although they were not targeted at the fleet and were more of a curiosity than a threat.[53]

Rover Patrols could be deadly. On 28 July at 2040, Avenger JZ 300 from 849 NAS, flying out of RAF Perranporth in Cornwall, was part of a patrol which spotted a small German convoy passing out to sea through the boom at Saint-Malo. Patiently the airmen watched until the three trawlers and four armed landing craft had steamed out of range of the German coastal defences. The weather was fine and the visibility excellent as the rugged US-built strike aircraft angled downwards into a shallow dive from 3,000ft, closing the target out of the sun in the face of 'intense and accurate' German fire. Within minutes, automatic fire riddled the Avenger's port wing, and one shell tore off the aircraft's port tailplane and elevator. Fifteen jagged holes shredded the rudder, and the pilot, Sub-Lieutenant P.T. White, had a narrow escape when a shell shattered the cockpit and burst on his headrest. The observer, 28-year-old Lieutenant Joseph Nixon, was not so lucky: the incoming fire shattered the bulkhead separating his compartment from the cockpit and he was killed 'instantaneously', two seconds before White released four 500lb bombs at 1,000ft. JZ 300 straddled a landing craft and a trawler, White claiming to have sunk the former and damaged the latter, before he nursed his battered aircraft back to Perranporth. Nixon, from Hove, left behind a wife, Peggy.[54]

With Sellar's Support Squadron and Coastal Forces forming an almost impenetrable barrier around the Bay, Petersen moved his E-boat flotillas back into British coastal waters to reach the constant flow of invasion traffic. Kapitänleutnant Jens Matzen's 6. *Sfltl* attacked convoy ETM46 from Southend to the Seine Bay on the night of 26/27 July. Skirting the escorting Royal Navy corvettes *Orchis* and *Potentilla*, Matzen's boats caught the vulnerable merchant ships off Dungeness, and torpedoed the freighters *Empire Beatrice* and *Fort Perrot*. Neither ship sank, but eight crew members died in the *Empire Beatrice*, which had to be beached near Dungeness. *Fort Perrot* caught fire but was towed to safety. MGBs caught Matzen's force after the attack, raking *S-90* with fire and wounding five of the crew.[55]

While Matzen attacked ETM46, six boats from 2. *Sfltl* sortied to distract the British forces around Le Havre, only to became embroiled in a fast-paced action with British MTBs which was frenetic even by the standards of Coastal Forces. At 0042, the experienced control ship HMS *Retalick* vectored MTBs *430*, *412* and *431* on to the approaching enemy 'at utmost speed'.[56] The two forces clashed off

Cap d'Antifer and in the confusion, *S-182* rammed *MTB-430*, which blew up, wrecking both boats. Coming up behind at high speed, *MTB-412* had no chance of avoiding the carnage and ploughed into *430*'s drifting wreck, sustaining such severe damage that the MTB had to be abandoned, *412*'s 21-year-old Sub-Lieutenant Derek Okey from Sevenoaks being fatally wounded in the melee. The collision left a further eleven British and eight German sailors dead, including *S-182*'s Commanding Officer, 28-year-old Kapitänleutnant Kurt Pinger. Seventeen Germans were taken prisoner.[57] Despite British claims of multiple 'kills', *S-182* was the only E-boat destroyed in thirty-eight naval actions and twenty air attacks during July 1944.[58] These fast and elusive opponents remained extremely difficult to catch, however great the Allied superiority in numbers, and verifying results in these hectic night actions was incredibly challenging.

Elsewhere, HMS *Cooke* caught 21-year-old Oberleutnant Gerhard Conrad's big, vulnerable Type VIID minelaying submarine *U-214* off Start Point and destroyed it with the loss of all forty-eight crew. In total, eleven U-boats sortied against the invasion traffic from French bases in July 1944. The limited successes they achieved came at a terrible cost – seven were sunk with the loss of more than 400 men killed or captured, and two more were forced to abort.[59] This failure was not inevitable and did not just derive from Allied numerical superiority. It was earned through constant vigilance and hard work by the escort groups. Every so often, a skilled, bold or lucky U-boat commander could still deliver a reminder that victory in the Seine Bay should still not be taken for granted.

Oberleutnant Hermann Stuckmann struck a serious blow on the night of 29/30 July, when his *U-621* fired a *Zaunkönig* into the LSI(S) HMS *Prince Leopold*, which had landed the 5th Ranger Battalion at Omaha on 6 June. There was 'an unholy thump', according to Petty Officer Richard Hughes, and the former Belgian ferry took on a list so severe that HMS *Chelmer*, which had come alongside to help pump her, had to cast off. After the embarked troops were put aboard a destroyer, the tug *Amsterdam* took the LSI(S) in tow and tried to get it home. Hughes and the rest of the ship's company remained aboard 'to try and keep the old wagon afloat' but in the end *Prince Leopold's* flooding was uncontrollable and the LSI capsized and sank 6 miles south of the Nab Tower, the recycled First World War fort now serving as a lighthouse east of the Isle of Wight.[60] Fourteen members of the ship's company died along with thirty military personnel. On the same day, the Luftwaffe bombed and sank the ASW trawler *Lord Wakefield* off Omaha Area. Skipper Henry Dodd went down with his command and thirty-three of his crew.

The following night the E-boats sortied again, running the same complex double-blind they had on 26/27 July. While *2.Sfltl* distracted the defender, *S-91*, *S-97* and *S-114* from Matzen's Dieppe-based *6.Sfltl* hit convoy FTM53, eleven MT ships, eight LSTs and a trawler bound from Juno Area to Tilbury. FTM53 was approaching Dungeness at 9 knots when Matzen's boats struck with *Flächenabsuchender Torpedo* (FAT), long-range pattern-running torpedoes, in one of the most effective German attacks of the Battle of the Seine Bay's closing phase. Matzen used a standard technique known as a *Stichanzatz* (stitch) where widely dispersed boats took station along a convoy route, guided by *B-Dienst* intelligence or Luftwaffe reconnaissance. Effective in 1942 when it was first conceived, in the circumstances of 1944, with fewer boats and a harried, much-diminished Luftwaffe, it was far harder to develop effectively, but on the night of 30/31 July the results were alarming.

British radar failures on land and afloat, coupled with disastrous delays in communication, 'mistakes in the disposition of the escort' and 'lack of initiative' meant that, despite a strong escort and the presence of three destroyers and thirteen Coastal Forces craft deployed on anti-E-boat patrols, Matzen reached his firing position unhindered. He was aided by a simple British signals failure: an intercept order was mistakenly sent to 'Call Sign FO.1', instead of Call Sign 'FO.i', the destroyer HMS *Campbell*, which was escorting the convoy. From such a small error, perhaps the result of overtired personnel, disaster sprang.[61]

At around 0130, almost simultaneously and without warning, torpedoes slammed into five freighters. Captain Owen John of the

SS *Samwake* recorded an 'extremely violent' explosion in Number 2 Hold which blew out all the hatches, his 2nd Officer recording 'a brilliant flash followed by a reddish glow reaching up to masthead height'. The 7,219-ton *Samwake* immediately heeled over 4 degrees to port, three holds filling with water thanks to a huge hole in the port side, roughly 10ft long, with buckled, ruptured plating extending even further. 'All available pumps were put on', John wrote later, 'but no impression was made owing to the rapid inflow of the water.' In a desperate attempt to save his ship, he began to transfer oil from the port to the starboard side to counter the list. 'All my crew were behaving extremely well', he recorded, 'there was no sign of panic.' There were no casualties and after sending all non-essential personnel to their boat stations John continued to run the pumps and try to keep his wounded freighter afloat. At 0250 he lowered *Samwake*'s lifeboats and sent most of his crew away, remaining aboard himself with 2nd Engineer Wells and another engineer, Patterson, to rig the auxiliary 'Donkey Boiler' and keep the pumps running unattended. John was glowing in his praise for these two men, 'the most outstanding of this fine crew . . . their gallantry set a fine example to all'.[62]

At 0300, everything was ready and the three men joined the others in the lifeboats. Remarkably, John and another team of volunteers boarded the ship again later in the night, to transfer ballast and try to correct *Samwake*'s worsening list, until they were peremptorily ordered away by a nearby destroyer. Their desperate fight to save the dying freighter was for nothing. 'At 0540 I saw my ship beginning to tip,' John wrote in his report; 'she dipped by the head, the stern reared up vertically and held for a few minutes, then very slowly she rolled over to starboard and disappeared at 0545 in a small fountain of water', the port navigation light still burning and a melancholy trickle of smoke still rising from the funnel.[63]

Captain R.S. Craston of the SS *Ocean Courier* was in his Chart Room when a FAT exploded deep inside Number 5 Hold, buckling the freighter's propeller shaft, throwing a shower of sand ballast high in the air and blasting a stored propeller right through the deck. The hold immediately flooded, but the mass of sand it held checked the force of the explosion and *Ocean Courier*'s bulkheads held out. As

Ocean Courier settled by the stern, 'I gave the general alarm', Craston recorded, 'and altered course to the northward, towards the beach, with the idea of beaching the vessel if necessary.' Ten minutes later, the broken propeller shaft finally failed and the engines stopped, leaving the freighter wallowing within sight of land. The torpedo had smashed the accommodation for *Ocean Courier*'s naval and military gunners, and a desperate effort began to rescue them from beneath the wreckage and sand. A volunteer rescue party led by 2nd Officer Pearson climbed down a small escape hatch and pulled three wounded survivors to freedom, but five gunners died in the mangled wreck of the mess deck.[64] As dawn broke a passing LST took off *Ocean Courier*'s wounded, and the veteran tug *Lady Brassey* (launched in 1913) towed the freighter to Dungeness.

Ocean Courier's sister ship *Ocean Volga* was also hit. Third Officer Leonard Fifield was on watch when he heard 'a bang just like somebody banging a saucepan' and the ship ahead swung violently out of line. 'I knew it was a torpedo,' Fifield recalled; 'I had to go hard a starboard to avoid hitting him. I turned through ninety degrees and I sounded the alarms, fortunately, to get everybody on deck and the Old Man had come up and then suddenly bang! We got it right on the bow because we'd swung into it.' *Ocean Volga* was badly flooded forward but able to steam for Southend unaided at 6 knots (11km/h), escorted by the minesweeper HMS *Pickle*.[65]

The 7,160-ton SS *Fort Dearborn* became the third victim of Matzen's attack when a FAT slammed into the port side between Numbers 2 and 3 Holds, under the bridge. *Fort Dearborn*'s wound was even more catastrophic, Captain R. Newlands estimating a hole measuring 15m by 9m in the side, which flooded two holds and the engine room, and as the freighter settled by the bow, he ordered his men to abandon ship; by 0145, everyone was clear. Remarkably, the stubborn ship refused to sink, a tribute to the Canadians who built her, and Newlands and a small team reboarded later that night. The corvette *Poppy* tried to tow *Fort Dearborn* but the big freighter was so far down by the head that the little warship could only pull her in circles. As dawn was breaking, salvation arrived in the form of the Admiralty tug *Lady Duncannon*, which took *Fort Dearborn* in tow, ably assisted by a pair of passing US tugs which lashed themselves to either side. Even then progress was glacial until the indefatigable *Lady Brassey* returned from Dungeness to join the rescue at about noon on the 31st. Between them, the four tugs hauled *Fort Dearborn* to Dungeness and beached the freighter at 1530.[66] The fourth victim, *Fort Kaskaskia*, reached Dungeness unaided despite 'a hole in our side the size of a bus', John Abrahams recalled, adding that he had been so convinced the ship would sink that he had ditched all the code books over the side. Incredibly, Abrahams had been sunk in a previous ship, the *Jersey City*, exactly four years before, on 31 July 1940.[67]

Matzen ran for home as soon as he had fired his torpedoes and although the destroyer HMS *Opportune* raced off in pursuit, the E-boats were too fast and escaped unscathed. This alarming success, which one Admiralty report even considered may have been down to the mythical 'W-boats', brought immediate retaliation.[68] On the night of 31 July the RAF returned to Le Havre, but the Germans were better prepared and there were fewer E-boats to hit on this occasion; some were at sea fighting a running battle with Royal Navy screening forces and the remainder were safe inside their reinforced concrete pens. Just three boats were damaged, including *S-132*, which was out of action for a fortnight.[69]

As the US Army raced out into Normandy and Brittany, sailors went with them to open up newly captured ports. The situation was fluid and fraught with danger, which could have tragic consequences. On 1 August, US Navy Captain Norman Ives, Quentin Walsh's CO at Cherbourg, set out with a group of US Navy officers and men for Granville. Reconnoitring Granville with ease, they carried on into Brittany the following day, following up on a rumour that the Germans had evacuated Saint-Malo. The rumour turned out to be just that. Approaching the port, Ives and his small party came across and captured a pair of stray German soldiers. Believing them to be demoralised stragglers, they had stopped to interrogate them, their vulnerable jeeps parked carelessly along the side of the road, when gunfire erupted around them. The two Germans were part of a far larger group, which surrounded the party. Ives, Lieutenant-Commander Arthur Hooper and four ratings were killed and another eight men were wounded; the remainder were surrounded under heavy fire until they were rescued by tanks from the 6th Armoured Division.[70] 'For operational purposes the party was annihilated,' Walsh recalled; 'as a result Admiral Wilkes ... gave me about three hundred more men to carry out the reconnaissance of Brittany as far as Brest.'[71]

The night of 2/3 August saw one of the most concentrated German attacks on the eastern flank of the Bay, which was meant to mark the debut of another new E-boat weapon, the TIIId *Dackel* (dachshund) very-long-range torpedo, which could be programmed to circle in a pattern at the end of its run. In addition, the Kriegsmarine deployed sixteen control and twenty-eight explosive *Linsen* explosive motor boats from *211.Kfltl* operating from Houlgate and an upgraded human torpedo, the *Marder*, which was similar to the earlier *Neger* but capable of submerging. The *Marder*s of *362.KFltl* were combined with the remaining *Neger*s of *361.Kfltl* to form a combined force of fifty-eight human torpedoes.[72] In addition the Luftwaffe contributed a strong air attack to distract the defences and dropped flares to mark targets. This kind of combined-arms operation could have been absolutely lethal had the Germans co-ordinated them in this way more consistently.

Another RAF raid on Le Havre sank *S-39* and *S-114* and damaged two others, limiting the available E-boats to four, all from *2.SFltl*, as well as preventing the *Dackel* torpedos from being loaded. The E-boats spent the night skirmishing frantically with British MTBs without getting near a worthwhile target; two boats collided and another was damaged, but they did buy the *K-Verbände* the time and space they needed to make their attack.[73] This time, they tried to work around the northern end of the Trout Line rather than push straight through it, but their losses were still dreadful: only ten control *Linsen*s and seventeen human torpedoes returned to base, *ML-181* alone claiming four *Linsen*s – apparently nicknamed Weasels by the Allies – destroyed.[74] German claims of success remained greatly exaggerated, totalling between 40,000 and 50,000 tons of Allied shipping, including a cruiser or troop transport, two destroyers, two corvettes and a merchant ship, which earned a further two Knight's Crosses for the *K-Verbände*.[75]

The real total was more modest but still a *Marder* hit the Hunt Class destroyer HMS *Quorn*. Lieutenant Ivan Hall, the Commanding Officer, recalled proceeding at a steady 8 knots (15km/h) up and down a patrol area which had been assigned him by Pugsley in his regular night defence signal. It was a bright, moonlit night when the destroyer was shaken by a huge explosion sometime around 0300. *Quorn* was turning to the north-east under full helm when the torpedo ripped open the starboard side and within fifty seconds the destroyer was on her beam ends: it was immediately clear that nothing could be done to save her. Hall ordered 'abandon ship' but 'I doubt if it got further than the wheelhouse.' Two minutes later the stricken destroyer righted itself and broke in two amidships; as Hall, the last to leave, dived from his now vertical bridge and swam clear, he watched both halves of his command plunge to the bottom, until just a few feet of the bow and stern remained above the water. Tragically, as he watched he saw men desperately trying to escape through the scuttles in the forward mess deck, 'which were of course too small'.[76]

Two very junior officers distinguished themselves in the sinking, a testament to the resilience of the 'citizen sailors' which characterised the Seine Bay fleet. Sub-Lieutenant Basil Pollard returned to the wrecked stern to cut free a Carley Float, then, despite 'not being a strong man', he swam around the scene, helping exhausted seamen to get aboard, as well as 'quelling' two men who had 'completely lost their heads ... one of whom attacked him'. Sub-Lieutenant Harry Schofield also returned to the sinking stern, to make the destroyer's depth charges safe and prevent them exploding in the water, which could have caused carnage among the survivors.[77] Both young officers were awarded OBEs.[78] Unfortunately, no attempt was made to rescue survivors until 0720 on what was a frantic night for the defenders of the Bay's eastern flank; as a consequence, well over half of the estimated 120 shocked and probably injured men who went into the water gave up their desperate fight to stay afloat and slipped away over the ensuing four and a half hours. Only 39 ratings and 6 officers survived; 130 officers and men lost their lives. A bitter Hall requested a full investigation as to why no earlier attempt was made to rescue survivors, concluding his report by writing that 'the behaviour and morale of the ship's company in the face of extreme hardship and increasing exhaustion was admirable'.[79]

Quorn's destruction was claimed by a *Marder* operator named Ferdinand Hoffman. 'I . . . fired my torpedo and hit the destroyer', he remembered. 'After my shot I turned at once and tried to reach the coast. I was terribly afraid.'[80] Hoffman abandoned his *Marder* when it was shot up by a British MGB; he tried to swim ashore but was pulled out of the water and taken prisoner.

On the same chaotic night, a *Marder* torpedoed the former cruiser HMS *Durban*, which had already been scuttled as part of the Gooseberry breakwater at Ouistreham, and a *Linsen* hit and sank the minesweeping trawler *Gairsay* with the loss of thirty-one officers and men. They also indirectly claimed *LCG(L)-764*, which was trying to recover a *Linsen*, 'for good reasons presumably', Royal Marine William Cockburn recorded dubiously, when it exploded alongside, blowing a hole in the port side and killing eight sailors and Royal Marines. Cockburn was spun around in his own gun mounting and briefly knocked out, before being half-carried to safety aboard an ML which nosed up alongside the sinking LCG.[81] This may well have been Graham Rouse's *ML-197*, which was certainly involved, Rouse recalling that 'It was a chaotic situation in the dark – we went alongside and took off some who were still on board and pulled out others who were in the water. I thought I could hear someone in the water shouting to get our attention – "ML! ML!" and I called back into the darkness to "Hang on". I do not know what happened to the owner of this voice.'[82]

The grim reality was that up to a point warships were expendable, particularly trawlers and the cheap, improvised LCGs. The Trout Line was there to keep the enemy away from the freighters, and in the main it was successful, although on the same chaotic night, human torpedoes seem to have been the most likely suspects for attacks on the freighters *Samlong* and *Fort Lac la Rouge*. The latter was in the middle of discharging cargo and crowded with sleeping Pioneer Corps stevedores, exhausted after working solidly until 2200 the previous night, when an explosion tore through Number 5 Hold on the starboard side at 0620, directly below the 'tween decks space where they were stretched out. Three Pioneers were confirmed killed and a further eight logged as missing. After salvage chief Commodore McKenzie had inspected the ship and agreed with the Master's assessment that *Fort Lac la Rouge* was not in immediate danger of sinking, the badly damaged freighter was towed to Juno Area and beached to complete unloading.[83]

Against these losses, the Allies could set the inexorable flow of men and materiel from North America, across the Atlantic and thence into the Seine Bay.

✳ 15 ✳
On to Le Havre
3 August–12 September 1944

In this operation we staked our all in many respects upon unknown factors, and to the skill with which the navies met the unexpected our initial victory was largely due.

General Dwight D. Eisenhower[1]

On 3 August, Convoy HX300 arrived in the UK from New York via Halifax, Nova Scotia. It was the largest trade convoy of the war. It totalled 167 ships carrying a staggering 1 million tons of cargo, including everything from grain and molasses to military vehicles, aircraft and fuel, and with the remaining U-boats expending themselves in near-suicidal attempts to interfere with the traffic in and out of the Seine Bay and the British coastal shipping routes which fed into it, they enjoyed a trouble-free passage. By 14 July, 1 million tons of stores and nearly 300,000 vehicles had been put ashore to support Eisenhower's armies, which had expanded to thirty-three divisions by the end of July.[2]

As if to drive home to the Germans the steady progress towards an Allied victory in the Bay, on 4 August HMS *Stayner* and HMS *Wensleydale* destroyed *U-671* south of Newhaven. Remarkably, three survivors came to the surface among the inevitable oil and wreckage, Oberleutnant zur See Hans Schaefer, Bootsmaat Bruno Ehlers and Maschinemaat Ernst Meyer, who related the grim story of the submarine's end to their interrogators: 'After the first of these attacks all lights were extinguished and water began to come into the boat. The second attack lifted the submarine and after it she remained heavy and on the bottom. The third attack apparently turned her on her side.' Encouragingly for the Allies, morale in the U-boat service was apparently starting to break under the appalling losses, the inter-rogators reporting that 'neither rating had any enthusiasm for service in submarines and Schaefer . . . was pessimistic regarding the outcome of the war'.[3]

Two days later, HMS *Loch Killin* sank *U-736* south-west of Lorient using the new 'Squid' anti-submarine mortar, and an Anglo-Canadian task force formed around the cruiser HMS *Bellona* annihilated a German convoy carrying troops from Saint-Nazaire, sinking or damaging every ship.[4] The action formed part of a much larger joint Royal Navy–RAF operation codenamed Kinetic. As the Allied armies swept across western France, German troops withdrew into the Biscay port cities of Brest, Saint-Nazaire, Lorient, La Rochelle and Royan, which Hitler had declared were fortresses to be defended to the last man, and the last remnants of the Kriegsmarine in the west were ordered to transfer with them. Kinetic's aim was the total annihilation of this ragtag collection of warships, and it was carried out with the full weight of Allied sea power: anti-submarine groups with strong cruiser/ destroyer forces operating around the clock under an air umbrella provided by Coastal Command and the escort carrier HMS *Striker*.[5]

On 7 August, the day Eisenhower moved his advanced HQ to Normandy, events on land took a dramatic shift once again when, against all logic, Hitler instructed his generals to launch Operation Lüttich, a counter-attack at Mortain, with the hopelessly ambitious objective of cutting off Patton's 3rd US Army, racing deep into Normandy and Brittany. The result was that most of the remaining German armoured divisions thrust themselves deep into a bag before running out of steam well short of their objective, thanks to a tena-cious American defence and outstanding air support. The bag would go down in history as the Falaise Pocket, its neck marked by the towns of Falaise to the north and Argentan to the south, and it would break the German Army in Normandy. 'As on former occasions', wrote Eisenhower, 'the fanatical tenacity of the Nazi leaders . . . led the Germans to cling too long to a position from which military wisdom would have dictated an earlier retreat.'[6] By 10 August, the Allies were planning a pincer movement to draw the neck of the bag closed, cutting off and annihilating much of the German Army, with Patton swinging east and pressing up to Argentan from the south and General Harry Crerar's 1st Canadian Army pushing towards Falaise from the north. The prospects for an end in Normandy looked good, but until it came, the fighting in the Bay would continue.

On the day that the Germans launched Lüttich, the former LSI *Amsterdam*, which had carried the Rangers to Pointe du Hoc before being converted to a Hospital Ship, was mined returning from Juno Area. 17-year-old Galley Boy Patrick Manning was fast asleep in the cabin he shared with another young Galley Boy when

> suddenly there was a muffled explosion, the lights went out, and the ship listed. We managed to get our trousers on and our life-jackets, but as we looked out of the porthole, all we could see was water and the deck was wet underfoot. There was a horrible smell of ether in the air. We found the cabin door but couldn't open it.[7]

Desperately the two boys kicked and banged on the door until they noticed that a broken bunk was holding it shut; tugging it free they opened the door and raced on deck to find that 'the ship seemed to be broken in the middle with one half listing one way and the other half the other. One of the funnels and the mast were down and the screws were out of the water. Only one LCA could get away to pick up survivors.'[8]

After preventing a disoriented Royal Army Medical Corps sergeant from jumping over the stern and killing himself on the still-revolving propellers, Manning jumped over the side and swam clear of the ship. Unable to board the overcrowded LCA, he paddled wearily around in the cold and the mist until the sound of screams and shouts drew his eyes back to the stricken *Amsterdam*. He recalled with horror:

> I looked around and could see some of the wounded soldiers jumping over the side, and there were two people stuck in

portholes – I was told afterwards that they were nurses. As I continued paddling, I heard a gushing noise then saw what looked like ashes shooting out of the funnel amid lots of noise. Then there was nothing, just wreckage floating in the water and deathly silence.[9]

Fifty-five patients, ten Royal Army Medical Corps staff, thirty members of the crew and eleven prisoners-of-war went down with the *Amsterdam*. Two military nurses were indeed among the dead, Sisters Mollie Evershead and Dorothy Field of the Queen Alexandra's Imperial Military Nursing Service; 27-year-old Evershed, from Soham in Cambridgeshire, and Field, who was 32 and from Ringwood, Hampshire, were seen by survivors repeatedly going back inside the sinking *Amsterdam*, helping to recover a remarkable seventy-five survivors. Both women were Mentioned in Despatches and later awarded the King's Commendation for Brave Conduct. They are the only women named on the British Normandy Memorial at Ver-sur-Mer.[10]

The following day, as part of Operation Kinetic, RAF Beaufighter strike aircraft from Coastal Command's 19 Group sank four German minesweepers near Saint-Nazaire. In exchange, Kapitänleutnant Karl-Heinz Lange's *U-667* torpedoed the Liberty ship *Ezra Weston*, travelling in convoy EBC66 from Milford Haven. *LST-644* came alongside and took off survivors, but believing *Ezra Weston* had been mined, Lieutenant Jack Radford, RCNVR, inexplicably took his corvette HMCS *Regina* alongside the LST and stopped engines to transfer them aboard his ship. Lange, still lurking in the vicinity and doubtless unable to believe his luck, fired a snapshot with a *Zaunkönig* and the battle-worn Flower Class corvette exploded and disappeared in under thirty seconds. Twenty-eight officers and men died, mostly in the engine room, a remarkably small total given the speed with which *Regina* exploded and sank. Most survivors were taken aboard *LST-644*, where 26-year-old Surgeon-Lieutenant Grant Gould, an intern from Ottawa Civic Hospital, treated them throughout the night, despite having a broken chest bone and being 'half-choked with fuel oil, and so painfully wounded that he had to take morphia himself'.[11] Gould was Mentioned in Despatches for his actions.

The *Linsen*s came out again from Honfleur on the night of 8/9 August in another operation coordinated with E-boats firing long-range *Dackel* torpedos. They claimed a destroyer, an escort vessel, an LST and six merchant ships, which was once again nonsense.[12] It must have been only too tempting for the very young, undertrained and probably terrified operators, travelling at speed in the dark and often under fire, to simply point their boats and get out of trouble as soon as they could. The only victim was the 20-year-old cruiser HMS *Frobisher*, which was hit by a *Dackel* at 0715 the following morning, shortly after Captain James Mudford had stood down his ship's company from action stations after the mayhem of the *Linsen* attack had passed. Although the powerful explosion 'whipped' the ship, and men were tossed about like skittles, there were fortunately no casualties, but it tore a huge hole in the port side forward and blasted across the full width of the ship, buckling and distorting the plates on the other side and the decks above. Interestingly, the initial report attributed the attack to a human torpedo but after parts of a torpedo firing pistol were recovered this was corrected to 'the new, unknown torpedo "slow worm"', apparently a British nickname for the *Dackel*. *Frobisher* was badly flooded, but the damage control parties did 'excellent work' and the cruiser was able to limp home the following day.[13]

Although by now most US warships had left the Bay, Bulkeley's PT Boats remained. Among their duties were regular patrols between Cherbourg, the Channel Islands and Saint-Malo, trying out the effective RN tactic of directing the PTs from a control ship. On the night that *Frobisher* was torpedoed five boats were out with the destroyer escort USS *Maloy*, divided into two forces deployed west of Jersey, *PT-508* and *PT-509* (codenamed Barracuda) and PTs *500*, *503* and *507* (Tunny). Embarked in *Maloy* with the PT Squadron 34 Commander Lieutenant Jack Sherertz was Peter Scott, along to assist as 'an old hand at this game'.[14] The night was calm, visibility was good and according to Lieutenant J.F. Queeny, Executive Officer of *PT-508*, 'the scene was of varying tones of gray accented by the brilliant white wash from the boats as they thundered along, exhausts rumbling their steady growl into an endless carpet of foam spreading astern'.[15]

At 0450 the force ran into a fog bank which at times reduced visibility to just 20m, just as *Maloy*'s radar picked up a German convoy 7 miles away making for Jersey at 12 knots.[16] Vectored in by *Maloy*, Group Tunny fired torpedoes by radar at 0535, range just under 2,000m, but missed. The PTs regrouped around *Maloy*, then Sherertz and Scott directed Barracuda to make another attack: *508* and *509* raced forward in line at 40 knots, crossing the German convoy's bow to attack from inshore. As they circled after firing, *509* ran out into an unexpected clear patch which revealed the full strength of the German force: two freighters escorted by six heavily armed minesweepers. Desperately Lieutenant Harry Crist man-oeuvred the catastrophically outgunned *509* towards the safety of the fog bank, inadvertently masking *508*'s guns as he did so, at the same time signalling that the enemy was dead ahead and he was 'directly in the middle'.[17]

The signal turned out to be Crist's last. As the German sweepers methodically raked the desperately jinking *509* with heavy fire, Crist turned *509* at speed, heading for the convoy; the senior German officer in *M-4626* accepted the challenge and turned to meet him. As the two warships hurtled towards each other, a German shell exploded in *509*'s flimsy wooden wheelhouse, the boat burst into flames, and rammed the German sweeper so hard that *509*'s bow wedged deep into the enemy ship's hull, the boat's racing engines keeping it wedged firmly in place.[18]

Sherertz transferred to *PT-503* and with *507* he searched the area for hours, skirmishing again with the Germans at 0800, but found no trace of the lost boat, although a floating body was found two days later and part of the hull later in the month.[19] Crist and thirteen of his men died, along with two men from *503*; five more sailors were wounded. Three German sweepers were badly damaged, four German sailors were killed and forty-one wounded.[20] Remarkably there was a survivor from *509*, Radar Mechanic 2nd Class John L. Page, who was knocked out in the action and awoke to find himself on the deck of his burning boat, looking up at the side of *M-4626*, from where angry Germans were firing small arms and tossing down grenades. He crawled painfully forward through a hail of fire until the German sailors saw him, stopped shooting and tossed him a line. By the time he was hauled aboard, aided by a German officer just minutes before the shattered *509* drifted away and blew up, he had thirty-seven separate wounds, including a broken arm and leg, and a bullet in his lung.[21]

As the final Canadian push to close the Falaise Pocket from the north began with Operation Totalise (7–10 August) and Patton continued to advance from the south, the assault on the Seine Bay from Le Havre continued. On the morning of the 11th, the Kriegsmarine scored one of their last significant successes in the Bay, and one which could have been a major setback had it occurred two months earlier, when the invaluable repair ship HMS *Albatross* was hit by one of ninety-one *Dackels* fired into the assault area between 4 and 18 August.[22] The torpedo exploded at 0700. Flooded for a third of her length, the former seaplane carrier heeled over to port and started to dip by the bow. 'Feared heavy loss of life', Rivett-Carnac signalled ominously to Ramsay on the morning of the incident and he was unfortunately correct. Sixty-seven members of the ship's company and of Port Repair Party 1530 were killed, and many more were injured or suffered from the effects of 'gassing'. 'Two lethal gases contributed to the concentration that proved so disastrous in a ship "battened down" for action', Captain Donald McGrath reported, 'the nitric acid given off by the torpedo warhead exploding under water and the carbon monoxide left in confined space after the ... explosion.' Respirators, he went on, were 'useless ... but kept out the smell'. The most effective antidote turned out to be bringing the gas casualties out onto the upper deck where the fresh air and sunshine speeded their recovery.[23]

Albatross was saved thanks to the extraordinary efforts of the 'disciplined and very steady' ship's company, many of whom McGrath recommended for awards, and good damage control. The latter could reasonably be expected from a ship which presumably had a high proportion of shipwrights and other specialists aboard and was at action stations when hit with all watertight doors, scuttles and portholes closed. The Dutch tug *Zwarte Zee* towed *Albatross* back to Portsmouth stern-first later the same day.[24] Ramsay was alarmed enough to fly to France the following day to discuss this 'latest underwater menace', which was correctly identified as a long-range torpedo, noting in his diary that 'a good system of nets appeared to be the only answer'.[25]

All of the Biscay ports were placed under siege within the first two weeks of August, with the Allied navies playing a key role in maintaining and supporting the besieging troops and blockading the garrisons. Middleton's US VIII Corps reached Brest on 7 August. LSTs started unloading supplies for Middleton's troops directly on to the beaches north of Brest on the 11th. On the night of 11/12 August, the all-Canadian 12th Escort Group, reinforced by the British destroyer HMS *Albrighton*, took part in another aggressive Kinetic sweep in Audierne Bay, to the south of the city. The 'bolting-on' of a strange warship with unfamiliar characteristics appears to have been rather unfortunate: in particular, *Albrighton* was nearly 10 knots slower than the Canadian destroyers *Qu'appelle*, *Restigouche*, *Skeena* and *Assiniboine*. Although the force set on fire and drove ashore three *Vorpostenboote*, in the high-speed melee the sluggish *Albrighton* got in the way, and *Skeena* rammed *Qu'appelle* hard on the starboard quarter, wrecking *Qu'appelle*'s steering and tearing away several metres of her own bow. 'For the future embarrassment of the enemy', *Albrighton*'s pained CO, Lieutenant John Hooker, concluded his report, 'such action close inshore against comparatively slow targets is better in every respect fought at slower speed.'[26]

Ashore, the battle to close the Falaise Pocket continued, Patton pushing up from the south until halted by Bradley on 13 August to reduce the risk of a confused 'blue on blue' encounter with his Allies, and the Canadians fighting their way south to Falaise in a new offensive, Operation Tractable, which began on the 14th. At sea, Operation Kinetic was building up to a crescendo under the command of Dalrymple-Hamilton, now flying his flag from the cruiser HMS *Diadem*. On the 12th *Diadem* and the destroyers HMS *Onslow* and the Polish ORP *Piorun* caught and sank *Sperrbrecher 7*, originally the freighter *Sauerland*, which was disabled and drifting after being attacked by Coastal Command Beaufighter strike aircraft 24 miles from La Rochelle. *Sperrbrecher* (literally 'barrage breaker') were merchant ships converted into heavily armed naval auxiliaries and filled with cork and other buoyant material, their role being to steam ahead of a convoy and detonate mines. 'The Polish destroyer went so close in order to accomplish this it was quite unbelievable', recalled Telegraphist Derek Wellman of *Onslow*, 'as if it was having a personal vendetta for the various disasters that had occurred in Poland.' On the same day, *Onslow* also accidentally shot down an RAF Liberator, although that was left out of the despatch subsequently submitted by war correspondent Stanley Maxted, who was embarked at the time.[27]

On the same day, the Admiralty decided to put a stop to the troublesome harassing fire from *Batterie Blücher*, the main coastal battery on Alderney, which was interfering with shipping coming in and out of Cherbourg, by bombarding it. The battleship *Rodney* manoeuvred carefully into position behind Cap de la Hague with the help of a US tug and then fired single shots spotted by an RAF Spitfire from 26 Squadron: this was the first time a British battleship had fired on Crown territory, and every possible precaution was being taken to prevent civilian casualties. Comparing this careful process with the indiscriminate bombardment of French towns earlier in the campaign is unavoidable although the circumstances were of course clearly very different. German seaman Helmut Lucke was on the other end of *Rodney*'s barrage that Saturday afternoon. 'We were all in the shower', he recalled; 'All off a sudden, like a big bang! So, we got out the shower . . . where we were staying there was a hill opposite [where] we'd built our foxholes.' The bombardment went on most of that Saturday afternoon, Lucke remembering that 'every three minutes we got a salvo, and I think all round . . . three or four people were killed . . . one or two they stood on top of the bunker to see what was going on'.[28] Although *Rodney*'s fire was accurate, with more than half of the seventy-five shells fired falling close to the battery, only one gun was temporarily put out of action, and *Batterie Blücher* was in action again by the end of the month.[29]

On 14 August, the formidable Karl-Heinz Lange in *U-667*, slayer of the *Ezra Weston* and HMCS *Regina*, added to his tally by torpedoing the US Navy's *LST-921* and the British *LCI(L)-99* in convoy EBC72, just off the North Devon coast. *LCI(L)-99* sank almost immediately with the loss of nine officers and men. Lange's second torpedo blew off *921*'s stern, killing two officers and forty-one men. The bow was towed into Falmouth so that the cargo could be unloaded but *921* never went to sea again, the hulk eventually being taken to Antwerp and used as a floating workshop. Lange was awarded the German Cross in Gold on 25 August for his extraordinary success, which went very much against the 'run of play' for U-boats in 1944, although he had little time to enjoy it: *U-667* was mined and sunk the following day in the Bay of Biscay with the loss of all aboard.[30]

Elsewhere on the night of the 14/15 August, the German evacuation of the Biscay ports was picking up pace, as was Operation Kinetic. Off the French resort of Les Sables-d'Olonne at 0300, Force 27, the cruiser HMS *Mauritius* and destroyers HMS *Ursa* and HMCS *Iroquois*, caught the German seaplane tender *Richthofen*, escorted by Kapitänleutnant Wilhelm Meentzen's veteran torpedo boat *T-24*, and a minesweeper. Once again, Meentzen fought hard and well, screening his charges with smoke and attempting to torpedo *Iroquois*, but *T-24* was heavily outgunned and by the time the Germans reached the security of the shore batteries *Richthofen* was on fire and *M-385* had been forced to beach.[31] Later the same night Force 27 drove a coastal tanker ashore, then engaged the minesweepers *M-275* and *M-385*, escorting the blockade runner *Tallus* heading southeast near Île d'Yeu, north-west of La Rochelle. The two destroyers confidently pushed close inshore but came under heavy fire from German coastal guns and the two sweepers, so they withdrew out to sea and *Mauritius* patiently pummelled the convoy at long range; by 0715 all three German ships were beached and on fire.

M-275 ended up on a sandbank, and the crew made their way ashore, although according to one survivor they reboarded at high water and went into Les Sables-d'Olonne, then made their way to La Pallice, all the time harried relentlessly from the air. In common with most of the Kriegsmarine's smaller units, eventually the battered sweeper was disarmed and the crew and anti-aircraft guns were sent to join the defences around the besieged port. At Saint-Nazaire the remaining ships of *6.Vorpostenflottille* were disarmed and their crews sent ashore to reinforce naval artillery units.[32] Overall, the air and sea elements of Operation Kinetic netted the Allies eleven large merchant ships, fifty-three coasters, minesweepers and other small naval craft, two destroyers and one torpedo boat sunk, and caused many more to be confined to port and disarmed.[33]

The following day, at 1435, Oberleutnant Gerhard Palmgren in *U-741* tried to emulate Lange's success when he torpedoed the Royal Navy's *LST-404*, steaming steadily back to Southend from the Seine Bay in convoy FTM68, carrying wounded soldiers and German POWs. The huge explosion was observed by Lieutenant Bryan Harris in the corvette HMS *Orchis*, escorting convoy FTC68 about four miles away to starboard. As *LST-413* closed the shattered *404* to take off survivors, the veteran corvette, commissioned in 1940, swept down like an avenging angel. Harris's ASDIC operator, Able Seaman Ron Goddard, picked up *U-741* at 1451, 2,500m away, and a few minutes later Harris dropped a pattern of five depth charges right over the submarine.[34]

Goddard regained contact as soon as *Orchis* passed over *U-741* and Harris ordered another pattern fired, then began a methodical 'deliberate' attack using his forward-firing Hedgehog anti-submarine mortar, operated with deadly efficiency by a team under the command of the 'skilful' and 'spirited' RNVR Lieutenant William Moss. *Orchis* crept slowly towards the submarine, now guided by the 'keen and efficient' Leading Seaman Harry Kay on the ASDIC, and Moss fired his mortar at 1525, resulting in a sinister patch of light-coloured oil rising to the surface. Concerned that this could be a ruse, Harris took *Orchis* in for a second run, aborted because of a technical problem, and then a third, at 1544. 'A very heavy explosion resulted', he wrote in his report, 'but [ASDIC] contact was still held. Very heavy oil now began to appear.'[35]

As Harris manoeuvred *Orchis* for a fourth attack, Kay picked up 'loud hissing noises' and three figures popped to the surface in the oil, two struggling frantically, the third motionless. Harris broke off his attack and attempted to rescue the survivors. One traumatised German sailor was recovered, but the other two could not be found. Harris marked the wreck with a Dan Buoy and left the site at 1730. He was awarded a Bar to his Distinguished Service Cross for his actions; Moss was also awarded a DSC and Kay a Distinguished

Service Medal.[36] This methodical action serves as a salutary reminder of the competence of Allied ASW forces but also of the constant need for vigilance. Even at this very late stage in the Battle of the Seine Bay, with the land battle for Normandy almost over, the Kriegsmarine had not yet given up the fight. The greatest threat in and around the Seine Bay was complacency.

On 15 August 1944 the Allies launched Operation Dragoon, the invasion of the Côte d'Azur in the South of France, between Cavalaire-sur-Mer in the west and Saint-Raphaël in the east. Dragoon was the final nail in the coffin for the beleaguered Wehrmacht in France. Normandy had absorbed most of its fighting strength and the defending 19th Army could do little other than withdraw to the north. US Admiral Kent Hewitt, in overall command, wrote later that 'compared to what we'd faced before, it wasn't bad. I think it was more or less a surprise landing . . . we received an amazing welcome . . . on the part of the French people.'[37] Doubtless it helped that many of the assault troops were Free French, a shrewd political decision. Tragically, Normandy assault force commander Rear-Admiral Don Moon, who was supposed to play the same role on the Riviera, had killed himself on 5 August 1944, apparently as a result of prolonged combat stress, a grim lonely journey which may have begun in April with the Tiger disaster.

Churchill, never a fan of the southern France landings – supposedly the codename was changed from Anvil to Dragoon because he had been 'dragooned' into it – nevertheless took the opportunity to witness it from the destroyer HMS *Kimberley*, some small compensation for being barred from seeing Neptune. Later, writing to King George VI, he expressed his concern about how long it would take to advance up the Rhône Valley and the impact of the campaign on operations in the north.[38] Churchill missed the key strategic point, which was that Anvil gave the Allies access to the huge and almost undamaged ports of Marseille and Toulon. Over time, many reinforcements from the USA would be delivered through the Mediterranean, eventually easing the supply problems caused by the enormous damage to some northern ports, and the Germans continued defence of others.[39]

Back in the Bay, the *K-Verbände* were still trying desperately to inter-fere with the flow of men and materiel. A *Marder* attack planned for the night of 15/16 August was aborted, but the human torpedoes came out again the following night, in the face of the usual determined opposition from the Trout Line; the CO of *LCF-33* recalled firing a Lewis gun straight into the plastic dome of one *Marder*: 'I could clearly see the German inside and the horror on his face.'[40] *LCF(L)-231* went one better, riddling a *Marder* with 20mm fire, killing the pilot and then capturing the craft for evaluation.[41] By now the Germans had taken to drifting dummy *Marders* into the Bay with the tide, with a human silhouette painted on the inside of a Plexiglass dome, along with, according to at least one account, the booby-trapped bodies of Allied servicemen.[42] In anticipation of the *Marders*' arrival, Allied sailors circled the fleet in the dark, periodically throwing hand grenades in the water. Forty-two human torpedoes set out from Villers on the night of the 16th, and only sixteen returned, the remainder killed or taken prisoner.[43]

Human torpedoes hit the indestructible *Courbet*, the operators apparently unaware that the old French battleship had been scuttled as part of the Gooseberry breakwater weeks before, and the freighter *Iddesleigh*, beached a few nights before after detonating a pressure mine, but the most serious loss of life that night came when the *K-Verbände* sank Landing Craft (Flak) *LCF-1*, which went down taking seventy-one officers, sailors and Royal Marines with her, almost the entire ship's company. Among them was 39-year-old Sub-Lieutenant Clifford Longley. Just two days earlier he had written to his beloved wife, Evelyn, at home in London with their son Michael, describing a run ashore to Ouistreham with his friend 21-year-old Royal Marine Lieutenant Peter Fairhurst, and their excitement that very shortly arrangements would be made for them to visit Bayeux; 'a decent sized place', he wrote, 'with plenty of shops and where it is sometimes possible to get food'. He ended by blessing the rough weather: 'about the only blessing the heavy seas bestow is that we are likely to be immune from sea attack'. It is doubtful either Longley or Fairhurst, who was also killed, ever saw Bayeux. Evelyn was notified of his death in a bleak standard letter on the 26th, the Admiralty expressing their 'deep regret and profound sympathy'.[44]

On 16 August, Hitler belatedly gave his generals permission to withdraw from the Falaise Pocket. The next day, Allied troops moved into Saint-Malo, apparently freeing up another urgently needed port, but unfortunately, as Albert Morrow, commanding the Canadian *MTB-726* discovered, the port was anything but safe. 'We could see fires burning each night there and the word was that Saint-Malo was captured,' he remembered. 'We decided just to find out what the score was.' Morrow was entering cautiously when, 'all of a sudden, point blank, a shell screamed across' and they beat a hasty retreat, 'running for our lives, zigging and zagging and laying smoke'.[45]

The approaches to Saint-Malo were, it transpired, controlled by a fort on the Île de Cézembre manned by a garrison of Kriegsmarine artillerymen from *Marineartillerie Abteilung 608*, and a group of Italian naval gunners, fascists from Mussolini's Salò Republic, commanded by a tough 47-year-old First World War veteran, Oberleutnant Richard Seuss – 'the mad Lieutenant', according to Morrow. Seuss held out for another fortnight, during which time he was awarded the Knight's Cross as well as courteously refusing an invitation to surrender, delivered in person by a Major Joseph Alexander, who rowed across on 18 August. While troops from the US 330th Infantry Regiment trained for an amphibious assault, Cézembre was pounded from the air with high explosive, napalm and phosphorus, bombarded by the battleships *Malaya* and *Warspite*, and shelled by artillery at Saint-Malo. Seuss surrendered on 2 September, just as the Americans were about to launch a full-scale amphibious assault using fifteen LCVPs shipped overland from Omaha Area, and was awarded the Oak Leaves to his Knight's Cross on the same day.[46]

E-boats hit convoy FTM70 on the night of 17/18 August 6 miles from Dungeness. Despite being sighted and engaged repeatedly throughout the night by groups of MTBs directed by HMS *Opportune*, and despite a strong close escort of two frigates, a mine-sweeper and a pair of MLs, the three raiders managed to torpedo the freighter *Fort Gloucester* and escape unscathed. As they retired towards France at speed and under fire, 'lots of own and enemy forces now became confused', according to Admiral Sir Henry Pridham-Wippell, Commander-in-Chief at Dover, 'making air attack impracticable'. Although strike aircraft turned up just after 0300, they were unable to find the E-boats, which slipped safely back into Boulogne. *Fort Gloucester* had no casualties and was able to be towed to safety.[47]

By August 1944, the sailors in the Seine Bay were exhausted, perhaps nobody more so than the hard-worked crews of the ferry craft, who were still working tirelessly in the former assault area, and of the larger landing craft, still trudging patiently to and fro in the 'Starlight' and 'Bluesky' convoys with their precious cargoes. It is worth reiterating that all of the actions described in the preceding pages were fought to protect them. Their story is not a thrilling one – often there was nothing to say – but their work remained as important as it had been on 6 June, and by August many ships and men were worn out. In a report written on the 8th, Commodore Hugh England, Commodore Depot Ships at Portsmouth, wrote that 'the appearance and discipline of [ferry craft] crews deteriorated after the assault and a certain amount of the men became slovenly'. He went on to explain the circumstances:

> Most of the NCOs and Coxswains were young and inexperienced and required constant supervision. Facilities aboard the Red Ensign [Merchant Navy] ships in which men lived during their rest periods did not lend themselves to the men keeping their appearance smart or clean and in some cases I observed a lack of keenness and determination ... due to the monotony of carrying out the same task day after day.[48]

Moving the men into better-equipped depot ships and camps ashore for rest breaks helped alleviate the problem, but the sailors carrying out the dirty, backbreaking and tedious work of delivering the build-up were reaching the end of their tether. Fortunately, the long Battle of the Seine Bay was finally ending.

On 18 August, Hitler ordered the whole of southern France evacuated except the besieged fortresses. On the same day the remaining U-boats were instructed to quit the Bay of Biscay for Norway, in some cases carrying out war patrols on the way. There were thirty boats in the Biscay ports, of which twenty-six were seaworthy. Four were sunk, but the remainder eventually slipped into Norwegian ports, their survival largely due to their schnorkels and the fact that the British were distracted by more aggressive boats operating around their coast.[49] This brought the direct submarine threat to the western flank of the Bay to an end, although U-boats on war patrols connected to the wider inshore campaign around the British coast remained a menace to the traffic in and out of the former assault area until the end of the campaign.

The danger had not yet passed entirely. On 18 August the barrage balloon ship HMS *Fratton*, veteran of many a coastal convoy, was hit in the Bay, apparently by a human torpedo, and sank in four minutes with the loss of thirty-one men. 19-year-old Stan Ford was blown into the water from his gun platform, with a fractured spine and injuries to both legs. In a BBC interview in 2022 he recollected:

> There was no reason why I should have survived . . . I didn't hear the explosion . . . I found myself in the water. There was carnage . . . but I survived. Very soon a rescue craft came by, hands came over the side to reach me and I was pulled aboard and that's the last I remember . . . nature took over and put me to sleep.[50]

He woke in hospital.

The following day, the Falaise Pocket finally closed, and Patton's armour reached the River Seine. The end was not far away. The decimated *Linsen* and *Neger K-Verbände* flotillas, no longer able to operate in the Bay with any effectiveness, became the next part of the Kriegsmarine to quit Normandy, when they were withdrawn to be redeployed. This left the remains of the *Marder*s and the newly arrived *Biber* one-man submarines, the first of which were about to arrive at Fécamp.

The frantic, see-saw battle against the U-boats continued, with the submarines now making the long and perilous journey from Norway to reach their patrol areas. British destroyers sank *U-413* off Brighton on the 20th. The following day Oberleutnant Hans-Joachim Förster's *U-480* struck back, torpedoing the RCN corvette HMCS *Alberni*, sister to the unfortunate *Regina*. Lieutenant Ian

Bell's *Alberni* was on a 'Spout Patrol' when Förster struck, firing an acoustic torpedo which detonated in the corvette's engine room on the port side. *Alberni* sank in about fifteen seconds taking fifty-nine officers and men with her.[51]

There were no signs of the Germans slackening the tempo of their assault on the eastern flank, whatever was going on ashore. Coastal Forces were in action again in the old battleground off Cap d'Antifer on the night of 20/21 August, MTBs *471*, *476* and *477* taking on a force of R-boats on a minelaying operation. All three boats took hits and five men were killed, *477*'s damage was so serious that the MTB had to be towed back to base. In exchange, they claimed three R-boats damaged. Mines remained a threat right up until the last days in the Bay – HMS *Orchis* fell victim to one off Courseulles on the 21st, with the loss of twenty-eight men. The corvette had to be beached in Juno Area and was declared a total loss; Lieutenant Bryan Harris apologised for the delay it caused to his report on the sinking of *U-741* six days earlier.[52] Förster in *U-480* struck again on the 22nd, sinking HMS *Loyalty* in the Channel with the loss of twenty men. The Algerine Class minesweeper was the last major Allied warship to be sunk due to enemy action in operations connected to the Battle of the Seine Bay. Förster went on to sink two merchant ships before leaving the Channel at the end of August.

Operation Kinetic reached its climax at the end of August. Force 27 sank Korvettenkapitän Ludolf Jacobi's entire *7.Vorpostenflotilla* off Belle Île on the 22nd. Seven patrol boats were sunk or driven ashore with the loss of 122 men killed, wounded or missing. Most of the 250 survivors swam ashore only to find themselves co-opted into the land fighting.[53] RAF Beaufighters from 19 Group's Strike Wing sank the last two seaworthy German destroyers at anchor off le Verdon, *Z-24* and *T.24*, the extraordinarily resilient torpedo boat of the RCN's erstwhile nemesis, Kapitänleutnant Wilhelm Meentzen's.

With the situation on land unravelling, the Germans switched their naval strategy in the east from reinforcing Le Havre to evacuating it. In response, Portsmouth Command reinforced the Coastal Forces patrols off the city with destroyers, and a frenetic series of night actions followed, fought under the guns of the German coastal batteries. They lasted until the end of the month, during which the British claimed ten landing craft, five coasters, three R-boats and an E-boat sunk or driven ashore, and another thirteen craft of all types damaged. One of the concluding acts of the Battle of the Seine Bay, this close blockade of Le Havre was also one of the most dramatic. On the night of 24/25 August alone, British MTBs and US PT Boats fought six distinct actions. On the following night, HMS *Thornborough* detected two E-boats at midnight and in a seamless procedure which was now second nature to these experienced, well-trained groups, vectored MTBs *450, 481* and *482* to intercept. The E-boats retired at speed to join a convoy forming up outside Fécamp and the MTBs followed them in, launching a high-speed attack at 0150. 'The MTBs engaged for ten minutes, stopping the convoy, setting one coaster on fire and heavily damaging one E-boat. They were illuminated and heavily engaged from shore throughout and 0202 withdrew under heavy fire.' The old Channel veteran, Capitaine de Corvette André Patou in the Free French destroyer *La Combattante*, took advantage of the chaos to creep in under cover of the MTBs' withdrawal, sinking two coasters and driving another ashore. Finally, as the two remaining escorts, a landing craft and an R-boat, returned to Fécamp, three more MTBs closed and sank both with torpedoes.[54]

The pattern continued on 27/28 August, paused on 28/29, when apparently no German traffic ran, and then ramped up again on the last night of the evacuation, 29/30 August, when the Kriegsmarine pulled the last of their warships back to Fécamp: nine R-boats and ten assorted landing craft and auxiliaries, covered by *8.Sfltl*. The undeniable success came at a cost in men and boats. The older MTBs started to break down after a week of high-tempo activity with limited opportunities for maintenance and on the last night, German coastal gunners hit the destroyer HMS *Cattistock* in the bridge, killing three ratings and the commanding officer, 26-year-old Richard Keddie, 'an inspiring and gallant officer who showed great promise'.[55] His two brothers, John and Wallace, were also killed during the Second World War, an unimaginable loss for his parents, Frederick and Annie.[56]

On the 25th, the Allies began a massive attack to try to take Brest. Bomber Command and the US 8th Air Force pounded the city from the air and sank fifteen ships at anchor, prompting the British Official Historian to write that 'by the 27th the German naval forces in the Bay of Biscay had almost ceased to exist'.[57] HMS *Warspite* was deployed to assist, firing more than 200 15-inch (380mm) shells into the city from a firing position on the other side of the island of Ushant.[58] Despite this the garrison did not finally surrender until 19 September.

Paris surrendered to De Gaulle's Free French troops on 25 August. They were accompanied by a detachment from Fleming's 30 Assault Unit who, acting on intelligence obtained from POW interrogations, raced to capture the Kriegsmarine HQ in the Château de la Muette, near the Bois de Boulogne, and the principal torpedo factory, seizing documents and protypes.[59] On the same day, in the Bay, *U-764* sank *LCT-1074* off Omaha Area with the loss of ten officers and men, and a full load of US tanks. Alfred Mead, an 18-year-old seaman, was one of only four survivors from the crew and recalled lying in a bunk on a US hospital ship wondering 'Will I survive if this one sinks?'[60] However, tragically, the worst losses suffered by Allied naval forces as the Battle of the Seine Bay reached its conclusion came two days later, and they were inflicted by the RAF, not by the Germans.

On the afternoon of 27 August, the fleet minesweepers of the 1st MSF were concluding a week-long routine sweep close to Le Havre, in preparation for the bombardment which would precede the Allied assault on the town. The operation was supposed to have been completed the day before, but Commander Trevor Crick, the Flotilla Commander, had sent his Navigating Officer over to the depot ship HMS *Ambitious* to advise that they would need an extra day. This alteration should have been signalled onwards to all other commands.[61] 'Today we finish the job,' Len East of HMS *Salamander* wrote in his diary. 'It is a flat calm and a hot sunny day.'[62] Just after noon, an RAF reconnaissance aircraft passed over. The pilot waved. The sunbathing sailors waved back.[63]

At 1335 the flotilla were steaming at 5 knots (9km/h) having just completed two laps of an LL (magnetic mine) sweep, with HM ships *Salamander*, *Jason* and *Britomart* in line abreast and HMS *Hussar* bringing up the rear, when sixteen Typhoon fighter-bombers from

263 and 266 Squadrons swept over the horizon, with four Polish Spitfires as top cover.[64] After weeks of almost unbroken Allied air superiority and repeated exhortations to avoid firing on friendly aircraft, nobody on the sweepers was the slightest bit concerned. On *Salamander*, the off-duty watch were sunbathing on the upper deck after a Sunday lunch of pork chops and roast potatoes, followed by pears and custard. On the bridge, lookouts turned their binoculars to the sound of aero engines and relaxed. The Tannoy crackled into life – 'friendly aircraft, carry on sunbathing'.[65]

The RAF strike aircraft had been despatched to attack a reported German force but the naval authorities had failed to warn them that 1st MSF were in the area. Ignoring the recognition signals being fired from the desperately manoeuvring sweepers, one after another the deadly fighter-bombers banked and swooped down to attack. *Salamander* was attacked four times. The first two Typhoons turned the water alongside into a boiling cauldron, swamping the bridge with water, but the third pilot was terribly accurate. Diving in steeply from about 120m, fine on the port bow, he unloaded eight rockets directly into the minesweeper, causing a secondary detonation of the depth charges which ripped away about thirty feet of the stern.[66]

Salamander came to a dead stop, on fire. *Hussar* and *Britomart* were also burning furiously, with the latter listing heavily to port. The Typhoons came in again, passing low over *Jason* and raking the sweeper with cannon fire from the bridge to the boat deck. 22-year-old Thomas Jackson raced on deck to his action station to see 'two Spitfires heading for the ship at sea level. The first one opened fire on the ship [and] I dived behind a locker.'[67]

The aircraft left at 1340. *Hussar* sank in twelve minutes, taking fifty-seven officers and men with her. *Britomart* was settling by the stern with a 'deep smoking hole' where the bridge had been.[68] Half an hour later, as the stunned and in many cases badly wounded ship's company abandoned ship, the sweeper rolled over and sank with the loss of twenty officers and men, including the commanding officer, Lieutenant-Commander Arthur Galvin, who had been notified of his long-awaited promotion only that day. To make matters worse, as the aircraft left German coastal gunners started ranging on the stopped ships, doubtless unable to believe their luck. *Jason*, which had two fatalities, laid a smokescreen, launched boats and started rescuing survivors, along with two accompanying Dan-laying trawlers, which had also been strafed and had suffered casualties. They were later joined by the destroyer *Pytchley*. Ernie Hammond was trying to pull survivors aboard *Jason* when the German shells started falling:

> I was on the bottom of one scrambling net, I had one leg in the rung to hold myself and one hand hauling the blokes up. I had this bloke, in another two seconds I would have got him back on board but ... the shells were coming over the funnel and dropping on the other side, a bit near, and the ship got underway. I had to leave him. His head just left me and he went in the propeller, poor bugger. Screaming, I've never heard a man scream so hard.[69]

Thomas Jackson volunteered to go out in *Jason*'s whaler, recalling 'vast areas of the sea on fire, bodies floating, cries for help'. Jackson and his comrades swam repeatedly out to pull men back to the boat until, exhausted and covered in oil, they could do no more: 'the smell was overpowering ... as we sat there it was quiet except for the cries of those burnt'.[70]

A subsequent enquiry established that the decorated and highly experienced RAF officer commanding the Typhoons had repeatedly questioned his orders to attack, believing the minesweepers to be friendly, but Rivett-Carnac's HQ had expressly ordered that the attack go ahead, as the message from *Ambitious* had not been passed on. The responsibility almost certainly rested with a doubtless over-worked and exhausted signaller 'who probably simply forgot to write (R) FOBAA [repeat to Flag Officer British Assault Area] in the address'.[71] The following day the destroyer HMS *Melbreak* was attacked by an unidentified aircraft which might also have been 'friendly', losing five officers and men. Mirroring the situation on land, as the 'front' at sea became more fluid and the known positions of friendly forces changed on a daily basis, the risk of 'blue on blue' incidents grew correspondingly greater.

At the end of August, SHAEF moved from the UK to France, officially opening for business just outside Granville on 1 September, with Montgomery reluctantly relinquishing his role as overall land forces commander to Eisenhower but retaining command of the Anglo-Canadian 21st Army Group, with Eisenhower activating Bradley's US 12th Army Group (1st, 3rd and 9th US Armies). The British joined the Americans on the River Seine, initiating a head-long flight back to the German frontier by the defeated remnants of the Wehrmacht in France, pursued by the Allied armies as fast as their desperately stretched supply line back to the Seine Bay would let them. Only the isolated garrisons in the Channel ports remained. The last E-boats, from *2. Sfltl*, left Le Havre on the 29th for Boulogne, only to abandon that port six days later, losing *S-184* to British coastal gunners while transiting the Strait of Dover. This was the day that 500 miles to the north-east the British captured the great Belgian port of Antwerp intact.

The latest addition to the *K-Verbände*, the *Biber* one-man submarines, launched their first and only attack into the former assault area on 29 August. Fourteen of the crudely built, unreliable boats went into the water, sighted nothing and were immediately returned to Germany, ending the story of the *K-Verbände* in the Bay. Caught up in the maelstrom of the collapse, several were shot up and one was found abandoned on the Amiens–Bapaume road, miles away in the heart of the old First World War battlefields, by Ian Fleming's trained scavengers from 30 Assault Unit.[72]

Ramsay flew out to join Eisenhower on 8 September, setting up his headquarters at a chateau near to SHAEF, newly christened 'HMS *Royal Henry*', which he recorded in his diary as 'better than hoped for', continuing 'no comfort as we know it except beds are good ... had good dinner but went to bed early as nowhere to sit'.[73] Wren Ginger Thomas joined the staff at *Royal Henry* shortly afterwards:

> We landed on the wonderful Mulberry harbour ... we had typed about it hundreds of times but were now seeing it for the first time. I remember travelling through St Lô and being astonished

at the amount of damage there had been to the places. I was used to bomb damage ... but the devastation here was breathtaking. As we travelled through Normandy, troops would stand outside their tents waving at us – they probably didn't see many girls around there!

It was a triumphant period, with all the months of exhausting work, danger and sacrifice finally bearing fruit for the sailors who had done so much, ashore and afloat, to deliver victory. Thomas had a 'wonderful time' working for Ramsay, remembering that 'morale amongst the staff was excellent'.[74]

And yet still Le Havre held on, under siege, its bombed and battered garrison stubbornly refusing to surrender, even as the war raced away to the north and the other Channel ports fell: movingly, Canadian troops returned to Dieppe as liberators on 1 September, and moved on to free Ostend on the 9th. Between 5 and 10 September, Bomber Command, *Warspite* and the monitor *Erebus* pounded the unfortunate city in advance of an assault. An estimated 2,000 French civilians died in the bombardment.

In the meantime, the entire complex infrastructure which made the Seine Bay function was dismantled with unseemly haste and moved north to keep up with the fighting. Juno Area closed on 7 September, and Rivett-Carnac moved his HQ up to Rouen, returning his Coastal Forces craft to the UK for redeployment. The Support Squadron Eastern Flank left the now-redundant Trout Line and returned to the UK for rest and refit 'having done four hours on, four hours off, 24/7' since June, according to Able Seaman Dick Blyth of *LCG(L)-1*.[75] After rest and refit, the hard-worked support landing craft moved to Ostend in October and distinguished them-selves supporting Operation Infatuate II, the landings at Walcheren on 1 November. Infatuate was part of a wider sequence of operations fought to clear the German defenders from the shores of the Scheldt Estuary and open up Antwerp for use, an extraordinary story which falls outside the scope of this narrative. Seaward patrols from the Bay were cancelled, with responsibility for defending traffic in and out of the former assault area passing to C-in-C Portsmouth.

Two days later, in a significant but largely unremarked milestone, ships which were homeward bound from Mulberry B at Arromanches sailed independently without escort for the first time since the summer of 1940.[76]

On 10 September the British 49th Infantry Division, supported by the specialised tanks of the 79th Armoured Division, launched Operation Astonia and stormed the wretched, mutilated remains of Le Havre, so long a thorn in the side of the Allied sailors fighting for their lives in the Bay. Fighting through the rubble against stubborn German defenders took two days and cost several hundred lives, but at 1145 on 12 September the garrison surrendered. On the same day the dogged sweeper crews and clearance parties moved into the devastated, mined and booby-trapped port to begin the painstaking task of reopening it. Able Seaman William Gostling was aboard the minesweeping launch *ML-206* to do a 'searching sweep'.

> This is a wire hawser between two ships and you've got a weak part like a fuse in it. You steam as close as you can to the sides of the harbour and every time the fuse breaks you know there's something down there. It may be a ship that Jerry's sunk, it could be mines, it could be anything.

After a day of this stressful, exhausting work, Gostling and his ship-mates anchored for a well-earned meal and a rest, only to have a series of mines with delayed or pre-set timers detonate around them. 'There were just big explosions everywhere and you just wondered "is the next one going to be underneath us?"' he recalled. *ML-206* remained in Le Havre for fourteen days, sweeping every day.[77]

Brest fell six days after Le Havre, followed by Boulogne on 22 September and Calais on the 30th. Allied troops started to capture the heavy gun batteries which had threatened the Channel for so long. Kriegsmarine officer Gunther Schran commanded the anti-aircraft guns at *Stp212 Batterie Friedrich August*, which capitulated on 23 September. 'We were completely surrounded by the Canadians,' he remembered; 'such was the mood amongst the soldiers ... in the heavy battery that it was useless to continue and the officers were actually threatened by our men to capitulate, otherwise they would probably revolt and shoot the officers and the NCOs. So, with tears in his eyes, the Old Man gave the order to hoist the white flag.' Schran continued firing until he was personally threatened with summary execution by his own sailors: 'on reflection of course [it] was stupid, although at the time I didn't think it was stupid, I thought I did my duty right to the end'.[78] The new ports would take weeks to be cleared of mines and obstructions, so Mulberry B, Omaha Beach and Cherbourg remained significant supply hubs throughout the winter, but they were no longer in the front line.

Seemingly in a heartbeat, after weeks of effort and sacrifice by Allied sailors to support their military comrades fighting in Normandy, the Seine Bay had become a backwater.

Conclusion

> Because it all went so smoothly, it may seem to some people that it was all easy and plain sailing. Nothing could be more wrong. It was excellent planning and execution.
>
> Admiral Sir Bertram Ramsay, 30 July 1944[1]

S adly, Ramsay never got to write a memoir describing the Battle of the Seine Bay in his own words. On 2 January 1945 he was killed when his aircraft crashed on take-off as he was setting off from an airfield near Paris for a conference with Montgomery in Brussels. Wren Ginger Thomas attended his funeral.

> We carried wreaths and marched behind the coffin, which was drawn on a gun carriage. We were all very upset because he had been like a friend to us. The night after the funeral there was a heavy snowfall, and all the wreaths were covered in snow and ice. Admiral Ramsay's family were due to spend some quiet time by his graveside the next day, and that morning the Wrens were sent out to shake the wreaths free of ice. I remember very clearly the smell of the flowers as we shook those wreaths.[2]

From the outset the premise of this book has been a simple one: that in the summer of 1944, sailors fought a long, exhausting and dangerous battle at sea which mirrored the Battle of Normandy on land. The great wars of the twentieth century permanently changed perceptions of decisive battle. From short, bloody encounters between fleets or armies lasting hours or at best a few days, like Waterloo or Trafalgar, they became long, gruelling campaigns, which pulled in not just the fighting soldier or sailor, but the planner and the supply rating, the technician and the engineer. Arguably the supreme example of this is the Battle of the Atlantic, the most important maritime campaign of the Second World War in the west, which lasted for years and involved hundreds of thousands of men and women, and thousands of ships, submarines and aircraft, operating across an inconceivably vast expanse of land and sea.

This book argues that the campaign fought to seize, exploit and defend the waters around Normandy, the Battle of the Seine Bay, was not just an overlooked naval battle, but the second most important naval campaign in the west, after that Atlantic struggle which enabled it. Defeat in the Seine Bay might have been unlikely but even a significant setback could have stalled the land battle and prolonged the war for months, opening the possibility of a negotiated peace with all the attendant consequences for the postwar world. Occasional triumphs by German warships, submarines and the *K-Verbände*, and the months-long attrition from mining, illustrate the risks only too well.

The Battle of the Seine Bay was not always overlooked. The writers of the immediate postwar period, notably Commander Kenneth Edwards and Vice-Admiral B.B. Schofield, wrote eloquently of the scale of the naval effort. However, their works were compromised by security restrictions, notably around ULTRA and the deception operations, and by what seems to have been a definite need to avoid dwelling on anything which went wrong or, more pertinently, which the enemy got right. As a consequence, their writing played down any sense of risk associated with the naval campaign, of 'peril' in the modern parlance, and thus they inadvertently brought to pass Ramsay's worst fear: that it was 'all easy and plain sailing'. So, the Battle of the Seine Bay became compressed into Operation Neptune, one day of tension and a long exercise in logistics, with sailors as taxi drivers and freight haulers. Subsequent writers have picked up this trend and thus the naval battle has been airbrushed from the narrative.

Nothing could be further from the truth. Almost every day, before, during and after D-Day, Allied sailors put their lives on the line and ships were lost or damaged protecting those long, fragile supply lines. Almost every day, the outnumbered, outgunned men of the Kriegsmarine tried their best to reach them. The British Naval Staff History cites 917 ships and smaller craft lost or damaged during Operation Neptune alone, including 26 warships of varying sizes lost to all causes, and another 84 damaged, many of which never returned to service.[3]

Counting casualties is never an exact science, particularly in the case of a campaign which has rarely been studied coherently before. The British Normandy Memorial records 2,234 Royal Navy sailors in its online roll of honour, and 179 Merchant Navy personnel; this only encompasses the period 6 June to 31 August 1944, and does not include Allied personnel.[4] The US Navy Bureau of Medicine and Surgery recorded a further 363 fatalities between 6 June and 28 September, and the US Coast Guard another 25.[5] The Commonwealth War Graves Commission lists 130 Canadian sailors who died between 6 June and 12 September 1944 and were almost certainly killed in operations in and around the Bay. More sailors died from the rest of the Commonwealth, Poland, France, Norway and many other countries. Imagine if these ships and men had been lost over a few hours, or a couple of days? Imagine if the ships had gone down in the Arctic, or miles out in the Atlantic, where survivors often died before rescue?

Undoubtedly, considering the sheer number of ships and vessels which took part, losses were relatively low, and certainly acceptable by the grim logic which applies in wartime. Even so, 917 craft lost or damaged out of around 7,000 ships and landing craft taking part is a significant percentage, and in any case misses the point, which is that it was not 'easy' if you were involved, either in a position of authority trying to control events, or at the sharp end on a ship in the Seine Bay. Every time a ship set off a mine or was torpedoed, most sailors would have wondered if they were next.

It surely felt like a battle to them.

Notes

Preface

1. Part of a signal sent by Montgomery to Admiral of the Fleet Sir Andrew Cunningham, the First Sea Lord (operational head of the Royal Navy) following the German surrender on Lüneburg Heath on 5 May 1945.
2. Hewitt, Nick, 'HMS *Belfast* and Operation Neptune June–July 1944', *The Mariner's Mirror*, vol. 94, no. 2 (May 2008), 188–201.
3. Hewitt, Nick, *Firing on Fortress Europe: HMS* Belfast *at D-Day* (Imperial War Museum, London, 2015).
4. Naval Staff Battle Summary No. 39 Operation 'Neptune': Landings in Normandy June 1944 (London, HMSO, 1994), 152.
5. The title emerged out of conversations with my friend Stephen Fisher, a fine historian of the Normandy campaign without whose encyclopaedic knowledge and extraordinary generosity this book would be significantly diminished. It is not, I have since learned, wholly original: John Frayn Turner, for example, used it in his venerable *D-Day: Invasion '44* (George G. Harrap, London, 1959, 218). Stephen's own books, *Embarking the D-Day Armada*, a unique analysis of the extraordinary infrastructure which was created in the United Kingdom prior to D-Day, and a new history of Sword Beach, should hopefully be available by the time this book goes to print, and will be indispensable reading for anyone interested in D-Day, the Battle of the Seine Bay and the Battle for Normandy.
6. Corelli Barnett's *Engage the Enemy More Closely: The Royal Navy in the Second World War* (Hodder & Stoughton, London, 1991) is perhaps the most readable general history of the British experience. Craig Symonds' *World War II at Sea* (Oxford University Press, Oxford, 2018) and Evan Mawdsley's *The War for the Seas: A Maritime History of World War II* (Yale University Press, New Haven, CT and London, 2020) both provide sweeping general histories of the worldwide naval campaigns which shaped the Second World War. The multi-volume British and US official histories by, respectively, Roskill and Morison

are indispensable. There are many more detailed works on specific campaigns; for a concise history of the Atlantic campaign, I would always recommend Marc Milner's *The Battle of the Atlantic* (Tempus, Stroud, 2005) and for the Mediterranean I would suggest Jack Green and Allesandro Massignani's *The Naval War in the Mediterranean* (Frontline Books, Barnsley, 2011).

7. See, for example, but not exclusively, Field Marshal Lord Alanbrooke, Alex Danchev and Daniel Todman, (eds), *War Diaries 1939–1945* (Weidenfeld and Nicolson, London, 2001); Winston S. Churchill, *The Second World War* (6 volumes, Cassell & Co., London, 1949–54); Dwight D. Eisenhower, *Crusade in Europe* (William Heinemann Limited, London, 1949); Craig L. Symonds, *Operation Neptune: The D-Day Landings and the Allied Invasion of Europe* (Oxford University Press, Oxford, 2016); Commander Kenneth Edwards, *Operation Neptune* (Collins, London, 1946); Vice-Admiral B.B. Schofield, *Operation Neptune* (Ian Allan, London, 1974), and the various multi-volume British and US official histories: Major L.F. Ellis, CVO, CBE, DSI, C, with Lieutenant-Colonel Warhurst, *Victory in the West* (HMSO, London, 1962–8); S.W. Roskill, *The War at Sea 1939–1945* (HMSO, London, 1954–6); Samuel Eliot Morison, *History of United States Naval Operations in World War II* (Castle Books, Edison, NJ, 2001); and various authors, *The US Army in World War II: European Theatre of Operations* (US Army Center of Military History, Washington, DC). For a very readable modern account see Rick Atkinson's excellent Liberation Trilogy – *An Army at Dawn*, *The Day of Battle* and *The Guns at Last Light* (Abacus, London, 2004–15).

Prologue

1. The National Archives (henceforth TNA) ADM 179/507 Overlord Reports Not Appearing Elsewhere: 11 HNMS Svenner Loss.
2. Kriegstagebuche der 5. Torpedobootsflottille 1.6.199 – 15.6.1944 (Naval Intelligence Department File P.G.70321).
3. Ibid.
4. D-Day Story Collection (henceforth DDS) 1995/100/79 Hoffmann Interview.
5. TNA ADM 53/120730 Log of HMS *Warspite* June 1944.
6. Lawrence Paterson, *Hitler's Forgotten Flotillas: Kriegsmarine Security Forces* (Seaforth, Barnsley, 2017), 289.
7. Ibid., 290.
8. TNA ADM 179/507 Overlord Reports not Appearing Elsewhere: 11 HNoMS *Svenner Loss*.
9. BBC People's War Archive A7535892 (henceforth BBCPW) HMS *Ramillies*.
10. Captain G.B. Middleton, RN, 'D-Day Operations: A Personal Recollection', *The Naval Review*, vol. 89, no. 1 (January 2001), 44.
11. TNA ADM 179/507 Overlord Reports Not Appearing Elsewhere: 11 HNMS Svenner Loss.
12. Imperial War Museum (henceforth IWM) Documents 2823 Private Papers of Captain J.R. Gower, DSC, RN. Gower's grandson is the former England cricket captain David Gower, OBE.
13. BBCPW A1070155 HMS *Ramillies* and A1125000 Wightman, Edward.

14. Ambrose, Stephen E., *D-Day June 6, 1944: The Battle for the Normandy Beaches* (Pocket Books, London, 2002), 266.

I The Long Road Back

1. History of COSSAC (Chief of Staff to Supreme Allied Commander) (The Historical Sub-Section, Office of Secretary, General Staff, Supreme Headquarters Allied Expeditionary Force, May 1944), 1.
2. See H.G. Wells' novel *The Shape of Things to Come* (Hutchinson, London, 1933).
3. See Nick Hewitt, *The Kaiser's Pirates: Hunting Germany's Raiding Cruisers 1914–15* (Pen & Sword, Barnsley, 2013).
4. Winston S. Churchill, *The Second World War Volume V: Closing the Ring* (Cassell & Co., London, 1952), 514.
5. The British referred to these craft as TLCs or Tank Landing Craft. This was adjusted to LCT (Landing Craft Tank) to conform with US nomenclature after the United States entered the war on 7 December 1941.
6. Winston S. Churchill, *The Second World War Volume II: Their Finest Hour* (Cassell & Co., London, 1949), 218.
7. See Christopher Buckley, *Norway; The Commandos; Dieppe* (HMSO, London, 1977) for the origins of the Commandos.
8. Field Marshal Lord Alanbrooke, Alex Danchev and Daniel Todman (eds), *War Diaries 1939–1945* (Weidenfeld & Nicolson, London, 2001), 236.
9. Ironclad was a response to concerns that the Japanese might seize Madagascar from Vichy, as they had with other French possessions in Asia, and use the island as a base from which to interdict British shipping in the Indian Ocean. It would also bring the Eastern and Western Axis powers dangerously close to a link-up. See Dr Tim Benbow, 'Menace to Ironclad: The British Operations against Dakar (1940) and Madagascar (1942)', *The Journal of Military History*, vol. 75 (July 2011), 523–36.
10. Samuel Eliot Morison, *History of United States Naval Operations in World War II: Volume XI The Invasion of France and Germany 1944–1945* (Castle Books, Edison, NJ, 2001), 7–10, and Major Ian Smith, RM, 'Co-operation and Conflict: The Anglo-American Alliance Before D-Day', *The Naval Review*, vol. 107, no. 4 (November 2019), 502.
11. Morison, *Invasion of France and Germany*, 10.
12. Naval Staff Battle Summary No. 33 B.R.1736 (26) Raid on Dieppe (Naval Operations) 19 August 1942 (Admiralty Historical Section, 1959), 4
13. See ibid., 55, for a summary of all lessons learned from Jubilee.
14. Colonel C.P. Stacey, *The Canadian Army 1939–1945: An Official Historical Summary* (Ministry of National Defence, Ottawa, 1948), 86.
15. Naval Staff Battle Summary No. 38 Operation 'Torch' (Admiralty Historical Section, 1948), 53.
16. Sir Frederick Morgan, KCB, *Overture to Overlord* (Mayflower, London, 1962), 69.
17. See Vice-Admiral B.B. Schofield, *Operation Neptune* (Ian Allan, London, 1974), 30, or Edwards, *Operation Neptune*, 30–1.
18. Hilary St George Saunders, *Royal Air Force 1939–1945: Volume III: The Fight Is Won* (HMSO, London, 1954), 3.

19. Winston S. Churchill, *The Second World War Volume IV: The Hinge of Fate* (Cassell & Co., London, 1951), 708.
20. Alanbrooke, *War Diaries 1939–1945*, 409.
21. See Samuel Eliot Morison, *History of United States Naval Operations in World War II: Volume IX, Sicily–Salerno–Anzio January 1943–June 1944* (Castle Books, Edison, NJ, 2001), 81, 85.
22. Correlli Barnett, *Engage the Enemy More Closely: The Royal Navy in the Second World War* (Hodder & Stoughton, London, 1991), 756–7. In *The Watery Maze* (Collins, London, 1961), his history of Combined Operations, Bernard Fergusson provides a vivid description of Rattle, which he calls 'in many ways ... the summit of Combined Operations Headquarters' achievement'. 'The plan for Overlord had been spinning ... like a roulette wheel', Fergusson writes; 'it was time it stopped and stopped, by a little manipulation, in the right place' (272–81).
23. See Chapters 3 and 12.

2 Owning the Channel

1. IWM Sound 26950 Howe, Bernard.
2. See the two-volume *Official Operational History of the Royal Canadian Navy in the Second World War 1939–1945* (Vanwell Publishing Limited, St Catharines, ON, 2002, 2007), jointly authored by a team of historians from the RCN's Directorate of History and Heritage, for the story of the RCN's remarkable transformation.
3. See Nick Hewitt, *Coastal Convoys 1939–1945: The Indestructible Highway* (Pen & Sword, Barnsley, 2008).
4. S.W. Roskill, *The War at Sea 1939–1945 Volume 2: The Period of Balance* (HMSO, London, 1956), 386.
5. For simplicity these craft will be referred to as 'E-boats' throughout.
6. IWM Sound 14771 Rushworth-Lund, Anthony John.
7. Ibid.
8. Roskill, *The War at Sea 1939–1945 Volume 2*, 392–94.
9. IWM Sound 13650 Morrow, Albert.
10. IWM Sound 26950 Howe, Bernard.
11. TNA ADM 199/1036 Coastal Forces Actions in the English Channel.
12. IWM Sound 13650 Morrow, Albert.
13. TNA ADM 1/12488 Operation Tunnel 22–3 October 1943.
14. Ibid.
15. Roger Hill, *Destroyer Captain: Memoirs of the War at Sea 1939–1945* (Granada, London, 1979), 153
16. Ibid., 164.
17. TNA ADM 1/13716 Coastal Forces Action on Night of 24/25 October 1943 Action Report.
18. https://weaponsandwarfare.com/2020/01/08/ s-boot-in-the-west-ii/ and Hans Frank, *German S-Boats in Action in the Second World War* (Seaforth, Barnsley, 2007), 63.
19. IWM Sound 9380 Lloyd-Davies, Felix Justin.

20. TNA ADM 1/29416 Operation 'Stonewall'. Interception of Blockade Runners. Services of HMS *Glasgow* and *Enterprise* December 1943.
21. Ibid.
22. IWM Sound 9380 Lloyd-Davies, Felix Justin.
23. IWM Sound 22147 Pitman, Albert.
24. TNA ADM 1/29416 Operation 'Stonewall'. Interception of Blockade Runners. Services of HMS *Glasgow* and *Enterprise* December 1943.
25. IWM Sound 22147 Pitman, Albert.
26. IWM Sound 9380, Lloyd-Davies, Felix Justin.
27. Ibid.
28. TNA ADM 1/29416 Operation 'Stonewall'. Interception of Blockade Runners. Services of HMS *Glasgow* and *Enterprise* December 1943.
29. IWM Sound 22147 Pitman, Albert.
30. TNA ADM 1/29416 Operation 'Stonewall'. Interception of Blockade Runners. Services of HMS *Glasgow* and *Enterprise* December 1943.
31. Ibid.
32. TNA ADM 199/261 Coastal Forces Actions: 29–30 January 1944.
33. BBC People's War (henceforth BBC PW) Record Number A3563444 Sprigg.
34. Scott, Peter, *Battle of the Narrow Seas* (Seaforth, Barnsley, 2009), 180. MacFarlane survived his injuries, and the war.
35. S.W. Roskill, *The War at Sea 1939–1945 Volume 3, Part 1: The Offensive 1st June 1943–31st May 1944* (HMSO, London, 1960), 289.
36. TNA ADM 199/263 Coastal Actions with Enemy Destroyers and Light Forces: Operation Tunnel Action with Elbing Class Destroyers 25–26 April 1944.
37. W.A.B. Douglas, R. Sarty, and M. Whitby, *A Blue Water Navy: The Official Operational History of the Royal Canadian Navy in the Second World War 1939–1945 Volume II Part 2* (Vanwell Publishing, St Catharines, ON, 2007), 224–6.
38. TNA ADM 199/263 Coastal Actions with Enemy Destroyers and Light Forces: Operation Tunnel Action with Elbing Class Destroyers 25–26 April 1944.
39. Douglas, Sarty and Whitby, *A Blue Water Navy*, 225.
40. TNA ADM 199/263 Coastal Actions with Enemy Destroyers and Light Forces: Operation Tunnel Action with Elbing Class Destroyers 25–26 April 1944.
41. Ibid.
42. ADM 199/263 Coastal Actions with Enemy Destroyers and Light Forces: Report of Action on Night of 28/29 April 1944 between HMC Ship HAIDA and ATHABASKAN and Two Enemy Destroyers.
43. Ibid.
44. Ibid.
45. Douglas, Sarty and Whitby, *A Blue Water Navy*, 229.
46. ADM 199/263 Coastal Actions with Enemy Destroyers and Light Forces: Report of Action on Night of 28/29 April 1944 between HMC Ship HAIDA and ATHABASKAN and Two Enemy Destroyers.
47. http://www.royalnavyresearcharchive.org.uk/SQUADRONS/838_Squadron.htm.
48. ADM 199/263 Coastal Actions with Enemy Destroyers and Light Forces: report of Action against E-boats 25/26 April HMS ROWLEY and FS LA COMBATTANTE.

49. ADM 1/15991 Actions Against E-Boats 13/14 May 1944: FS LA COMBATTANTE MTBs 680, 608, https://www.findagrave.com/memorial/122500844/klaus-donitz and http://www.s-boot.net/englisch/sboats-kin-channel44.html.
50. Naval Staff Battle Summary No. 39 Operation 'Neptune', 48–9.
51. Chris O'Flaherty, *Naval Minewarfare: Politics to Practicalities* (The Choir Press, Gloucester, 2019), 70. I am grateful to Captain O'Flaherty, an experienced Royal Navy mine warfare officer, for making me aware of his work and providing me with a copy of his invaluable book.
52. TNA ADM 199/261 Coastal Forces Actions: Operation KN.6 Minelaying Carried Out 19–20 May 1944 MTBs 249, 251, 246, 247.
53. IWM Sound 28735 Rickman, Eric 'Ricky'
54. Ibid.
55. Ibid.
56. TNA ADM 358/4341 MTB 732 (Sunk by La Combattante).
57. IWM Sound 26950 Howe, Bernard.

3 Backroom Boys and Girls

1. BBC PW ID 2524402 Thomas, Ginger.
2. Robert W. Love, Jr, and John Major (eds), *The Year of D-Day: The 1944 Diary of Admiral Sir Bertram Ramsay* (University of Hull Press, Hull, 1994), xxxiii.
3. Edwards, *Operation Neptune*, 34.
4. Sir Frederick Morgan KCB, *Overture to Overlord* (Mayflower, London, 1962), 131. Eisenhower made this very clear in his generous introduction to Morgan's memoir, writing that '[Morgan] was charged with making the best plan possible out of the means . . . allocated by the Combined Chief of Staff.'
5. Ibid., 74. The observer was US Major-General Ray Barker.
6. Eisenhower, Dwight D., *Report by the Supreme Commander to the Combined Chiefs of Staff on the Operations in Europe of the Allied Expeditionary Force 6 June 1944 to 8 May 1945* (HMSO, London 1946), 6–7, 2
7. Field Marshal Montgomery the Viscount of Alamein, *Memoirs* (Collins, London, 1958), 210–11.
8. See F.H. Hinsley, *British Intelligence in the Second World War: Abridged Edition*, HMSO, London, 1993), 436.
9. Love and Major, *The Year of D-Day*, 3.
10. National Museum of the Royal Navy (henceforth NMRN) 2004.11-5 Operation Neptune Seniority List.
11. Love and Major, *The Year of D-Day*, 37, 53 and 64.
12. Naval Staff Battle Summary No. 39 Operation 'Neptune', 13.
13. TNA DEFE 2/418 Naval Commander Force J Report.
14. Admiral Sir Bertram H. Ramsay, KCB, MVO, 'The Assault Phase of the Normandy Landings: Official Despatch Submitted to the Supreme Commander, Allied Expeditionary Force, on the 16th October 1944, by Admiral Sir Bertram H. Ramsay, KCB, MVO, Allied Naval Commander-in-Chief, Expeditionary Force in Supplement to the London Gazette of Tuesday, the 28th of October 1947', 5113.
15. Naval Staff Battle Summary No. 39 Operation 'Neptune', 14, author's emphasis.

16. NMRN 2004.11-5 Assault Group J.2 Operation Order for Operation Neptune.
17. Edwards, *Operation Neptune*, 70–1.
18. Naval Staff Battle Summary No. 39 Operation 'Neptune', 53.
19. Ibid., 54.
20. Ibid., 55.
21. Ibid., 55–6.
22. See Fisher, *Sword Beach*.
23. Geoffrey Sanders, *Soldier, Sailor* (The Bombardment Units Association/John Jennings, Gloucester, 1947), 96.
24. Lieutenant (jg) Coit N. Coker, 'Fire Control on Omaha Beach', *The Field Artillery Journal* (September 1946).
25. See Adrian R. Lewis, *Omaha Beach: A Flawed Victory* (Tempus, Stroud, 2004) for a forensic analysis of this and a myriad of other tensions between British and US doctrines, some of which had serious consequences on D-Day.
26. Naval Staff Battle Summary No. 39 Operation 'Neptune', 55.
27. Ibid., 57.
28. DDS H194/1986/9 Neptune Bombardment and Fire Support Plan.
29. Ibid.
30. Every German defensive position from Norway to the Spanish border was allocated a WN number.
31. DDS H194/1986/9 Neptune Bombardment and Fire Support Plan.
32. Ibid.
33. Ibid.
34. Ibid.
35. Ibid.
36. DDS H9/1985/4 HMS *Warspite* Bombardment Information and http://www.atlantikwall.co.uk/atlantikwall/kva_g_d2_trouville_wntrou017.php.
37. Ibid.
38. Edwards, *Operation Neptune*, 70.
39. Naval Staff Battle Summary No. 39 Operation 'Neptune', 13.
40. NMRN UC 405/5359 The Story of the Mulberries, by Hickling, Rear-Admiral H, and MacKillop, Brigadier I L H, (War Office, 1947), 4.
41. NMRN UC 405/5359 The Story of the Mulberries, by Hickling, Rear-Admiral H, and MacKillop, Brigadier I L H, 1.
42. Guy Hartcup, *Code Name Mulberry: The Planning, Building and Operation of the Normandy Harbours* (David & Charles, Newton Abbot, 1977), 58.
43. Barnett, *Engage the Enemy More Closely*, 759.
44. NMRN UC 405/5359 The Story of the Mulberries, by Hickling, Rear-Admiral H, and MacKillop, Brigadier I L H, 19.
45. Edwards, *Operation Neptune*, 61.
46. NMRN UC 405/5359 The Story of the Mulberries, by Hickling, Rear-Admiral H, and MacKillop, Brigadier I L H, 8.
47. Ibid.
48. Rear-Admiral Edward Ellsberg, *The Far Shore* (Panther, London, 1964), 61.
49. Basil Liddell Hart, *The Other Side of the Hill* (Cassell, London, 1973), 392.
50. Many of the complex challenges connected to Pluto and Mulberry were overcome at the Combined Operations Experimental Establishment (COXE, or 'Coxy') at Instow, in north Devon (see Fergusson, *The Watery Maze*, 192–5).

COXE found answers to an inconceivable range of other conundrums, from beaching and extracting landing craft and LSTs, to unloading cargo ships and waterproofing vehicles. The extraordinary photographic archive of this important but largely unrecognised organisation is held by the National Museum of the Royal Navy in Portsmouth.

51. Barnett, *Engage the Enemy More Closely*, 762.
52. Barnett, *Engage the Enemy More Closely*, 781–96.
53. Naval Staff Battle Summary No. 39 Operation 'Neptune', 62.
54. TNA DEFE 2/418 Naval Commander Force J Report.
55. Barnett, *Engage the Enemy More Closely*, 800.
56. https://library.columbia.edu/libraries/ccoh Interview 4076899 Kirk, Alan Goodrich. Reproduced in Paul Stillwell (ed.), *Assault on Normandy: First Person Accounts from the Sea Services* (Naval Institute Press, Annapolis, MD, 1994), 23–8. Also see Lewis, *Omaha Beach*.
57. Andrew Gordon, 'Bertram Ramsay and Staff Work', *The Naval Review*, vol. 102 (August 2014), 242.
58. BBCPW 2524402 Thomas, Ginger.
59. Ibid.
60. The D-Day Story (henceforth DDS) Record Number H666/1990.
61. The origins of BIGOT are obscure but it pre-dates Overlord. The most common theory is that it relates to operations in the Mediterranean which were planned from Gibraltar, when outbound documents were stamped TO GIB and material being sent back to the UK was reversed, to BIGOT, but this has never been established beyond doubt.
62. BBC PW ID A2843840 Cartwright, Kathleen.
63. IWM Sound 23180 Nichol, Paulina.
64. IWM Sound 32390 Checketts, Harold.
65. See, for example, John Ross, *The Forecast for D-Day* (Lyons Press, Guilford, CT, 2014) and Stagg's own memoir, *Forecast for Overlord* (Ian Allan, London, 1971).
66. IWM Sound 32390 Checketts, Harold.
67. TNA ADM 223/162 Weekly Intelligence Reports No. 213 7th April 1944.
68. Ibid.
69. Ibid.
70. Jonathan Falconer, *The D-Day Operations Manual* (Haynes, Sparkford, 2013), 14.
71. BBC PW ID 2524402 Thomas, Ginger. Remarkably, many of the postcards survive today in the collections of the Imperial War Museum.
72. See Falconer, *D-Day Operations Manual*, 16.
73. 'Endeavour', 'Can We Afford the Non-Fighting Part of the Navy', *The Naval Review*, vol. 78 (July 1990), 211–12.
74. For a meticulously researched and comprehensive analysis of POSTAGE ABLE and other COPP survey missions see https://www.coppsurvey.uk/.
75. Commander N.C. Glen, 'Normandy', *The Naval Review*, vol. 93 (November 2005), 411–12.
76. Ibid., 411–12.
77. Ibid. Self-heating soup cans had a tube of cordite, the propellent from small arms ammunition, running through the middle, which could be lit using a cigarette. It is hard to imagine this technique passing 2023 food hygiene regulations!

78. TNA ADM 1/16493 'Walterboote': Small German High Speed Submarine.

79. TNA ADM 219/211 E-Boat Attacks on Coastal Convoys: Comparison with Possible Threat from Walter Boat.

80. TNA ADM 1/16493 'Walterboote': Small German High Speed Submarine. See also Douglas, Sarty and Whitby, *A Blue Water Navy*, 216.

81. Thaddeus Holt, *The Deceivers: Allied Military Deception in the Second World War* (Folio Society, London, 2008). See also Mary Katherine Barbier, *D-Day Deception: Operation Fortitude and the Normandy Invasion* (Stackpole, Mechanicsburg PA, 2009).

82. There are many books about GARBO and the other double agents. See, for example: R. Hesketh, *Fortitude: The D-Day Deception Campaign* (Penguin, London, 2002); Ben Macintyre, *Double Cross: The True Story of the D-Day Spies* (A&C Black, London, 2012); S. Talty, *Agent Garbo: The Brilliant, Eccentric Secret Agent Who Tricked Hitler and Saved D-Day* (Houghton Mifflin, Boston, MA, 2012).

83. Holt, *The Deceivers*, 407–8 and 413–14. Starkey was not wholly planned as a deception, according to Morgan it was also the plan developed to respond to any sudden change in circumstances – either a German or a Russian collapse – in 1943. Morgan, *Overture to Overlord*, 85.

84. Morgan, *Overture to Overlord*, 104.

85. Holt, *The Deceivers*, 332 and 460.

86. Falconer, *D-Day Operations Manual*, 27–32.

4 Build, Borrow and Beg

1. Love and Major, *The Year of D-Day*, 11.

2. See Morgan, *Overture to Overlord*, 144, and Edwards, *Operation Neptune*, 45.

3. Naval Staff Battle Summary No. 39 Operation 'Neptune', 35–8.

4. TNA ADM 179/508 Overlord LCT Bases.

5. This debate is summed up well in Symonds, *Operation Neptune*, 146–8.

6. Morison, *Invasion of France and Germany*, 53.

7. Norman Scarfe, *Assault Division: A History of the 3rd Division from the Invasion of Normandy to the Surrender of Germany* (Spellmount, Staplehurst, 2004), 49.

8. TNA ADM 179/507 Overlord Reports Not Appearing Elsewhere: A LCI(L) Sqn. Villiers went on to write forty-four books, and command square-rigged sailing ships for the films *Moby Dick* and *Billy Budd*, as well as serving as Chairman and President of the Society for Nautical Research and as a Trustee of the National Maritime Museum.

9. IWM Sound 34087, Perks, Leslie William 'Bill'.

10. Quoted in Symonds, *Operation Neptune*, 166.

11. Stillwell, *Assault on Normandy*, 154.

12. Ibid., 154–5.

13. C.B.S.C, 'LST: Landing Ship Tank', *The Naval Review*, vol. 35 (August 1947), 234.

14. Ibid.

15. Ibid.

16. IWM Sound 21575 Watkins, Dennis.

17. IWM Sound 21967 Noble, Ernest.

18. IWM Sound 27251 Parker, Stan.
19. C.B.S.C, 'LST: Landing Ship Tank', 234.
20. IWM Sound 16406 Bell, Henry.
21. IWM Sound 8739 Madden, Colin Duncan.
22. Lewis Johnman and Hugh Murphy, *British Shipbuilding and the State Since 1918: A Political Economy of Decline* (University of Exeter Press, Exeter, 2002), 67.
23. IWM Sound 20156 Hall, Alice.
24. BBC PW A2724879 Miles, Bill
25. Johnman and Murphy, *British Shipbuilding and the State*, 83–4.
26. IWM Sound 33568 Humphries, George.
27. IWM Sound 22195 Rogers, Albert.
28. Ibid.
29. TNA ADM 179/508 Overlord LCT Bases.
30. TNA ADM 179/507 Overlord Reports Not Appearing Elsewhere: Flag Officer British Assault Area.
31. See https://www.naval-history.net/WW2MiscRNLandingBarges for a breakdown of the various barge conversions.
32. TNA ADM 179/511 Overlord Reports Southampton. The types of ship included merchant ship conversions landing craft of all sizes and Coastal Forces craft.
33. TNA ADM 179/415 Admiral Superintendent Portsmouth Report on Operation Overlord, 1.
34. Ibid.
35. TNA ADM 199/532 Reports of Proceedings 1943–1944: HMS *Centurion* Passage Home 13th March–13th May 1944.
36. TNA ADM 179/415 Admiral Superintendent Portsmouth Report on Operation Overlord, 3.
37. IWM Sound 27267 Luff, Frank.
38. Ibid.
39. Report by Allied Naval Commander-in-Chief Expeditionary Force on Operation NEPTUNE (London, 1944), 128.
40. See Love and Major, *The Year of D-Day*, 69. See also Tim Benbow, 'Battleships, D-Day and Naval Strategy', *War in History*, vol. 29, no. 3 (July 2022), for an excellent analysis of the complex, multifaceted and often overlooked roles of battleships in the Seine Bay.
41. Benbow, 'Battleships, D-Day and Naval Strategy'.
42. https://library.columbia.edu/libraries/ccoh Interview 4076899 Kirk, Alan Goodrich, 259.
43. Carleton F. Bryant, 'Battleship Commander', in Stillwell, *Assault on Normandy*, 183.
44. William B. Kirkland Jr, *Destroyers at Normandy: Naval Gunfire Support at Omaha Beach* (Naval Historical Foundation, Washington, DC, 1994), 10.
45. Captain Robert J. Bulkeley, *At Close Quarters: PT Boats in the United States Navy* (Naval History Division, Washington, DC, 1962), 350.
46. Wendy Tebble, 'The Development and Role of Inshore Fire Support Craft in Amphibious Operations 1939–1945', 21 and 45. Unpublished M.Phil Thesis at the Department of War Studies, Kings College, London, 2003. I am extremely grateful to Professor Andrew Lambert for bringing this

52. Ibid.
53. Ibid.
54. IWM Sound 30008 Capon, John.
55. TNA ADM 199/261 Coastal Forces Actions\Attack by E-boats on Convoy T-4 (Exercise Tiger) 27–28 April 1944.
56. Kapitän zur See Gunther Rabe, *S-130*, quoted in Greg H. Williams, *The US Navy at Normandy: Fleet Organisation and Operations in the D-Day Invasion* (McFarland & Company, Jefferson, NC, 2020), 46.
57. Ken Small with Mark Rogerson, *The Forgotten Dead* (Bloomsbury, London, 1989), 22–3.
58. TNA ADM 199/261 Coastal Forces Actions\Attack by E-boats on Convoy T-4 (Exercise Tiger) 27–28 April 1944.
59. Small, *The Forgotten Dead*, 49–51.
60. Williams, *The US Navy at Normandy*, 47.
61. Small, *The Forgotten Dead*, 69–74.
62. TNA ADM 199/261 Coastal Forces Actions\Attack by E-boats on Convoy T-4 (Exercise Tiger) 27–28 April 1944.
63. BBC PW A356558 Smith, William.
64. IWM Sound 12734 Wellman, Derek.
65. TNA ADM 199/261 Coastal Forces Actions\Attack by E-boats on Convoy T-4 (Exercise Tiger) 27–28 April 1944.
66. See, for example, Roskill, *The War at Sea 1939–1945 Volume 3, Part 2*, 294; Morison, *Invasion of France and Germany*, 66.
67. Yung, *Gators of Neptune*, 166.
68. TNA ADM 199/261 Coastal Forces Actions\Attack by E-boats on Convoy T-4 (Exercise Tiger) 27–28 April 1944.
69. Ibid.
70. Ibid.
71. ADM 199/1556 Admiralty War History Cases and Papers Operation Neptune/Aggressive Measures against German E-boats and Destroyers May 1944.
72. Love and Major, *The Year of D-Day*, 64–5.

6 Final Days

1. TNA ADM 223/162 Weekly Intelligence Reports No. 216 28th April 1944.
2. DDS 1995/100/81 Interview with Admiral Krancke.
3. TNA 223/449 Allied Invasion German Reactions 1944.
4. Frank, *German S-Boats in Action*, 109.
5. Grand Admiral Karl Dönitz, *Memoirs: Ten Years and Twenty Days* (Naval Institute Press, Annapolis, MD, 2012), 396.
6. Clay Blair, *Hitler's U-boat War: The Hunted 1942–1945* (Cassell, London, 2000), 402.
7. Herbert Werner, quoted in Blair, *Hitler's U-boat War*, 314.
8. Michael Salewski, *Die deutsche Seekriegsleitung 1935–1945, Band II, 1942–1945* (Bernard & Graefe Verlag, Munich, 1975), 415.
9. I am grateful to Dr Tim Benbow for drawing my attention to this point.

10. Grand Admiral Erich Raeder, *My Life* (United States Naval Institute Press, Annapolis, MD, 1960), 281.
11. Lawrence Paterson, *Hitler's Forgotten Flotillas*, 279–82.
12. Friedrich Ruge, 'The Invasion of Normandy', in Dr Hans-Adolf Jacobsen and Dr Jürgen Rohwer, *Decisive Battles of World War II: The German View* (André Deutsch, London, 1965), 325.
13. IWM Sound 17433 Lucke, Helmut.
14. *Fuehrer Conferences on Naval Affairs: 1944* (Admiralty, London, July 1947), 9.
15. DDS 167/1990 Neptune Monograph Prepared by Commander Task Force 122, 43.
16. Ibid.
17. Ibid., and Morison, *Invasion of France and Germany*, 56.
18. Generalleutnant Hans Speidel, *We Defended Normandy* (Herbert Jenkins, London, 1951), 66.
19. Friedrich Ruge, *Rommel in Normandy* (Presidio, London, 1979), 35.
20. Speidel, *We Defended Normandy*, 67.
21. Ruge, 'The Invasion of Normandy', 328.
22. Ultra and other signals intelligence gave the Allies a comprehensive picture of German defensive minelaying in early 1944, including details of which specific types were deployed in which areas. Ultra also facilitated an interception of Kriegsmarine minelaying craft on 23 May, which left two sunk and three damaged, and 'irreparably crippled' German minelaying in the Seine Bay. See Hinsley, *British Intelligence in the Second World War*, 461–2.
23. Ruge, *Rommel in Normandy*, 38.
24. Naval Staff Battle Summary No. 39 Operation 'Neptune', 49.
25. Ruge, *Rommel in Normandy*, 38–9.
26. DDS 1995/100/81 Interview with Admiral Krancke.
27. Ruge, 'The Invasion of Normandy', 327.
28. B.H. Liddell Hart (ed.), *The Rommel Papers* (Collins, London, 1953), 458.
29. NMRN CRTY 2019/59/24 Reports on Operation Neptune/Admiralty Docket – Summary of the Lessons Learned During Operation Neptune.
30. Ruge, *Rommel in Normandy*, 20.
31. See Lewis, *Omaha Beach*, 119–46.
32. NMRN CRTY 2019/59/24 Reports on Operation Neptune/Admiralty Docket – Summary of the Lessons Learned During Operation Neptune.
33. Ibid.
34. Eisenhower, *Report by the Supreme Commander*, 14.
35. Cajus Bekker, *The Luftwaffe War Diaries* (Corgi, London, 1972), 453.
36. DDS 167/1990 Neptune Monograph, 48.
37. See Hinsley, *British Intelligence in the Second World War*, 464.
38. Jak P. Mallman Showell, *German Naval Codebreakers* (Ian Allan, Hersham, 2003), 129.
39. Stillwell, *Assault on Normandy*, 183.
40. Commander Michael Chichester, 'The Greatest Amphibious Operation in History (and a great naval bombardment)', *The Naval Review*, vol. 82, no. 2 (April 1994), 102.
41. Ibid.
42. Quoted in George Evans, *The Landfall Story* (The Acorn Press, Liverpool, 1972), 62. *LCT-7074* is the last remaining Landing Craft Tank that took part

32. IWM Sound 33902 Michell, Richard.
33. 'M.S.X.', 'D-Day in a Minesweeper', 133.
34. BBC PW A8809879 Ward, Joseph.
35. BBC PW A4250521 Hasker, Leslie.
36. TNA DEFE 2/418 Force J Report.
37. Brendan Maher, *A Passage to Sword Beach* (Naval Institute Press, Annapolis, MD, 1996), 118.
38. Ibid.
39. 'Ramsay Despatch', 5115.
40. 'M.S.X.', 'D-Day in a Minesweeper', 134.
41. TNA DEFE 2/418 Force J Report\Enclosure 11 Reports of Proceedings\Minesweepers\9 MS Flotilla.
42. Williams, *The US Navy at Normandy*, 121–2.
43. Quoted in Douglas, Sarty and Whitby, *A Blue Water Navy*, 249.
44. 'M.S.X.', 'D-Day in a Minesweeper', 135.
45. IWM Sound 33323 Gostling, William.
46. TNA ADM 179/504 Report of Proceedings Naval Commander Force S.
47. Ibid.
48. Wilfred Granville and Robin A., Kelly, *Inshore Heroes: The Story of HM Motor Launches in Two World Wars* (W.H. Allen, London, 1961), 247.
49. TNA DEFE 2/414 Report Naval Commander Eastern Naval Task Force Parts I–VI.
50. 'Ramsay Despatch', 5114.
51. TNA ADM 179/504 Report of Proceedings Naval Commander Force S.
52. TNA DEFE 2/418 Force J Report.
53. TNA ADM 179/505 Report of Proceedings Naval Commander Force G.
54. IWM Sound 20009 Perry, Leslie, quoted in Hewitt, *Firing on Fortress Europe*, 58.
55. IWM Sound 24907 Simpson, Charles, quoted in Hewitt, *Firing on Fortress Europe*, 66.
56. TNA DEFE 2/416 & 417 Naval Commander Force G Report\Enclosure 2 Captain G2 Report\9 591 LCA (HR) Flotilla.
57. Ibid.
58. IWM Sound 9956 Irwin, Hugh and www.cwgc.org.uk.
59. TNA DEFE 2/419 Naval Commander Force S Report.
60. IWM Sound 9956 Irwin, Hugh.
61. Ibid.
62. IWM Sound 11331 Dosch, Theron.
63. BBC PW A2096723 Watts, R.G. A Wireman was a naval rate introduced in wartime, to reflect the skills of civilian electricians who were not technically trained naval electrical engineers.
64. BBC PW A2541601 Lowndes, Tony.
65. BBC PW A8532100 Small, Dennis.
66. Ibid.
67. Ibid.
68. NMRN CRTY 2019/59/24 Reports on Operation Neptune/Admiralty Docket – Summary of the Lessons Learned During Operation Neptune.
69. BBC PW A7015925 Milton, Frank.

70. TNA DEFE 2/416 & 417 Naval Commander Force G Report\Enclosure 2 Captain G2 Report.
71. BBC PW A7015925 Milton, Frank.
72. Ibid.
73. Ibid.
74. *Yorkshire Post*, via http://pompeypensioners.org.uk.
75. IWM Sound 18684 Bird, Peter.
76. TNA ADM 358/2666 Sinking of LBV 42.
77. 'Ramsay Despatch', 5114.
78. Paul Lund and Harry Ludlam, *Out Sweeps: The Exploits of the Minesweepers in World War II* (New English Library, London, 1979), 176.

8 Into the Fire

1. 'Ramsay Despatch', 5116.
2. 'Ramsay Despatch', 5117.
3. Naval Staff Battle Summary No. 39 Operation 'Neptune', 90.
4. 'Ramsay Despatch', 5116.
5. Naval Staff Battle Summary No. 39 Operation 'Neptune', 91.
6. Morison, *Invasion of France and Germany*, 95.
7. Naval Staff Battle Summary No. 39 Operation 'Neptune', 93.
8. https://www.uss-corry-dd463.com/.
9. Williams, *The US Navy at Normandy*, 225.
10. Ibid., 225–6.
11. Ibid., 226–8.
12. http://www.uss-corry-dd463.com/d-day_u-boat_photos/corry_loss_initial_rpts.
13. Morison, *Invasion of France and Germany*, 96, and Williams, *The US Navy at Normandy*, 226, both repeat the mine error. There is detail about this controversy at https://www.uss-corry-dd463.com/.
14. TNA ADM 53/119404 Log of HMS *Erebus* June 1944. Apparently, this was attributed to faulty fuses fitted to shells manufactured in the US by Crucible Steel. http://www.navweaps.com/Weapons/WNBR_15-42_mk1.php.
15. Williams, *The US Navy at Normandy*, 230–1.
16. See Peter Caddick-Adams, *Sand and Steel: A New History of D-Day* (Arrow, London, 2019). Roosevelt, son of the 26th US President and distantly related to President Franklin Delano Roosevelt, was at 56 the oldest American to land on D-Day.
17. Morison, *Invasion of France and Germany*, 101.
18. Fane, *The Naked Warriors*, 63–4.
19. TNA ADM 53/119404 Log of HMS *Erebus* June 1944.
20. IWM Sound 21558 Miller, Alan.
21. Ibid.
22. Morison, *Invasion of France and Germany*, 104.
23. Commodore James E. Arnold, 'NOIC Utah', in Stillwell, *Assault on Normandy*, 90.
24. Ibid.
25. Caddick-Adams, *Sand and Steel*, 559.

26. Morison, *Invasion of France and Germany*, 131.
27. Ibid.
28. Stillwell, *Assault on Normandy*, 183.
29. IWM Sound 9380 Lloyd-Davies, Felix Justin.
30. Morison, *Invasion of France and Germany*, 119.
31. IWM Sound 13097 Howe, Kenneth.
32. Morison, *Invasion of France and Germany*, 121.
33. Sabin, Lorenzo 'Close in Support at Omaha Beach', in Stillwell, *Assault on Normandy*, 59. Lewis, in *Omaha Beach*, 300–7, provides Sabin's verdict on the British-built craft he was in charge of. Gun and rocket craft had some value, but the LCFs were in Sabin's opinion 'hardly worth the time, trouble and money'. Fundamentally Sabin believed that because the US sailors had insufficient time to familiarise themselves with their charges, their impact at Omaha was limited.
34. See Lewis, *Omaha Beach*, for a detailed exploration of this argument. In summary, the US Navy favoured a long, devastating bombardment as practised in the island battles of the Pacific. The US Army preferred a short bombardment to retain tactical surprise, in line with British doctrine they had learned in the Mediterranean.
35. Bryant, 'Battleship Commander', in Stillwell, *Assault on Normandy*, 184.
36. Administrative History of U.S. Naval Forces in Europe 1940–1946: Volume 5 Operation Neptune (London, 1946), 517, from http://www.ibiblio.org/hyperwar/.
37. Captain Richard H. Crook, 'Traffic Cop', in Stillwell, *Assault on Normandy*, 64.
38. Naval Staff Battle Summary No. 39 Operation 'Neptune', 94.
39. Dean Rockwell, 'DD Spelled Disaster', in Stillwell, *Assault on Normandy*, 70.
40. Ibid.
41. Morison, *Invasion of France and Germany*, 134
42. Ibid., and Williams, *The US Navy at Normandy*, 147.
43. Caddick-Adams, *Sand and Steel*, 644.
44. Williams, *The US Navy at Normandy*, 148.
45. Crook, 'Traffic Cop', 65.
46. Morison, *Invasion of France and Germany*, 138.
47. Lewis, Clifford W, in the Coast Guard 'Compass', quoted in Williams, *The US Navy at Normandy*, 251.
48. BBC PW A7920029 Gaskin, John.
49. BBC PW A1929468 Green, Jimmy.
50. Ibid.
51. Ibid.
52. Kershaw, *The Bedford Boys*, 226.
53. IWM Sound 25199 Benbow, Hilaire.
54. Ibid.
55. Ibid.
56. Commander F.D. Fane, *The Naked Warriors* (Panther Books/Hamilton and Company, London, 1958), 60. See also Lewis, *Omaha Beach: A Flawed Victory*, 245–64. Lewis argues that there were not enough Navy NCDUs available, that the Army's Engineer Special Brigades were inadequately prepared to clear beach obstacle in water, and that the requirement for a landing in daylight left inadequate time to clear the obstacles. Ultimately he holds Bradley and Montgomery responsible for what he calls the 'near-defeat' at Omaha (262)

57. Fane, *The Naked Warriors*, 55–6.
58. Orval Wakefield, 'Naval Combat Demolition Unit', in Stillwell, *Assault on Normandy*, 95.
59. Lieutenant-Commander Paul S. Fauks, 'My Only Job Was to Stay Alive', in Stillwell, *Assault on Normandy*, 80.
60. Administrative History of U.S. Naval Forces in Europe 1940–1946: Volume 5, 521.
61. 'Ramsay Despatch', 5116.
62. Bradley, *A Soldier's Story*, 271.
63. IWM Sound 25199 Benbow, Hilaire.
64. Morison, *Invasion of France and Germany*, 141.
65. USS *Baldwin* Action Report, quoted in Kirkland, *Destroyers at Normandy*, 42.
66. Martin Sommers, 'The Longest Hour in History', *The Saturday Evening Post*, 8 July 1944, quoted in Morison, *Invasion of France and Germany*, 143.
67. Coker, 'Fire Control on Omaha Beach'.
68. Ibid.
69. Comdesdiv 36 Action Report, p7, quoted in Morison, *Invasion of France and Germany*, 148.
70. Comdesdiv 36 Action Report, quoted in Kirkland, *Destroyers at Normandy*, 28.
71. Morison, *Invasion of France and Germany*, 145.
72. Coker, 'Fire Control on Omaha Beach', 148.
73. *Carmick* Action Report, quoted in Kirkland, *Destroyers at Normandy*, 63.
74. *Doyle* deck log, quoted in Kirkland, *Destroyers at Normandy*, 65.
75. 'Ramsay Despatch', 5116.
76. Bradley, *A General's Life*, 251, quoted in Kirkland, *Destroyers at Normandy*, 75.

9 Resolute and Seamanlike

1. Naval Staff Battle Summary No. 39 Operation 'Neptune', 90
2. IWM Documents 2067 Brooke Smith, Lieutenant Peter W., quoted in Hewitt, *Firing on Fortress Europe*, 71.
3. IWM Sound 26747 Painter, Gordon, quoted in Hewitt, *Firing on Fortress Europe*, 73.
4. http://www.atlantikwall.co.uk/atlantikwall/fnc_wn32_marefontaine_bttr.php.
5. TNA ADM 199/1655, quoted at http://www.atlantikwall.co.uk/atlantikwall/fnc_wn32_marefontaine.
6. TNA ADM 179/505 Report of Proceedings Naval Commander Force G\ Appendix C Report on Bombardment.
7. IWM Sound 27181 Bartlett, Thomas.
8. Hill, *Destroyer Captain*, 260.
9. Commander William Donald, *Stand by for Action* (New English Library, London, 1975), 160.
10. TNA ADM 179/505 Report of Proceedings Naval Commander Force G\ Appendix C Report on Bombardment.
11. Ibid.
12. IWM Sound 9956 Irwin, Hugh.
13. Ibid.
14. IWM Sound 20117 Hill, Richard.

15. Ibid.
16. Ibid.
17. Ibid.
18. TNA ADM 179/505 Report of Proceedings Naval Commander Force G\ Appendix C Report on Bombardment.
19. IWM Sound 20117 Hill, Richard.
20. TNA DEFE 2/416 & 417 Naval Commander Force G Report\Appendix A Narrative.
21. Ibid., Enclosure 1 Captain G1 Report\5 Senior Officer Jig Green Report.
22. Ibid., Appendix A Narrative.
23. Ibid., Enclosure 2 Captain G2 Report\10 LCOCU 3 & 4.
24. https://www.mcdoa.org.uk/Operation_Neptune_The_LCOCU_Frogmen. htm.
25. TNA ADM 179/505 Report of Proceedings Naval Commander Force G\ Appendix C Report on Bombardment.
26. TNA DEFE 2/416 & 417 Naval Commander Force G Report\Enclosure 1 Captain G1 Report\17 D Sqn 28 & 53 LCT Flotillas.
27. Ibid.
28. https://www.combinedops.com.
29. TNA DEFE 2-416 & 417 Naval Commander Force G Report\Enclosure 1 Captain G1 Report\10 Group VII 33 & 49 LCT Flotillas.
30. Ibid., Enclosure 2 Captain G2 Report\3 Senior Officer King Red Report. The 88mm guns, like Tiger tanks, acquired almost mythic status in Normandy. Just as almost every enemy tank shot at by a soldier was misidentified as a 'Tiger', almost every gun which fired at sailors was an 'Eighty-Eight'.
31. TNA DEFE/2-416 & 417 Naval Commander Force G Report\Enclosure 6 332 Support Flotilla.
32. Caddick-Adams, *Sand and Steel*, 727.
33. TNA DEFE 2/416 & 417 Naval Commander Force G Report\Enclosure 2 Captain G2 Report\6 SS Empire Lance & 540 LCA Flotilla.
34. Ibid., 1 Summary.
35. Holman, *Stand by to Beach*, 74–5; BBC PW A2844272 Tandy, George, and BBC PW A2431397 Williams, Eddie.
36. See Caddick-Adams, *Sand and Steel*, 734.
37. TNA DEFE 2/418 Force J Report\Enclosure 4 Gunnery.
38. Ibid.
39. Ibid., Enclosure 11 Reports of Proceedings\Bombardment\HMS *Diadem*.
40. Ibid., 26th Destroyer Flotilla.
41. Ibid.
42. DDS H87/1991/91 Holmes, Frank.
43. Tebble, 'Inshore Fire Support Craft', 226.
44. TNA ADM 179/504 Report of Proceedings Naval Commander Force S\ Appendix 1 Bombardment and Support.
45. TNA ADM 202/449 Landing Craft Reports Overlord\4 US Marine Report.
46. Ibid.
47. TNA DEFE 2/418 Force J Report\Enclosure 4 Gunnery.
48. Naval Staff Battle Summary No. 39 Operation 'Neptune', 99 and TNA DEFE 2/418 Force J Report\Enclosure 1 Embarkation, Passage & Assault.

49. TNA DEFE 2/418 Force J Report\Enclosure 1 Embarkation, Passage & Assault.
50. Ibid., Enclosure 11 Reports of Proceedings\Group J1\526 LCA Flotilla.
51. Ibid., 557 LCA Flotilla.
52. BBC PW A5018032 Turner, Frederick.
53. Ibid.
54. TNA DEFE 2/418 Force J Report\Enclosure 11 Reports of Proceedings\ Group J1.
55. IWM Sound 10086 Ashcroft, Gerald.
56. http://www.6juin1944.com/assaut/juno/tables.pdf.
57. IWM Sound 10086 Ashcroft, Gerald.
58. Ibid.
59. Ibid.
60. BBC PW A3230010 Newman, Dennis.
61. Ibid.
62. BBC PW A2541601 Lowndes, Tony.
63. TNA DEFE 2/418 Force J Report\Enclosure 11 Reports of Proceedings\ LCOC Units.
64. Ibid., Enclosure 1 Embarkation, Passage & Assault.
65. TNA ADM 199/1556 Admiralty War History Cases and Papers Operation Neptune\Countermeasure to Beach Obstacles.
66. IWM Sound 33568 Humphries, George, and DDS H108-1991.2 LCT 513.
67. TNA DEFE 2/418 Force J Report\Enclosure 11 Reports of Proceedings\ Group J2\30 LCT Flotilla.
68. IWM Sound 20064, Dye, Ralph.
69. Ibid.
70. Ibid.
71. Douglas, Sarty and Whitby, *A Blue Water Navy*, 261.
72. TNA DEFE 2/414 Report Naval Commander ETF Parts I-VI.
73. TNA ADM 179/507 Overlord Reports Not Appearing Elsewhere\19 A LCI (L) Sqn.
74. TNA ADM 199/1659 Reports on Operation Neptune. Miscellaneous Reports not Enclosed in Main Report\HMS *Scylla* Report of Proceedings.

10 Sword and the Follow-Up Waves

1. IWM Sound 17394 Gueritz, Teddy.
2. TNA ADM 53/120730 Log of HMS *Warspite* June 1944.
3. TNA ADM 179/504 Report of Proceedings Naval Commander Force S\ Appendix 1 Bombardment and Support.
4. Ibid.
5. TNA ADM 53/120730 Log of HMS *Warspite* June 1944; TNA ADM 179/504 Report of Proceedings Naval Commander Force S\Appendix 1 Bombardment and Support; and S.W. Roskill, *HMS* Warspite: *The Story of a Famous Battleship* (Futura, London, 1974), 278.
6. TNA ADM 179/504 Report of Proceedings Naval Commander Force S\ Appendix 1 Bombardment and Support.
7. Crosley, *They Gave Me a Seafire*, 118.

15. TNA WO 106/4316 Summary of Naval Report on Operation Neptune\9 The Build Up.
16. IWM Sound 11467 Whitehorn, Derek.
17. 'Ramsay Despatch', 5109, and Edwards, *Operation Neptune*, 96.
18. Edwards, *Operation Neptune*, 78–9.
19. Ibid., 80.
20. TNA ADM 179/507 Overlord Reports Not Appearing Elsewhere\5 Captain Southbound Sailings.
21. Hewitt, *Coastal Convoys*, 203.
22. 'Ramsay Despatch', 5117.
23. Edwards, *Operation Neptune*, 198.
24. BBC PW A2541601 Lowndes, Tony.
25. DDS 2005-1490-1499 Jarman LBF 310.
26. IWM Sound 18200 Maxted, Dennis.
27. Hore, 'The Logistics of Neptune', 246.
28. BBC PW A2372302 Gray, Louis.
29. BBC PW A2697230 Douglas, Frank.
30. IWM Sound 20332 Le Roy, René.
31. Naval Staff Battle Summary No. 39 Operation 'Neptune', 121–3.
32. https://library.columbia.edu/libraries/ccoh Interview 4076899 Kirk, Alan Goodrich, 342.
33. Yung, *Gators of Normandy*, 200–1.
34. TNA Beach and Ferry Groups.
35. IWM Sound 14147 Fifield, Leonard.
36. 'Ramsay Despatch', 5119.
37. BBC PW 4179341 Yates, Norman.
38. TNA DEFE 2/414 Report Naval Commander ETF Parts I–VI.
39. Bulkeley, *At Close Quarters*, 356.
40. Naval Staff Battle Summary No. 39 Operation 'Neptune', 123.
41. TNA DEFE 2/418 Force J Report\Enclosure 11 Reports of Proceedings\ NOIC Juno Beach Reports\G RNO Courselles & Bomb Disposal.
42. Ibid., and Naval Staff Battle Summary No. 39 Operation 'Neptune', 123.
43. Dr Frank A. Blazich Jr, 'D-Day's Magic Boxes: US Navy Pontoon Technology in Operation Overlord', unpublished paper delivered at the Normandy 75 Conference in Portsmouth, July 2019.
44. Eisenhower, *Report by the Supreme Commander*, 32.
45. Edwards, *Operation Neptune*, 204–5.
46. DDS H292-1995-1-5 Holladay, Blockship Empire Bunting.
47. NMRN UC 405/5359 The Story of the Mulberries, by Hickling, Rear-Admiral H, and MacKillop, Brigadier I L H, 2.
48. Naval Staff Battle Summary No. 39 Operation 'Neptune', Appendix A 61–3.
49. Moran Towing is still active today https://www.morantug.com/.
50. IWM Sound 10626 Barnes, Albert.
51. IWM Sound 13040 Bungard, Kenneth.
52. Ellis, Major L.F., CVO, CBE, DSI, C, with Warhurst, Lieutenant-Colonel, *Victory in the West Volume 1*, 264.
53. Naval Staff Battle Summary No. 39 Operation 'Neptune', 128, and J.F. Hutchings, 'The Story of Force Pluto', *The Naval Review*, vol. 34 no. 4 (November 1946), 324.

54. Naval Staff Battle Summary No. 39 Operation 'Neptune', 139.
55. BBC PW A2231281 Summers, Hendry.
56. TNA ADM 179/507 Overlord Reports Not Appearing Elsewhere\4 Captain Northbound Sailings. Captain McCourt was awarded the Distinguished Service Cross for his actions but sadly lost his life when the *Wallace Rose* was sunk in a collision in 1954. https://www.shipsnostalgia.com/threads/wallace-rose.35651/.
57. Ellsberg, *The Far Shore*, 279.
58. TNA DEFE 2/416 & 417 Naval Commander Force G Report\Appendix I Build Up Period, and Love and Major, *The Year of D-Day*, 93.
59. IWM Sound 35800 Male, Herbert.
60. Naval Staff Battle Summary No. 39 Operation 'Neptune', 139.
61. www.naval-history.net and www.cwgc.org/find-records/find-war-dead/casualty-details/2811467/brian-gofton-hutton-gee/.
62. IWM Sound 18803 Simpson, Eric.
63. IWM Sound 2219 Rogers, Albert.
64. BBC PW A2501010 Williams, John.
65. Naval Staff Battle Summary No. 39 Operation 'Neptune', 140.
66. Ellsberg, *The Far Shore*, 281.
67. IWM Sound 6827 White, Bruce.
68. IWM Sound 17642 Beckett, Alan.
69. Naval Staff Battle Summary No. 39 Operation 'Neptune', 141, and NMRN UC 405/5359 The Story of the Mulberries, by Hickling, Rear-Admiral H, and MacKillop, Brigadier I L H, 29.
70. Tony Booth, *Admiralty Salvage in Peace and War 1906–2006* (Pen & Sword Maritime, Barnsley, 2007), 133.
71. TNA ADM 179/507 Overlord Reports Not Appearing Elsewhere\10 HMS *Albatross*.
72. TNA ADM 1/29724 Salvage of SS Empire Lough in the English Channel 24.6.44.
73. TNA DEFE 2/416 & 417 Naval Commander Force G Report\Appendix I Build Up Period.
74. Naval Staff Battle Summary No. 39 Operation 'Neptune', 142 and Appendix H(3).
75. DDS 2005-219 Wilson LST 425. The file also contains the 4 August 1944 clipping from the *Evening Standard*.
76. Naval Staff Battle Summary No. 39 Operation 'Neptune', 11.

12 Guarding the Bay

1. *Fuehrer Conferences*, 34
2. Michael Salewski, *Die deutsche Seekriegsleitung 1935–1945, Band II, 1942–1945* (Bernard & Graefe Verlag, Munich, 1975), 424.
3. DDS 1995/100/81 Krancke Interview.
4. Dönitz, *Memoirs*, 422.
5. Paterson, *Hitler's Forgotten Flotillas*, 287–8.
6. See Dr Tim Benbow, 'The Contribution of Royal Navy Aircraft Carriers and the Fleet Air Arm to Operation "Overlord", 1944', *War in History*, vol. 26, no. 2 (2019), 265–86, for further detail on why aircraft carriers were not used in the Seine Bay.

7. V.E. Tarrant, *The Last Year of the Kriegsmarine May 1944–May 1945* (Arms & Armour Press, London, 1994), 60–1.
8. Dönitz, *Memoirs*, 422.
9. Herbert A. Werner, *Iron Coffins: A U-Boat Commander's War 1939–1945* (Cassell, London, 1999), 213–19.
10. TNA ADM 223/73 Channel Ultras 1944–45.
11. Blair, *Hitler's U-Boat War*, 582.
12. TNA ADM 219/138 Directorate of Naval Operational Studies Report No 56/44 Notes on Escort Group Ops in the Channel June 6th to July 10th, 1944.
13. Werner, *Iron Coffins*, 223.
14. NMRN, Neville, Marine H, LCF 32, in Records of LCG and LCF Association.
15. DDS H676/1990 Uridge.
16. Scott, *Battle of the Narrow Seas*, 193.
17. TNA ADM 199/1659 Reports on Operation Neptune. Miscellaneous Reports not Enclosed in Main Report\FDT 217 Report of Proceedings.
18. BBC PW A2501010 Williams, John.
19. J.G. Sharples, '*Emerald* on D-Day', letter *The Naval Review*, vol. 82, no. 3 (July 1984), 284.
20. Rudi Schmidt, *Achtung – Torpedos Los! Der Strategische und Operative Einsatz des Kampfgeschwader 26* (Bernard & Graefe Verlag, Koblenz, 1991), 194–5, 202.
21. TNA DEFE 2/414 Report Naval Commander ETF Part II Defence of the Assault Area.
22. See Cornelius Ryan, *The Longest Day* (New English Library, Sevenoaks, 1982), 206–8.
23. TNA DEFE 2/414 Report Naval Commander ETF Part II Defence of the Assault Area and Tarrant, *The Last Year of the Kriegsmarine*, 68.
24. TNA DEFE 2/414 Report Naval Commander ETF Part II Defence of the Assault Area.
25. Ibid.
26. O'Flaherty, *Naval Minewarfare*, 53.
27. See Hewitt, *Firing on Fortress Europe*, for a detailed account of life on the gunline aboard a bombarding warship.
28. Hans Von Luck, *Panzer Commander* (Frontline Books, London, 2013), 141–2, and Caddick-Adams, *Sand and Steel*, 777.
29. Quoted in Michael Reynolds, *Steel Inferno: 1st SS Panzer Corps in Normandy* (Spellmount, Staplehurst, 1997), 88.
30. Ibid., 113.
31. IWM Sound 18537 Neilson, Ian.
32. DDS 1995/100/79 Hoffman Interview.
33. TNA ADM 199/1659 Reports on Operation Neptune. Miscellaneous Reports not Enclosed in Main Report\Coastal Forces Reports of Proceedings.
34. Frank, *German S-Boats in Action*, 110, and http://www.s-boot.net/englisch/sboats-km-channel44.html.
35. Williams, *The US Navy at Normandy*, 300–2.
36. TNA ADM 179/509 Portsmouth Command Coastal Forces Operation Overlord/Appendix 1 Summaries of Action Reports.
37. See Captain Chris O'Flaherty, Royal Navy, *Crash Start: The Life and Legacy of Lieutenant Richard Guy Ormonde Hudson DSC Royal Naval Volunteer Reserve* (The Choir Press, Gloucester, 2019).

38. IWM Sound 21200 Barker, Tom.
39. IWM Sound 20094 Lester, George.
40. Ibid.
41. TNA ADM 179/509 Portsmouth Command Coastal Forces Operation Overlord/Appendix 1 Summaries of Action Reports and TNA ADM 358/4351 Sinking of LCT 875.
42. https://www.ibiblio.org/hyperwar/USN/ships/logs/DD/dd726-Knuepfer.html.
43. Ibid.
44. Williams, *The US Navy at Normandy*, 322–7.
45. IWM Sound 8739 Madden, Colin.
46. TNA DEFE 2/418 Force J Report\Enclosure 11 Reports of Proceedings\Group J1\HMS *Lawford* and https://www.naval-history.net/xDKCas1944-06JUN1.htm for casualties. Archaeological evidence gathered by Ministry of Defence damage assessment expert David Manley for the television series *Wreck Detectives* in 2008 proved that *Lawford* was probably sunk by a radio-controlled glider bomb dropped by a second aircraft some distance away.
47. TNA ADM 199/1659 Reports on Operation Neptune. Miscellaneous Reports not Enclosed in Main Report\Captain of Patrols ROP.
48. TNA ADM 179/504 Report of Proceedings Naval Commander Force S\1 The Narrative\Phase 3 Post Assault.
49. Blair, *Hitler's U-boat War*, 582–5.
50. Williams, *The US Navy at Normandy*, 333–41.
51. Quoted in BBC PW A2041804 Ward, Peter.
52. Douglas, Sarty and Whitby, *A Blue Water Navy*, 276–7.
53. Basil Jones, 'A Matter of Length and Breadth', in *The Naval Review* Volume 37 Number 2 (May 1950), 139.
54. Ibid.
55. Tarrant, *The Last Year of the Kriegsmarine*, 63.
56. Douglas, Sarty and Whitby, *A Blue Water Navy*, 278.
57. Tarrant, *The Last Year of the Kriegsmarine*, 65.
58. Jones, 'A Matter of Length and Breadth', 141.
59. Love and Major, *The Year of D-Day*, 85.
60. James Foster Tent, *The E-Boat Threat: Defending the Normandy Invasion Fleet* (Airlife, Shrewsbury, 1996), 135.
61. Williams, *The US Navy at Normandy*, 344.
62. Tent, *The E-Boat Threat*, 137.
63. Williams, *The US Navy at Normandy*, 357–66.
64. IWM Sound 10626 Barnes, Albert.
65. TNA ADM 199/1659 Reports on Operation Neptune/Miscellaneous Reports not Enclosed in Main Report\Coastal Forces Reports of Proceedings.
66. DDS H139-1999-1 Dearden, A W P.
67. Ibid.
68. Ibid.
69. TNA ADM 179/509 Coastal Forces D-Day\Appendix 1 Summaries of Action Reports.
70. http://www.rodericktimms.royalnavy.co.uk/flag_battleship.html.
71. IWM Sound 21200 Barker, Tom.
72. Blair, *Hitler's U-Boat War*, 582–3.

73. https://www.history.navy.mil/research/library/online-reading-room/title-list-alphabetically/g/gaf-invasion-normandy.html.
74. IWM Sound 29556 Haskell-Thomas, Brian.
75. TNA ADM 199/532 Reports of Proceedings 1943–44\ORP *Piorun* and HMS *Ashanti* Action with Enemy Minesweepers 14 June 1944.
76. Ibid.
77. Tent, *The E-Boat Threat*, 135.
78. Ibid., 143–55.
79. 'Ramsay Despatch', 5120.
80. Ruge, *Rommel in Normandy*, 189.
81. TNA ADM 219/153 Notes on Air Attacks on Le Havre and Boulogne.
82. Tent, *The E-boat Threat*, 196.
83. BBC PW A5386016 Popham, Sam.
84. TNA ADM 219/153 Notes on Air Attacks on Le Havre and Boulogne.
85. See Tent, *The E-Boat Threat*, for a forensic account of this raid, its context and consequences.
86. TNA ADM 199/1659 Reports on Operation Neptune. Miscellaneous Reports not Enclosed in Main Report\Coastal Forces Reports of Proceedings.

13 Battle for Cherbourg

1. Naval Staff Battle Summary No. 39 Operation 'Neptune', 149.
2. Roskill, *HMS Warspite*, 281.
3. IWM Sound 26526 Pickering, Eric.
4. TNA ADM 358/4359 Loss of HMS *Mourne* 15 June 1944.
5. TNA ADM 267/117 Damage Reports. Department of Naval Constructors\Blackwood.
6. Ibid.
7. Ibid.
8. Roskill, *The War at Sea 1939–1945 Volume 3, Part 2*, 58.
9. Richard Woodman, *Keepers of the Sea: The Story of the Trinity House Yachts and Tenders* (Chaffcutter Books, Ware, 2005), 152–3. *Juno* still exists, aground by the River Neath, at the time of writing.
10. TNA DEFE 2/420 Force S Reports\10 NOIC Sword.
11. Williams, *The US Navy at Normandy*.
12. https://www.cwgc.org/find-records/find-war-dead/casualty-details/2438685/charles-alfred-rickett/.
13. DDS 641/1999 Scales AB R T.
14. BBC PW A2688212, Taylor A A.
15. TNA ADM 267/117 Damage Reports. Department of Naval Constructors\La Surprise.
16. BBC PW A4022489 Wagstaffe, Sydney.
17. TNA DEFE 2/414 Report Naval Commander ETF Parts I-VI.
18. Naval Staff Battle Summary No. 39 Operation 'Neptune', 145.
19. Admiral of the Fleet Sir Philip Vian, *Action this Day: A War Memoir* (Frederick Muller, London, 1960), 150.
20. TNA ADM 199/1659 Reports on Operation Neptune. Miscellaneous Reports not Enclosed in Main Report\HMS *Scylla* Report of Proceedings.

21. https://uboat.net/allies/warships/ship/105.html.
22. TNA ADM 267/38 Damage Reports. Department of Naval Constructors\
    Swift.
23. IWM Sound 2173 Shrimpton, Bob, quoted in Hewitt, *Firing on Fortress
    Europe*, 149.
24. IWM Sound 28458 Rouse, Graham.
25. TNA ADM 267/38 Damage Reports. Department of Naval Constructors\
    Swift.
26. BBC PW A5386016 Popham, Sam, and TNA ADM 358/4364 Loss of MMS
    Number 8.
27. https://www.cwgc.org/find-records/find-war-dead/casualty-details/2219252/
    herbert-john-tredgett/.
28. DDS 97/12 The Sinking of the SS Derrycunihy T72/MTS.
29. Ibid.
30. DDS 97/12 The Sinking of the SS Derrycunihy T72/MTS, and Booth,
    Admiralty Salvage, 137.
31. TNA DEFE 2/414 Report Naval Commander ETF Parts I-VI and Naval
    Staff Battle Summary No. 39 Operation 'Neptune', 145.
32. Morison, *The Invasion of France and Germany*, 173.
33. Ibid.
34. IWM Sound 8739 Madden, Colin.
35. Edwards, *Operation Neptune*, 182.
36. BBC PW 7823775 Howarth, Eric.
37. Ibid.
38. All ground forces in Normandy remained under the command of Montgomery's
    21st Army Group until 1 September 1944, when Eisenhower assumed the
    overall command of Allied land forces.
39. Jacobsen and Rohwer, *Decisive Battles of World War Two*, 342.
40. Ellis, *Victory in the West*, 493, and Naval Staff Battle Summary No. 39 Operation
    'Neptune', Appendix H(3).
41. Showell, *German Naval Codebreakers*, 133.
42. Quoted in Naval Staff Battle Summary No. 39 Operation 'Neptune', 148.
43. Ellis, *Victory in the West Volume 1*, 287–8, and Speidel, *We Defended Normandy*,
    106.
44. Bradley, *A Soldier's Story*, 312.
45. Ibid.
46. TNA ADM 1/79464 Bombardment of Cherbourg Commander Support
    Force Operation Plan.
47. Ibid.
48. Ibid.
49. Bryant, 'Battleship Commander', in Stillwell, *Assault on Normandy*, 185.
50. TNA ADM 1/79464 Bombardment of Cherbourg Commander Support
    Force Operation Plan/Report of Proceedings 9th MS Flotilla.
51. Morison, *Invasion of France and Germany*, 198.
52. TNA ADM 1/79464 Bombardment of Cherbourg Commander Support
    Force Operation Plan/Report of Proceedings 9th MS Flotilla.
53. Ibid.
54. TNA ADM 1/29800 Awards for ML 141 at Cherbourg.
55. IWM Sound 9380 Lloyd-Davies, Felix.

56. Holman, *Stand by to Beach*, 189.
57. Morison, *Invasion of France and Germany*, 201.
58. Ibid., 202.
59. Irvin Airey, 'A Strange Place for a Marine', in Stillwell, *Assault on Normandy*, 191.
60. Bryant, 'Battleship Commander', in Stillwell, *Assault on Normandy*, 185.
61. Morison, *Invasion of France and Germany*, 208. *Laffey* went on to have an extraordinary combat record in the Pacific. The destroyer is still afloat today and open to the public as a museum ship at Patriot's Point, Charleston, South Carolina. Bryant's flagship *Texas* is also a museum ship, undergoing a multi-million dollar restoration in Galveston at the time of writing.
62. Morison, *Invasion of France and Germany*, 211.
63. Bryant, 'Battleship Commander', in Stillwell, *Assault on Normandy*, 186.
64. IWM Sound 9380 Lloyd-Davies, Felix. The US Navy was entirely 'dry' (alcohol free) in 1944.
65. Morison, *Invasion of France and Germany*, 211, and Chester Wilmot, *The Struggle for Europe* (The Reprint Society, London, 1956), 360.
66. Bulkeley, *At Close Quarters*, 357.
67. IWM Sound 17433 Lucke, Helmut.
68. Naval Staff Battle Summary No. 39 Operation 'Neptune', 152.
69. Roland G. Ruppenthal, *US Army in World War II European Theatre of Operations – Logistical Support of the Armies: Volume II September 1944 to May 1945* (Department of the Army, Washington, DC, 1959), 66.
70. Ibid., 67–9.
71. Morison, *Invasion of France and Germany*, 217.
72. IWM Sound 26848 Broomfield, Claude.
73. Maher, *A Passage to Sword Beach*, 147–8.
74. Granville and Kelly, *Inshore Heroes*, 255.
75. Ruppenthal, *US Army in World War II: Volume II*, 63.
76. Ibid., 78–88
77. Love and Major, *The Year of D-Day*, 96.
78. 'Ramsay Despatch', 5122.
79. https://uboat.net/boats/u1191.htm.
80. TNA ADM 267/117 Damage Reports. Department of Naval Constructors\Pink.
81. Scott, *The Battle of the Narrow Seas*, 198.
82. TNA ADM 199/1659 Reports on Operation Neptune. Miscellaneous Reports not Enclosed in Main Report\Coastal Forces Reports of Proceedings.
83. TNA ADM 199/532 Reports of Proceedings 1943–44\HMCS *Huron* and HMS *Eskimo* Action with Enemy Trawlers 27–28 June 1944.
84. Ibid., and Douglas, Sarty and Whitby, *A Blue Water Navy*, 300–1.
85. Blair, *Hitler's U-boat War*, 619.
86. BBC PW A2668647, Froggatt, Jim.
87. IWM Sound 19571 Fetherstone-Dilke, Charles.
88. Blair, *Hitler's U-boat War*, 586
89. *Lehrgeschwader* literally translates as Training Wing. *LG1* was roughly equivalent to an RAF Operational Training Unit.
90. Peter Taghon, *Die Geschichte des Lehrgeschwaders 1* (VDM Heinz Nickel, Zweibrücken, 2004), 350.

91. TNA ADM 179/509 Coastal Forces D-Day\Appendix 1 Summaries of Action Reports and http://www.s-boot.net/englisch/sboats-km-channel44.html.
92. Naval Staff Battle Summary No. 39 Operation 'Neptune', 152.
93. https://www.cwgc.org/find-records/find-war-dead/casualty-details/2367239/richard-beattie/.
94. Roskill, *The War at Sea 1939–1945 Volume 3, Part 2*, 127. The Reichsmarine became the Kriegsmarine in 1935, two years after the Nazis came to power.
95. TNA ADM 1/29742 Operation Dredger Action with German Forces 5–6 July 1944.

14 Last Resort

1. TNA ADM 223/594 German Secret Weapons off Anzio (*Neger*).
2. Dönitz, *Memoirs*, 369.
3. *Linsen* means lentils. *Neger* is an unpleasant racial epithet and was intended to be a pun on the craft's designer, Mohr, which translates as 'of Moorish ancestry'.
4. Lawrence Paterson, *Weapons of Desperation: German Frogmen and Midget Submarines of World War II* (Pen & Sword, Barnsley, 2018), 12, 16.
5. TNA ADM 223/594 German Secret Weapons off Anzio (*Neger*).
6. Paterson, *Weapons of Desperation*, 36–9.
7. http://www.southseasubaqua.org.uk/diving-projects/project-cato/497-project-cato-final-report.
8. Quoted in Paterson, *Weapons of Desperation*, 42.
9. TNA ADM 358/4371 Attack on HMS *Trollope* 6 July 1944.
10. Paterson, *Weapons of Desperation*, convincingly argues that Gerhold was responsible for *Trollope's* destruction, drawing on an interview held at Explosion Museum of Naval Firepower in Gosport.
11. TNA ADM 267/118 Department of Naval Constructors/HMS *Magic*, via Project Cato Final Report.
12. Ibid.
13. Ibid.
14. Ibid.
15. Quoted in Paterson, *Weapons of Desperation*, 42.
16. TNA HWI/3076 Ultra Decrypts Neger and the Orne Bridges. This doubtless made interesting reading for Winston Churchill when he was passed the intercepts on 15 July.
17. Roskill, *The War at Sea 1939–1945 Volume 3, Part 2*, 127.
18. https://www.combinedops.com.
19. TNA ADM 179/509 Coastal Forces D-Day\Appendix 1 Summaries of Action Reports and https://www.cwgc.org/find-records/find-war-dead/casualty-details/2438348/john-collins/.
20. Paterson, *Weapons of Desperation*, 44–5.
21. In British service *Dragon* was named after the fire-breathing monster, but the same word means 'Dragoon' in Polish.
22. TNA ADM 1/12348 Future Employment of HMS *Dragon*.
23. TNA ADM 267/76 Damage Reports Department of Naval Constructors\Dragon.

24. ADM 217/536 HMS *Pennywort* Report of Proceedings (Loss of *Dragon*).
25. TNA ADM 267/76 Damage Reports Department of Naval Constructors\ Dragon.
26. IWM Docs 20637 Brooke-Smith, Peter, quoted in Hewitt, *Firing on Fortress Europe*, 162.
27. Paterson, *Weapons of Desperation*, 44–5.
28. Edwards, *Operation Neptune*, 237.
29. IWM Sound 27251 Parker, Stan.
30. TNA ADM 267/117 Damage Reports. Department of Naval Constructors\ Pylades. At the time, *Pylades* was believed to have been mined, but in 2004 Ministry of Defence damage assessment expert David Manley established beyond doubt that the sweeper was torpedoed.
31. IWM Sound 27251 Parker, Stan.
32. BBC PW A3922175 Bailey, Fred.
33. IWM Sound 27251 Parker, Stan.
34. Roskill, *The War at Sea 1939–1945 Volume 3, Part 2*, 122.
35. Edwards, *Operation Neptune*, 234–5.
36. Ibid., 294.
37. TNA ADM 179/509 Coastal Forces D-Day\Appendix 1 Summaries of Action Reports. *MTB-416* was the renumbered *MGB-81*, which is still afloat in Portsmouth today. Beautifully restored, MGB-81 is owned and operated by Portsmouth Naval Base Property Trust.
38. Ibid.
39. IWM Sound 18774 Southerst, Herbert.
40. Ibid.
41. TNA ADM 267/38 Damage Reports. Department of Naval Constructors\ Isis.
42. Quoted in Paterson, *Weapons of Desperation*, 48–9.
43. Ibid., 48–9.
44. BBC PW A452021 Hasker, Leslie.
45. IWM Sound 17509 Cassidy, Geoffrey.
46. Roskill, *The War at Sea 1939–1945 Volume 3, Part 2*, 123, and Symonds, *Operation Neptune*, 350.
47. The 'red ball' was a marker identifying both trucks and routes as high priority; only trucks marked with the red ball could use red ball roads.
48. Love and Major, *The Year of Victory*, 110.
49. Roskill, *The War at Sea Volume 3, Part 2*, 121.
50. Quoted in Roskill, *HMS* Warspite, 282.
51. Wilson, 'A Short Life and a Merry One', 252.
52. TNA ADM 199/839 Operations by Naval Air Squadrons.
53. Ibid.
54. TNA ADM 199/839 Operations by Naval Air Squadrons\849 Squadron, https://www.naval-history.net/ and https://www.cwgc.org. I am very grateful to my former colleague Barbara Gilbert at the Fleet Air Arm Museum for identifying the pilot in this incident.
55. Frank, *German S-Boats in Action*, 117, http://www.s-boot.net/englisch/sboats-km-channel44.html; and http://www.convoyweb.org.uk/.
56. TNA ADM 179/509 Coastal Forces D-Day\Appendix 1 Summaries of Action Reports.

57. Ibid. and http://www.s-boot.net/englisch/sboats-km-channel44.html.
58. *Kriegstagebuch Marinegruppenkommando West* 01.01.1942 – 31.07.1944, *Bundesarchiv/Militärchiv* (BAMA) RM/35/II 52-64, quoted in Frank, *German S-Boats in Action*, 117.
59. Blair, *Hitler's U-boat War*, 605–6.
60. IWM Sound 25525, Hughes, Richard.
61. TNA ADM 199/261 Coastal Forces Actions\Convoy FTM 53 E-boat Attack 30–31 July 1944.
62. TNA ADM 199/2147 Merchant Navy Survivors' Reports 1 January 1944–31 December 1944, 219, 221.
63. Ibid., 221.
64. Ibid., 226–8.
65. IWM Sound 14147 Fifield, Leonard.
66. TNA ADM 199/2147 Merchant Navy Survivors' Reports 1 January 1944 – 31 December 1944, 222–3.
67. BBC PW A4414420 Abrahams, John.
68. TNA ADM 199/261 Coastal Forces Actions\Convoy FTM 53 E-boat Attack 30–31 July 1944.
69. http://www.s-boot.net/englisch/sboats-km-channel44.html.
70. Morison, *The Invasion of France and Germany*, 298–9, and Walsh, 'The Capture of Cherbourg', in Stillwell, *Assault on Normandy*, 201.
71. Walsh, 'The Capture of Cherbourg', in Stillwell, *Assault on Normandy*, 201.
72. Paterson, *Weapons of Desperation*, 50.
73. http://www.s-boot.net/englisch/sboats-km-channel44.html.
74. Granville and Kelly, *Inshore Heroes*, 253.
75. Paterson, *Weapons of Desperation*, 52.
76. TNA ADM 267/38 Damage Reports. Department of Naval Constructors\Quorn.
77. Ibid.
78. TNA ADM 1-29770 Decorations following loss of HMS *Quorn*.
79. TNA ADM 267/38 Damage Reports. Department of Naval Constructors\Quorn.
80. https://uboat.net/allies/warships/ship/4628.html.
81. BBC PW 4040245 Cockburn, William.
82. BBC PW A3504953 Rouse, Graham.
83. TNA ADM 199/2147 Merchant Navy Survivors' Reports 1 January 1944–31 December 1944, 236–7.

15 On to Le Havre

1. Eisenhower, *Report by the Supreme Commander*, 65.
2. Ibid., 66, and Ellis, *Victory in the West Volume 1*, map facing 386.
3. TNA ADM 199/1462 Sinking of U-671, quoted in Hewitt, *Coastal Convoys*, 211.
4. Roskill, *The War at Sea Volume 3, Part 2*, 130.
5. Ibid., 302.
6. Eisenhower, *Report by the Supreme Commander*, 54.
7. BBC PW A4368639 Manning, Patrick.

Conclusion

1. Love and Major, *The Year of D-Day*, 114.
2. BBC PW A2524402 Thomas, Ginger.
3. Naval Battle Summary No. 39 Operation 'Neptune', 132.
4. https://www.britishnormandymemorial.org/roll-of-honour/.
5. Williams, *The US Navy at Normandy*, 401.

Bibliography

ADM 1/12348 Future Employment of HMS *Dragon*

ADM 1/12488 Operation Tunnel 22–23 October 1943

ADM 1/13716 Coastal Forces Action on Night of 24/25 October 1943 Action Report

ADM 1/1572 HMS *Wensleydale* Actions with E-boats 10 June and 12–16 June 1944

ADM 1/15991 Actions Against E-Boats 13/14 May 1944: FS *LA COMBATTANTE* MTBs 680, 608

ADM 1/15991 FS *La Combattante* Action vs E-boats 12–13 May 1944

ADM 1/16493 'Walterboote': Small German High Speed Submarine.

ADM 1/16836 Captured German Midget Submarine *Biber* – Technical Evaluation

ADM 1/17110 Oyster Mines Trials Run on MTBs

ADM 1/29389 Awards to Officers and Men of HMS *Whitshed* Convoy Protection

ADM 1/29416 Operation 'Stonewall'. Interception of Blockade Runners. Services of HMS *Glasgow* and *Enterprise* December 1943.

ADM 1/29617 Award HMS *Quorn* action with E-boats May 1944

ADM 1/29724 Salvage of SS *Empire Lough* in the English Channel 24.6.44

ADM 1/29742 Operation Dredger Action with German Forces 5–6 July 1944

ADM 1/29770 Decorations following loss of HMS *Quorn*

ADM 1/29800 Awards for *ML-141* at Cherbourg

ADM 1/29878 Sinking of *U-741* by HMS *Orchis*

ADM 1/29885 Sinking of *U-678* 9 July 1944

ADM 1/29955 HMS *Stayner* and MTBs *724* and *738*. Destruction of 3 x E-boats 18–19 Sept 1944

ADM 1/29982 Awards for Mining of HMS *Albatross*

BIBLIOGRAPHY

ADM 1/79464 Bombardment of Cherbourg Commander Support Force Operation Plan
ADM 116/511 Bombardment of Heavily Defended Coasts
ADM 179/415 Overlord Report Admiral Superintendent Portsmouth
ADM 179/427 Overlord Report HMS *Vectis*
ADM 179/429 Overlord Report NOIC IoW
ADM 179/430 Overlord Report FOIC Southampton
ADM 179/431 Overlord Report FOIC Portland
ADM 179-455 Instructions for Escort of Overlord Convoys
ADM 179/482 Operations Frog and Deer
ADM 179/504 Report of Proceedings Naval Commander Force S
ADM 179/505 Report of Proceedings Naval Commander Force G
ADM 179/507 Overlord Reports Not Appearing Elsewhere
ADM 179/508 Overlord LCT Bases
ADM 179/509 Portsmouth Command Coastal Forces Operation Overlord
ADM 179/511 Overlord Reports Southampton.
ADM 179/518 Gilkicker Comms Report
ADM 179/524 C-in-C Portsmouth Overlord Narrative and Reports
ADM 186/809 POW Interrogation Reports 1944
ADM 189/147 German Oyster Mine Docket No 7 1944
ADM 199/1556 Admiralty War History Cases and Papers Operation Neptune
ADM 199/261 Coastal Forces Actions
ADM 199/263 Coastal Actions with Enemy Destroyers and Light Forces
ADM 199/349 Far East and Channel Convoy Reports
ADM 199/532 Reports of Proceedings 1943–1944
ADM 199/839 Operations by Naval Air Squadrons
ADM 199/1036 Coastal Forces Actions in the English Channel
ADM 199/1462 Sinking of *U-671*
ADM 199/1556 Admiralty War History Cases and Papers Operation Neptune
ADM 199/1659 Reports on Operation Neptune. Miscellaneous Reports not Enclosed in Main Report
ADM 199/2147 Merchant Navy Survivors' Reports 1 January 1944–31 December 1944
ADM 202/449 Landing Craft Reports Overlord
ADM 217/536 HMS *Pennywort* Report of Proceedings (Loss of *Dragon*)
ADM 219/88 Reports Blockade Runners and Interceptions
ADM 219/138 Directorate of Naval Operational Studies Report No 56/44 Notes on Escort Group Ops in the Channel June 6th to July 10th, 1944
ADM 219/143 Operational Implications of the German Oyster Mines
ADM 219/153 Notes on Air Attacks on Le Havre and Boulogne
ADM 219/211 E-Boat Attacks on Coastal Convoys: Comparison with Possible Threat from Walter Boat
ADM 223/4 Admiralty Intelligence Reports and Papers
ADM 223/6 Command of Kriegsmarine Small Battle Units
ADM 223/73 Channel Ultras 1944–45
ADM 223/162 Weekly Intelligence Reports 213–225 1944
ADM 223/163 Weekly Intelligence Reports 226–238 1944
ADM 223/438 Allied Invasion German Movements and Intentions 1942–1944
ADM 223/449 Allied Invasion German Reactions 1944

ADM 223/583 Human Torpedoes (Italian)

ADM 223/594 German Secret Weapons off Anzio

ADM 223/703 Problems and Tasks Confronting the Directors of German Naval Warfare

ADM 226/50 Reports Issued under supervision of R W L Gawn. Unit X and Oyster

ADM 230/44 Firefighting Arrangements during Operation Overlord

ADM 243/14 Minelaying in European waters. Operation Pasture 15 August–3 September 1944

ADM 267/76 Damage Reports: Bomb, Mine and Torpedo Volume 19

ADM 267/77 Damage Reports: Bomb, Mine and Torpedo Volume 20

ADM 267/95 Damage Reports: Bomb, Mine and Torpedo Volume 38

ADM 267/117 Damage Reports: Bomb, Mine and Torpedo Volume 60

ADM 267/118 Damage Reports: Bomb, Mine and Torpedo Volume 61

ADM 267/133 Damage Reports: Bomb, Mine and Torpedo Volume 76

ADM 280/920 Delta Sweeps (Countermeasures Against Oyster Mines)

ADM 358/3010 Loss of Hospital Ship *Amsterdam* 07.08.44

ADM 358/2666 Sinking of *LBV-42*

ADM 358/4301 Loss of *MTB-700* December 1943

ADM 358/4329 MTBs *602, 608* and *614* Action 29.3.44

ADM 358/4333 Loss of HMS *Wallasea* 6 January 1944

ADM 358/4335 MTBs *671, 632, 617* Action 24 April 1944

ADM 358/4351 Sinking of *LCT-875*

ADM 358/4341 *MTB-732* (Sunk by *La Combattante*)

ADM 358/4359 Loss of HMS *Mourne* 15 June 1944

ADM 358/4364 Loss of MMS Number 8

ADM 358/4371 Attack on HMS *Trollope* 6 July 1944

ADM 358/4364 Loss of MMS Number 8

ADM 358/4391 Attack on HMS *Melbreak* 28 August 1944

ADM 53/119404 Log of HMS *Erebus* June 1944

ADM 53/120730 Log of HMS *Warspite* June 1944

DEFE 2/414 Report Naval Commander Eastern Naval Task Force Parts I–VI

DEFE 2/416 and 417 Naval Commander Force G Report

DEFE 2/418 Naval Commander Force J Report

DEFE 2/419 and 2/420 Naval Commander Force S Report

HWI/3076 Ultra Decrypts Neger and the Orne Bridges.

WO 106/4316 Summary of Naval Report on Operation Neptune

D-Day Story Collection

167/1990 Neptune Monograph Prepared by Commander Task Force 122

1990/10/1–8 Convoy ETC37 Sailing Orders

1995/100/29 Long. USS *Amesbury*

1995/100/42 Paul. *LST-983*

1995/100/79 Hoffmann. Kriegsmarine

1995/100/81 Krancke. Kriegsmarine

2001/181–199 Longley. *LCF-1*

2005/219 Wilson *LST-425*

2010/2019 *LST-522*

2013/19 Broomhead. HMS *Gorgon*
2016/433/11 *LST-323*
272/1992. Crooks. *LST-529*
402/1997 DD97/41 Albert. Royal Canadian Navy
641/1999 Scales. HMS *Talybont*
642/1996 Ellison. US Steam Tug 761
DD2000/3a Williams. WRNS
DD2005/105 Marlow. *MTB-630*
DD2005/108 2005/1490-1499 Jarman. *LBF-310*
DD2006/1991/1 2006/1701 Barker. HMS *Argonaut*
DD96/52 130/1996 Human Torpedoes (Extract)
DD97/12 SS *Derrycunihy*
DD97/34 389/1991 Hornsby. High Speed Launch
H108/1991-2 *LCT-513*
H133/1991 McCormack. *ML-204*
H139/1999/1 Dearden. SS *Lucy Stone*
H194/1986/9 Neptune Bombardment and Fire Support Plan
H26/1994 Stevenson. HMS *Argonaut*
H295/1995/1-5 Holladay. Blockship *Empire Bunting*
H303/1988 Cutler HMS *Largs*
H492/1989/19 Little
H544/1990 Wildman. HMS *Largs*
H661/1990 Brunning. *X20*
H662/1990 Burnley. RN Kite Balloons
H666/1990 Cowey. HMS *Dryad* and COSSAC
H676/1990 Uridge. SS *Thysville*
H690/1990 Brooks. HMS *Largs*
H87/1995/1 Holmes. HMS *Venus*
H9.1985.4 HMS *Warspite* Bombardment
No reference. Clarke. Portsmouth Dockyard General Order

National Museum of the Royal Navy

CRTY 2019/59/24 Reports on Operation Neptune/Admiralty Docket – Summary
   of the Lessons Learned During Operation Neptune
MM 1975/354 Operation Order, Operation Neptune, Assault Group J2, Captain
   R J O Otway-Ruthven RN
N/N Royal Marines Museum: Papers of the LCG&F Association
RMM 1986/2005a Adams: RM Landing Craft Coxswain
RNM 02/56/1 Winterton, Commander D W
RNM 1990/86/5 Copy memorandum dated office of the Flag Officer
   Commanding, Dover 4.6.1944 addressed by Vice-Admiral H. Pridham Wippell
   to all ships companies at Dover
RNM 1990/86/6*1 and 2 Two Naval signals sent by Vice-Admiral H. Pridham
   Wippell Flag Officer commanding, Dover on 6.6.1944
RNM 2004/11 A collection of papers relating to the service of Lieutenant-
   Commander Arthur Bradfield RNR as Commanding Officer of HMS *St Helier*
RNM 2014.8/10. Brooker, William. HMS *Nelson*

RNM 2014/26 Bound volume about Operation Neptune entitled 'Naval Operations Orders 1-22'. Memorandum No. X/0927/30. Copy No.160

RNSM A1944/19 Notes dated February 1944 on towing X-craft and transferring X-craft crews at sea

RNSM A1977/93 Personal memorabilia of Admiral Sir W J W Woods, HMS *Centurion*

RNSM A1994/066 U-boats sunk in D-Day build-up. Article from Shipping periodical, May 1994

RNSM A1995/215 Midget Submarines on D-Day

UC 405/5359 The Story of the Mulberries, by Hickling, Rear-Admiral H, and MacKillop, Brigadier I L H

BBC People's War Archive https://www.bbc.co.uk/history/ ww2peopleswar/

Abrams, John. SS *Fort Kaskaskia*. A4414420
Anonymous. RN Beach Signals Unit. A3375209
Anonymous. HMS *Windsor*. A2705717
Anonymous. *LCT-883*. A4095678
Arnison, Jim. HMS *Argonaut*. A2478431
Attwood, Frank. HMS *Glenroy*. A2692884
Bailey, Fred. HMS *Pylades*. A3922175
Bailey, Syd. Combined Operations. A4888966
Baker, Jim. Royal Marines. A3918233
Bee, Ronald. *MGB-326*. A4398861
Blyth, Dick. *LCG(L)-1*. A4326699
Boot, Alan. HMS *Burdock*. A2773668
Boothroyd, Margaret. WRNS. A2939646
Brown, Rhoda. WRNS. A2522251
Buck, Ray. SS *Empire Capulet*. A2166293
Burkett, Clifford. RAF High Speed Launches. A3406808
Cartwright, Kathleen. WRNS. A2843840
Chaffer, Dennis. *LCF-34*. A2843912
Clarke, George. MV *Sagacity*. A5675538
Clarke, Roland. *MGB-67*. A2945621
Cockburn, William. *LCG(L)-764* A4040245 A4045952
Cooper, Richard. *MMS-44*. A2593019
Corney, Leslie. HMS *Speedwell*. A2748855
Criddle, George. HMS *Britomart*. A4137293
Croft, Peter. HMS *Gozo*. A8763159
Crowe, Marjorie. WRNS. A2358993
Currie, Daniel. HMS *Swift*. A4578537
Dale, Joan. WRNS. A2734157
Doré, John. Tug *King's Cross*. A2710540
Douglas, Frank. *LBK-1*. A2697230
Dove, John. RN Deception. A2213902
East, Len. HMS *Salamander*. A4511107
Eastmead, Norman. RAF High Speed Launch. A5717810
Emery, John. HMS *Largs*. A4022902
Ensor, Geoff. SS *Cap Tourane*. A2496477

Farram, Herbert. *LCI(L)-241*. A2047682
Farrar, Harry. *LCT-941*. A2638604
Field, D. HMS *Eglinton*. A2673948
Flowers, Freda. WRNS. A6439034
French, Mick. HMS *Ramilles*. A7535892
Friday, Leslie. HMS *Gazelle*. A2665406
Froggatt, Jim. HMS *Maid of Orleans*. A2668647
Gaskin, John. RN Landing Craft. A7920029
Gibbs, William. SS *Fort Biloxi*. A5803355
Goodwin, Lewis. HMS Largs. A7360995 and A2225378
Gordon, Ian. HMS *Lawford*. A4524941
Goss, Peter. RN LST. A4427750, A4427778 A4427156
Goulding, Peter. HMS *Plucky*. A1104788
Gray, Louis. *HDML-1383*. A2372302
Green, Jimmy. HMS *Empire Javelin* and LCAs. A1929468
Griffiths, Morgan. HMS *Vidette*. A5342348
Grudgings, Peter. LCT(R) A8565492
Hall, Geoffrey. Mulberry Harbour. A8249385
Hamilton, Ian. HMS *Rodney*. A4131929
Harmer, Doug *LCT(R)-436*. A2106686
Harrison, Roger. RN LCT. A2068805
Hasker, Leslie. HMS *Chamois*. A4250521
Heath, Jack. *LCT-522*. A4371059
Hill, Arthur. *LCVP-1028*. A2044847 A2044838 A2549243 A2044883
Hill, Thomas. SS *Empire Battleaxe*. A7414832
Hook, Stan. RN LCT. A1140751
Horton, Elsie. WRNS. A2366138
Hough, Stan. HMS *Prinses Astrid*. A1979067 A2667215
Howarth, Eric. HMS *Eskimo*. A7823775 A7823261
Howorth, Ashworth. SS *Empire Arquebus*. A2693153
Humphries, Margueritte. WRNS. A8174018 A8174180
Hutchinson, Cyril. *LBV-43*. A4599066 A4599057
Hutton, Reg. *LCT-651*. A2084582
Isaacs, Len. LCT. A2734085
Jackson, Thomas. HMS *Jason*. A2669196
Kay, Tom. DEMS Gunner. A2048753
King, Harry. *LCF-30*. A2626346
Kirby, Edward. RN Landing Craft. A2720233
Kirkby, George. HMS *Prinses Astrid*. A2649765
Lamming, Ronald. HMS *Orestes*. A5262374
Lea, Alfred. HMS *Neave*. A4248380
Lemon, Harry. RN LCI(L) A2665406
Leonard, Alfred. SS HMS *Cricketer*. A4023181
Lomax, Jack. HMS *Grey Shark*. A6674105
Lowndes, Tony. 802 LCV(P) Flotilla. A2541601
Lutman, Ken. HMS *Lawford*. A4865556
Manning, Patrick. SS *Amsterdam*. A4368639
Martin, Kay. WRNS. A2872811
Mayes, John. RN LBV Flotilla. A2127791

Mead, Alfred. *LCT-1074*. A152926
Mercer, Victor. *MMS-247*. A4347029
Miles, Bill. HMS *Prinses Margaret* LSI(H) and LCA. A2724879
Milton, Frank. 700LCP(L) Flotilla. A7015925
Morgan, John. RN LCM. A2707544
Moseley, Ernie. HMS *Wensleydale*. A6982464 A6982617
Moxey, Jack. *ML-269*. A4053944
Neal, Leslie. RN ML. A8483952
Newman, Dennis. *LCI(S)-536*. A3230010
Nutter, Thomas. HMS *Belfast*. A4024441
O'Sullivan. HMS *Lawford*. A6054734
Oakley, Ken. RN Beach Commando. A2654156
Parker, Raymond. HMS *Enterprise*. A5366441
Parker, Stan. HMS *Pylades*. A5183525
Pateman, William. RN LCF. A4401866
Pearce, Frank. *Motor Fire Vessel 79*. A2660122
Perkins, Dorothy. WRNS. A4060333
Phippen, Bob. HMS *Empire Halberd*. A4659249 A4659401 A4659500
Pine, Winifred. WRNS. A2621837
Plater, HMS *Prinses Astrid*. A1979067
Polglaze, Charles, HMS *Aristocrat*. A2717075
Popham, Sam. HMS *Recruit*. A5385800 A5386016
Quirk, Neville. HM Drifter. A5560913
Ramus, Alfred. HMS *Cockatrice*. A2730728
Rank, Edmund. HMS *Qualicum*. A6649275
Reeve, John. RN HDML. A4519271
Richardson, Robert. *LBO-36*. A2323324
Rogers, Ivy. WRNS. A7217976
Rouse, Graham. *ML-197*. A3504953
Rushton, John. RN LCT. A2806698
Russell, John. 15th MSF. A7015358
Sales, Aubrey. *Southampton Salvor*. A5720186
Sanders, Rena. WRNS. A3187235
Scarr, Desmond. SS *Derrycunihy*/43rd Reconnaissance Regiment. A5847393
Scott-Douglas, H. HMS *Ekins*. A1318079 A1092287
Scrivener, Frank. HMS *Prinses Astrid*. A1979067
Slater, Edward. HMS *Thornbrough*. A7435604
Small, Dennis. RN LCM. A8532100
Smart, Richard. HMS *Chamois*. A2866151
Smith, Sydney. *LCG-11*. A2682254
Smith, William. *ML-303*. A356558
Spencer, Dennis. HMS *Warspite*. A4523708
Sprigg, Leslie. *MTB-695* A3563444
Stockton, J. HMS *Prinses Astrid*. A1979067
Stonebridge, W. HMS *Stevenstone*. A3509381
Stott, George. RN LCA. A6676167
Summers, John and Hendry. MV *Dawlish*. A2231281
Sutcliffe, Malcolm. Royal Navy. A3672713
Tandy, George. LCA 786 and 539 Assault Flotilla. A2844272

Taylor, A.A. ML 292. A2688212 A2682010
Taylor, Noel. RN Commandos. A8190173
Thomas, Ginger. WRNS. A2524402
Thompson, James. Rosedown and Thompsons (Civilian). A7626134
Titley, Sam. LST. A3545868
Turner, Frederick. 556th LCA Flotilla. A5018032
Van Damme, Robert. SS *Julia*. A2640647
Viewing, Gerry. HMS *Wrestler*. A3886734
Vincent, Paddy. HMS *Duke of York*. A4477737
Wagstaffe, Sydney. HMS *Fury*. A4022489
Walker, Peter. HMS *Bellona*. A2363267
Wallace, Em. WRNS. A2513305
Ward, Bert. HMT *St Martin*. A2876457 A4455984
Ward, Joseph. HMS *Pique*. A8809879
Ward, Peter. HMS *Beagle*. A2041804 A2041282
Watts, R.G. *LCT-2455*. A2096723
Wightman, Edward. HMS *Ramilles* A1070155 A1125000 A1070074 A1074377
   A1077680
Wilkinson, Colin. HMS *Narborough*. A2865008
Williams, C.A. HMS *Chamois*. A2359451
Williams, Eddie. HMS *Empire Halberd* and *LCA-602*. A2431397
Williams, John. HMS *Diadem*. A2501010
Wilson, George. SS *Cameronia*. A2635643
Woodley, George. HMS *Dryad*. A7305103
Wright, Norman. RN Shore Party. A2731051
Yates, Norman. Admiralty Pilot. A4179341
Yeatman, Jack. HMT *Pearl*. A2023291

Imperial War Museum

IWM Documents 2823 Private Papers of Captain J.R. Gower, DSC, RN
IWM Documents 20637 Brooke-Smith, Peter

IWM SOUND ARCHIVE

Adams, Eric. HMS *Whitaker*. 24572
Adcock, Alan. Royal Engineers and Mulberry Harbour. 14141
Aisher, Owen. *MTB-758*. 10814
Alexander, Robert. HMS *Enterprise*. 21647
Ashcroft, Gerald. *LCT-517*. 10086
Banks, Cyril. HMS *Ready*. 34094
Barker, John, HMS *Arethusa*. 11888
Barker, Tom. HMS *Duff*. 21200
Barlow, John. Southwick House. 11732
Barney, Stephen. HMS *Urania*. 32870
Barnes, Albert. HMT *Storm King*. 10626
Bartlett, Thomas. HMS *Bulolo*. 27181
Bayly, Patrick. HMS *Mauritius*. 12590
Beasley, Eric. HMS *Limbourne*. 11255
Beckett, Alan. Royal Marines and Mulberry Harbour. 17642

BIBLIOGRAPHY

Bell, George. HMS *Domett*. 21137
Bell, Henry. *LST-320*. 16406
Benbow, Hilaire. HMS *Vigilant*. 25199
Bennett, Albert. HMS *Blankney*. 26845
Bennett, Joseph. HMS *Keppel*. 12413
Berryman, 'Dick'. Naval Gunfire Observer. 20579
Bird, Peter. *LBV-45*. 18684
Bone, John. *MTB-777*. 12400
Brazier, Len. HMS *Louis*. 26610
Brend, Raymond. *LST-319*. 18622
Bridge, John. Naval Party 1500. 15560
Briggs, Keith. Royal Marines LCOCU. 16696
Briggs, Ted. HMS *Hilary*. 10751
Broomfield, Claude. HMS *Spragge*. 26848
Bungard, Kenneth. Royal Navy and Mulberry Harbour. 13040
Burnett, Francis. *LSI-518*. 21014
Burnett, Roy. HMS *Salamander*. 25433
Byrne, Tom. HMS *Lennox*. 20334
Capon, John. HMS *Obedient*. 30008
Carlill, John. HMS *Mauritius*. 34427
Checketts, Harold. RN and Southwick House. 32390
Clark, Eric. HMS *Gorgon*. 31298
Coaker, Reginald. HMS *Urania*. 17117
Cockram, Tommy. HMS *Duff*. 25041
Cole, Jack. HMS *Sweetbriar*. 20277
Cowley, Horace. HMS *Queen Emma*. 22134
Craig, James, HMS *Jervis*. 27727
Cross, Stanley. *MTB-666*. 17235
Curtis, Rupert. Convoy S9. 22489
Czieselsky, Heinz. Kriegsmarine. 20517
D'Arcy, Michael. HMS *Gore*. 24573
Dick, Charles. HMS *Bentley*. 25275
Dosch, Theron. US *LST-345*. 11331
Dowell, Howard. *LCF-32*. 18576
Downing, Alexander. *ML-202*. 10936
Dreyer, Christoper. Coastal Forces Staff. 8984
Dye, Ralph. 3 Bombardment Unit, Royal Artillery. 20064
Farmer, Harold. *LST-164*. 20500
Fetherstone-Dilke, Charles. HMS *Hotham*. 19571
Fifield, Leonard. SS *Ocean Volga*. 14147
Fisher, James, HMS *Bellona*. 30137
Fitzgerald, HMS *Black Prince*. 10804
Franklin, Bill. HMS *Nelson*. 27052
Franklin, Maurice. 98th LAA Regiment, Royal Artillery. 27797
Freeman, John. SS *Fort Norman*. 34104
Fry, William. *LST-409*. 18579
Godwin, Patrick. HMS *Fitzroy*. 23324
Goetsch, Klaus. Kriegsmarine Kleinekampfverbände. 12591
Gostling, William. *ML-206*. 33323

BIBLIOGRAPHY

Greet, Geoffrey. Naval Beach Section. 33206
Gritten, John. Admiralty Correspondent. 21560
Gueritz, Teddy. Acting Beachmaster, Fox Beach Group. 17394
Hall, Alice. Welder, Hawthorn Leslie. 20156
Hamilton, Kenneth. HMS *Dacres*. 15240
Hamilton, Malcom. 617 Squadron RAF. 18264
Hammond, Ernie. HMS *Jason*. 19103
Hampden, John. LC(S). 35799
Harris, Raymond. 476 Assault Flotilla. 13268
Haskell-Thomas, Brian. HMS *Magpie*. 29556
Hays, Frank, 21649
Heathfield-Robinson, Douglas. RASC DUKW driver. 28197
Heron, Reginald. LCG Flotilla. 22835
Hill, Richard. *LCS(M)-117* and 524 Assault Flotilla. 20117
Hilse, Rolf. Kriegsmarine *U-740*. 26952
Hitchcock, Don. HMS *Narborough*. 23345
Honour, George. HMS *X-23*. 9709
Hook, Sydney. *LST-403*. 18547
Howard, William. HMS *Bellona*. 30014
Howe, Bernard. *MTB-739*. 26950
Howe, Kenneth. FFS *Georges Leygues*. 13097
Howell, Peter. HMS *Poole*. 34101
Hughes, Richard. HMS *Prince Leopold*. 25525
Humphries, George. *LCT-523*. 33568
Hunter, Don. SS *Empire Pickwick*. 34098
Hutchinson, Frederick. HMS *Warspite*. 10888
Irwin, Hugh. 591 LCA(HR) Flotilla. 9956
Jarman, William. *LBE-49*. 18627
Jesse, Ron. HMS *Belfast*. 25186
Jewett, Frederick. HMS *Vigilant*. 22614
Johnson, Harry. HMS *Bulolo*. 14256
Keen, George. HMS *Hotspur*. 28887
Lane, Ray. HMS *Seymour*. 27050
Langford, Frederick 'Sam'. RN Shore Party. 14143
Le Roy, René. LCOCU 5. 20332
Lennox-Hamilton, Malcolm. 617 Squadron RAF. 18624
Lester, George. HMS *Kingsmill*. 20094
Lines, Eric. *LCT(R)-447*. 26843
Lloyd-Davies, Felix. HMS *Glasgow*. 9380
Longhurst, Victor 'Vic'. 103 LCT Flotilla. 21656
Lowndes, Tony. 802 LCVP Flotilla. 28680
Lücke, Helmut. Kriegsmarine Hafenschutzflotilla. 17433
Luff, Frank. HMS *Hilary*. 27267
Luff, Jim. HMS *Gore*. 24195
Lunn, Robert. RASC DUKW Driver. 27730
McMillan, John, Gold Beach Group. 22616
Madden, Colin Duncan. HMS *Lawford*. 8739
Male, Herbert 'Bertie'. *LCT-628*. 35800
Marker, Sid. HMS *Cubitt*. 26621

BIBLIOGRAPHY

Maxted, Dennis. *LBV-327*. 18200
Michell, Richard. HMS *Sidmouth*. 33902
Miller, Alan. HMS *Erebus*. 21558
Mills, Charles. Southwick House. 11767
Morrow, Albert. *MTB-672*. 13650
Muggleton, Charles. 3rd LBV Flotilla. 33059
Neilson, Ian. Royal Artillery Air Observation Post. 18537
Nichol, Paulina. WRNS. 23180
Nicolson, David. RN Beach Repair Party. 12074
Noble, Ernest. HMS *Gazelle*. 21967
Oakley, Ken. Fox RN Beach Commando. 17294
Painter, Gordon. HMS *Belfast*. 26747
Parker, Stan. HMS Pylades. 27251
Perks, Leslie William 'Bill'. HMS *Walker*. 34087
Perry, Leslie. Suffolk Regiment. 20009
Pickering, Eric. HMS *Aylmer*. 26526
Pitman, Albert. HMS *Glasgow*. 22147
Plummer, Derek. HMS *Impulsive*. 25054
Raven-Hill, Lucien 'Tod'. *LCG-18*. 30095
Repard, David. HMS *Byron*. 22161
Reynolds, Don. HMS *Virago*. 27243
Rickman, Eric 'Ricky'. 854 Squadron, Fleet Air Arm. 28735
Rogers, Albert. *LBV(M)-121*. 22195
Rouse, Graham. *ML-197*. 28458
Rush, Bernard. 7th LBV Flotilla. 32113
Rushworth-Lund, Anthony. 841 Squadron, Fleet Air Arm. 14771
Schram, Gunther. Kriegsmarine Coast Artillery. 13582
Seeley, Margaret. WRNS. 11737
Shrimpton, Bob. HMS *Belfast*. 2173
Simpson, Charles. HMS *Belfast*. 24907
Simpson, Eric. 9th LBV Flotilla. 18803
Sivelle, Henry. *LCI(L)-169*. 178389
Southerst, Herbert. HMS *Cam*. 18774
Sutton, Thomas. *LCT-2233*. 14217
Swainson, Anthony. LCT(R). 27177
Tarbitt, John. 519th Assault Flotilla. 28767
Taylor, Sidney. HMS *Seagull*. 19532
Thomas, George. HMS *Rodney*. 15110
Thompson, Peter. *LST-304*. 12935
Till, Dennis. *LCT-1094*. 27071
Turner, Wilfred. RN Landing Barges. 24711
Walsh, Ronald. HMS *Kingsmill*. 27308
Walter, Arthur. Director of Ports and Inland Waterways, 21st Army Group. 12555
Walters, Arthur. *LCT-627*. 32959
Watkins, Dennis. HMS *Retalick*. 21575
Wellman, Derek. HMS *Onslow*. 12734
White, Bruce. Director of Ports and Inland Water Transport, War Office. 6827
Whitehorn, Derek. Fort Southwick. 11467
Wright, Jack. RN LCT. 26978

BIBLIOGRAPHY

Official Despatch Submitted to the Supreme Commander, Allied Expeditionary Force, on the 16th October 1944, in Supplement to the *London Gazette* of Tuesday, the 28th of October 1947'.

Roskill, Captain S.W., *The War at Sea 1939–1945 Volume 2: The Period of Balance* (HMSO, London, 1956).

Roskill, Captain S.W., *The War at Sea 1939–1945 Volume 3, Part 1: The Offensive 1st June 1943–31st May 1944* (HMSO, London, 1960).

Roskill, Captain S.W., *The War at Sea 1939–1945 Volume 3, Part 2: The Offensive 1st June 1944–14th August 1945* (HMSO, London, 1961).

Ruppenthal, Roland G., *US Army in World War II European Theatre of Operations – Logistical Support of the Armies: Volume II September 1944 to May 1945* (Department of the Army, Washington, DC, 1959).

Seuss, Richard, and Blumenson, Martin, *The US Army in World War II: Breakout and Pursuit* (US Army Center of Military History, Washington, DC, 1961).

Stacey, Colonel C.P., *The Canadian Army 1939–1945: An Official Historical Summary* (Ministry of National Defence, Ottawa, 1948).

Books and Articles

Alanbrooke, Field Marshal Lord, Danchev, Alex, and Todman, Daniel (eds), *War Diaries 1939–1945* (Weidenfeld & Nicolson, London, 2001).

Ambrose, Stephen E., *D-Day June 6, 1944: The Battle for the Normandy Beaches* (Pocket Books, London, 2002).

Atkinson, Rick, *The Guns at Last Light: The War in Western Europe 1944–1945* (Abacus, London, 2015).

Barbier, Mary Katherine, *D-Day Deception: Operation Fortitude and the Normandy Invasion* (Stackpole, Mechanicsburg PA, 2009).

Barnett, Correlli, *Engage the Enemy More Closely: The Royal Navy in the Second World War* (Hodder & Stoughton, London, 1991).

Beevor, Anthony, *D-Day: The Battle for Normandy* (Penguin/Viking, London, 2009).

Bekker, Cajus, *The Luftwaffe War Diaries* (Corgi, London, 1972).

Benbow, Tim, 'Battleships, D-Day and Naval Strategy', *War in History*, vol. 29, no. 3 (July 2022), 684–703.

Benbow, Tim, 'The Contribution of Royal Navy Aircraft Carriers and the Fleet Air Arm to Operation "Overlord", 1944', *War in History*, vol. 26, no. 2 (2019), 265–86.

Benbow, Tim, 'Menace to Ironclad: the British Operations against Dakar (1940) and Madagascar (1942)', *The Journal of Military History*, vol. 75 (July 2011), 769–809.

Blair, Clay, *Hitler's U-boat War: The Hunted 1942–1945* (Cassell, London, 2000).

Blazich, Dr Frank A., Jr, 'D-Day's Magic Boxes: US Navy Pontoon Technology in Operation Overlord', unpublished paper delivered at the Normandy 75 Conference in Portsmouth, July 2019.

Boog, Horst, Krebs, Gerhard, and Vogel, Detlef, *Das Deutsche Reich und der Zweite Weltkrieg Band 7: Das Deutsche Reich in der Defensive: Strategischer Luftkrieg in Europa, Krieg im Westen und in Ostasien, 1943–1944/45* (Deutsche Verlags-Anstalt, Stuttgart, 2001).

BIBLIOGRAPHY

Booth, Tony, *Admiralty Salvage in Peace and War 1906–2006* (Pen & Sword Maritime, Barnsley, 2007).

Bradley, Omar, *A Soldier's Story of the Allied Campaigns from Tunis to the Elbe* (Eyre & Spottiswoode, London, 1951).

Bradley, Omar, *A General's Life* (Simon & Schuster, New York, 1983).

Buckley, Christopher, *Norway; The Commandos; Dieppe* (HMSO, London, 1977).

Bulkeley, Captain Robert J., *At Close Quarters: PT Boats in the United States Navy* (Naval History Division, Washington, DC, 1962).

Burn, Lambton, *Down Ramps!* (Carroll & Nicholson, London, 1947).

Caddick-Adams, Peter, *Sand and Steel: A New History of D-Day* (Arrow, London, 2019).

Carrell, Paul, *Invasion! – They're Coming!: The German Account of the Allied Landings and the 80 Days' Battle for France* (Corgi, London, 1974).

Carter, Tom, *Beachhead Normandy: An LCT's Odyssey* (Potomac Books, Washington, DC, 2012).

Chalmers, W.S., *Full Cycle: The Biography of Admiral Sir Bertram Home Ramsay* (Hodder & Stoughton, London, 1959).

Churchill, Winston S., *The Second World War Volume II: Their Finest Hour* (Cassell & Co., London, 1949).

Churchill, Winston S., *The Second World War Volume IV: The Hinge of Fate* (Cassell & Co., London, 1951).

Churchill, Winston S., *The Second World War Volume V: Closing the Ring* (Cassell & Co., London, 1952).

Churchill, Winston S., *The Second World War Volume VI: Triumph and Tragedy* (Cassell & Co., London, 1954).

Coker, Lieutenant (jg) Coit N., 'Fire Control on Omaha Beach', *The Field Artillery Journal* (September 1946).

Crosley, Commander R. 'Mike', *They Gave Me a Seafire* (Airlife, Shrewsbury, 1986).

De Guingand, Major-General Sir Francis, *Operation Victory* (Hodder & Stoughton, London, 1950).

Dear, I.C.B., and Foot, M.R.D. (eds), *The Oxford Companion to World War II* (Oxford University Press, Oxford, 2001).

D'Este, Carlo, *Decision in Normandy: The Unwritten Story of Montgomery and the Allied Campaign* (Penguin, London, 2001).

D'Este, Carlo, *Patton: A Genius for War* (Harper Perennial, New York, 1996).

Donald, Commander William, *Stand by for Action* (New English Library, London, 1975).

Dönitz, Grand Admiral Karl, *Memoirs: Ten Years and Twenty Days* (Frontline Books, Barnsley, 2012).

Edwards, Commander Kenneth, *Operation Neptune* (Collins, London, 1946).

Eisenhower, Dwight D., *Crusade in Europe* (William Heinemann Limited, London, 1949).

Eisenhower Foundation (eds), *D-Day: The Normandy Invasion in Retrospect* (University Press of Kansas, Wichita, 1971).

Elliott, E., *Allied Minesweeping in World War II* (Patrick Stephens Ltd, Cambridge, 1997).

Ellsberg, Rear-Admiral Edward, *The Far Shore* (Panther, London, 1964).

Evans, George, *The Landfall Story* (The Acorn Press, Liverpool, 1972).

BIBLIOGRAPHY

Falconer, Jonathan, *The D-Day Operations Manual* (Haynes, Sparkford, 2013).

Fane, Commander F.D., *The Naked Warriors* (Panther Books/Hamilton & Company, London, 1958).

Fergusson, Bernard, *The Watery Maze: The Story of Combined Operations* (Collins, London, 1961).

Fisher, Stephen, *Sword Beach: The Untold Story of D-Day's Forgotten Battle* (Bantam, London, 2024).

Ford, Ken, *D-Day Commando: From Normandy to the Maas with 48 Royal Marine Commando* (Sutton Publishing, Stroud, 2003).

Fowler, Will, *The Last Raid: The Commandos, Channel Islands and the Final Nazi Raid* (The History Press, Cheltenham, 2016).

Frank, Hans, *German S-Boats in Action in the Second World War* (Seaforth, Barnsley, 2007).

Granville, Wilfred, and Kelly, Robin A., *Inshore Heroes: The Story of HM Motor Launches in Two World Wars* (W.H. Allen, London, 1961).

Greenwood, Trevor, *D-Day to Victory: The Diaries of a British Tank Commander* (Simon & Schuster, London, 2012).

Hartcup, Guy, *Code Name Mulberry: The Planning, Building and Operation of the Normandy Harbours* (David & Charles, Newton Abbot, 1977).

Hastings, Max, *Overlord: D-Day and the Battle for Normandy 1944* (Michael Joseph, London, 1984).

Hawkins, Desmond (ed.), *War Report D-Day to VE Day: Despatches by the BBC's War Correspondents with the Allied Expeditionary Force 6 June 1944–5 May 1945* (Ariel Books/BBC, London, 1985).

Hewitt, Nick, *Coastal Convoys 1939–1945: The Indestructible Highway* (Pen & Sword, Barnsley, 2008).

Hewitt, Nick, *Firing on Fortress Europe: HMS* Belfast *at D-Day* (Imperial War Museum, London, 2015).

Hewitt, Nick, 'HMS *Belfast* and Operation Neptune June–July 1944', *The Mariner's Mirror*, vol. 94, no. 2 (May 2008), 188–201.

Hill, Roger, *Destroyer Captain: Memoirs of the War at Sea 1942–45* (Mayflower, London, 1979).

Holbrook, David, *Flesh Wounds* (Corgi, London, 1966).

Holland, James, *Normandy '44: D-Day and the Battle for France* (Corgi, London, 2020).

Holman, Gordon, *Stand by to Beach* (Hodder & Stoughton, London, 1945).

Holt, Thaddeus, *The Deceivers: Allied Military Deception in the Second World War* (Folio Society, London, 2008).

Howarth, David, *Dawn of D-Day* (Fontana, London, 1971).

Jacobsen, Dr Hans-Adolf, and Rohwer, Dr Jürgen, *Decisive Battles of World War II: The German View* (André Deutsch, London, 1965).

Jary, Sydney, *18 Platoon* (Sydney Jary Limited, Carshalton, 1987).

Johnman, Lewis, and Murphy, Hugh, *British Shipbuilding and the State Since 1918: A Political Economy of Decline* (University of Exeter Press, Exeter, 2002).

Johnson, Garry, and Dumphie, Christopher, *Brightly Shone the Dawn: Some Experiences of the Invasion of Normandy* (Frederick Warne, London, 1980).

Keegan, John, *Six Armies in Normandy* (Penguin, London, 1988).

Kershaw, Alex, *The Bedford Boys: One Small Town's D-Day Sacrifice* (Simon & Schuster, London, 2003).

BIBLIOGRAPHY

Kershaw, Ian, *The End: Germany 1944–45* (Penguin, London, 2012).

King, Fleet Admiral Ernest J., and Whitehill, Commander Walter Muir, *Fleet Admiral King: A Naval Record* (Eyre & Spottiswoode, London, 1953).

Kirkland, William B. Jr, *Destroyers at Normandy: Naval Gunfire Support at Omaha Beach* (Naval Historical Foundation, Washington, DC, 1994).

Ladd, James, *Commandos and Rangers of World War II* (Book Club Associates, London, 1979).

Lee, David, *Beachhead Assault: The Story of the Royal Naval Commandos in World War II* (Greenhill Books, London, 2004).

Lewis, Adrian R., *Omaha Beach: A Flawed Victory* (Tempus, Stroud, 2004).

Liddell Hart, Basil, *The Other Side of the Hill* (Cassell, London, 1973).

Liddell Hart, B.H. (ed.), *The Rommel Papers* (Collins, London, 1953).

Love, Robert W., Jr, and Major, John (eds), *The Year of D-Day: The 1944 Diary of Admiral Sir Bertram Ramsay* (University of Hull Press, Hull, 1994).

Lund, Paul, and Ludlam, Harry, *Out Sweeps: The Exploits of the Minesweepers in World War II* (New English Library, London, 1979).

Lund, Paul, and Ludlam, Harry, *Trawlers Go to War* (New English Library, London, 1972).

Lund, Paul, and Ludlam, Harry, *The War of the Landing Craft* (New English Library, London, 1976).

Maher, Brendan, *A Passage to Sword Beach* (Naval Institute Press, Annapolis, MD, 1996).

Mawdsley, Evan, *The War for the Seas: A Maritime History of World War II* (Yale University Press, New Haven, CT, and London, 2020).

Miller, Russell, *Nothing Less Than Victory: The Oral History of D-Day* (Penguin, London, 1994).

Montgomery, Field Marshal the Viscount of Alamein, *Memoirs* (Collins, London, 1958).

Morgan, Sir Frederick, KCB, *Overture to Overlord* (Mayflower, London, 1962).

The Navy and the Y Scheme (HMSO, London, 1944).

Neillands, Robin, *The Battle of Normandy 1944* (Cassell, London, 2003).

Nudd, Derek, *Castaways in Question: British Naval Interrogators from WW1 to Denazification* (self-published, 2020).

O'Flaherty, Captain Chris, Royal Navy, *Crash Start: The Life and Legacy of Lieutenant Richard Guy Ormonde Hudson DSC Royal Naval Volunteer Reserve* (The Choir Press, Gloucester, 2019).

O'Flaherty, Captain Chris, Royal Navy, *Naval Minewarfare: Politics to Practicalities* (The Choir Press, Gloucester, 2019).

Ovary, Richard, *Why the Allies Won* (Pimlico, London, 2006).

Paterson, Lawrence, *Hitler's Forgotten Flotillas: Kriegsmarine Security Forces* (Seaforth, Barnsley, 2017).

Paterson, Lawrence, *Weapons of Desperation: German Frogmen and Midget Submarines of World War II* (Pen & Sword, Barnsley, 2018).

Picot, Geoffrey, *Accidental Warrior: In the Front Line from Normandy till Victory* (Penguin, London, 1993).

Prysor, Glyn, *Citizen Sailors: The Royal Navy in the Second World War* (Penguin, London, 2012).

Raeder, Grand Admiral Erich, *My Life* (United States Naval Institute Press, Annapolis, MD, 1960).

BIBLIOGRAPHY

Rankin, Nicolas, *Churchill's Wizards: The British Genius for Deception 1914–1945* (Faber & Faber, London, 2009).

Reynolds, Michael, *Steel Inferno: 1st SS Panzer Corps in Normandy* (Spellmount, Staplehurst, 1997).

Roskill, S.W., *HMS* Warspite*: The Story of a Famous Battleship* (Futura, London, 1974).

Ross, John, *The Forecast for D-Day* (Lyons Press, Guilford, CT, 2014).

Ruge, Friedrich, *Rommel in Normandy* (Presidio, London, 1979).

Ruge, Friedrich, *Sea Warfare 1939–1945: A German Viewpoint* (Cassell, London, 1957).

Ryan, Cornelius, *The Longest Day* (New English Library, Sevenoaks, 1982).

Salewski, Michael, *Die deutsche Seekriegsleitung 1935–1945, Band II, 1942–1945* (Bernard & Graefe Verlag, Munich, 1975).

Sanders, Geoffrey, *Soldier, Sailor* (The Bombardment Units Association/John Jennings, Gloucester, 1947).

Saunders, Hilary St George, *Royal Air Force 1939–1945: Volume III: The Fight Is Won* (HMSO, London, 1954).

Scarfe, Norman, *Assault Division: A History of the 3rd Division from the Invasion of Normandy to the Surrender of Germany* (Spellmount, Staplehurst, 2004).

Schmidt, Rudi, *Achtung – Torpedos Los! Der Strategische und Operative Einsatz des Kampfgeschwader 26* (Bernard & Graefe Verlag, Koblenz, 1991).

Schofield, Vice-Admiral B.B., *Operation Neptune* (Ian Allan, London, 1974).

Schulman, Milton, *Defeat in the West* (Pan, London, 1988).

Scott, Peter, *Battle of the Narrow Seas: The History of Light Coastal Forces in the Channel and North Sea 1939–1945* (Seaforth, Barnsley, 2009).

Showell, Jak P. Mallman, *German Naval Codebreakers* (Ian Allan, Hersham, 2003).

Small, Ken, with Rogerson, Mark, *The Forgotten Dead* (Bloomsbury, London, 1989).

Speidel, Lieutenant-General Hans, *We Defended Normandy* (Herbert Jenkins, London, 1951).

Stafford, David, *Ten Days to D-Day: Countdown to the Liberation of Europe* (Little, Brown, London, 2003).

Stagg, James, *Forecast for Overlord* (Ian Allan, London, 1971).

Stillwell, Paul (ed.), *Assault on Normandy: First Person Accounts from the Sea Services* (Naval Institute Press, Annapolis, MD, 1994).

Symonds, Craig L., *Operation Neptune: The D-Day Landings and the Allied Invasion of Europe* (Oxford University Press, Oxford, 2016).

Symonds, Craig L., *World War II at Sea* (Oxford University Press, Oxford, 2018).

Taghon, Peter, *Die Geschichte des Lehrgeschwaders 1* (VDM Heinz Nickel, Zweibrücken, 2004).

Tarrant, V.E., *The Last Year of the Kriegsmarine May 1944–May 1945* (Arms & Armour Press, London, 1994).

Tebble, Wendy, 'The Development and Role of Inshore Fire Support Craft in Amphibious Operations 1939–1945'. Unpublished M.Phil Thesis at the Department of War Studies, Kings College, London, 2003.

Tent, James Foster, *The E-Boat Threat: Defending the Normandy Invasion Fleet* (Airlife, Shrewsbury, 1996).

Trigg, Jonathan, *D-Day through German Eyes: How the Wehrmacht Lost France* (Amberley, Stroud, 2019).

Turner, John Frayn, *Invasion '44: The Full Story of D-Day* (Corgi, London, 1974).

Vian, Admiral of the Fleet Sir Philip, *Action This Day: A War Memoir* (Frederick Muller, London, 1960).

Von Luck, Hans, *Panzer Commander* (Frontline Books, London, 2013).

Warner, Philip, *The D-Day Landings* (William Kimber, London, 1980).

Wells, H.G., *The Shape of Things to Come* (Hutchinson, London, 1933).

Werner, Herbert A, *Iron Coffins: A U-Boat Commander's War 1939–1945* (Cassell, London, 1999).

Williams, Greg H., *The US Navy at Normandy: Fleet Organisation and Operations in the D-Day Invasion* (McFarland & Company, Jefferson, NC, 2020).

Wilmot, Chester, *The Struggle for Europe* (The Reprint Society, London, 1956).

Wilson, Andrew, *Flamethrower* (Corgi, London, 1973).

Woodman, Richard, *Keepers of the Sea: The Story of the Trinity House Yachts and Tenders* (Chaffcutter Books, Ware, 2005).

Yung, Christopher D., *Gators of Neptune: Naval Amphibious Planning for the Normandy Invasion* (Naval Institute Press, Annapolis, MD, 2006).

Online Sources

http://pompeypensioners.org.uk
http://www.6juin1944.com/
http://www.atlantikwall.co.uk/
http://www.rodericktimms.royalnavy.co.uk/
http://www.royalnavyresearcharchive.org.uk/
http://www.s-boot.net/
http://www.southseasubaqua.org.uk/
http://www.uss-corry-dd463.com/
https://library.columbia.edu/
https://uboat.net/
https://weaponsandwarfare.com/
https://www.blatherwick.net/documents/RoyalCanadianNavyCitations/
https://www.britishnormandymemorial.org/roll-of-honour/
https://www.combinedops.com
https://www.coppsurvey.uk/
https://www.cwgc.org/
https://www.findagrave.com/
https://www.history.navy.mil/
https://www.history.uscg.mil/
https://www.hmsmedusa.org.uk/
https://www.german-navy.de/kriegsmarine/ships/torpedoboats/flottentorpedo-boot1939/t27/history.html
https://www.ibiblio.org/hyperwar/
https://www.mcdoa.org.uk/
https://www.naval-history.net/
https://www.squadron34.com/
https://www.unithistories.com
https://www.worldnavalships.com/
Abrahams, John, 322

Index

INDEX

INDEX

2. 'Ramsay Despatch', 5114, and https://www.hmsmedusa.org.uk/medusa-history/medusa-at-d-day/.
3. TNA DEFE 2/420 Force S Reports – Attachment 1 X23 Op Gambit Report and TNA DEFE 2/418 Force J Report – Enclosure 11 Reports of Proceedings\X20 Operation Gambit.
4. IWM Sound 9709 Honour, George.
5. Lieutenant-Commander G.B. Honour, 'Operation Gambit: An Eye-Witness Report', *The Naval Review*, vol. 81, no. 1 (January 1993), 84, and TNA DEFE 2/418 Force J Report – Enclosure 11 Reports of Proceedings\X20 Operation Gambit.
6. TNA DEFE 2/420 Force S Reports – Attachment 1 X23 Op Gambit Report and TNA DEFE 2/418 Force J Report – Enclosure 11 Reports of Proceedings\X20 Operation Gambit.
7. Ibid. The author had the extraordinary privilege of diving to the seabed off Normandy with Jim Booth in 1993 while making a television documentary, *D-Day's Sunken Secrets*. The last time the former COPPist had been in a submarine was June 1944.
8. 'Ramsay Despatch', 5114.
9. https://www.hmsmedusa.org.uk/medusa-history/medusa-at-d-day.
10. Ibid. *HDML-1387* survives today, beautifully restored and operating in Portsmouth harbour as HMS *Medusa*, the name it was given as a postwar survey craft.
11. Commander H. St A. Malleson, 'The Decca Navigator System on D-Day, 6 June 1944: An Acid Test', *The Naval Review* vol. 72, no. 3 (July 1984), 249 (reprinted from *The Journal of Naval Science*, vol. 7, no. 4).
12. BBC PW A5717810 Eastmead, Norman.
13. IWM Sound 28458 Rouse, Graham.
14. BBC PW A3504953 Rouse, Graham.
15. IWM Sound 28458 Rouse, Graham.
16. BBC PW A3504953 Rouse, Graham.
17. IWM Sound 28458 Rouse, Graham.
18. IWM Sound 19532 Taylor, Sidney.
19. BBC PW A5385800 Popham, Sam.
20. O'Flaherty, *Naval Minewarfare*, 70.
21. *Fuehrer Conferences on Naval Affairs 1944* (Admiralty, London, 1947), 29.
22. TNA ADM 189/147 German Oyster Mine Docket No 7 1944.
23. Naval Staff Battle Summary No. 39 Operation 'Neptune', 41.
24. Ibid., 49.
25. TNA WO 106/4316 Summary of Naval Report on Operation Neptune\14 Minesweeping.
26. 'Ramsay Despatch', 5115.
27. E. Elliott, *Allied Minesweeping in World War II* (Patrick Stephens, Cambridge, 1997), 107, quoted in O'Flaherty, *Naval Minewarfare*, 71.
28. BBC PW A2593019 Cooper, Richard.
29. IWM Sound 33902 Michell, Richard.
30. TNA WO 106/4316 Summary of Naval Report on Operation Neptune\14 Minesweeping.
31. 'M.S.X.', 'D-Day in a Minesweeper', *The Naval Review*, vol. 34 no. 2 (May 1946), 134.

in Operation Neptune. Painstakingly restored by the National Museum of The Royal Navy between 2014 and 2020, *LCT-7074* is now open to the public and operated by The D-Day Story in Portsmouth.

43. Roger Hill, *Destroyer Captain*, 251.
44. Ibid.
45. Gordon Holman, *Stand by to Beach!* (Hodder & Stoughton, London, 1945), 29.
46. http://www.6juin1944.com/assaut/juno/tables.pdf.
47. IWM Sound 8739 Madden, Colin Duncan.
48. BBC PW A2843912 Chaffer, Dennis.
49. IWM Sound 34427 Carlill, John.
50. TNA DEFE 2/418 Force J Report.
51. IWM Sound 28680 Lowndes, Tony.
52. TNA DEFE 2/420 Force S Reports.
53. Love and Major, *The Year of D-Day*, 81.
54. TNA DEFE 2/420 Force S Reports.
55. IWM Sound 27071 Till, Dennis.
56. Naval Staff Battle Summary No. 39 Operation 'Neptune', 81.
57. Williams, *The US Navy at Normandy*, 108–9.
58. Horst Boog, Gerhard Krebs and Detlef Vogel, *Das Deutsche Reich und der Zweite Weltkrieg Band 7: Das Deutsche Reich in der Defensive: Strategischer Luftkrieg in Europa, Krieg im Westen und in Ostasien, 1943–1944/45* (Deutsche Verlags-Anstalt, Stuttgart, 2001).
59. See Alex Kershaw, *The Bedford Boys: One Small Town's D-Day Sacrifice* (Simon & Schuster, London, 2003).
60. BBC PW A1929468 Green, Jimmy.
61. Williams, *The US Navy at Normandy*, 109.
62. NMRN CRTY 2019/59/24 Reports on Operation Neptune/Admiralty Docket – Summary of the Lessons Learned During Operation Neptune.
63. BBC PW 4179341 Yates, Norman.
64. BBC PW A6439034 Flowers, Freda.
65. NMRN 1990/86/6*1 & 2 Two Naval signals sent by Vice-Admiral H. Pridham-Wippell Flag Officer commanding, Dover on 6 June 1944.
66. TNA DEFE 2/416 & 417 Naval Commander Force G Report.
67. IWM Sound 25186 Jesse, Ron, quoted in Nick Hewitt, *Firing on Fortress Europe*, 57.
68. BBC PW A8532100 Small, Dennis.
69. Symonds, *Operation Neptune*, 238.
70. Love and Major, *The Year of D-Day*, 83.
71. BBC PW A4477737 Vincent, Paddy.
72. IWM Sound 18624 Lennox-Hamilton, Malcolm.
73. IWM Sound 22161 Repard, David.
74. Commander A.J.W. Wilson, 'A Short Life and a Merry One: One Small Craft's D-Day', *The Naval Review*, vol. 82, no. 3 (July 994), 251.
75. Holt, *The Deceivers*, 490–1.

7 Crossing to the Bay

1. Naval Staff Battle Summary No. 39 Operation 'Neptune', 49.

15. Slapton Sands was first used as an amphibious training area in 1938. Tebble, 'Inshore Fire Support Craft', 63.
16. BBC PW A4659249 Phippen, Bob.
17. IWM Sound 28680 Lowndes, Tony. Unknowingly, I lived in this hotel, the Pendragon, in 2014–15!
18. Ibid.
19. Ibid.
20. Tom Carter, *Beachhead Normandy: An LCT's Odyssey* (Potomac Books, Washington, DC, 2012), 26–8.
21. Ibid., 32.
22. Stillwell, *Assault on Normandy*, 160.
23. Quoted in Douglas, Sarty and Whitby, *A Blue Water Navy*, 125.
24. BBC PW A2731051 Wright, Norman.
25. Quoted in David Lee, *Beachhead Assault* (Greenhill Books, London, 2004), 40.
26. Ibid., 44.
27. Ibid., 45.
28. IWM Sound 20332 Le Roy, René.
29. Wakefield, Orval, 'Combat Demolition Unit', in Stillwell, *Assault on Normandy*, 93. The NCDUs were the ancestors of today's US Navy SEAL (Sea Air Land) Teams.
30. IWM Sound 27730 Lunn, Robert.
31. IWM Sound 20579 Berryman, 'Dick'.
32. Ibid., and Sanders, *Soldier, Sailor*, 1.
33. IWM Sound 20579, Berryman, 'Dick'.
34. IWM Sound 25186 Jesse, Ron.
35. Commander R. 'Mike' Crosley, *They Gave Me a Seafire* (Airlife, Shrewsbury, 1986), 113.
36. IWM Sound 8739 Madden, Colin Duncan.
37. Ibid.
38. Christopher D. Yung, *Gators of Neptune: Naval Amphibious Planning for the Normandy Invasion* (Naval Institute Press, Annapolis, MD, 2006), 155.
39. IWM Sound 8739 Madden, Colin Duncan.
40. Ibid.
41. TNA ADM 179/504 Report of Proceedings: Naval Commander Force S.
42. Ibid.
43. IWM Sound 18684 Bird, Peter.
44. TNA ADM 179/505 Report of Proceedings: Naval Commander Force G.
45. See Lewis, *Omaha Beach*, for a robust if polemical argument that this compromise was deeply problematic. Lewis makes a well-argued case that using US techniques from the Pacific, involving among other things a prolonged preliminary bombardment lasting hours or even days, would have delivered a cleaner victory and saved lives in Normandy.
46. Love and Major, *The Year of D-Day*, 42.
47. Ibid., 63.
48. BBC PW A1929468 Green, Jimmy.
49. IWM Sound 28680 Lowndes, Tony.
50. Yung, *Gators of Neptune*, 157–8.
51. TNA ADM 199/261 Coastal Forces Actions\Attack by E-boats on Convoy T-4 (Exercise Tiger) 27–28 April 1944

comprehensive (and in my opinion very publishable) study of the Support Landing Craft to my attention.

47. TNA DEFE2/324, 11–19, quoted in Tebble, 'Inshore Fire Support Craft', 149

48. Dr Alfred Vagts, *Landing Operations* (Military Service Publishing Co., Harrisburg, PA, 1946), quoted in Tebble, 'Inshore Fire Support Craft', 120.

49. Tebble, 'Inshore Fire Support Craft', 35 and 89.

50. Paul Lund and Harry Ludlam, *The War of the Landing Craft* (New English Library, London, 1976), 95. For a full account of the Milford Haven disaster see this book, 93–106.

51. IWM Sound 26843 Lines, Eric.

52. TNA ADM 199/1556 Admiralty War History Cases and Papers Operation Neptune: Overlord and Anvil Provision of Small Craft.

53. Ibid., 182.

54. Ibid., 258

55. Morison, *Invasion of France and Germany*, 55.

56. Naval Staff Battle Summary No. 39 Operation 'Neptune', Appendix A, 7–12.

57. Again, Stephen Fisher's *Embarking the D-Day Armada* (forthcoming) will provide a comprehensive account of this process.

58. TNA ADM 179/508 Overlord LCT Bases.

59. Morison, *Invasion of France and Germany*, 62.

60. Ibid., 63, and Ramsay, 'The Assault Phase of the Normandy Landings, Official Despatch Submitted to the Supreme Commander, Allied Expeditionary Force, on the 16th October 1944, by Admiral Sir Bertram H. Ramsay, KCB, MVO, Allied Naval Commander-in-Chief, Expeditionary Force in Supplement to the London Gazette of Tuesday, the 28th of October 1947' (henceforth 'Ramsay Despatch'), 5113.

5 Finding Sailors

1. TNA ADM 179/505 Report of Proceedings: Naval Commander Force G

2. Roskill, *The War at Sea 1939–1945 Volume 3, Part 2: The Offensive Part 2 1st June 1943–31st May 1944* (HMSO, London, 1961), 10.

3. Major L.F. Ellis, CVO, CBE, DSI, C, with Lieutenant-Colonel Warhurst, *Victory in the West Volume 2: The Defeat of Germany* (HMSO, London, 1968), 158.

4. 'Duilius', 'Review of Royal Marine Operations 1939–1945', *The Naval Review* vol. 33, no. 3 (August 1945), 184–5.

5. *The Navy and the Y Scheme* (HMSO, London, 1944), 7.

6. Ibid.

7. IWM Sound 29556 Haskell-Thomas, Brian.

8. IWM Sound 35800 Herbert Gordon 'Bertie' Male.

9. Ibid.

10. IWM Sound 18627 Jarman, William.

11. IWM Sound 18684 Bird, Peter.

12. Ibid.

13. BBC PW A8532100 Small, Dennis.

14. BBC PW A2724879 Miles, Bill.

BIBLIOGRAPHY

Sharples, J.G., '*Emerald* on D-Day', letter to *The Naval Review*, vol. 82, no. 3 (July 1984).

'T.A.B.C.', 'HMS *Ajax* at War 1940–1945', vol. 37, no. 2 (1949).

Turner, Graham, 'The Loss of HMS *Charybdis* 23 October 1943', vol. 79, no. 4 (October 1991).

White, W.D.S., 'A Cruiser at War', vol. 83, no. 4 (October 1995).

Wilson, Commander A.J.W., 'A Short Life and a Merry One: One Small Craft's D-Day', vol. 82, no. 3 (July 1994).

Other

BBC, 'We Were There', https://www.bbc.co.uk/news/av/uk-63582384.

Kriegstagebuche der 5. Torpedobootsflottille 1.6.199 – 15.6.1944 (Naval Intelligence Department File P.G.70321).

Official Publications

Douglas, W.A.B., Sarty, R., and Whitby, M., *A Blue Water Navy: The Official Operational History of the Royal Canadian Navy in the Second World War 1939–1945 Volume II Part 2* (Vanwell Publishing, St Catharines, ON, 2007).

Douglas, W.A.B., Sarty, R., and Whitby, M., *No Higher Purpose: The Official Operational History of the Royal Canadian Navy in the Second World War 1939–1945 Volume II Part 1* (Vanwell Publishing, St Catharines, ON, 2002).

Eisenhower, Dwight D., *Report by the Supreme Commander to the Combined Chiefs of Staff on the Operations in Europe of the Allied Expeditionary Force 6 June 1944 to 8 May 1945* (HMSO, London, 1946),

Ellis, Major L.F., CVO, CBE, DSI, C, with Warhurst, Lieutenant-Colonel, *Victory in the West Volume 2: The Defeat of Germany* (HMSO, London, 1968).

Fuehrer Conferences on Naval Affairs: 1944 (Admiralty, London, July 1947)

Hinsley, F.H., *British Intelligence in the Second World War: Abridged Edition* (HMSO, London, 1993).

Morison, Samuel Eliot, *History of United States Naval Operations in World War II: Volume IX The Sicily-Salerno-Anzio January 1943–June 1944* (Castle Books, Edison, NJ, 2001).

Morison, Samuel Eliot, *History of United States Naval Operations in World War II: Volume XI The Invasion of France and Germany 1944–1945* (Castle Books, Edison, NJ, 2001).

Naval Battle Summary, *The Campaign in NW Europe June 1944–May 1945* (HMSO, London, 1994).

Naval Battle Summary, *The Invasion of the South of France – Operation 'Dragoon', 15th August 1944* (HMSO, London, 1994).

Naval Staff Battle Summary No. 33 B.R.1736 (26), *Raid on Dieppe (Naval Operations) 19th August 1942* (Admiralty Historical Section, 1959).

Naval Staff Battle Summary No. 38, *Operation 'Torch'* (Admiralty Historical Section, 1948).

Naval Staff Battle Summary No. 39, *Operation 'Neptune': Landings in Normandy June 1944* (HMSO, London, 1994).

Ramsay, Admiral Sir Bertram H., KCB, MVO, Allied Naval Commander-in-Chief, Expeditionary Force, 'The Assault Phase of the Normandy Landings:

BIBLIOGRAPHY

The Naval Review

'AJWW', 'Some Notes on Operation Neptune', vol. 82, no. 2 (April 1994).

Aylen, I.G., 'Recollections of Assault Unit No. 30 – 1', vol. 65, no. 4 (October 1977).

'B.J.'. 'Birthday Party', vol. 38, no. 3 (August 1950).

Borthwick, Mrs David (sic), 'The Commodore Landing Craft Base's Barge Crew', vol. 73 no. 1 (January 1985).

Chichester, Commander Michael, 'The Greatest Amphibious Operation in History (and a great naval bombardment)', vol. 82, no. 2 (April 1994).

Clitherow, Chichester, 'LST: Landing Ship Tank', vol. 35 (August 1947).

Creasy, Rear-Admiral George, and 'LGD', 'Admiral Sir Bertram H Ramsay, KCB, KBE, MVO: Two Tributes', vol. 33, no. 1 (February 1945).

Dickinson, H.W., 'Operation Aquatint: The British at Omaha Beach', vol. 96, no. 2 (May 2008).

Dolphin, Captain George, "The Normandy Landings – 6 June 1944", vol. 65, no. 3 (July 1977).

'Duilius', 'Review of Royal Marine Operations 1939–1945', vol. 33, no. 3 (August 1945).

Edwards, Kenneth, 'The Navy's Job in the Channel', vol. 32, no. 4 (November 1944).

'Endeavour', 'Can We Afford the Non-Fighting Part of the Navy?', vol. 78 (July 1990).

Glen, Commander N.C., 'Normandy', vol. 93 (November 2005).

Gordon, Andrew, 'Bertram Ramsay and Staff Work', vol. 102 (August 2014).

Habershon, D.B., 'D-Day Operations: A Personal Reflection', vol. 89, no.1 (January 2001).

Honour, Lieutenant-Commander G.B., 'Operation Gambit: An Eye-Witness Report', vol. 81, no. 1 (January 1993).

Hore, Captain P.G., 'The Logistics of Neptune', vol. 82, no. 3 (July 1994).

Hutchings, J.F., 'The Story of Force Pluto', vol. 34, no. 4 (November 1946).

Jones, Basil, 'A Matter of Length and Breadth', vol. 37, no. 2 (May 1950).

'J.S', 'A Journey to France', vol. 68, no. 3 (July 1980).

Malleson, Commander H. St A., 'The Decca Navigator System on D-Day, 6 June 1944: An Acid Test' (reprinted from *The Journal of Naval Science*, vol. 7, no. 4), vol. 72, no. 3 (July 1984).

'Memor', 'The Assault Phase of the Normandy Landings (Operation Neptune) – Supplement to the *London Gazette* of the 28th of October, 1947', vol. 36, no. 1 (February 1948).

Middleton, Captain G.B., RN, 'D-Day Operations: A Personal Recollection', vol. 89, no. 1 (January 2001).

'M.S.X', 'D-Day in a Minesweeper', vol. 34, no. 2 (May 1946).

'Onlooker', 'HM Navigation School 1903–1968', vol. 56, no. 3 (July 1968).

Pallot, J., 'Operation Neptune', vol. 82, no. 2 (April 1994).

Popham, F.H. (Sam), 'HMS *Recruit* 7th MSF June 1944', vol. 88, no. 4 (October 2000).

Smith, Major Ian, RM, 'Co-operation and Conflict: The Anglo-American Alliance Before D-Day', vol. 107, no. 4 (November 2019).

at-Normandy/. Clark was awarded the Distinguished Service Cross by the British.

39. TNA ADM 179/504 Report of Proceedings Naval Commander Force S\Enclosures\10 200 and 201 LCI(S) Flotilla.
40. TNA DEFE 2/420 Force S Reports\3 Group S3 Assault\Assault Group 10 Stores and 2nd Priority Vehicles.
41. IWM Sound 21649 Hays, Frank.
42. Naval Staff Battle Summary No. 39 Operation 'Neptune', 104.
43. IWM Sound 25054 Plummer, Derek.
44. IWM Sound 17294 Oakley, Ken.
45. TNA DEFE 2/420 Force S Reports\10 NOIC Sword.
46. IWM Sound 17394 Gueritz, Teddy.
47. Ibid.
48. Naval Staff Battle Summary No. 39 Operation 'Neptune', 116.
49. DDS H303.1988 Cutler HMS *Largs*.
50. BBC PW A7360995 Goodwin, Lewis.
51. Evans, George, *The Landfall Story*, 63.
52. Ibid.
53. Lt-General Orwin C. Talbott, 'Shipwrecked in the Channel', in Stilwell, *Assault on Normandy*, 121.
54. Ibid.
55. IWM Sound 23345 Hitchcock, Don.
56. Naval Staff Battle Summary No. 39 Operation 'Neptune', 13.
57. I.C.B. Dear and M.R.D. Foot (eds), *The Oxford Companion to World War II* (Oxford University Press, Oxford, 2001), 667.
58. 'Ramsay Despatch', 5117.

11 The Battle of the Build-Up

1. *Grimsby Daily Telegraph*, 2 June 1944 via British Library.
2. Naval Staff Battle Summary No. 39 Operation 'Neptune', 13.
3. Ibid., 115.
4. Captain George Dolphin, 'The Normandy Landings – 6 June 1944', *The Naval Review*, vol. 65, no. 3 (July 1977), 244.
5. Captain P.G. Hore, 'The Logistics of Neptune', *The Naval Review*, vol. 82, no. 3 (July 1994), 246.
6. Edwards, *Operation Neptune*, 201.
7. TNA ADM 179/507 Overlord Reports Not Appearing Elsewhere\4 Captain Northbound Sailings.
8. Ibid.
9. TNA ADM 199/1659 Reports on Operation Neptune. Miscellaneous Reports not Enclosed in Main Report\Naval Commander Force J\Ferry Craft.
10. IWM Sound 18579 Fry, William.
11. Ibid.
12. TNA ADM 179/508 Overlord LCT Bases\16 Disembarkation of Casualties.
13. TNA ADM 179/431 Overlord FOIC Portland\1 Staff and Specialist Officer Reports\10 Commander Local Defence and TURCO.
14. IWM Sound 8739 Madden, Colin Duncan.

8. Ibid., 119.
9. TNA DEFE 2/414 Report Naval Commander ETF Parts I–VI.
10. Middleton, 'D-Day Operations: A Personal Recollection', 45.
11. TNA ADM 179/482 Operations Frog and Deer.
12. TNA ADM 179/504 Report of Proceedings Naval Commander Force S\
Appendix 1 Bombardment and Support. No. 9 Para fired a prearranged signal
flare, variously described as yellow and red-green-red, and sent off a pigeon,
but neither method reached *Arethusa*.
13. IWM Sound 12590 Bayly, Patrick.
14. TNA ADM 179/504 Report of Proceedings Naval Commander Force S\
Appendix 1 Bombardment and Support.
15. BBC PW A432669 Blyth, Dick.
16. TNA ADM 179/504 Report of Proceedings Naval Commander Force S\
Appendix 1 Bombardment and Support, and http://www.atlantikwall.co.uk/
atlantikwall/fn_gr_wn20_la_breche.php.
17. TNA ADM 179/504 Report of Proceedings Naval Commander Force S\
Appendix 1 Bombardment and Support.
18. Sanders, *Soldier, Sailor*, 109.
19. IWM Sound 25054 Plummer, Derek.
20. TNA ADM 179/504 Report of Proceedings Naval Commander Force S\
Appendix 1 Bombardment and Support.
21. I am grateful to Dr Tim Benbow for reminding me of this point.
22. TNA ADM 179/504 Report of Proceedings Naval Commander Force S\.
23. Ibid., Enclosures\1 Captain Group S Three.
24. Ibid.
25. Lambton Burn, *Down Ramps!* (Carroll and Nicholson, 1947), quoted on
https://www.coppsurvey.uk/latest-news/down-ramps-lct-947-on-d-day.
Dunbar and Barbarian were the names of tanks.
26. TNA ADM 179/504 Report of Proceedings Naval Commander Force S\
Enclosures\1 Captain Group S Three.
27. Naval Staff Battle Summary No. 39 Operation 'Neptune', 103.
28. TNA ADM 179/504 Report of Proceedings Naval Commander Force S\
Enclosures\1 Captain Group S Three and www.cwgc.org.
29. TNA ADM 179/504 Report of Proceedings Naval Commander Force S\
Enclosures\1 Captain Group S Three.
30. Ibid.
31. BBC PW A264765 Kirkby, George.
32. BBC PW A 2668647 Froggatt, Jim.
33. TNA ADM 179/504 Report of Proceedings Naval Commander Force
S\Enclosures\1 Captain Group S Three.
34. Ibid.
35. TNA ADM 179/504 Report of Proceedings Naval Commander Force
S\Enclosures\10 200 and 201 LCI(S) Flotilla.
36. IWM Sound 34422 Curtis, Rupert.
37. Ibid.
38. TNA ADM 179/504 Report of Proceedings Naval Commander Force S\
Enclosures\2 Captain Group S Two and https://www.history.uscg.mil/
Browse-by-Topic/Notable-People/Award-Recipients/Coast-Guard-Heroes-

45. IWM Sound 13650 Morrow, Albert.
46. https://fr.wikipedia.org/wiki/Richard_Seuss and Blumenson, Martin, *The US Army in World War II: Breakout and Pursuit* (US Army Center of Military History, Washington, DC, 1961), 411, from http://www.ibiblio.org/hyperwar. Apparently so much unexploded ordnance remains on the island that, even today, access is still largely prohibited.
47. TNA ADM 199/261 Coastal Forces Actions\Coastal Forces Action 17–18 August 1944.
48. TNA ADM 179/507 Overlord Reports Not Appearing Elsewhere\3 Commodore Depot Ships August.
49. Tarrant, *The Last Year of the Kriegsmarine*, 107–11.
50. BBC, 'We Were There', https://www.bbc.co.uk/news/av/uk-63582384.
51. Douglas, Sarty and Whitby, *A Blue Water Navy*, 365–8.
52. TNA ADM 1/29878 Sinking of U741 by HMS *Orchis*.
53. Roskill, *The War at Sea Volume 3, Part 2*, 131, and Paterson, *Hitler's Forgotten Flotillas*, 297.
54. TNA ADM 179/509 Coastal Forces D-Day\Appendix 1 Summaries of Action Reports.
55. Ibid.
56. John and Wallace Keddie, both in the Royal Air Force, died in 1941 and 1942 respectively. https://www.cwgc.org/find-records/find-war-dead/casualty-details/1802488/wallace-arthur-robert-keddie/.
57. Roskill, *The War at Sea 1939–1945 Volume 3, Part 2*, 131.
58. Roskill, *HMS Warspite*, 282.
59. Derek Nudd, *Castaways in Question: British Naval Interrogators from WWI to Denazification* (self-published, 2020), 131.
60. BBC PW A152926 Mead, Alfred.
61. Lund and Ludlam, *Out Sweeps*, 180.
62. BBC PW A4511017 East, Len.
63. Lund and Ludlam, *Out Sweeps*, 182.
64. TNA ADM 267/133 Damage Reports. Department of Naval Constructors. Bomb, Mine and Torpedo\HMS *Salamander*.
65. BBC PW A4511017 East, Len.
66. TNA ADM 267/133 Damage Reports. Department of Naval Constructors. Bomb, Mine and Torpedo\HMS *Salamander*.
67. BBC PW A2669196 Jackson, Thomas.
68. Lund and Ludlam, *Out Sweeps*, 184.
69. IWM Sound 19103 Hammond, Ernie.
70. BBC PW A2669196 Jackson, Thomas.
71. Lund and Ludlam, *Out Sweeps*, 192.
72. Paterson, *Weapons of Desperation*, 67.
73. Love and Major, *The Year of D-Day*, 134.
74. BBC PW A252402 Thomas, Ginger.
75. BBC PW A4326699 Blyth, Richard.
76. Roskill, *The War at Sea 1939–1945 Volume 3, Part 2*, 136.
77. IWM Sound 33323 Gosling, William.
78. IWM Sound 13582 Schran, Gunther.

8. Ibid.
9. Ibid.
10. https://www.britishnormandymemorial.org/news-story/marking-nhs-72-the-story-of-two-brave-nurses/.
11. https://www.blatherwick.net/documents/RoyalCanadianNavyCitations/.
12. Paterson, *Weapons of Desperation*, 55–6.
13. TNA ADM 267/77 *Damage Reports* Department of Naval Constructors HMS *Frobisher*.
14. Morison, *The Invasion of France and Germany*, 299.
15. Quoted in ibid. 299.
16. Squadron 34 War Diary with after action report at https://www.squadron34.com/.
17. Ibid. and Bulkeley, *At Close Quarters*, 360.
18. Morison, *The Invasion of France and Germany*, 300.
19. Bulkeley, *At Close Quarters*, 360.
20. https://www.squadron34.com/.
21. Bulkeley, *At Close Quarters*, 361–2.
22. Frank, *German S-Boats in Action*, 117.
23. TNA ADM 267–133 *Damage Reports*. Department of Naval Constructors. Bomb, Mine and Torpedo\HMS *Albatross*.
24. Ibid. and https://www.worldnavalships.com/forums/thread.php?threadid= 17102. Remarkably *Albatross* was repaired and converted into a passenger ship, surviving until 1954.
25. Love and Major, *The Year of D-Day*, 121.
26. TNA ADM 199/532 Reports of Proceedings 1943–44\12th Escort Group 7–12 August 1944 and collision between HMCS *Skeena* and *Qu'Appelle*.
27. IWM Sound 12734 Wellman, Derek.
28. IWM Sound 17433 Lucke, Helmut.
29. Fowler, Will, *The Last Raid: The Commandos, Channel Islands and the Final Nazi Raid* ('The History Press, Cheltenham, 2016). A British warship would not shell Crown territory again until the Falklands War in 1982.
30. https://uboat.net/allies/merchants/ship/3317.html.
31. Douglas, Sarty and Whitby, *A Blue Water Navy*, 312.
32. Paterson, *Hitler's Forgotten Flotillas*, 297–9.
33. Tarrant, *The Last Year of the Kriegsmarine*, 109.
34. TNA ADM 1/29878 Sinking of U741 by HMS *Orchis*.
35. Ibid.
36. Ibid.
37. Admiral H. Kent Hewitt, 'A Warm Welcome in Southern France', in Stilwell, *Assault on Normandy*, 223.
38. Churchill, *The Second World War Volume VI: Triumph and Tragedy*, 85–6.
39. Naval Battle Summary, The Invasion of the South of France – Operation 'Dragoon', 15th August 1944 (HMSO, London, 1994), 56.
40. Lund and Ludlum, *The War of the Landing Craft*, 194.
41. DDS 130/1996 Human Torpedoes (Extract).
42. Sub-Lieutenant Ray Browning of LCF-34, quoted in Tebble, 'Inshore Fire Support Craft', 224.
43. Paterson, *Weapons of Desperation*, 57.
44. DDS 2001/189/181/199 Longley Letters LCF 1.